D1553147

Indonesia

Paul Dixon

Credits

Footprint credits

Editor: Jo Williams
Production and layout: Emma Bryers
Maps: Kevin Feeney

Managing Director: Andy Riddle
Commercial Director: Patrick Dawson
Publisher: Alan Murphy
Publishing Managers: Felicity Laughton, Jo Williams, Nicola Gibbs
Marketing and Partnerships Director: Liz Harper
Marketing Executive: Liz Eyles
Trade Product Manager: Diane McEntee
Account Managers: Paul Bew, Tania Ross
Advertising: Renu Sibal, Elizabeth Taylor
Trade Product Co-ordinator: Kirsty Holmes

Photography credits

Front cover: Dreamstime
Back cover: Shutterstock

Printed and bound in the United States of America

Publishing information

Footprint *Focus Indonesia*
1st edition
© Footprint Handbooks Ltd
September 2012

ISBN: 978 1 908206 90 9
CIP DATA: A catalogue record for this book is available from the British Library

® Footprint Handbooks and the Footprint mark are a registered trademark of Footprint Handbooks Ltd

Published by Footprint
6 Riverside Court
Lower Bristol Road
Bath BA2 3DZ, UK
T +44 (0)1225 469141
F +44 (0)1225 469461
footprinttravelguides.com

Distributed in the USA by Globe Pequot Press, Guilford, Connecticut

Every effort has been made to ensure that the facts in this guidebook are accurate. However, travellers should still obtain advice from consulates, airlines, etc, about travel and visa requirements before travelling. The authors and publishers cannot accept responsibility for any loss, injury or inconvenience however caused.

The content of Footprint *Focus Indonesia* has been taken directly from Footprint's *Southeast Asia Handbook* which was researched and written by Andrew Spooner and Paul Dixon.

Contents

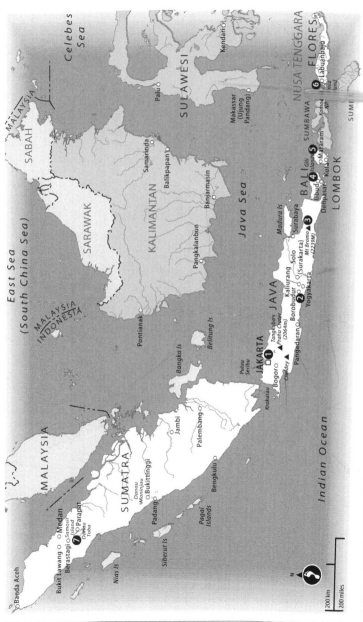

Indonesia is one of those countries mothers wince at when hearing that their child is planning a visit. Indeed, the past decade has seen this country, the world's fourth most populous, in the headlines for all the wrong reasons. However, for a traveller the archipelago has always promised great adventure and has given the contemporary era thrilling tales of swashbuckling mariners, bloodthirsty headhunters, unheard of wealth and glorious birds of paradise. It has lured some of the great anthropologists, writers and scientists to delve deep into its myriad cultures and shady jungles for meaningful answers. Nowadays, there are still many adventures to be had: trekking through virgin rainforest, diving deep canyon walls as manta rays glide past and raving in hip clubs with the beautiful urban elite. Whilst parts of the country may seem completely devoid of tourists, this provides a great opportunity to learn some *Bahasa*, mingle with the welcoming and extraordinarily resilient locals and have an experience that often feels more genuine than those on the well-worn tourist trails of mainland Southeast Asia.

With up to 17,000 islands (depending on the tide) and hundreds of different languages, Indonesia is the world's largest archipelago, one that was bound together by the Dutch and cemented as a nation by independence in 1945. While there are many who seek to find differences between the people in this unlikely nation, there are plenty of obvious links. Despite having the world's largest Muslim population, Indonesia is not an Islamic state although the religion is undoubtedly one of the most vital chains that binds the people. One of the great sensory memories of Southeast Asia is the scent of clove-laden *kretek* cigarettes, which permeates the entire country from the swankiest Jakarta restaurant to the bumpiest Sumatran bus. The enjoyment of these unique cigarettes is another of the unmistakable bonds between the people of this huge country.

Planning your trip

Getting to Indonesia

Air
The main international gateway into Indonesia is Jakarta's **Soekarno-Hatta International Airport**, with Bali and Medan (Sumatra) also popular. **Garuda**, the national flag carrier, flies between Jakarta, other Asian cities and Australia. It was banned from flying into Europe and the USA for a few years and many Indonesian carriers were still banned as this book went to press. **Garuda** has started operating flights from Amsterdam to Jakarta and is planning to start direct flights from several more European destinations. Most of the major European carriers have reduced the number of flights to Jakarta; there are no direct flights from the USA or UK to Indonesia. The large majority of travellers transit via the Middle East or Southeast Asia. **AirAsia**, www.air asia.com, **Singapore Airlines**, www.singaporeair.com, **Malaysia Airlines**, www.malaysia airlines.com, and **Thai Airways**, www.thaiairways.com, all offers good connections to Jakarta and other places throughout Indonesia.

Overland
A daily ferry operates from Penang in Malaysia to Belawan (the port of Medan) in Indonesia (Sumatra, the northern island), sailing at 0900 and arriving at 1300. Returning, it sails from Belawan (Medan) at 1030 and arrives in Penang at 1430. The fare is about RM90. See www.langkawi-ferry.com. Details of all these journeys can be found at www.seat61.com.

Transport in Indonesia

Air
The most convenient and comfortable way to travel is by air. **Garuda** (www.garuda-indonesia.com) and **Merpati** (www.merpati.co.id) service all the main provincial cities. Merpati tends to operate the short-hop services to smaller destinations, particularly in eastern Indonesia.

The other main domestic airlines are **Lion Air** (www.lionair.co.id), proud owner of a fleet of sparkling B737-900s, and **Indonesia AirAsia** (www.airasia.com). Other key players are **Batavia Air** (www.batavia-air.co.id) and **Sriwijaya** (www.sriwijayaair-online.com). All these airlines cover major destinations in Indonesia. Smallest of all are **DAS, SMAC** and **Deraya** (www.deraya.co.id) and **Susi Air** (www.susiair.com), which tend to service smaller towns in Java and the outer islands, especially Kalimantan and Sumatra. In Nusa Tenggara, travellers often have to use Merpati, or one of the local outfits such as **Trans Nusa** (www.transnusa.co.id) and **Indonesia Air Transport** (www.iat.co.id).

By international standards, flights in Indonesia are cheap. It is also considerably cheaper buying tickets in Indonesia than it is purchasing them abroad. Airlines such as Garuda, Lion Air, Batavia Air and AirAsia have an online booking system for use with Visa or MasterCard. Garuda flights can be reserved online. Offices in larger towns will usually accept credit card payment, although smaller branch offices in out-of-the-way places will often only take cash payment. Some airlines give student reductions. During holiday periods, flights are booked up some time ahead. ▶▶ *For details of domestic airport tax, see page 15.*

Boat

The national shipping company is **Pelayaran Nasional Indonesia (PELNI)** ① *Jln Gajah Mada 14, Jakarta, T021 633 4342, www.pelni.co.id*. Many travel agents also sell PELNI tickets and, although they levy a small surcharge, may be far more convenient. PELNI operates a fleet of modern passenger ships that ply fortnightly circuits throughout the archipelago. The ships are well run and well maintained, have an excellent safety record, and are a comfortable and leisurely way to travel. Each accommodates 500-2250 passengers in five classes, has central air conditioning, a bar, restaurant and cafeteria. The unprecedented growth in the domestic airline industry in the past few years has seen PELNI profits take a beating, with more and more routes being cut annually. Note that sailing with PELNI can take some planning as departures in more remote parts of the country can be as far apart as two weeks. Check the PELNI website for the lastest schedule.

Rail

Passenger train services are limited to Java and certain areas of Sumatra. Trains are usually slow and often delayed. Single track connects many major cities. First class is air conditioned with a dining car. There are two main trunk routes on Java: Jakarta–Cirebon–Semarang–Surabaya and Jakarta–Bandung–Yogyakarta–Solo (Surakarta)–Surabaya. The principal services are identified by name, for example, the *Bima* is the air-conditioned night-express from Jakarta via Yogya and Solo, to Surabaya (12 hours); the *Mutiara Utara* is the northern route train to Surabaya via Semarang; the *Senja Utama Solo* is the express train to Yogya and Solo; while the *Senja Utama Semarang* is the express train to Cirebon and Semarang. There are three classes: **Eksekutif** is first class, with air conditioning, reclining seats and breakfast included. **Business** (*bisnis*) is fan-cooled, with pillows provided; and **Ekonomi**, with rather run-down, well-used coaches, broken fans and windows that may or may not open – this class is subject to overcrowding. All three classes can be booked. Reservations should be made well in advance; it is often easier through a travel agent in the town where you are staying. Fares and timetables can be found at www.kereta-api.co.id (only in Indonesian) – for schedules, train names and fares head to the 'Jadwal & Tarif' link.

Road

Bicycle In some of the more popular tourist destinations, guesthouses and some tour companies hire out bicycles. These vary in quality – check the brakes before you set off. Expect to pay about 25,000Rp per day for a locally or Chinese-built mountain bike.

Bus Road transport in Indonesia has improved greatly in recent years, and main roads on most of the islands are generally in reasonably good condition though somewhat overcrowded. In many areas main roads may be impassable during the rainy season and after severe storms.

Most Indonesians get around by bus. The network is vast and although it is not always quick or comfortable, buses are the cheapest way to travel. There are a range of bus alternatives from **Bis Ekonomi** (dirt cheap, cramped but a good way to mingle with Indonesians), to **Bis VIP** (icy cold, fully reclinable seats with plenty of space). Visitors are most likely to find themselves on fairly comfy **Bis Malam**, air-conditioned buses that plough the roads of the archipelago each night and deposit red-eyed passengers at their desination at dawn just in time for morning prayers.

Avoid the seats at the front, which are the most dangerous if there is a crash. Roads are often windy and rough, and buses are badly sprung (or totally un-sprung). Despite harrowingly fast speeds at times, do not expect to average much more than 40 kph except on the best highways. Overnight buses are usually faster and recommended for longer journeys. However, air-conditioned overnighters can be very cold and a sarong or blanket is useful.

Tickets can be obtained from bus company offices or through travel agents; shop around for the best fare – bargaining is possible. It is sensible to book a day or so ahead for longer journeys. During Ramadan and at Lebaran, all forms of public transport are packed. **Shuttle buses** or **Travels** are found in the main tourist areas on Bali and Lombok and increasingly between the major cities in Java. In Bali they operate almost exclusively for the benefit of foreigners connecting the most popular destinations, with a fixed daily timetable. They will pick up and drop off passengers at their hotels and take a great deal of the hassle out of travel.

Car and motorbike hire Cars can be hired for self-drive or with a driver. Motorbike hire is available at many beach resorts and increasingly in other towns. It is illegal to ride without a helmet, although this can just be a construction worker's hard hat. Many machines are poorly maintained: check brakes and lights before paying.

Taxi Taxis are metered in the major cities. Drivers often cannot change large bills. All registered taxis, minibuses and rental cars have yellow number plates; black number plates are for private vehicles, and red are for government-owned vehicles.

Other forms of local road transport
Bajaj Small three-wheeled motor scooters similar to the Thai tuk-tuk. They are probably the cheapest form of 'taxi' after the becak, but are only available in big cities.
Becaks Becaks or bicycle rickshaws are one of the cheapest, and most important, forms of short-distance transport in Indonesia. Literally hundreds of thousands of poor people make a living driving becaks. However, they are now illegal in central Jakarta and often officially barred from main thoroughfares in other large cities. Bargain hard and agree a fare before boarding.
Bemos These are small buses or adapted pickups operating on fixed routes. They usually run fixed routes for fixed fares (it varies between towns, but around 3000Rp), but can also be chartered by the hour or day.
Ojeks Motorcycle taxis. Ojek riders, often wearing coloured jackets, congregate at junctions, taking passengers pillion to their destination. Agree a price before boarding and bargain hard.

Oplets Larger versions of bemos carrying 10-12 passengers. They have a bewildering number of other names – daihatsu in Semarang, angkuta in Solo, microlets in Jakarta, while in rural areas they tend to be called colts. In larger cities, bemos/colts often follow fixed routes. They are sometimes colour coded, sometimes numbered, sometimes have their destinations marked on the front – and sometimes all three. For intra-city trips there is usually a fixed fare (it varies between towns, but around 3000Rp) although it is worth asking one of your fellow passengers what the *harga biasa* (normal price) is, or watch what is being handed to the driver or his sidekick by fellow passengers. In the countryside, routes can vary and so do fares; be prepared to bargain. Oplets can also be chartered by the hour or day (bargain hard).

Maps

Locally, maps may not be available beyond the larger cities, and often the quality is poor.
Nelles A good series of maps of the major islands and island groups.
Periplus Travel Maps A recent series of maps to the major islands including some to individual provinces. Good on tourist site information and often with good city insets.

Where to stay in Indonesia

Tourist and business centres usually have a good range of accommodation for all budgets. Bali, for example, has some of the finest hotels in the world – at a corresponding price – along with excellent mid- and lower-range accommodation. However, visitors venturing off the beaten track may find hotels restricted to dingy and overpriced establishments catering for local businessmen and officials. The best-run and most competitively priced budget accommodation is found in popular tourist spots – like Bali and Yogya. It is almost always worth bargaining. This is particularly true for hotels in tourist destinations that attract a fair amount of local weekend business: the weekday room rate may be 50% less than the weekend rate. All hotels are required to display their room rates (for every category of room) on a *daftar harga*, or price list. This is invariably either in public view in the reception area or will be produced when you ask about room rates. Indonesians prefer to be on the ground floor, so rooms on higher floors are usually cheaper. In cheaper accommodation, the bed may consist only of a bottom sheet and pillow with no top sheet.

Terminology can be confusing: a *losmen* is a lower price range hotel (in parts of Sumatra and in some other areas, *losmen* are known as *penginapan*); a *wisma* is a guesthouse, but these can range in price from cheap to moderately expensive; finally, a *hotel* is a hotel, but can range from the cheap and squalid up to a Hilton.

With the economy faring well in Indonesia in recent years, and a more affluent middle class emerging, mid-range and top-end hotels are being built at an extraordinary rate, many offering excellent promotion rates and possessing all the mod cons an international traveller requires. The backpacker market has seen less money being poured into it than, for example, in Malaysia and Thailand, and these places can often seem to be a bit bleak and tawdry compared to cheaper digs elsewhere in Southeast Asia. The exception to this is in Bali and some parts of Lombok, where the backpacker market is still pulling in the rupiah and there are a few gems to be found.

Bathing and toilets

Baths and showers are not a feature of many cheaper *losmen*. Instead a *mandi* (a water tank and ladle) is used to wash. The tub is not climbed into; water is ladled from the tub and

Price codes

Where to stay

$$$$	over US$100	$$$	US$46-100
$$	US$21-45	$	US$20 and under

Price codes refer to the cost of a standard double/twin room in high season.

Restaurants

$$$	over US$12	$$	US$6-12	$	under US$6

Price codes refer to the cost of a two-course meal, not including drinks.

splashed over the head. The traditional Asian toilet is of the squat variety. (Toilets are called *kamar kecil* – the universal 'small room' – or *way say*, as in the initials 'WC'.) Toilet paper is not traditionally used; the faithful left hand and water suffice. In cheaper accommodation you are expected to bring your own towels, soap and toilet paper.

Food and drink in Indonesia

Food

The main staple across the archipelago is rice. Today, alternatives such as corn, sweet potatoes and sago, which are grown primarily in the dry islands of the East, are regarded as 'poor man's food', and rice is the preferred staple.

Indonesians will eat rice – or *nasi* (milled, cooked rice) – at least three times a day. Breakfast is often left-over rice, stir-fried and served up as *nasi goreng*. Mid-morning snacks are often sticky rice cakes or *pisang goreng* (fried bananas). Rice is the staple for lunch, served up with two or three meat and vegetable dishes and followed by fresh fruit. The main meal is supper, which is served quite early and again consists of rice, this time accompanied by as many as five or six other dishes. *Sate/satay* (grilled skewers of meat), *soto* (a nourishing soup) or *bakmi* (noodles, a dish of Chinese origin) may be served first.

In many towns (particularly in Java), *sate, soto* or *bakmi* vendors roam the streets with carts containing charcoal braziers, ringing a bell or hitting a block (the noise will signify what he or she is selling) in the early evenings. These carts are known as *kaki lima* (five legs). *Pedagang* (vendor) *kaki lima* also refers to hawkers who peddle their wares from stalls and from baskets hung from shoulder poles.

Larger foodstalls tend to set up in the same place every evening in a central position in town. These *warungs*, as they are known, may be temporary structures or more permanent buildings, with simple tables and benches. In the larger cities, there may be an area of *warungs*, all under one roof. Often a particular street will become known as the best place to find particular dishes like *martabak* (savoury meat pancakes) or *gado gado* (vegetable salad served with peanut sauce). It is common to see some *warungs* labelled *wartegs*. These are stalls selling dishes from Tegal, a town on Java's north coast. More formalized restaurants are known simply as *rumah makan* (literally 'eating houses'), often shortened to just 'RM'. A good place to look for cheap stall food is in and around the market or *pasar*; night markets or *pasar malam* are usually better for eating than day markets.

Feast days, such as Lebaran marking the end of Ramadan, are a cause for great celebration and traditional dishes are served. *Lontong* or *ketupat* are made at this time (they are both versions of boiled rice – simmered in a small container or bag, so that as it cooks, the rice is compressed to make a solid block). This may be accompanied by *sambal goreng daging* (fried beef in a coconut sauce) in Java or *rendang* (curried beef) in Sumatra. *Nasi kuning* (yellow rice) is traditionally served at a *selamatan* (a Javanese celebration marking a birth, the collection of the rice harvest or the completion of a new house).

In addition to rice, there are a number of other common ingredients used across the country. Coconut milk, ginger, chilli peppers and peanuts are used nationwide, while dried salted fish and soybeans are important sources of protein. In coastal areas, fish and seafood tend to be more important than meat. As Indonesia is more than 80% Muslim, pork is not widely eaten (except in Chinese restaurants) but in some areas, such as Bali, Christian Flores and around Lake Toba in Sumatra, it is much more in evidence.

Regional cuisines

Although Indonesia is becoming more homogeneous as Javanese culture spreads to the Outer Islands, there are still distinctive regional cuisines. The food of Java embraces a number of regional forms, of which the most distinctive is **Sundanese**. *Lalap*, a Sundanese dish, consists of raw vegetables and is said to be the only Indonesian dish where vegetables are eaten uncooked. Characteristic ingredients of Javanese dishes are soybeans, beef, chicken and vegetables; characteristic flavours are an interplay of sweetness and spiciness. Probably the most famous regional cuisine, however, is **Padang** or **Minang** food, which has its origins in West Sumatra province. Padang food has 'colonized' the rest of the country and there are Padang restaurants in every town, no matter how small. Dishes tend to be hot and spicy, using quantities of chilli and turmeric, and include *rendang* (dry beef curry), *kalo ayam* (creamy chicken curry) and *dendeng balado* (fried seasoned sun-dried meat with a spicy coating). In **Eastern Indonesia**, seafood and fish are important elements in the diet, and fish grilled over an open brazier (*ikan panggang* or *ikan bakar*) and served with spices and rice is a delicious, common dish. The **Toraja** of Sulawesi eat large amounts of pork, and specialities include black rice (*nasi hitam*) and fish or chicken cooked in bamboo (*piong*). There are large numbers of Chinese people scattered across the archipelago and, like other countries of the region, **Chinese** restaurants are widespread.

Drink

Water must be boiled for at least five minutes before it is safe to drink. Hotels and most restaurants should boil the water they offer customers. Ask for *air minum* (drinking water). Many restaurants provide a big jug of boiled water on each table. In cheaper establishments it is probably best to play safe and ask for bottled water, although consider the environmental impact of this.

'**Mineral water**' – of which the most famous is *Aqua* ('aqua' has become the generic word for mineral water) – is available in all but the smallest and most remote towns. Check the seal is intact before accepting a bottle. Bottled water is cheap: a 1.5 litre bottle costs around 3500Rp. Bottled water is considerably cheaper at supermarkets than at the many kiosks lining the streets.

Western **bottled and canned drinks** are widely available in Indonesia and are comparatively cheap. Alternatively, most restaurants will serve *air jeruk* (citrus **fruit juices**) with or without ice (*es*). The **coconut milk** is a good thirst quencher and a good source of potassium and glucose. Fresh fruit juices vary greatly in quality; some are little more than water, sugar and ice. Ice in many places is fine, but in cheaper restaurants and away from tourist areas many people recommend taking drinks without ice. Javanese, Sumatran,

Sulawesi or Timorese *kopi* (coffee), fresh and strong, is an excellent morning pick-you-up. It is usually served *kopi manis* (sweet) and black; if you want to have it without sugar, ask for it *tidak pakai gula*. The same goes for other drinks habitually served with mountains of sugar (like fruit juices). *Susu* (milk) is available in tourist areas and large towns, but it may be sweetened condensed milk. *Teh* (tea), usually weak, is obtainable almost everywhere. *Teh jahe* (hot ginger tea) is a refreshing alternative.

Although Indonesia is a predominantly Muslim country, alcohol is widely available. The two most popular **beers** – light lagers – are the locally brewed *Anker* and *Bintang* brands. Wine is becoming more popular. A reasonable bottle can be had for around US$15. Imported **spirits** are comparatively expensive, however, a number of local brews including *brem* (rice wine), *arak* (rice whisky) and *tuak* (palm wine) are available.

Shopping in Indonesia

Indonesia offers a wealth of distinctive handicrafts and other products. Best buys include textiles (batik and *ikat*), silverwork, woodcarving, *krisses* (indigenous daggers), puppets, paintings and ceramics. Bali has the greatest choice of handicrafts. It is not necessarily the case that you will find the best buys in the area where a particular product is made; the larger cities, especially Jakarta, sell a wide range of handicrafts and antiques from across the archipelago at competitive prices.

Tips on buying
Early morning sales may well be cheaper, as salespeople often believe the first sale augurs well for the rest of the day. Except in the larger fixed-price stores, bargaining (with good humour) is expected; start at 60% lower than the asking price. Do not expect to achieve instant results; if you walk away from the shop, you will almost certainly be followed, with a lower offer. If the salesperson agrees to your price, you should feel obliged to purchase – it is considered very ill mannered to agree on a price and then not buy the article.

What to buy
Centres of batik-making are focused on Java. Yogyakarta and Solo (Surakarta) probably offer the widest choice. There is also a good range of batik in Jakarta. The traditional hand-drawn batiks (*batik tulis*) are more expensive than the modern printed batiks. *Ikat* is dyed and woven cloth found on the islands of Bali, Lombok and Nusa Tenggara, although it is not cheap and is sometimes of dubious quality. *Wayang* is a Javanese and Balinese art form and puppets are most widely available on these islands, particularly in Yogyakarta and Jakarta. Baskets of all shapes and sizes are made for practical use, out of rattan, bamboo, sisal, and nipah and lontar palm. The intricate baskets of Lombok are particularly attractive. Woodcarving ranges from the clearly tourist oriented (Bali), to fine classical pieces (Java), to 'primitive' (Papua). The greatest concentration of woodcarvers work in Bali, producing skilful modern and traditional designs. For a more contemporary take on Indonesian fashion, head to the *distros* of Bandung for some seriously unique T-shirts and accessories.

Essentials A-Z

Accident and emergency
Ambulance T118, Fire T113, Police T110.

Customs and duty free
The duty-free allowance is 2 litres of alcohol, 200 cigarettes or 50 cigars or 100 g of tobacco, along with a reasonable amount of perfume.

Prohibited items include narcotics, arms and ammunition, pornographic objects or printed matter.

Embassies and consulates
For Indonesian embassies and consulates abroad and for foreign embassies in Indonesia, see http://embassy.goabroad.com.

Internet
Any town of any size will have an internet café. Costs vary from 3000Rp-20,000Rp per hr. Indonesia is a surpisingly well-wired country and many hotels, cafés and even convenience stores offer Wi-Fi (though frustratingly hotels often charge for access). Smartphones, particularalarly Blackberry and their BBM (Blackberry messenger service) have taken off here in recent years.

Language
The national language is Bahasa Indonesia, which is written in Roman script. There are 250 regional languages and dialects, of which Sundanese (the language of West Java and Jakarta) is the most widespread. In Padang and elsewhere in West Sumatra, the population speak Minang, which is also similar to Bahasa. About 70% of the population can speak Bahasa, which is relatively easy to learn. English is the most common foreign language, with some Dutch and Portuguese speakers.

The best way to learn Indonesian is to study it intensively in Indonesia. In Jakarta and Bali, a variety of short and long courses (including homestay programmes in Bali) are available through The Indonesia-Australia Language Foundation (IALF), T021 521 3350, www.ialf.edu. In Yogyakarta, another centre where overseas students study Indonesian, courses are run by the Realia Language School, T0274 583229, www.realians.com, which is recommended. It is cheaper if a group learns together.

Media
The best English-language newspaper is the *Jakarta Post* (www.thejakartapost.com). The *Jakarta Globe* (www.thejakartaglobe. com) also offers coverage of the country and beyond and often publishes some interesting travel features on Indonesian destinations. The *Asian Wall Street Journal* and the *International Herald Tribune* can be purchased in Jakarta and some other major cities and tourist destinations; so too can the *Singapore Straits Times*.

Radio Republik Indonesia (*RRI*) broadcasts throughout the country. News and commentary in English is broadcast for about 1 hr a day. Shortwave radios will pick up *Voice of America*, the *BBC World Service* and *Australian Broadcasting*.

Televisi Republik Indonesia (*TVRI*) is the government-run channel. There are also private stations showing news and occasional English-language films and documentaries.

Money → *For latest rates, visit www.xe.com.*
The unit of currency in Indonesia is the rupiah (Rp). When taking US$ in cash, make sure the bills are new and crisp, as banks in Indonesia can be fussy about which bills they accept (Flores and Sumatra are particularly bad). Larger denomination US$ bills also tend to command a premium exchange rate. In more out of the way places it is worth making sure that you

have a stock of smaller notes and coins – it can be hard to break larger bills.

Two of the better banks are **Bank Negara Indonesia (BNI)** and **Bank Central Asia (BCA)**. BNI is reliable and efficient and most of their branches will change US$ TCs. Banks in larger towns and tourist centres have ATMs. Cash or traveller's cheques (TCs) can be changed in most tourist centres at a competitive rate. Credit cards are widely accepted.

Tipping is commonplace in Indonesia, and small bills are often handed over at the end of every transaction to smooth it over and ensure good service, Indeed, it can often seem that the whole country is founded on tipping, an informal way of channelling money through society so that lower earners can supplement their meagre earnings and are motivated into action. A 10% service charge is added to bills at more expensive hotels. Porters expect to be tipped about 2000Rp a bag. In more expensive restaurants, where no service is charged, a tip of 5-10% may be appropriate. Taxi drivers (in larger towns) appreciate a small tip (1000Rp). *Parkirs* always expect payment for 'watching' your vehicle; 1000Rp.

Cost of travelling
Indonesia is no longer the bargain country it was 10 years ago. Whilst it is still cheap by Western standards tourists can now expect to dig deeper for their meals and accommodation. Visitors staying in 1st-class hotels and eating in top-notch restaurants will probably spend between US100 and US$150 a day. Tourists on a mid-range budget, staying in cheaper a/c accommodation and eating in local restaurants, will probably spend between US$50-80 a day. A backpacker, staying in fan-cooled guesthouses and eating cheaply, could scrape by on US$20-25 a day, though this leaves little room for wild partying. Indonesia has seen prices spiral in recent years, particularly for food and this is reflected in the increased costs that travellers now have to bear when visiting the country.

Post
The postal service is relatively reliable; though important mail should be registered. Every town and tourist centre has either a *kantor pos* (post office) or postal agent, where you can buy stamps, post letters and parcels.

Safety
Despite the recent media coverage of terrorist plots and attacks, riots and other disturbances in Indonesia, it remains a safe country and violence against foreigners is rare. Petty theft is a minor problem.

Avoid carrying large amounts of cash; TCs can be changed in most major towns.

Beware of the confidence tricksters who are widespread in tourist areas. Sudden reports of unbeatable bargains or closing down sales are usual ploys.

Civil unrest The following areas of Indonesia have seen disturbances in recent years and visits are not recommended: Maluku (around Ambon), Central Sulawesi (around Palu and Poso). Both these places have been victims of sectarian violence. However, these incidents have been localized and almost never affected foreign visitors. Embassies ask visitors to exercise caution when travelling in Aceh, a region recovering from a long internal conflict.

Flying After a series of accidents the EU banned many Indonesian airlines from entering its air space over continuing concerns of poor maintenance and safety. The Indonesian government and airline companies have taken this very seriously and the last few years have seen brand new Boeings and Airbuses being rolled out by **Lion Air** and **Garuda**. The airlines considered acceptable by the EU are **Batavia**, **Garuda** and **Indonesia AirAsia**. Many European embassies advise against domestic air travel. For the latest information, see www.fco.gov.uk/en and www.travel.state.gov/travel/warnings.html.

Tax

Expect to pay 11% tax in the more expensive restaurants, particularly in tourist areas of Bali and Lombok. Some cheaper restaurants serving foreigners may add 10% to the bill.

Airport tax 75,000Rp-150,000Rp on international flights (Jakarta and Denpasar are both 150,000Rp), and anywhere between 10,000Rp and 30,000Rp on domestic flights, depending on the airport.

Telephone → *Country code +62.*

Operator T101. International enquiries T102. Local enquiries T108. Long-distance enquiries T106. Every town has its communication centres (**Wartel**), where you can make local and international calls and faxes.

Mobile phones Known as hand-phones or HP in Indonesia, use has sky rocketed and costs are unbelievably low. It usually costs around 15,000Rp to by a Sim card with a number. Top-up cards are sold at various denominations. If you buy a 10,000Rp or 20,000Rp card, the vendor will charge a few more thousand, in order to gain some profit. If you buy a 100,000Rp card, you will pay a few thousand less than 100,000Rp. This is standard practice throughout the country. Beware of vendors in Kuta, Bali who try and sell Sim cards at highly inflated prices. Reliable operators include **Telkomsel**, **IM3** and **Pro XL**. If you want to buy a dirt cheap phone in country, look for the Esia brand which offers bargain basement phone and credit packages.

Visas and immigration

Visitors from several nations, including Malaysia, The Philippines and Singapore are allowed a visa-free stay of 30 days in Indonesia. Visitors from nations including the following are able to get a US$25

30-day **Visa On Arrival** (**VOA**): Australia, Canada, France, Germany, Holland, Ireland, Italy, New Zealand, Portugal, Spain, United Kingdom and the USA. Check with your embassy. Pay at a booth at the port of entry. These visas are extendable at immigration offices in the country for an extra 30 days. In Bali many travel agents offer to extend visas, for a fee. Visitors wishing to obtain a VOA must enter and leave Indonesia though certain ports of entry, including the following:

Sea ports Batam, Tanjung Uban, Belawan (Medan), Dumai, Jayapura, Tanjung Balaikarimun, Bintang Pura (Tanjung Pinang), and Kupang.

Airports Medan, Pekanbaru, Padang, Jakarta, Surabaya, Bali, Manado, Adisucipto in Yogyakarta, Adisumarmo in Solo, and Selaparang in Mataram, Lombok.

A US$10 VOA (7 days) is available for visitors to the Riau islands of Batam and Bintan.

60-day visitor visas (B211) are available at Indonesian embassies and consulates around the world (a ticket out of the country, 2 photos and a completed visa form is necessary). Costs vary. They can be extended giving a total stay of 6 months (must be extended at an immigration office in Indonesia each month after the initial 60-day visa has expired; take it to the office 4 days before expiry). To extend the visa in Indonesia, a fee of US$25 is levied and a sponsor letter from a local person is needed. To obtain a 60-day visitor visa in Singapore, a one-way ticket from Batam to Singapore is adequate: purchase from the ferry centre at HarbourFront in Singapore.

It is crucial to check this information before travelling as the visa situation in Indonesia is extremely volatile. Travellers who overstay their visa will be fined US$20 a day. Long-term overstayers can expect a fine and jail sentence. See www.indonesianembassy.org.uk for more information.

All visitors to Indonesia must possess a passport valid for at least 6 months from their date of arrival in Indonesia, and they should have proof of onward travel. It is not uncommon for immigration officers to ask to see a ticket out of the country. (A Batam–Singapore ferry ticket or cheap Medan–Penang air ticket will suffice).

Contents

Indonesia

Java

Java is Indonesia's political, economic and cultural heartland. With 60% of the country's population, the capital Jakarta, and the great bulk of Indonesia's industrial muscle, Java is the critical piece in the Indonesian jigsaw. It was here that many of the early, pre-colonial empires and kingdoms were based – reflected in monuments such as Borobudur and Prambanan, and in many smaller temples. Cities like Yogyakarta and Solo remain vibrant artistic and cultural centres, while Bogor and Bandung show more clearly the hand of the relatively short-lived Dutch presence. The latter, particularly, is renowned for its art deco architecture. Jakarta, as Indonesia's capital, has the most restaurants, the largest museums, and the widest array of shopping, but it is not a particularly enticing city.

The hand of humans has always had to contend with the forces of nature and nowhere is this clearer than in the battle against Java's volcanoes. From Krakatau off the west coast of Java to Gunung Bromo in East Java, a spine of active volcanoes runs through the island. While these volcanoes periodically bring destruction, they also provide the basis for a string of hill resorts and towns, and the fertile soil needed for feeding this incredibly densely populated island.

Jakarta

Jakarta is Indonesia's centre of commerce and communications, of manufacturing activity and consumption, of research and publishing. It has the highest per capita income and the greatest concentration of rupiah billionaires. Jakarta is not often rated very highly as a tourist attraction, but if visitors can tolerate the traffic, then it is possible to spend an enjoyable few days visiting the excellent museums, admiring the architectural heritage of the Dutch era, strolling through the old harbour or discovering some of the many antique, arts and crafts shops. Night owls are invariably bowled over by the city's nightlife, which offers superb variety, from sipping top-notch vintages in lounge bars to downright dirty clubbing.

Today, Jakarta is a sprawling, cosmopolitan city, with a population of over 9,580,000 (2010 census)– making it by far the largest city in Indonesia. Metropolitan Jakarta, known as Jabodetabek (metropolitan Jakarta includes the satellite cities of Bogor, Depok, Tangerang and Bekasi), has an estimated population of 28 million, making it one of the 10 largest metropolitan areas on earth. Growth has been rapid. Jakarta is perceived by the poorer rural Indonesians as a city paved with gold, and they have flocked to the capital in their thousands.

The central area is dominated by office blocks, international hotels, flashy condominium developments, shopping malls and wide, tree-lined roads. Off the main thoroughfares, the streets become smaller and more intimate, almost village-like. These are the densely inhabited kampungs where immigrants have tended to live – one-storey, tile-roofed houses crammed together and linked by a maze of narrow paths. Initially, kampungs developed their own identity, with people from particular language and ethnic groups, even from particular towns, congregating in the same place and maintaining their individual identities. Today those distinctions are less obvious, but the names of the kampungs are a reminder of their origins: Kampung Bali, Kampung Aceh (North Sumatra) and Kampung Makassar (Ujung Pandang), for example.

Arriving in Jakarta → *Phone code: 021.*

Getting there

Jakarta's **Soekarno-Hatta Airport** ⓘ *25 km northwest of the city, T021 550 5177, www. jakartasoekarnohattaairport.com,* is where most visitors arrive. It connects Jakarta with all other major cities and towns in the country, as well as regional and global destinations. Budget carriers flying into Jakarta include **AirAsia** (from Singapore, KL in Malaysia, Bangkok and Phuket in Thailand), and **Jetstar Asia** (from Singapore). State-owned **Garuda**, **Merpati** and all international airlines operate from Terminal 2. Domestic airlines use Terminal 1. Terminal 3 is used by **Indonesia AirAsia**.

Facilities at the airport include car rental, currency exchange booths, ATMs, left-luggage facilities (outside the Arrivals hall), hotel booking counter, a taxi desk, tourist information desk (with maps), the **Transit Hotel**, the **Transit Restaurant**, fast-food outlets, a 24-hour post office, long-distance calls, and internet and cell phone connectivity facilities.

Metered taxis to the centre of town cost about 90,000Rp (plus toll fees of 11,500Rp). Only taxis with official Taxi Bandara stickers on their windscreens are allowed to pick up passengers at the airport. The airport authorities hand out complaints cards for visitors to complete, setting out the toll charges and surcharges applicable. Allow at least an hour to reach the airport from the centre of town, more at peak times. **Damri** ⓘ *T021 550 1290, www.damri.co.id,* runs air-conditioned buses from Terminal 2 F/E to Jakarta's Gambir railway station every 15-30 minutes from 0500-1830 (one hour, 20,000Rp).

The **Gambir railway station** is also a major arrival point in Jakarta. There is a **Blue Bird** taxi rank just to the north of the station, which charges a 4500Rp surcharge. The journey to Jalan Jaksa costs around 20,000Rp (the centre for budget accommodation). Alternatively, those with little luggage will be able to manage the 10-minute walk. Air-conditioned Damri buses also run to Blok M, Jalan Bulungan, and Kemayoran. There are also buses running to Bogor (35,000Rp) and Bandung (70,000Rp), for those that want to avoid Jakarta. Many of the first-class hotels lay on transport.

Tourist information
The **Jakarta Tourist Office** ① *Jakarta Theatre Building, Jln MH Thamrin 9, T021 314 2067, Mon-Sat 0900-1800, www.jakarta-tourism.go.id*, supplies maps and information.

Places in Jakarta → *For listings, see pages 27-36.*

Kota or Old Batavia
① *From the Hotel Indonesia roundabout or the Sarinah building take TransJakarta bus corridor 1 to Jakarta Kota Station or a taxi.*

The city of Jakarta developed from the small area known as **Kota**, which stretches from the Pasar Ikan (Fish Market) to Jalan Jembatan Batu, just south of Kota train station. The area is about 8 km north of both Monas and many of the city's hotels and guesthouses. North of Pasar Ikan was the old harbour town of **Sunda Kelapa** ① *admission to harbour area 1500Rp, daily 0800-1800*, which thrived from the 12th century to 1527 and is still worth a visit today. *Sunda* refers to the region of West Java and *Kelapa* means coconut. Impressive Bugis or Makassar schooners dock here on their inter-island voyages and can be seen moored along the wharf. Gradually, they are being supplanted by modern freighters, but for the time being at least it is possible to see these graceful ships being loaded and unloaded by wiry barefoot men, who cross precariously between the wharf and the boats along narrow planks. Boatmen will offer visitors the chance to ride in a small boat around the harbour, which gives a fascinating glimpse into life on the water. A 30-minute trip should cost between 40,000Rp and 50,000Rp, but hard bargaining is required. It is also sometimes possible to arrange a passage on one of the boats to Kalimantan and elsewhere.

On the southern edge of Sunda Kelapa and close to the Lookout Tower (see below) is the original, and still functioning, **Pasar Ikan**. The market is an odd mixture of ship chandlers, tourist stalls and food outlets. Among the merchandise on sale are sea shells, toy *kijangs*, carvings and unfortunate stuffed animals. Close by at Jalan Pasar Ikan 1 is the **Bahari (Maritime) Museum** ① *T021 669 3406, Tue-Sun 0900-1500, 2000Rp,* which was one of the original Dutch warehouses used for storing spices, coffee and tea. Today it is home to an unimpressive maritime collection. However, upstairs is an interesting display of photographs dating from the late 19th and early 20th centuries, recording life on board the steamships that linked Batavia with Holland. The museum is worth a visit for the building rather than its contents. Other warehouses behind this museum were built between 1663 and 1669.

Overlooking the fetid **Kali Besar** (**Big Canal**), choked with rubbish and biologically dead, is the **Uitkijk** (**Lookout Tower**) ① *daily 0900-1700, 2000Rp*, built in 1839 on the walls of the Dutch fortress Bastion Culemborg (itself constructed in 1645). The tower was initially used to spy on (and signal to) incoming ships, and later as a meteorological post – a role it continued to fill until this century. From the top of the tower there are views north over the port of Sunda Kelapa and south to the city, over an area of poor housing and urban desolation.

Jakarta

→ Jakarta maps
1 Jakarta, page 21
2 Kota, page 22
3 Jakarta centre, page 24

Where to stay 🛏
Kamar Kamar 1

Restaurants 🍴
Anatolia 1
Apartment 2
Gourmet Garage 3
Kinara 4
Loewy 5
Trattoria 6

Bars & clubs 🍸
CJs 8
Elbow Room 7
Red Square 11
Stadium 12
Vin + 13
Vino Embassy 14

Less than 1 km from the Bahari Museum and Sunda Kelapa, south along either Jalan Cangkeh or Jalan Kapak, is one of the last **Dutch-era drawbridges** across the Kali Besar. It was built over two centuries ago and is known as the 'Chicken Market Bridge', but it has been allowed to fall into disrepair. Continuing south for another 200 m or so, walking past old Dutch warehouses, godowns and other commercial buildings, is **Fatahillah Square**, or **Taman Fatahillah**. This was the heart of the old Dutch city and the site of public executions and punishments – hangings, death by impalement and public floggings. It was also a bustling market place. In the middle of the square is a small, domed building (rebuilt in 1972), the site of the old drinking fountain. The Dutch were unaware that the water from this fountain was infested and it contributed to the city's high incidence of cholera and consequently high mortality rate. On the south side of the square is the **Fatahillah Museum**, on the site of the first City Hall built in 1620. A second hall was constructed in 1627 and today's building was completed in 1710. A fine example of Dutch architecture (reminiscent of the old city hall of Amsterdam), it became a military headquarters after independence and finally, in 1974, the **Museum of the History of Jakarta** ① *T021 692 9101, Tue-Sun 0900-1500, 2000Rp*. It is a lovely building but, like so many Indonesian museums, the collection is poorly laid out. It contains Dutch furniture and VOC memorabilia. In the courtyard behind the museum, two *ondel-ondel* figures stand outside another room of rather down-at-heel exhibits. Below the main building are the prison cells.

The **Wayang Museum** ① *on the west side of the square at Jln Pintu Besar Utara 27, T021 682 9560, Tue-Sun 0900-1500, 2000Rp*, was previously called the Museum of Old Batavia. All that remains of the original 1912 building is its facade. Until 1974 it housed the collection now in the Fatahillah Museum and today contains a good collection of *wayang kulit* and *wayang golek* puppets. Well-made examples are sold here for US$22-77. Performances of *wayang kulit* or *wayang golek* are occasionally held here (enquire at tourist office). West from the Wayang Museum and over the Kali Besar (canal) is the **Toko Merah** or **Red House**. This was once the home of Governor-General Gustaaf van Imhoff. There are some other interesting 18th-century Dutch buildings in the vicinity.

On the north side of Fatahillah Square is an old Portuguese bronze cannon called **Si Jagur**, brought to Batavia by the Dutch after the fall of Melaka in 1641. The design of a clenched fist is supposed to be a symbol of cohabitation and it is visited by childless women in the hope that they will be rendered fertile. On the east side of the square is the **Balai Seni Rupa (Fine Arts Museum)**, formerly the Palace of Justice at Jalan Pos Kota 2. Built in the 1860s, it houses a poor exhibition of paintings by Indonesian artists. The building is shared with the **Museum Keramik** ① *T021 690 7062, Tue-Sun 0900-1500, 2000Rp*, a collection of badly displayed ceramics. The most stylish place to eat and drink on the square is at the **Café Batavia** – itself something of an architectural gem in Indonesian terms. It was built in stages between 1805 and 1850 and is the second oldest building on the square (after the City Hall). Particularly fine is the renovated Grand Salon upstairs, made of Java teak. The café was opened at the end of 1993 and is frequented by foreigners and the Indonesian wealthy. There is a **tourist information office** next to the café and, next to this, a **clothes market,** which functions every day except Sunday.

East of Kota railway station on the corner of Jalan Jembatan Batu and Jalan Pangeran is the oldest church in Jakarta, **Gereja Sion** ① *admission by donation in the adjacent church office*, also known as the 'old Portuguese Church' or 'Gereja Portugis'. It was built for the so-called 'Black Portuguese' – Eurasian slaves brought to Batavia by the Dutch from Portuguese settlements in India and Ceylon. These slaves were promised freedom, provided that they converted to the Dutch Reformed Church. The freed men and women became a social group known as *Mardijkers* (Liberated Ones). The church was built in 1693 and is a fine example of the Baroque style, with a handsome carved wooden pulpit and an elaborately carved organ. The four chandeliers are of yellow copper.

2 Kota

➡ Jakarta maps
1 Jakarta, page 21
2 Kota, page 22
3 Jakarta centre, page 24

Where to stay 🛏
Batavia 1

Restaurants 🍴
Café Batavia 1

200 metres
200 yards

Central Jakarta

South of Fatahillah Square is **Glodok**, or **Chinatown**. This lies outside the original city walls and was the area where the Chinese settled after the massacre of 1740. Despite a national ban on the public display of Chinese characters that was only rescinded in August 1994, Glodok's warren of back streets still feels like a Chinatown, with shophouses, enterprise and activity, and temples tucked behind shop fronts. Midway between Fatahillah Square and Merdeka Square is the **National Archives** or **Arsip Nasional**. This building (which no longer holds the National Archives) was erected in 1760 as a country house for Reiner de Klerk, a wealthy resident who subsequently became governor-general. Since 1925, it has been owned by the state and now houses an interesting collection of Dutch furniture.

The enormous **Medan Merdeka** (**Liberty Square**) dominates the centre of Jakarta. It measures 1sq km and is one of the largest city squares in the world. In the centre of Medan Merdeka is the **National Monument** (**Monas**), a 137-m-high pinnacle meant to represent a *lingga* and thus symbolize fertility and national independence. This massive obelisk was commissioned by President Sukarno in 1961 to celebrate Indonesia's independence from the Dutch. Construction entailed the bulldozing of a large squatter community to make way for the former president's monumental ambitions. It is known among residents of the city, rather irreverently, as Sukarno's Last Erection. Covered in Italian marble, it is topped by a bronze flame (representing the spirit of the revolutionaries), coated in 35 kg of gold leaf. Take the lift to the observation platform for magnificent views over the city. In the basement below the monument is a **museum** ① *T021 384 2777, daily 0830-1700 (closed last Mon of the month), 7500Rp for the museum and trip to the top of the structure; for 2750Rp visitors can access the museum and the lower part of the structure, ticket booth to the north of the monument; avoid going at weekends when there are long queues and general mayhem, as tourists from all over the country descend on the site for a visit.* This houses dioramas depicting the history of Indonesia's independence. The entrance to the museum is north of the road immediately in front of the monument (access is through an underground tunnel), where there is a **statue of Diponegoro** (a Javanese hero) on horseback. He was held prisoner by the Dutch at the Batavia town hall, before being exiled to Manado in North Sulawesi.

On the west side of the square is the neoclassical **National Museum** ① *T021 386 8172, Sun, Tue-Thu 0830-1430, Fri 0830-1130, Sat 0830-1330, 750Rp, guided English-language tours available at 1030 on Tue and Thu, see the Jakarta Post for details as times and days vary, or call the Indonesian Heritage Society on T021 572 5870.* Established in 1860 by the Batavian Fine Arts Society, it is an excellent museum and well worth a visit. Set around a courtyard, the collection consists of some fine stone sculpture (mostly of Hindu gods), a textile collection, and a collection of mainly Chinese ceramics found in Indonesia. Next to the ceramics is a display of bronzeware, including some magnificent Dongson drums and krisses. The pre-history room is well laid out. Its collection includes the skull cap and thigh bone of Java Man, a rare example of *Homo erectus*. The ethnographic collection includes an excellent range of masks, puppets, household articles, musical instruments and some models of traditional buildings representing cultures from several of the main islands in the archipelago. There is also a handicraft shop.

On the north side of the square is the neoclassical **Presidential Palace** or **Istana Merdeka**, built in 1861 and set in immaculate gardens. Originally named **Koningsplein Paleis**. President Sukarno resided at the Istana Merdeka, but President Suharto moved to a more modest residence and the building is now only used for state occasions. Behind the palace is the older **State Palace** (**Istana Negara**), next to the Bina Graha (the presidential

3 Jakarta centre

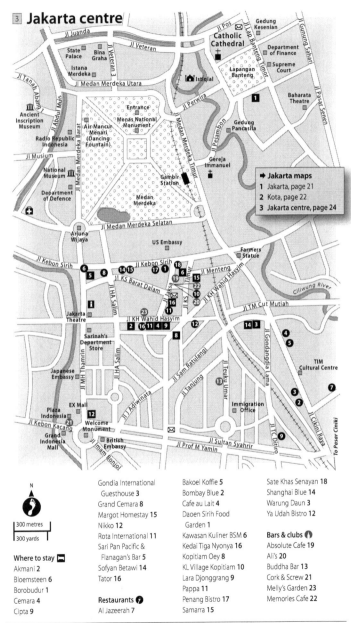

→ Jakarta maps
1 Jakarta, page 21
2 Kota, page 22
3 Jakarta centre, page 24

Where to stay 🛏
Akmani **2**
Bloemsteen **6**
Borobudur **1**
Cemara **4**
Cipta **9**
Gondia International
 Guesthouse **3**
Grand Cemara **8**
Margot Homestay **15**
Nikko **12**
Rota International **11**
Sari Pan Pacific &
 Flanagan's Bar **5**
Sofyan Betawi **14**
Tator **16**

Restaurants 🍴
Al Jazeerah **7**
Bakoel Koffie **5**
Bombay Blue **2**
Cafe au Lait **4**
Daoen Sirih Food
 Garden **1**
Kawasan Kuliner BSM **6**
Kedai Tiga Nyonya **16**
Kopitiam Oey **8**
KL Village Kopitiam **10**
Lara Djonggrang **9**
Pappa **11**
Penang Bistro **17**
Samarra **15**
Sate Khas Senayan **18**
Shanghai Blue **14**
Warung Daun **3**
Ya Udah Bistro **12**

Bars & clubs 🍸
Absolute Cafe **19**
Ali's **20**
Buddha Bar **13**
Cork & Screw **21**
Melly's Garden **23**
Memories Cafe **22**

office building). This palace was built for a Dutchman at the end of the 18th century and was the official residence of Dutch governors-general, before the Koningsplein Palace was built. To get to the State Palace, walk down Jalan Veteran 3 and turn west on Jalan Veteran.

In the northeast corner of Medan Merdeka is the impressive **Istiqlal Mosque**, finished in 1978 after more than 10 years' work. The interior is simple and is almost entirely constructed of marble. It is the principal place of worship for Jakarta's Muslims and reputedly the largest mosque in Southeast Asia, with room for more than 10,000 worshippers. Non-Muslims can visit the mosque when prayers are not in progress. Facing the mosque, in the northwest corner of Lapangan Banteng, is the strange neo-Gothic **Catholic Cathedral**; its date of construction is unknown, but it was restored in 1901.

From the south corner of Lapangan Banteng, Jalan Pejambon runs south past **Gedung Pancasila**, the building where Sukarno gave his famous *proklamasi*, outlining the five principles of Pancasila. At the southern end of Jalan Pejambon, backing onto Merdeka Square, is the **Gereja Immanuel**, an attractive circular domed church built by Dutch Protestants in the classical style in 1835.

West of the city centre

The **Textile Museum** ① *Jln Satsuit Tuban 4, near the Tanah Abang Market (and railway station), T021 560 6613, Tue-Sun 0900-1500, 2000Rp*, is housed in an airy Dutch colonial house set back from the road. It contains a good range of Indonesian textiles, both batik and *ikat*.

South of the city centre

The **Adam Malik Museum** ① *29 Jln Diponegoro, west from the junction with Jln Surabaya, Tue-Sat 1000-1300, Sun 0930-1300, 2500Rp, get there by bus or taxi*, houses a private, quirky collection that includes cameras, radios, walking sticks and watches, as well as Chinese ceramics, woodcarving from Papua, stone carvings from Java, ostentatious furniture, guns, krisses and some interesting Russian icons. The problem with this museum is its lack of discrimination. The interesting and the commonplace, the skilled and the inept, are all massed together.

A night-time drive, or perhaps even a walk, down **Jalan Latuharhary** in Menteng, reveals a seedier – or at least an alternative – side of life in Jakarta. Transvestites, dressed up to the nines, and known as *banci* (meaning hermaphrodite or homosexual) or *waria*, hawk their wares. Foreign visitors may be astonished not only by their beauty, but also by the fact that this is countenanced in an otherwise relatively strict Muslim society. Transvestites have, in fact, a long and honourable tradition not just in Indonesia but throughout Southeast Asia.

The large, wholesale **Pasar Cikini**, in the district of Menteng, is worth a visit to see the range of fruit, vegetables, fish and other fresh products trucked in from the surrounding countryside and the coast for sale in Jakarta. The second floor houses a gold market.

Around Jakarta

Taman Mini-Indonesia

① *T021 840 9214, www.tamanmini.com, park admission 9000Rp plus additional charges for major attractions, daily 0800-1700, 18 km and a rather arduous journey by public transport from the city centre – take a TransJakarta bus corridor 7 from Kampung Melayu to Kampung Rambutan terminal and from there an angkot to the park (1-1½ hrs), or a taxi from town for about US$18.*

This is a 120-ha 'cultural park', 10 km southeast of Jakarta (but closer to 20 km from the centre). Completed in 1975, there are 27 houses, each representing one of Indonesia's provinces and built in the traditional style of that region, although the building materials used are modern substitutes. Frustratingly, no translation of the descriptions is offered. All the houses are set around a lake with boats for hire. It is possible to drive around the park on weekdays or, alternatively, walk, take the mini train, cable car or horse and cart (small charges for these). The cable car takes passengers over the lake, upon which there is a replica of the whole archipelago. The **Keong Mas Theatre** ① *daily 1100-1700, from 30,000Rp*, (so-called because its shape resembles a golden snail) presents superb not-to-be-missed films on Indonesia, projected on an enormous IMAX screen. Check *Jakarta Post* for details of screenings. The **Museum Indonesia** ① *0900-1500, 5000Rp*, a Balinese-style building, houses a good collection of arts and crafts and costumes from across the archipelago. The **Museum Komodo** ① *0800-1500, 10,000Rp*, is, as the name suggests, built in the form of the *Varanus komodiensis*, better known as the Komodo dragon. It houses dioramas of Indonesian fauna and flora. There's also an aquarium, an insectarium, an orchid garden, aviaries and a swimming pool.

Pulau Seribu → *For listings, see pages 27-36.*

Pulau Seribu, or 'Thousand Islands', clearly named by the mathematically challenged, actually consists of 112 small islands. Just to the west of Jakarta, off Java's north coast, they are becoming increasingly popular as a tourist destination. The Dutch VOC had a presence on the islands from the 17th century, building forts, churches and shipyards.

Pulau Onrust is one of the closest islands to the mainland. It was used by the Dutch from the early 17th century and became an important ship repair centre; by 1775 as many as 2000 people were living on the island. But in the 1800s the British sacked and burnt the small settlement, so that today only ruins remain. **Pulau Bidadari** also has ruins of a fort and leper hospital built by the VOC. It lies 15 km from Ancol (45 minutes by speedboat). **Pulau Laki** is one of the inner islands situated 3 km offshore from Tanjung Kait west of Jakarta.

Venturing further north into the Java Sea, there are a succession of privately owned resorts including **Pulau Ayer**, **Pulau Putri**, **Pulau Pelangi**, **Pulau Kotok** and **Pulau Panjang**, in that order. They have beautiful beaches and offer snorkelling, scuba-diving, jet skiing and windsurfing.

Krakatau → *For listings, see pages 27-36.*

Krakatau is the site of the largest volcanic eruption ever recorded. The explosion occurred on the morning of the 27 August 1883, had a force equivalent to 2000 Hiroshima bombs, and resulted in the death of 36,000 people. A tsunami 40 m high, radiating outwards at speeds of reportedly over 500 kph, destroyed coastal towns and villages. The explosion was heard from Sri Lanka to Perth in Australia and the resulting waves led to a noticeable surge in the English Channel. The explosion was such that the 400-m-high cone was replaced by a marine trench 300 m deep.

Rupert Furneau writes in his book *Krakatoa* (1965): "At 10 o'clock plus two minutes, three-quarters of Krakatau Island, 11 square miles of its surface, an area not much less than Manhattan, a mass of rock and earth one and one-eighth cubic miles in extent, collapsed into a chasm beneath. Nineteen hours of continuous eruption had drained the magma from the chamber faster than it could be replenished from below. Their support removed, thousands of tons of roof rock crashed into the void below. Krakatau's three cones caved in. The sea bed reared and opened in upheaval. The sea rushed into the gaping hole. From the raging cauldron of seething rocks, frothing magma and hissing sea, spewed an immense quantity of water ... From the volcano roared a mighty blast, Krakatau's death cry, the greatest volume of sound recorded in human history".

In 1927, further volcanic activity caused a new island to rise above the sea – **Anak Krakatau** (Child of Krakatau). Today this island stands 200 m above sea level and visitors may walk from the east side of the island upon the warm, devastated landscape through deep ash, to the main crater. It remains desolate and uninhabited, though the other surrounding islands have been extensively recolonized (a process carefully recorded by naturalists; the first visitor after the 1883 explosion noted a spider vainly spinning a web). Check that the volcano is safe to visit and take thick-soled walking shoes (Krakatau is still avowedly active: between 1927 and 1992 it erupted no less than 73 times). There is good snorkelling and diving in the water around the cliffs; the undersea thermal springs allow abundant marine plant growth and this attracts a wealth of sea creatures, big and small.

The sea crossing is calmest and the weather best from April to June and September to October. Between November and March there are strong currents and often rough seas.

Note Anak Krakatau is currently highly active and tourists are NOT permitted to climb the crater. This is due to spewing molten rocks and potentially fatal toxic gases. Tourists can land on Anak Krakatau for a wander, at their own risk. Check the latest information before heading out, as the volcano has been put on the highest alert several times in the past year.

Jakarta listings

For hotel and restaurant price codes and other relevant information, see pages 9-12.

● Where to stay

Jakarta *p19, maps p21, p22 and p24*
Jalan Jaksa and around
This small street has been the backpackers' headquarters for years, with a large selection of budget lodgings, cheap eateries and plenty of travel agents. Don't come here expecting Thailand's Khaosan Rd or the tourist quarter of Ho Chi Minh; this street is decidedly low key. Slightly more salubrious hotels are located in the streets around Jln Jaksa.
$$$ The Akmani, Jln Wahid Hasyim 91, T021 3190 5335, www.akmanihotel.com. Slick hotel with excellent promo rates and a good range of facilities including pool and bar with pleasant outdoor seating, gym, restaurant and Wi-Fi access (chargeable). The rooms are modern and sleek and the more

expensive rooms on the higher floors offer excellent city views. Recommended.
$$$ Cemara Hotel, Jln Wahid Hasyim 69, T021 314 7580, www.hotelcemara.com. Newish place with 60 modern rooms with flatscreen cable TV and bathrooms with tub. Good discounts available. Breakfast not included. Wi-Fi available (chargeable).
$$$-$$ Cipta Hotel, Jln Wahid Hasyim 53, T021 390 4701, www.ciptahotel.com. Excellent service, although the mint walls and green carpet in some rooms are nauseating. Rooms are clean and spacious with cable TV and fridge. Wi-Fi is available for free in the café downstairs for 10,000Rp per hr. Tax and breakfast included in the price.
$$$-$$ Grand Cemara, Jln Cemara 1, T021 390 8215, www.hotelcemara.com. For those who have travelled halfway around the world to get to Indonesia, this hotel is a fairly comfy mid-range spot to get over the jetlag. Rooms are clean, and come with fridge and cable TV, and some have baths. Expensive

internet available in the room. Spa service available. Breakfast not included in the price.

$$ Hotel Tator, Jln Jaksa 37, T021 3192 3940. Selection of a/c and fan rooms, which are a little faded but compare better than most of the other cheap Jaksa options.

$$ Margot Homestay, Jln Jaksa 15C, T021 391 3830. Well-run place with a selection of a/c rooms with TV and decrepit furniture. There's a fair restaurant by the reception.

$$ Rota International Hotel, Jln Wahid Hasyim 63, T021 315 2858. Plenty of choice, with a selection of clean a/c rooms (some are a bit dark, ask to see a selection) with TV and bath around a massive central courtyard.

$ Bloemsteen Hostel, Jln Kebon Sirih Timur 1, 175 (just off Jln Jaksa), T021 3192 3002. This has been the budget traveller's most popular choice for years now, and justifiably remains in pole position with small, spotless rooms and clean shared bathrooms. There is a pleasant balcony upstairs. It's often very busy, so booking ahead is wise.

Menteng and Cikini
There's a range of mid-priced accommodation scattered throughout this area.

$$$-$$ Hotel Sofyan Betawi, Jln Cut Meutia 9, T021 314 0695, www.sofyanhotel. com. Popular with Indonesian business people. Has clean, comfortable rooms (some are a bit dark), with TV and bath. Broadband.

$ Gondia International Guesthouse, Jln Gondangdia Kecil 22, T021 390 9221. Set down a small alley off Jln Gondangdia, this friendly place has decent, simple a/c rooms with TV and a small but pleasant garden.

Soekarno-Hatta Airport
$$$ Jakarta Airport Hotel, Terminal 2 (above Arrivals area), T021 559 0008, www.jakartaairporthotel.com. Super location in airport for those with a layover, or arriving late at night. Rooms are smart and have a/c and cable TV. There is also a half-day (maximum 6 hrs stay) rate of US$75.

Elsewhere
$$$$-$$ Hotel Borobudur, Jln Lapangan Banteng Selatan, T021 380 5555, www.hotelborobudur.com. This old dame is aging well, with friendly rather than stuffy service and a huge selection of rooms. The 693 rooms are set in rambling corridors reminiscent of *The Shining*, seemingly endless. Standard rooms are comfy, although a little aged. There is a raised seating area by the window with views over the hotel's extensive grounds.

$$$$-$$$ Hotel Nikko, Jln MH Thamrin 59, T021 230 1122, www.nikkojakarta.com. Japanese minimalist style is in evidence aplenty here in the gorgeous design. Rooms are clean, modern with top fabrics and plenty of space. Facilities include pool, fitness centre and restaurants, some with amazing views of the skyline. There is a shuttle bus from here to Plaza Indonesia (no more than 5 mins' walk), which gives some idea of the clientele.

$$$$-$$$ Sari Pan Pacific, Jln MH Thamrin, T021 390 2707, www.panpacific. com/jakarta. Busy business hotel, with intriguing facade. The carpeted a/c rooms are well decorated, although the beds look ancient, and have cable TV, bath and broadband access. Facilities include pool and fitness centre. Breakfast for 1 included in the price.

$$$ The Batavia Hotel (formerly Omni Batavia), Jln Kali Besar Barat 44-46, T021 690 4118, www.batavia-hotel.com. Stuck out on a limb down in Kota, this 4-star place is handy for a quick sightseeing trip around the old city, but not much else, and getting a cab from here takes some time. However, the price is not bad considering the good service, and clean rooms with cable TV and big, comfy beds. Pool, fitness centre.

$$ Kamar Kamar, Jln RS Fatmawati 37K, T021 751 2560, www.kamar-kamar.com. New backpacker hostel with a variety of rooms, though mostly dorms, to the south of the city centre. Very comfortable and with a good rooftop café with occasional live music. Free Wi-Fi throughout. Recommended.

Jakarta *p19, maps p21, p22 and p24*
Jakarta is the best place in Indonesia to eat, with a diverse collection of restaurants spread out all over the city and a growing middle class willing to dip ever deeper into their pockets to fulfil gourmet fantasies.

Go to www.sendokgarpu.com to check what's currently hot in the Jakarta dining and nightlife scene.

Jalan Jaksa and around
$$$-$$ Samarra, Jln Kebon Sirih 77, T021 391 8690. Open 1100-2300. Gorgeous Arabic decor lends a sense of opulence to this restaurant serving Arab-Indonesian fusion food. The speciality of the house is *sate* served with numerous delectable sauces. There is an excellent wine list and sheesha pipes are available. Belly dancers on Fri and Sat evenings. Recommended.
$$$-$$ Shanghai Blue, Jln Kebon Sirih 79, T021 391 8690. Open 1100-2300. Owned by the same group that runs **Samarra** next door, the decor here is similarly beautiful with modern, funky Chinese seating, 1920s portraits of Shanghainese ladies adorning the walls and sultry lighting. The fare is Betawi (local Jakarta)-Chinese fusion, with some interesting spins on the local cuisine. Marci, a renowned local singer, charms audiences on Wed and Fri nights.
$$ Kedai Tiga Nyonya, Jln Wahid Hasyim 73, T021 830 8360. Open 1100-2200. Peranakan (Straits Chinese) cuisine in a homely setting. This is a good place to try some *asam pedas* (hot and sour) dishes, or *soka* (soft crab).
$$ Kopitiam Oey, Jln Agus Salim 18. Open 0700-2300. Located in a freshly painted pink shophouse, this is a café offers a fantastic range of Indonesian breakfast dishes and light meals throughout the day.

Those in the mood for something heavy will want to dig in to the biryanis on offer.
$$ Penang Bistro, Jln Kebon Sirih 59, T021 319 0600. Open 1100-2200. Malaysian favourites served in sleek, clean a/c setting. Dishes include Hainan chicken rice, *roti canai* (Indian bread served with curry) and *kangkung belachan* (water spinach with prawn-based chilli sauce).
$$ Ya Udah Bistro, Jln Johar 15 Gondangia, T021 314 0349. Popular hang-out with a lengthy menu of central European favourites. The Strammer Max, described as a German trucker's breakfast is sure to keep energy levels high for a morning of exploring. Recommended.
$ Daoen Siri Food Garden, Jln Kebon Sirih 41, T021 316 1200. Collection of stalls serving an enticing array of regional Indonesian cuisine inside a rather wobbly looking traditional thatched structure.
$ Kawasan Kuliner BSM, in a lane next to the Sari Pan Pacific connecting Jln Thamrin and Jln Agus Salim. A lane lined with tables and *kaki lima* stalls serving a huge variety of cheap Indonesian fare. Popular with office workers at lunchtime and a fun introduction to Indonesian street fare.
$ KL Village Kopitiam, Jln Jaksa 21-23, T021 314 8761. Open 0700-0100. Outdoor Malaysian eatery that has shaken up the scene on Jaksa with its delicious curries, *nasi lemak* (rice cooked in coconut milk with side dishes), and good-value set meals.
$ Pappa Restaurant, Jln Jaksa 41, T021 3192 3452. Open 24 hrs. Cheap Western and Indonesian fare served round the clock to feed the hordes of drunken English teachers who need a burger and just 1 more beer before home.
$ Sate Khas Senayan, Jln Kebon Sirih 31A, T021 3192 6238. Open 1000-2200. This is an excellent place to try *sate*. Set in a spotless clean environment, the restaurant serves up divine portions of chicken and beef *sate* along with good Javanese rice dishes, and some divine icy delights for dessert.

Kemang

Affectionately and somewhat optimistically known as Little Bali, this area is a popular haunt for expats with money to burn on top-class dining. Traffic around here is notoriously nightmarish, and it can take almost 1 hr to get here from central and north Jakarta.

$$$-$$ Anatolia, Jln Kemang Raya 110A, T021 719 4617. Open 1100-2300. Sumptuous Ottoman decor, sheesha pipes and superb Turkish cuisine make this one of the city's most respected restaurants.

$$$-$$ Gourmet Garage, Jln Kemang Raya, T021 719 0875. Open 1000-2300. Smart collection of stalls including an oyster bar and a Japanese counter. There is a supermarket downstairs selling cheeses, meats, bread and all the things homesick Westerners crave.

$$$-$$ Kinara, Jln Kemang Raya 78B, T021 719 2677. This place does Moghul architecture proud with its wonderful facade and interior. Tasty fare; the tandoori is well worth trying.

Elsewhere

$$$ The Apartment, Menara Gracia, GF, Jln HR Rasuna Said. Open 0830-2400. Homesick meat fans will want to head here for their delectable steak and eggs and wagyu beef cheek. Trades well on its novelty of offering diners a choice of apartment room to dine in including a jacuzzi and a bedroom.

$$$ Lara Djonggrang, Jln Teuku Cik Di Tiro 4, Menteng, T021 315 3252. Superlative Indonesian dining experience and ideal for those with a little cash to splash and some romance in mind. Excellent array of Javanese fare including Javanese baby chicken and *soto daging madura* (beef slices in a coconut broth with candlenut paste and lime). Recommended.

$$$-$$ Al Jazeerah Restaurant, Jln Raden Saleh 58, T021 314 6108. Open 1000-2300. This street is packed full of authentic Arab eateries, and this is one of the best with dishes such as hummous, tabbouleh and plenty of kebabs on offer. No booze.

$$ Bombay Blue, Jln Cikini Raya 40, T021 316 2865. Open 1200-2300. Slick decor and tasty Indian cuisine. Long menu featuring a good range of non-veg and veg dishes.

$$ Café Batavia, Taman Fatahillah, T021 691 5531. Open 0800-0100. Business is no longer as brisk as it once was, but this place still remains a classic venue, for a drink if nothing else. The bar is resonant with times past, with high ceilings, slowly whirring ceiling fans and 1920s class. Fare is Asian and Western.

$$ Loewy, Jln Lingkar Mega Kuningan E42 No 1, T021 2554 2378. Open 1100-0200. Belgian bistro with an excellent selection of wines and coffees and the city's finest selection of single malt whiskies. Notable dishes include steak, 3-cheese fondue and lamb shank. Recommended.

$$ Trattoria, Menara Karya Building, Jln HR Rasuna Said 1-2, Mega Kuningan, T021 579 4472. Open 0900-2330. Excellent value authentic Italian cuisine, with good house wine and a rather tasty complimentary chocolate liqueur providing the icing on the cake. Recommended.

$$-$ Warung Daun, Jln Cikini Raya 26, T021 391 0909. Open 1100-1000. Popular with Indonesian ladies that lunch, the MSG-free fare, with organic vegetables, is a sure-fire winner. The cuisine is Sundanese and Javanese and features tasty *ikan gurame* (fried carp) and some creative vegetarian dishes.

$ Bakoel Koffie, Jln Cikini Raya 25, T021 3193 6608. Open 1000-2400. Spacious café with pleasant outdoor seating area and newspapers to browse. Plenty of coffees and cakes to indulge in.

$ Café Au Lait, Jln Cikini Raya 17, T021 3983 5094. Open 0800-2400. European-style café, with high ceilings, free Wi-Fi access and a wide range of coffee, cakes, sandwiches and simple pasta dishes. Occasional live music in the evenings.

There are also a large number of foodstalls, such as on **Jln HA Salim**, which has a great number of cheap regional restaurants; **Jln Mangga Besar**, with night-time *warungs*; **Grand Indonesia mall**, which has an excellent foodcourt in the basement and **Pasar Raya**, Blok M, with a variety of reliably good 'stalls' (not just Indonesian) in the basement. The top floor of **Sogo**, in the Plaza Indonesia, has similar stalls; and **Café Tenda Semanggi**, in the middle of the Central Business District, near Bengkel Night Park (taxi drivers know it), is an open-air area that has been used for a cluster of upmarket foodstalls, serving mainly Indonesian cuisine. A really happening place with great atmosphere. People come here more for the vibe than the food. Open 1800-0100.

❶ Bars and clubs

Jakarta *p19, maps p21, p22 and p24*
If you want to have just 1 massive night out in Indonesia, it has to be in Jakarta, where the sun sets early and the night is long. There is a staggering choice of drinking venues to suit all and sundry. Nightlife is a very friendly affair, and many who go out on the tiles in Jakarta ending up slurping noodles at 0600 with a new group of friends and an impending hangover on the way.

Jalan Jaksa and around
Jln Jaksa has a reputation as being quite downmarket, and the bars conform to that stereotype, with plenty of hookers and local hangers-on. However, an evening out here can be great fun, slightly anarchic and is a great way to meet interesting characters.
Absolute Café, Jln Jaksa 5, T021 3190 9847. Open 1600-0400. A/c bar with pool tables, TVs screening football and cheap drinks popular with the English teaching crowd.
Ali's, Jln Jaksa 25, T021 3190 0807. Open 1000-0300. Known as the African expat's bar of choice, this dark bar has TVs, plenty of nooks, crannies and a small dance floor.
Melly's Garden, IBEC Building, Jln Wahid Hasyim 84-88. Lively student hangout with good music, filthy toilets and decent selection of food and drinks. Good spot to mingle with

the young intelligentsia away from the sighty more seedy overtones of Jln Jaksa.
Memories Café, Jln Jaksa 17, T021 316 2548. Open 0900-0300. A Jaksa stalwart, this bar has seen it all. Bar-girls flock here to join other drinkers in antics and occasional karaoke numbers.

Elsewhere
Buddha Bar, Jln Teuku Umar 1, Menteng. Open 1800-0100. This place caused a storm when it first opened with local Buddhist societies deploring the use of the Buddha's image in a drinking establishment. Nevertheless, after the furore settled down, this plush place has settled into its groove with cool beats and stylish decor
CJs, Hotel Mulia, Jln Afrika Asia Senayan, T021 574 7777. Open 1600-0300. Good live music at this raucous club popular with expats and bar-girls on the prowl.
Cork and Screw, Plaza Indonesia, 1st floor, Jln Thamrin, T021 3199 6659. Open 1100-0200. One of the hottest spots in the city, with over 250 different wines from all over the world. Daily 'Happy Pouring' between 1600 and 1800 offering the chance to sample a selection of featured wines. Excellent wine at good prices, and some fine food. Gets packed at weekends.
Elbow Room, Jln Kemang Raya 24, T021 719 4274. European beer and fondue operation with plenty of friendly vibes, varied menu, live music and one-for-one happy hour on weekdays.
Red Square, Plaza Senayan Arcadia Unit X-210, Jln New Delhi, Pintu 9, T021 5790 1281, www.redsquarejakarta.com. This highly successful lounge bar is currently the place to be seen, with sleek and ultra-modern interior featuring groovy lighting. Vodka-based drinks fly off the shelves.
Stadium, Jln Hayam Wuruk 111, T021 626 3323, www.stadiumjakarta.com. Mon-Thu 2000-0600, Fri-Sun 24 hrs. One of Southeast Asia's most notorious clubs, attracting a loyal crowd of wide-eyed worshippers. This dark venue is a confusing maze, with

numerous floors and plenty of sin, echoing with techno beats. There really is nowhere else quite like it. Recommended.

Vin +, Jln Kemang Raya, Jln Kemang Raya 45. Open 1600-0200. Fashionable spot to sip wine and people watch.

Vino Embassy, Jln Kemang Raya 67, T021 719 1333. Open 1600-0200. Swish little bar, with dim lights and massive selection of wine.

Entertainment

Jakarta *p19, maps p21, p22 and p24*
For a schedule of events, look in the 'Where to Go' section of the *Jakarta Post* and the paper's website. The tourist office should also have an idea of what's going on in the city.

Cinemas

The Indonesian way is to provide subtitles rather than to dub, so soundtracks are generally in English. Films usually cost between 20,000Rp and 25,000Rp. Good cinemas can be found in the **Jakarta Theatre Building** (Jln MH Thamrin 9) and at the **Grand Indonesia** mall and **EXMall**.

Cultural shows

Erasmus Huis, Jln HR Rasuna Said S-3, T021 524 1069, www.mfa.nl/erasmushuis/en. Next to the Dutch embassy, cultural events, including interesting lectures, are held here.
Gedung Kesenian, Jln Gedung Kesenian 1, T021 380 8282. This centre organizes *wayang orang* performances, piano recitals, theatre and other cultural events, a modern art gallery is attached to the theatre. Check the website or local media for schedule.
Taman Ismail Marzuki (or **TIM**), just off Jln Cikini Raya, T021 3193 7325, www.taman ismailmarzuki.com. This complex is the focal point of cultural activities in the city with performances almost every night, the centre contains exhibition halls, 2 art galleries, theatres, cinema complex and a planetarium.

Festivals

Jakarta *p19, maps p21, p22 and p24*
Ramadan There is an exodus from Jakarta during this time and services may be reduced. The upside is that there is no traffic.
20 Apr Anniversary of Taman Mini, performances of traditional music and dance.
May Jakarta International Cultural Performance, a festival of music and dance from around Indonesia and also from other areas of Southeast Asia.
22 Jun Anniversary of Jakarta, commemorates the founding of Jakarta. Followed by the Jakarta Fair, www.jakarta fair.biz, which takes place in the PRJ Arena, Kemayoran and lasts for 1 month. Exhibitions, live music and performances, art installations and millions of people milling about.
Aug Jalan Jaksa Street Fair, 7 days of entertainment, including dance and music, Betawi art and plenty of fun and games.
Dec Jakarta International Film Festival, www.jiffest.org, selection of contemporary world and documentary films, as well as Indonesian language and animated pictures. Check local media or website for screenings.

Shopping

Jakarta *p19, maps p21, p22 and p24*
Fixed-priced stores are becoming more common in Jakarta, but bargaining is still the norm wherever there is no marked price. When buying antiques and handicrafts, bargain down to 30-40% of the original asking price, especially on Jln Surabaya. Shopping malls are a way of life in Jakarta, an escape from the traffic and smog, and new shopping malls are being constructed all the time. Some of the most convenient include **Grand Indonesia**, Jln MH Thamrin 1, with banks, designer clothes stores, bookshops and restaurants (recommended); **Plaza Indonesia**, Jln MH Thamrin Kav 28-30, with top brands, good dining options and beautiful people; **EX Mall**, Jln MH Thamrin Kav 28-30, favouring younger shoppers with

high street brands, cinema and fast-food joints; and **Plaza Senayan**, Jln Asia Afrika, 1000-2200. Suave and sophisticated and deliciously cool, with a cinema.

Batik Ardiyanto, Pasar Raya (3rd floor), Jln Iskandarsyah 11/2; **Batik Keris**, Danar Hadi, Jln Raden Saleh 1A; **Batik Semar**, Jln Tomang Raya 54; **Government Batik Cooperative (GKBI)**, Jln Jend Sudirman 28; **Iwan Tirta**, Jln Panarukan 25 or Hotel Borobudur; 1 floor of Pasar Raya (Blok M), is devoted to batik; **Pasar Tanar Abang**, a market west of Merdeka Square, has good modern textiles, batik and *ikat* by the metre; **Srikandi**, Jln Melawai VI/6A.

Bookshops Jakarta is a good place to stock up on reading material, with excellent bookshops such as Kinokuniya in several malls.

Handicrafts Sarinah Department Store has 2 floors of handicrafts and batik from across Indonesia and is located on Jln MH Thamrin (at the intersection with Jln KH Wahid Hasyim). This is a great place to stock up on gifts for home, although if you are heading to other destinations in Java or Bali, it's best to wait, as prices are considerably higher in Jakarta.

Supermarket There is a **Hero** super-market beneath the Sarinah building on Jln MH Thamrin, which sells necessities. Most of the malls have supermarkets.

⏱ What to do

Jakarta *p19, maps p21, p22 and p24*
Language courses
IALF, Sentra Mulia, Jln Rasuna Said Kav X-6 No 8, T021 521 3350, www.ialf.edu. Offers a variety of Bahasa Indonesia courses.

Tour operators
Most larger hotels have travel agents; this list is not comprehensive. Most will arrange city tours, out-of-town day tours and longer tours throughout Indonesia.

For agents and companies geared to the needs of those on a lower budget, Jln Jaksa is probably the best bet. Bus and train tickets are booked for destinations across the archipelago and other services provided.
Astrindo Tours and Travel, 45-47 Jln Kebon Sirih, T021 230 5151. Professional outfit offering tailor-made tours.
Bayu Buana, Jln Kemang Raya 114, T021 7179 0662, www.bayubuanatravel.com. Branches all over the city, can arrange tickets, tours and help with visas.
Divalina Tour and Travel, Jln Jaksa 35, T021 314 9330.
Indonesian Heritage Society, T021 572 5870, may be offering city tours. These have been discontinued, but might start up again in the near future. There is a US$22 membership, worthwhile if you want to join several tours or are going to be based in the city.
Krakatau Tours, www.krakatau-tour.com, Office Sunset View Carita, Jln Raya Carita KM10, T0813 8666 88 11. Package tours to Krakatau and Ujong Kulon NP.
Robertur Kencana, Jln Jaksa 20, T021 314 2926. Gets the thumbs up from a lot of travellers.

⊖ Transport

Jakarta *p19, maps p21, p22 and p24*
Air
Daily flights to most major cities in Indonesia. Fares are generally good value flying out of Jakarta. **Lion Air** (www.lionair.co.id) and **AirAsia** (www.airasia.com) offer online booking. Those looking for a spectacular flight over the mountains of West Java to Bandung or Panganadaran will want to look into flying in one of **Susi Air's** Cessna Caravans. These flights depart daily from Halim Airport in east Jakarta. Jakarta to **Pangandaran** flights cost around US$65. Book at **Susi Air Jakarta**, BNI 46 Building 32nd floor, Jln Sudirman Kav I, T021 3929 726.

Bajaj

Bajaj, orange motorized 3-wheelers, Indian made, pronounced *bajai:* sometimes known as 'panzer' bajaj because of their tank-like behaviour. There have been rumours that the government would like to do away with bajajs, as they have been deemed 'anti-humane'. They are already barred from Jakarta's main thoroughfares. Nonetheless, they remain the cheapest way to get around other than by bus or on foot. Negotiate the price furiously before boarding and expect to pay a minimum of 10,000Rp for a short journey.

Many bajaj now run on CNG (Compressed Natural Gas), similar to ones seen in Delhi, and are significantly greener than the standard (painted red) smoke belching motorized models. The government eventually hopes to replace all motorized bajaj with CNG vehicles in an attempt to help clear some of the city's horrific air pollution. CNG bajaj are painted blue.

Boat

Jakarta's port is Tanjung Priok, 15 km from the city centre. Take bus No 60 from Jln Pos or bus No P14 from Jln Kebon Sirih, off Jln Jaksa. Or take a taxi. Allow at least 1 hr. It is less than 1 km from the bus station at Tanjung Priok to the dock. The state-owned shipping company PELNI has its head office at Jln Gajah Mada 14, T021 633 4342/45. Its ticket office is at Jln Angkasa 20, T021 421 1921. Check the latest schedule at www.pelni.co.id. A counter on the 2nd floor of the building is much less crowded for ticket purchase (entrance on right of building). 2 photocopies of passport are required (photocopying shop on left of building, as you face it). The PELNI ships *Kelud* (for **North Sumatra**, **Riau**), *Leuser* (**Kalimantan**, **Java**), *Dobonsolo* (**Sulawesi**, **Kalimantan**), *Bukit Raya* (**Kalimantan**, **Riau**) *Ciremai* (**Sulawesi**, **Maluku**, **Papua**), *Lambelo* (**Sulawesi**, **Maluku**, **Riau**), *Sirimau* (**Sulawesi**, **Nusa Tenggara**), and *Bukit Sigantung* (**Nusa Tenggara**, **Maluku**, **Sulawesi**, **Papua**), dock here.

Bus

Local Most fares around town are 2500Rp. Crowded, especially during rush hour, and beware of pickpockets.

The **Jakarta Transjarkarta** bus lines have taken a little away from the stress of city travelling, with clean a/c buses travelling along designated corridors that are for these buses only. There are 10 lines running at the moment, although 5 more are in construction. Fares from point to point are 3500Rp, including any transits.
Corridor 1: Blok M–Jln Jend Sudirman–Jln MH Thamrin–Merderka Barat–Harmoni–Jln Gajah Mada–Stasiun Kota.
Corridor 3: Kalideres (bus terminal)–Daan Mogot–Tomang Raya–Harmoni.
Corridor 7: Kampung Rambutan (bus terminal)–Otto Iskandardinata–Letjend MT Haryono.

Booking bus tickets: private bus companies have their offices at these terminals. Travel agents along Jln Jaksa will help tourists get tickets. Another option is to ring the company and reserve a ticket, and pay for it on arrival at the terminal. Your hotel should be able to help you do this. Make sure you find out which terminal your bus from Jakarta departs from. Companies worth trying include: **Lorena**, Jln Hasyim Ashan 15C, T021 634 1166, and **Pahala Kencana**, Komp. Gading Bukit Indah Blok C No 1, Jl Bukit Gading Raya Kelapa Gading, T021 451 7375.

Long distance There are 4 city bus terminals, all some distance from the city centre. **Kalideres Terminal**, on the west edge of the city, 15 km from the centre, serves the west coast, including **Merak** with a handful of connections on to **Sumatra** (most Sumatra buses depart from the Pulo Gadung terminal). Take Transjakarta busway corridor 3 buses to get here. Kampung Rambutan, about 15 km south of the city, serves **Bogor**, **Bandung** and other towns and cities in West Java. Take Transjakarta busway corridor 7 buses to get here. Pulo Gadung Terminal, 12 km east of the centre at the junction of Jln Bekasi Timur Raya and Jln Perintis Kemerdekaan, serves Central and East Java including the towns of **Cirebon** (5 hrs), **Yogya** (12 hrs), **Surabaya** (15 hrs) and **Malang** (18 hrs). Pulo Gadung is also the main bus terminal for **Sumatra**, with buses going to all the major towns – even as far as **Banda Aceh**, some 3000 km north. **Bali** is served from Pulo Gadung. Lebakbulus Terminal has buses going to **Bandung** and **Bali**. This terminal is 10 km south of the city.

Fares from Jakarta include: **Denpasar** (24 hrs) US$38, **Surabaya** (18 hrs) US$24, **Probolinggo** (20 hrs) US$26, **Yogyakarta/Surakarta** (12-14 hrs) US$18 and **Padang** (32 hrs) US$36.

Car hire
Most international companies strongly recommend a driver and local expats believe it is pure madness to attempt tackling the streets of Jakarta oneself. Visitors do, though, and survive. Cars with driver can be hired by the day for about US$65. **Avis**, Jln Diponegoro 25, T021 314 2900, also desks at Soekarno-Hatta Airport and the Borobudur Intercontinental Hotel. **Bluebird**, Jln Hos, Cokroaminoto T021 794 4444. **National**, Kartika Plaza Hotel, Jln MH Thamrin 10, T021 333423/314 3423. **Toyota Rentacar**, Jln Gaya Motor 111/3, Sunter 11, T021 650 6565.

Minibus
Also known as Travels. Door-to-door services are offered by **4848**, Jln Prapatan 34, T021 364 4488, and **Media Taxi**, Jln Johar 15, T021 314 0343. Fares to **Bandung** are US$8 and to **Yogya** US$19. Bear it mind that it can take an excruciating amount of time to pick people up in a city of Jakarta's size, and then there is the traffic to contend with, making this a more stressful and less scenic option than the train ride.

Taxi
This is the most comfortable and convenient way to get around the city.

There are numerous companies in Jakarta. **Blue Bird**, T021 7917 1234/794 1234, www.bluebirdgroup.com, is the only company worth using. They can be distinguished by the large Blue Bird Taxi sticker on the windscreen. There are plenty of imitators who have taken to painting their taxis blue, and whose drivers will try to hustle as much as they can. Flag fall is 6000Rp and 3000Rp for each subsequent km (after the first). Blue Birds can be found outside most major hotels, shopping malls and condo complexes. Tipping is normal, so round up to the nearest 1000Rp if you wish.

Train
Jakarta has 6 railway stations, which are more central than the bus stations. The main station is Gambir, on the east side of Merdeka Square (Jln Merdeka Timur). There is an English-speaking information service that advises on timetables and costs, T021 692 9194. Regular connections with **Bogor** (1 hr 20 mins) economy class only, 2500Rp, or the non-stop a/c Pakuan Express trains (50 mins) from 0730-1640, 11,000Rp.

For **Bandung**, (2½ hrs) there are the useful Parahiyangan trains, departing 6 times a day from Gambir (*bisnis* 30,000Rp/*eksekutif* 60,000Rp). For **Yogyakarta** (8 hrs) there is the Taksaka, 2 a day (*eksekutif* US$24). The *eksekutif*-only Argo Lawu departs at 2000 and calls in at **Yogya** before **Surakarta (Solo)** at 0430 (US$25 for either city). The Argo Dwipangga does the same trip departing at 0800 and arriving at **Solo** at 1606 (US$24).

There are numerous trains to **Surabaya** (10 hrs) including the Argo Anggrek, 2 daily at 0930 (arrives at 1730) and 2130 (arrives at 0730) on *eksekutif* class for US$31.

There is 1 daily train to **Malang**, the Gajayana departing at 1730 and arriving the following morning at 0859, US$35.

Those travelling to **Bogor** and staying in Jln Jaksa or Jln Wahid Hasyim will find it more convenient to jump on a *Pakuan Ekspres* train departing from Gongdangdia station, a 10-min walk from the southern end of Jln Jaksa.

Pulau Seribu *p26*
Air
There is an airstrip on Pulau Panjang. The trip takes 25 mins from **Jakarta**. Boat transfers to other islands.

Boat
A regular ferry service goes to **Onrust** and **Bidadari**, leaving Marina Jaya at Ancol at 0700 and returning from the islands at 1430. The journey takes 30 mins-1 hr. If you do not want to take the package option, then go to either Onrust or Bidadari and find a fisherman to take you out for the day to explore the outer islands. It should cost around US$50. Most of the resorts have their own boats, which pick up from Ancol in the mornings. People on day trips can also take these boats.

Krakatau *p26*
Boat
It may be possible to charter boats from Anyer, Carita and Labuan. Locals have gained a reputation for overcharging and then providing unseaworthy boats. (It is said that 2 Californian women spent 3 weeks drifting in the Sunda Strait, living on sea water and toothpaste, before being washed ashore near Bengkulu in West Sumatra.) A 2-engine speed boat suitable for 6-8 people should cost US$150-200. Bargain hard, and make sure you see the boat before handing over any cash. The boatsmen on the beach outside the Mutiara Carita Hotel in Labuan near Carita have a good range of vessels.

❶ Directory

Jakarta *p19, maps p21, p22 and p24*
Banks Most of the larger hotels will have money-changing facilities, and banks and money changers can be found throughout the city centre; for example, in shopping centres. Jln Jaksa also has many money changers, with competition keeping the rate good. Useful banks for visitors include **BNI** and **Lippo Bank** (both with ATMs accepting Visa and MasterCard) on Jln Kebon Sirih. There are ATMs all over the city. Also a money changer with fair rates on the 1st floor of **Sarinah** department store.
Embassies and consulates For Indonesian embassies and consulates abroad and for foreign embassies in Indonesia, see http://embassy.goabroad. com. **Emergencies** 24-hr emergency ambulance service: T118. **Police:** 24-hr emergency T110, Jln Jend Sudirman 45, T021 523 4333. Tourist Police, Jakarta Theatre Building, Jln MH Thamrin 9, T021 566000. **Immigration** Central Immigration, Jln Terminal 2, Cengkareng (near the airport) T021 550 7233. Kemayoran, Jln Merpati Kemayoran 3, T021 654 1209. Also an office on Jln Rasuna Said, T021 525 3004. These places will extend visas, but get there at 0800 prompt.
Medical services Clinics: Global Doctor, Jln Kemang Raya 87, T021 719 4565, www.globaldoctorjakarta.com, 24-hr. English-speaking doctors at reasonable rates (US$19 for consultation plus treatment costs). Also SOS Medika Klinik, Jln Puri Sakti 10, T021 750 5973, www. sos-bali.com/sos-medika-cipete.php, 24 hr. Hospitals: RS Jakarta, Jln Jend Sudirman Kav 49, T021 573 2241. RS MMC Kuningan, Jln HR Rasuna Said KC21, T021 520 3435 (24-hr emergency room). **Pharmacy:** Guardian Pharmacy, Plaza Indonesia, Pondok Indah Mall or Blok M Plaza. There are a couple of pharmacies on Jln Wahid Hasyim. **Telephone** Telkom, Jakarta Theatre Building, Jln M H Thamrin 81. Open every day, 24 hrs. Numerous **Warpostel** and other telephone offices dotted around.

Bogor

Bogor is centred on the lush botanical gardens, with views over red-tiled roofs stacked one on top of the other and toppling down to the Ciliwung River, which runs through the middle of the town. The Ciliwung, which has cut a deep gorge, has also become a convenient place to discard rubbish, marring some of the views in the process. The town has a large Christian community and a surprising number of Western fast-food outlets and department stores. These serve the population of wealthy Indonesians who live here and commute into Jakarta. A scattering of old colonial buildings is still to be found around town – for instance, set back from the road on Jalan Suryakencana.

The town lies 290 m above sea level in an upland valley, surrounded by Gunungs Salak, Pangrango and Gede. Average temperatures are a pleasant 26°C, significantly cooler than Jakarta, but rainfall is the highest in Java at 3000-4000 mm per year. The Dutch, quite literally sick to death of the heat, humidity and the swampy conditions of Jakarta, developed Bogor as a hill retreat.

Arriving in Bogor → *Phone code: 0251.*

Getting there

Bogor is just 60 km south of Jakarta and with a fast toll road is easily reached on a day trip from the capital. However, it is worth staying here for longer than just a few hours. Bogor is a thriving commuter town and, for many, the first stop from the airport for tourists who only want to see Jakarta on day trips from Bogor (rather than the other way around). The bus station is south of the famous botanical gardens, a longish walk or short *angkot* ride from the town centre, and there are frequent connections with Jakarta's Kampung Rambutan terminal and Soekarno-Hatta International Airport. There are also buses on to Bandung via the Puncak Pass (three hours) and further afield to Yogya, Solo and Bali. The train station is close to the town and there are regular connections with Jakarta's Gambir, Gongdangdia (for Jalan Jaksa and Jalan Wahid Hasyim) and Kota stations. It is best to avoid visiting at weekends as the roads get jammed due to the influx of oxygen-starved visitors from Jakarta gasping for fresh air. ➤➤ *See Transport, page 41.*

Getting around

Bogor is a small town and because it is much cooler here than Jakarta, walking is pleasant, but there are plenty of useful *angkot* routes. Bogor's **tourist office** ① *T0251 836 3433, daily 0900-1700,* is easy to miss, in the bizarre Taman Topi complex on Jalan Kapten Muslihat. The staff are helpful and have a good map as well as tips on the city. They arrange a number of interesting tours around West Java, and up to the summit of Gunung Salak.

Places in Bogor → *For listings, see pages 39-42.*

Botanical gardens (Kebun Raya)
① *T0251 832 2187, www.bogorbotanicgardens.org, daily 0800-1700, 9500Rp.*
The superb botanical gardens dominate the centre of the city, covering an immense 87 ha and housing 2735 plant species. The gardens are thought to have been established under the instructions of Sir Stamford Raffles. Certainly, Raffles was a keen botanist; however, it

was the Dutch Governor-General Van der Capellen who commissioned the transformation of the gardens into arguably the finest in Asia. The botanist Professor Reinhardt, from Kew Gardens in England, undertook the major portion of the work in 1817. The gardens became world renowned for their research into the cash crops of the region (tea, rubber, coffee, tobacco and chinchona – from the bark of which quinine is derived). The giant water lily, as well as a variety of orchids, palms and bamboos, can be seen. It used to be possible to see the giant Rafflesia flower, but it has now died.

Presidential Palace (Istana Bogor)

ⓘ *Those planning to visit the Istana Bogor must think ahead, only groups of 30 or more are admitted after permission has been secured through the Istana or the tourist office at least a week ahead of the planned visit, guests must be formally dressed and children under 10 are not admitted because of the value and fragility of the objects; if visitors can meet all these requirements they deserve a prize. In Jakarta, applications can be made through the Sekretariat Negara, on Jln Veteran 16, www.setneg.go.id.*

Deer graze in front of the imposing Presidential Palace or Istana Bogor, which lies within the botanical gardens, directly north of the main gates (there is also an entrance on Jalan Ir H Juanda). The palace was a particular favourite of President Sukarno and contains a large collection of his paintings, sculptures and ceramics (he had a passion for the female nude). Sukarno lived here under 'house arrest' from 1967 until his death in 1970. Today, it is used as a guesthouse for important visitors and high-level meetings.

Museums

The **Zoological Museum** ⓘ *daily 0800-1700,* is on the left of the entrance to the botanical gardens and was founded in 1894. It contains an extensive collection of stuffed, dried and otherwise preserved fauna (over 15,000 species), of which only a small proportion is on show at any one time. The museum also has a library. There is a **Herbarium** ⓘ *Mon-Thu 0800-1330 and Fri 0800-1000, 2000Rp,* associated with the botanical gardens, on Jalan Ir H Juanda, across the road from the west gate to the gardens. It is said to have a collection of two million specimens, which seems suspiciously inflated.

Markets

Jalan Otista (also known as Otto Iskandardinata) is a road running along the south edge of the botanical gardens. The street is lined with stalls selling fruit, rabbits (not to eat), some batik, children's clothes and unnecessary plastic objects. The main market area is along **Jalan Dewi Sartika**, where stalls, hawkers, shoppers, and angkots struggle for space. It's a fascinating area to walk around, absorb the atmosphere and people-watch.

Gong foundry

ⓘ *Jln Pancasan 17, T0251 832 4132, near the river and southeast of the botanical gardens.*

The gong foundry is one of the few foundries left in Indonesia – on one side of the street is the foundry, and on the other the gong stands are carved from wood. Visitors can watch metalsmiths making gongs in the traditional manner – a process that takes between one and three days per gong. The factory is about a 35-minute walk southeast from the town centre. Walk south down Jalan Empang and then turn right onto Jalan Pahlawan. Next door to the foundry, in addition to selling gongs, traditional puppets of high quality are on offer – and at far lower prices than in Jakarta. About 200 m on from the gong foundry is a small **tofu factory**, a fascinating insight into the simple process of tofu making. Fresh tofu is sold to local villages. Enday Media, a *wayang golek* puppet maker, has his home and **factory** ① *Kampung Sirnagalih 60, T0251 835 8808,* and offers *wayang* shows to groups. Visits can be arranged through the tourist office or through Selfi at Abu Pensione.

Jalan Batutulis
① *Admission by donation, daily 0800-1600, take an Angkutan (Green Colt) No 02.*
A **batutulis** (inscribed stone), dating from the 16th century and erected by one of the sons of a Pajajaran king, is housed in a small shrine 3 km south of town on Jalan Batutulis (which runs off Jalan Bondongon).

City tours in and around Bogor
Bogor is a great place to join a tour to absorb some *kampung* ambience, try a bit of Sundanese food and trek off into the untouristed national parks and forests of West Java. Town tours are offered by the tourist office and Selfi at **Abu Pensione** and typically take in the tofu factory, gong foundry, a trip to visit the *wayang golek* puppet maker and try a little local cuisine. The *sop buah* (fruit salad with 12 different locally grown fruits) is a real gastronomic treat and worth ensuring appears on any city tour itinerary. Prices for city tours start at around 225,000Rp per person. Toursts rarely venture into the depths of West Java, a genuine shame given the beauty of the province. Asep (T0818 0809 5615) at the tourist information office in Taman Topi runs a selection of trips into the Gunung Salak and Harimun national parks, offering the chance to spot some wildlife, stay with a local family and climb Gunung Salak. Prices start at 1,200,000Rp per person. He also does longer tours from Bogor ending in Bandung, Pangandaran or Yogya.

Around Bogor

Taman Safari
① *T0251 825 0000, www.tamansafari.com, daily 0900-1700, 125,000Rp (100,000Rp for children under 5). Take a bus heading for Cisarua and ask to be let off at the turning to the park, motorbike taxis ply the route from the main road to the park gates.*
Just before Cisarua, 2.5 km off the main road, is an open-air safari park. It also houses a mini zoo and offers amusement rides, elephant and horse riding, various animal shows throughout the day, a waterfall, swimming pool, restaurant and camping facilities. There is also a weekend **night safari** ① *Sat 1830-2100, 150,000Rp, under 5s 125,000Rp.*

Bogor listings

For hotel and restaurant price codes and other relevant information, see pages 9-12.

🛏 Where to stay

Bogor *p37*
Given its proximity to Jakarta, Bogor is unsurprisingly well endowed with good mid-range and high-end hotels. There are fairly slim pickings at the lower end of the market.

$$$$-$$$ Royal Hotel, Jln Ir H Juanda 16, T0251 834 7123, www.royalhotelbogor. com. Spanking new hotel in the heart of town with rooms offering breathtaking views of the mountains beyond. Rooms are modern, well furnished and have Wi-Fi access. The real draw here is the pool with plenty of loungers from which to watch the sun setting around Gunung Salak. Excellent discounts available. Recommended.

$$$$-$$$ Sahira Butik Hotel, Jln Paledang 53, T0251 832 2413, www.sahira butikhotel.com. This place has plenty of palatial overtures, friendly staff and fair discounts at weekends. The standard rooms are large and have private balcony. Wi-Fi access available. Pool. Recommended.

$$$ Hotel Salak, Jln Ir H Juanda 8, T0251 835 0400, www.hotelsalak.co.id. Top-notch hotel with formal but comfortable rooms, all carpeted and with Wi-Fi and cable TV. Spa, travel agent, pool and gym.

$$$ Terra Nostra, Jln Salak 8, T0251 833480. Small boutique hotel with a variety of rooms and suites and Balinese flourishes. Some of the suites are sightly on the small side, but could be handy for a family. Wi-Fi offered throughout.

$$$-$$ Hotel Mirah, Jln Pangrongo 9A, T0251 834 8040. The rooms are a little overpriced, given the competition in town. More expensive ones come with cable TV and are nicely decorated. Further down the price range, rooms are still acceptable, although lose some of the mod cons and become increasingly faded.

$$$-$$ Hotel Pangrango, Jln Pajajaran 32, T0251 832 1482, www.hotel-pangrango. co.id. Popular with Indonesian business folk, this 5-storey behemoth has 97 rooms, including budget rooms (with outside bathroom), TV and a/c (centralized-no individual control). The a/c standard rooms are spacious and have TV, fridge and bath. Wi-Fi access in lobby (expensive). Pool.

$$ Crawford Lodge, Jln Pangrango 2, T0251 322429. This place is worth a look for those interested in relieving some 1970s fantasies. It's a little like sleeping in a museum, but the rooms are clean enough and there is an inviting though small pool out the back

$$ Pakuan Palace Hotel, Jln Pakuan 5, T0251 832 3062, hopakuan@indo.net.id. The comfy standard rooms are not bad, with TV, a/c and hot water. Spending a little more will get international cable TV. Pool with outdoor seating. Take angkot No 6 to get here.

$$ Wisma Srigunting, Jln Pangrango 21A, T0251 339 660. Offers 6 rooms set in a spotless though dated and regal family home covered with family photos. The rooms (all a/c) are massive and have fridge and TV, and equally large bathrooms. Some rooms smell a little damp.

$$-$ Abu Pensione, Jln Mayor Oking 15, T0251 832 2893. This place is the best budget bet in town, with a wide variety of clean a/c and fan rooms, some filled with the sound of the gushing river below. The rooms are a little scruffy round the edges and could definitely do with some love The owner, Selfi, is a fountain of local information and great company. She offers excellent tours around town for a glimpse of local life.

$$-$ Wisma Pakuan, Jln Pakuan 12, T0251 319430. Friendly, with helpful staff and large clean a/c and fan rooms with TV around a pleasant garden. Recommended. Take angkot No 6 to get here.

🍴 Restaurants

Bogor *p37*

Local specialities include *asinan Bogor* (sliced fruit in sweet water and *tuge goreng*, fried beansprouts served with a spicy chilli sauce). Bogor, like many towns, has a profusion of Padang restaurants, but in this case they are almost all owned by one man and the food is virtually the same, so there is nothing to choose between them gastronomically.

The best food is to be found in the leafy suburb of villas around Jln Pangrango. Prices are fairly high here, but match the setting.

The area around the **Giant** shopping centre on Jln Pajajaran has plenty of fast-food options, further down the street towards Jln Otista, there are a few *nasi Padang* restaurants (**Trio** is very popular).

$$$-$$ Kembang Desa, Jln Pangrango 30, T0251 832 9348, www.kembangdesaresto. com. Open 1000-2200. Delightful restaurant serving a range of classical Indonesian dishes from around the archipelago. Highlights include the Tangkapan *ikan di muara angke*

(a gorgeous grilled seafood extravaganza) and the rice platters, offering the chance to try different regional dishes. There is a pleasant garden out the back and nightly musical entertainment. We are promised a bar is on the way too. Recommended.

$$$-$$ Saung Mirah, Jln Pangrango 32, T0251 832 7675. Sundanese restaurant offering up tasty *gurame* (grilled carp) and other Sundanese delights in a modern setting.

$$-$ Ali Baba, Jln Pangrango 13, T0251 348111. Open 1000-2200. This is the place to satisfy hummous cravings, with a fair menu of Middle Eastern standards.

$$-$ Buitenzorg Kedai Kita, Jln Pangrango 21, T0251 324160. Open 0800-2300. Relaxed eatery with eclectic menu of pizza, steaks and delicious Sundanese and Javanese dishes. Locals flock here for the coffee menu which includes beans from Sumatra, Timor and Sulawesi.

$$-$ Gumati, Jln Paledang 26, T0251 324318. Open 1000-2300. Brilliant views and superb array of Sundanese food to choose from. There are a few concessions to Western tastes with steaks and some simple pastas. Beautiful views over the mountains from the restaurant. Recommended.

$$-$ Jezz Café and **Ikkito Japanese Restaurant**, Jln Salak 16, T0251 711 1661. 2 restaurants on one lot. **Jezz Café** serves cold beer and decent pizza and has pleasant outdoors seating. Its neighbour, **Ikkito**, is well regarded for its *teppanyaki* and *shabu shabu*.

$$-$ Met Liefde, Jln Pangrango 16, T0251 338909. Open 0900-2300 (2400 at weekends). Waitresses in Dutch outfits, displays of clogs and a beautiful garden with outdoor seating. This is a fine spot for a bit of wining and dining for very reasonable prices. The menu is mainly Western, with plenty of Dutch desserts and a good range of juices. Live music at weekends. Recommended.

$ Pia, Jln Pangrango 10, T0251 324169. Open 0800-2200. Pies of every form to consume in a friendly outdoor setting,

from chocolate to apple, the house special. There are also plenty of savoury offerings.

$ Pondok Bambu Kuring, Jln Pajajaran 43, T0251 323707. Open 0930-2130. Large restaurant with *lesehan* (low tables) seating. Menu features a lot of good East Javanese seafood dishes with plenty of prawn and squid dishes and some tasty *ikan gurame*.

$ Salak Sunset Café, Jln Paledang 38, T0251 356045. Open 1100-2300. Average Western and Indonesian dishes, with some good snacks including *pisang koreng keju coklat* (fried banana with cheese and chocolate), but the real reason to come here is for the amazing sunset views over the town, perfect for sharing with an icy Bintang.

Shopping

Bogor *p37*
Batik Batik Semar, Jln Capten Muslihat 7.

Handicrafts Kenari Indah, Jln Pahlawan. Pasar Bogor, Jln Suryakencana.

Market Kebon Kembang, Jln Dewi Sartika. **Wayang Golek**, Enday Media Kp Sirnagalih 60, T0251 358808.

What to do

Bogor *p37*
Tour operators
Maghfiroh, Gedung Alumni IPB, Jln Pajajaran 54, T0251 393234.
Vayatour, Jln Pajajaran 23, T0251 256861, www.vayatour.com. Also **Natatour** upstairs, which can book AirAsia flights.

Transport

Bogor *p37*
Bogor is 60 km south of Jakarta. A fast toll road makes the trip to Bogor rapid, though scenically unexciting.

Bus

The station is just off Jln Raya Pajajaran, south from the botanical gardens and opposite the intersection with the toll road from Jakarta. Frequent connections with Jakarta's **Kampung Rambutan** (9000Rp non a/c, 14,000Rp a/c). Bear in mind that Kampung Rambutan is still quite a distance to the centre of Jakarta, making the train trip a much more sensible option. Green angkots from here to the centre of town cost 2500Rp. Regular connections with **Bandung**, via the Puncak Pass, 3 hrs. For travel to Bandung, **Deva Transport**, Jln Taman Yasmin Raya, T0251 753 2582, offers a door-to-door service (3 hrs, 75,000Rp). Phone and book, pay at the end of the journey. Private car companies have also started offering this door-to-door service, with a maximum of 3 passengers. **Bintang Travel**, T0251 915 6699, charges 75,000Rp. This saves the hassle of lugging bags to the bus station and also of getting from the bus station in Bandung into town, which can be a real hassle. For a/c buses to **Yogya**, **Solo** and **Bali**, it is best to go to use one of the well-established bus companies such as **Lorena** (Jln Raya Tajur 106, T0251 835 6666) and **Pahala Kencana** (Jln Siliwangi 118, Sukasari, T0251 835 3265). Bookings can be made over the phone, or through one of their agents at the bus terminal. Routes include **Denpasar** (27 hrs, US$38), **Yogya/Solo** (15 hrs, US$18), **Surabaya** (19 hrs, US$25), **Padang** (30 hrs, US$38) and **Probolinggo** (21 hrs, US$28). Also connections with **Merak**, **Labuan** and the popular surfers' beach at **Pelabuhanratu**. A very fast, efficient service runs from the Damri Airport Bus Terminal on Jln Pajajaran to Soekarno-Hatta Airport (every 20 mins from 0300-2000, 35,000Rp).

Car hire

Car and driver are available for charter from **Abu Pensione**, Jln Mayor Oking 15.

Colt (angkutan/angkot)

Omnipresent green machines; there seem to be more of them than there are passengers. Fixed fare of 2500Rp around town; destinations marked on the front. Blue angkots run to out-of-town destinations and are useful for those who fancy heading up to the tea plantations around **Cisarua** in **Puncak**, which have spectacular views and cool, fresh air.

Train

The station (a colonial building) is northwest of the botanical gardens on Jln Rajapermas, also known as Jln Stasiun. Regular connections every 30 mins or so with **Jakarta's Gambir** station. The uncomfortable economy trains take around 1hr 20 mins and cost 2500Rp. Much better are the regular **Pakuan Express** a/c trains that take just under 1 hr and cost 11,000Rp. The first train leaves Bogor at 0540 and the final train out is at 1715. Trains leave from Jakarta's **Kota** station, but also stop at **Gambir** and sometimes **Gongdangdia** (for Jln Jaksa or Jln Wahid Hasyim) on their way through the capital, en route to Bogor. Note that there are no trains on to Bandung.

❶ Directory

Bogor *p37*
Banks ATMs can be found all over town.
Emergency Police: Jln Capten Muslihat 16. PHKA: Jln Ir H Juanda 9 (also for permits to visit national parks). **Immigration** Jln Jend A Yani 65, T0251 832 2870.
Medical services Hospital: RS PMI Bogor, Jln Pajajaran 80, T0251 839 3030, is run by the Palang Merah Indonesia (Indonesian Red Cross). There is a good selection of specialist doctors here. Pharmacy: Guardian, inside Giant supermarket (2nd floor), Jln Pajajaran.
Telephone Wartels all over town.

Bandung

Set in a huge volcanic river basin at an altitude of 768 m and surrounded by mountains, Bandung has one of the most pleasant climates in Java, where the daytime temperature averages 23°C. The town centre is modern, unattractive and overcrowded, and some patience is needed in seeking out the town's main attraction: namely, its fine collection of art-deco architecture, built between 1920 and 1940 when Bandung was the most sophisticated European town of the Dutch East Indies.

The fourth largest city in Indonesia, Bandung is also the capital of the province of West Java. The city has a population of over 2,900,000, with a further 4,000,000 living in the surrounding area, making this one of the most densely populated regions of Java. Such has been the growth of the city that in 1987 its administrative boundaries were extended, doubling the area of the city overnight. Bandung is regarded as the intellectual heart of Java, with over 50 universities and colleges situated in the area. Modern Bandung has the same traffic problems as Jakarta and walking the city is no longer a pleasant stroll; roads are often bumper to bumper with traffic. The heart of the city is looking decidedly rundown nowadays, though those of an artistic orientation should keep an eye out for some genuinely excellent graffiti artwork on shopfronts and walls.

Arriving in Bandung → *Phone code: 022.*

Getting there

Bandung is 187 km southeast of Jakarta, 400 km west of Yogya. The airport is 4 km from town, but most people arrive here by train or bus. The train station is in the centre of town and there are services travelling west to Jakarta and east to Surabaya. Less conveniently located are Bandung's two long-distance bus terminals. The **Leuwi Panjang** terminal is 5 km south of town and serves destinations to the west, including Jakarta. The **Cicaheum** terminal is on the edge of town to the east, and buses from here run to Yogya, Solo, Surabaya and Bali and to towns on Java's north coast including Cirebon and Semarang. Both bus terminals are linked to the centre of town by bemo. The recently completed Cipularang toll road has brought Jakarta within a speedy two hours of Bandung, and at weekends it can seem as if half the capital has arrived there.▸▸ *See Transport, page 52.*

Getting around

Roads are often jammed and the complicated one-way system can be confusing to the uninitiated. However, because Bandung is more than 700 m above sea level, the climate is far cooler than lowland cities like Jakarta and Surabaya and walking is an option. Colts and town buses provide the main means of local transport. Taxis and car hire companies are also found here.

Tourist information

In their office in the northern side of the Masjid Agung on Jalan Asia Afrika, the staff of the **Bandung Visitor Information Centre** ⓘ *T022 420 6644, Mon-Sat 0900-1700 and Sun 0900-1400,* can tell you anything you want to know about Bandung and the surrounding area. The office organizes custom-made tours to suit each visitor's interests; for example, an architectural tour of the town, a pre-historic tour, a trip to the volcanoes, or a tour to visit Sundanese ethnic minorities. Staff are very helpful, particularly the English-speaking Ajid Suryana. There is also an office at the railway station.

Places in Bandung → *For listings, see pages 48-53.*

If you want to photograph these buildings, bear in mind that several are occupied by the military and sensitivities are acute.

Colonial art deco
Bandung is recognized as one of three cities in the world with 'tropical art deco' architecture (the others being Miami, Florida and Napier, New Zealand). The Bandung Society for Heritage Conservation has a register of well over 600 category I and II monuments in Bandung. Of all the art deco architects the one most closely associated with Bandung is Wolff Schoemacher. He graduated with Ed Cuypers from the Delft Technical University in the Netherlands, and then moved to Bandung where he designed hundreds of buildings. In theory, any building over 50 years old is protected and the Mayor of Bandung is said to be appreciative of the need to preserve this heritage. But with the cowboy atmosphere that pervades many other towns and cities, the preservationists will need to be ever watchful.

The most impressive art deco building, lying in the centre of town, is the **Savoy Homann Hotel** on Jalan Asia Afrika, built in 1938 by AF Aalbers and still retaining period furniture and fittings. It has been meticulously renovated at a cost of US$2 million so that visitors can savour a hotel that numbers Charlie Chaplin, Ho Chi Minh and Zhou En-lai among its guests. From the exterior it has been likened to a radio; the interior to an ocean liner. Aalbers is said to have wanted to remind Dutch guests of the ships that brought them to the country. Opposite is the **Preanger Hotel**, built in 1889 but substantially redesigned by Wolff Schoemacher in 1928. The remaining art deco wing faces Jalan Asia Afrika. West on Jalan Asia Afrika is the **Gedung Merdeka** ① *Mon-Fri 0900-1500, free,* also known as the Asia Afrika building. Originally built in 1895, it was completely renovated in 1926 by Wolff Schoemacher, Aalbers and Van Gallen Last, and today houses an exhibition of photographs of the first Non-Aligned Movement conference held here in 1955 (hence the name of the street).

Jalan Braga is often said to be Bandung's colonial heart. Sadly though, most of the original facades have been disfigured or entirely replaced. North of the railway line, also on Jalan Braga, is the **Bank of Indonesia**, designed by Ed Cuypers in the 1920s. Either side are church buildings designed by Schoemacher.

North of the centre
The north suburbs of Bandung are the most attractive part of the city; leafy and green, this is University Land. **Gedung Sate** on Jalan Diponegoro was built in the 1920s and is one of Bandung's more imposing public buildings, with strong geometric lines and a formal garden. Within the building, but rather hidden away, is the **Museum Post and Philately** ① *Jln Cilaki 37, Mon-Fri 0900-1500, free.* Almost opposite is the **Geological Museum** ① *No 57, T022 720 3205, Mon-Thu 0900-1530, Sat-Sun 0900-1330, adult 2000Rp, student 1500Rp,* reputed to be the largest in Southeast Asia. It houses skeletons of pre-historic elephants, rhinos, fossilized trees and a meteor weighing 156 kg that fell on Java in 1884. Most notably, it is home to the skull of 'Java Man'. Unfortunately, there's no information in English. Also north of the city centre on Jalan Taman Sari, the **Bandung Institute of Technology** or ITB was built by Maclaine Pont in 1918 and represents another

good example of the architecture of the art deco era. Off Jalan Taman Sari, just before the ITB travelling north, is the **Kebun Binatang** ① *daily 0800-1600, 10,000Rp, very crowded on Sun and holidays*, Bandung's **zoo** housing Komodo dragons among other beasts. It is set in beautiful surroundings and is well worth a visit. Not far south of the zoo is the rather bizarre '**Jean Street**' on Jalan Cihampelas. Shopkeepers vie for the most elaborate shopfront in an attempt to lure trade. It is a most surreal experience to wander amongst this collection of larger-than-life plaster Rambos, Superman leaping though a wall, and a huge Spiderman casting a web, helicopters, James Bonds and other figures and images, and worth a visit even if you are not intending to shop. There are not just jeans for sale here: all types of

Bandung

Where to stay 🛏	Trio 2	Momiji 1
Arion Swiss Belhotel 1		Sapuldi 11
By Moritz 22	**Restaurants** 🍴	Sederhana Bintaro 7
De'Tropis Guesthouse 4	Cihampelas Walk 9	Warung Laos 8
Grand Preanger 5	Dapur Ku 2	
Gunter 6	Fa Fa Bapau 10	**Bars & clubs** 🍸
Savoy Homann 19	Kartika Sari 12	Classic Rock Café 13
Scarlet Dago 7	Kiosk 3	Embassy 14
Scarlet Kebon Kawang 8	London Bakery 5	North Sea 6
Serena 3	Maung Dodol 4	

500 metres
500 yards

clothes, DVDs and merchandise for Bandung's large population of students and trendies are available. The streets are also lined with stalls selling fresh coconuts and durian ice cream – which emits the usual overwhelming smell. To get to the street, take an Angkutan kota running up Jalan Pasir Kaliki and then walk through Jalan Prof Eyckman (Jean Street itself is one-way running south). **Jalan Pasar Selatan** is a more recent imitation of the original, lined with stores selling denim.

South of the centre
South of town, the **Museum of West Java (Negeri Propinsi Jawa Barat)** *① Mon-Sat 0800-1600, 1000Rp,* is on the corner of Jalan Otto Iskandarinata and the ring road. It houses artefacts tracing the development and history of West Java.

One of the minarets of the **Masjid Agung** *① Jln Jend Sudirman, Sat and Sun only 0900-1700, 2000Rp,* can be climbed for fine views of the city, and the mountains that surround it. Ajid, at the tourist information office (in the north side of the mosque) can also arrange for tours of the huge mosque, but remember to dress conservatively. Men in shorts will not be allowed to enter.

Markets
Like many Indonesian cities, Bandung has a number of markets. **Pasar Kota Kembang** runs along a narrow lane linking Jalan Asia-Afrika and Jalan Dalem Kaum, and specializes in clothes, shoes and accessories. **Pasar Baru** is in Chinatown and is a good place to buy textiles, including batik; the basement houses a vegetable market. **Jalan Pasar Utara** is a food market selling snacks and many West Javanese culinary specialities. Bandung's largest **flower market**, supplied from the many upland nurseries around the city, is on Jalan Wastukencana.

Further north still (7 km) is the **Dago Teahouse** *① 1500Rp daily, early morning until 2200, catch a Dago colt up Jln Ir H Juanda (the colts terminate at Terminal Dago, not far from the Tea House), the Tea House is behind the Pajajaran University housing complex.* It was renovated in 1991, and provides a cultural hall and open-air theatre for evening Sundanese dance performances. There are good views of the city from here and an excellent restaurant. On Saturday nights, Jalan Dago gets crowded with the city's cool young things who hang out snacking, gossiping and listening to loud music around their customized cars.

Around Bandung

Most visitors who venture out of the city travel north into the volcanic **Priangan Highlands** that surround Bandung, to see neat tea plantations, colossal craters and natural hot springs.

Villa Isola
① Regular minibuses and colts ply this route out of Bandung. Either travel direct from the train station or via Terminal Ledeng at the northern edge of the city.
This lies on the route north of Jalan Setiabudi, 6 km from the city centre, and is yet another fine art deco building, set on a hill overlooking the city.

Lembang
Lembang, 16 km north of Bandung, is a popular resort town on an upland plateau with restaurants, hotels and pony drawn carts. It is famous for its pleasant climate and

abundance of fresh flowers and fruit. The town can be used as a base to explore the uplands and visit such places as the Tangkuban Prahu Crater and the Ciater Hot Springs (see below). Garden nurseries line the road into Lembang and the town also supports the internationally respected **Bosscha Observatory** ① *visits must be prearranged, regular minibuses connect Lembang with Bandung's Terminal Ledeng, on Jln Dr Setiabudi on the northern edge of the city, to get to Terminal Ledeng, take a colt going up Jln Pasir Kaliki, there are also colts running direct to Lembang from the train station in the centre of town.*

Tangkuban Prahu Crater

① *Daily 50,000Rp. Guides are unnecessary for the well-defined path to the Domas Crater, but for off-path treks (inadvisable without a guide because of the emissions of sulphurous gases) official guides are available from the tourist information centre at the crater (0700-1700) and cost in the region of 100,000Rp. Beware of the many charlatan guides. Take a bus or colt heading for Subang from either the Leuwi Panjang terminal or from the minibus stop opposite the train station; ask to be dropped off at the entrance to the crater (about 25 km from the city), hitch or walk (3.5 km) from here. At the weekend there are colts that go all the way to the summit.*

Tangkuban Prahu Crater (the capsized boat crater) is one of the most popular tourist sights in the vicinity of Bandung and possibly the most accessible volcanic crater in Indonesia. The route up to the volcano from Lembang passes through rich agricultural land, with terraces of market garden crops clawing their way up the hillsides, chincona trees (the bark is used to produce quinine), teak and wild ginger. The entrance to the 'park' is 9 km from Lembang. The drive from the gate snakes through a forest of giant pines. Some 3 km from the gate is the lower car park (with restaurant and tourist stalls). From here the road continues upwards for another 1 km to the rim of the impressive **Ratu Crater**. Alternatively, there is a footpath from the lower car park to the Ratu Crater (1.5 km), and another from there to the smaller **Domas Crater** (1 km). Another path links the Domas and Ratu Craters (1.2 km). It is also possible to walk all the way round the Ratu Crater. Despite being visited by numerous tour buses and inhabited by large numbers of souvenir sellers, the natural splendour of the volcano makes the trip worthwhile. Ratu rises to an altitude of 1830 m, and the crater drops precipitously from the rim. Bursts of steam and the smell of sulphur bear witness to the volcanic activity latent beneath the surface.

The curious shape of the summit of Tangkuban Prahu has given rise to the Sundanese *Legend of Prince Sangkuriang*, who unknowingly fell in love with his mother, Dayang Sumbi. She tried to prevent their marriage, insisting that her betrothed create a lake and canoe before sunrise on their wedding day. Sangkuriang seemed to be endowed with magical powers and he nearly achieved this impossible task when Dayang Sumbi called upon the gods to hasten the sun to rise, in order to prevent their forbidden union. Sangkuriang was so angry that he kicked his nearly finished canoe, which landed upside down on the horizon, thus creating this silhouette. The wildlife in the surrounding forest includes a small population of native gibbons. At the summit, hawkers sell *angklungs* (hand-held bamboo chimes) to bemused tourists while tapping out *Auld Lang Syne* or *Happy Birthday*. They also vigorously proffer wooden carvings and animals made of small seashells and herbal remedies such as *kayu naga*. This resembles green, hairy twiglets, and is reputedly good for rheumatism and backache. The twiglets are boiled in water and the resultant malodorous brew is drunk.

Ciater Hot Springs

① T0260 471 700. Open daily 24 hrs. Entrance 16,000Rp, 20,000Rp – 40,000Rp to bathe depending on class. Take a colt or bus towards Subang, ask to be let off at Air Panas Ciater; the hotel and springs are 150 m off the main road.

Ciater Hot Springs are 6.5 km on from Tangkuban Prahu, the road following the mountainside and winding through tea plantations. There are brilliantly clear hot-water pools and waterfalls here situated on the side of a hill. Unfortunately, the complex is run down.

Ciwidey

① Regular connections from the Kebon Kelapa terminal, 1½ hrs.

Ciwidey is a small town about 14 km southwest of Bandung. It is much less touristy and more rural than Ciater – and well worth the effort of getting there. Continuing along the road, up the Ciwidey Valley, the route climbs up past Cimanggu (at the 42 km marker) where there is a small park and hot pools fed from Gunung Patuha (2400 m). The hillsides here are planted with tea bushes. Among the largest estates are the **Rancabali** and **Malabar** estates.

Bandung listings

For hotel and restaurant price codes and other relevant information, see pages 9-12.

⊜ Where to stay

Bandung *p43, map p45*
Bandung lacks the quality budget accommodation of other Javanese cities, and those in search of clean comfortable digs are advised to spend a little more money here. Many of the city's hotels are scattered conveniently near the train station around Jln Kebonjati and Jln Kebon Kawung. The cost of a room in mid-range and more expensive places increases by around 20% at weekends.

$$$$-$$$ Arion Swiss Belhotel, Jln Otto Iskandarinata 16, T022 424 0000, www.swiss-belhotel.com. Top-class lodgings with tastefully decorated rooms with cable TV, broadband access and all mod cons. Spa, fitness centre and rooftop swimming pool.

$$$$-$$$ Grand Preanger, Jln Asia Afrika 81, T022 423 1631, www.preanger.aerowisata.com. A/c, restaurant (excellent food), pool, original art deco wing (1928), refurbished to a high standard and offering the most interesting rooms, central location, fitness centre, good facilities and well run.

$$$$-$$$ Scarlet Dago, Jln Siliwangi 5, Dago, T022 2500 3000, www.hotelscarletdago.com. On the edge of town and slightly away from the smog and exhaust fumes is this tasteful modern hotel. Rooms are swanky, the more pricey ones are huge and have massive open balconies. Wi-Fi access in the lobby. Decent weekday promo rates.

$$$ Savoy Homann, Jln Asia Afrika 112, T022 423 2244, www.savoyhomann-hotel.com. The wonderful art deco exterior of this hotel is immediately charming, proving that ageing places of style can be maintained in this country. Rooms are spacious and stylish, and have internet access and cable TV. Discounts available. Recommended.

$$$-$$ Hotel Scarlet Kebon Kawang, Jln H Mesri 11, T022 423 6146. Sprawling mid-range place with clean though slightly dark rooms. Handy for the train station for those arriving late. Good value for the mid-range bracket.

$$$-$$ Hotel Trio, Jln Gardujati 55-61, T022 603 1055, hoteltrio@bdg.centrin.net.id. Crowded with rooms, the **Trio** is popular with Chinese Indonesians and gets very busy at weekends. Rooms are all spotless and well maintained and come with TV and a/c. The more expensive rooms are huge and have a bath and fridge, with plenty of natural light. Pool. Discounts available (20-30%).

$$ De'Tropis Guest House, Jln Windu 6, T021 730 8034, www.detropis.com. Clean and friendly guesthouse set in a neighbourhood compound 20 mins' walk from the town centre. Rooms are well furnished and have cable TV and Wi-Fi access. The staff are friendly and very helpful, making this one of the better mid-range options in town. Decent breakfast and free tea and coffee all day. Recommended.

$$ Hotel Gunter, Jln Otto Iskandarinata 20, T022 420 3763. Faded 1960s hotel with rooms surrounding an immaculate cat-filled garden. Rooms are tatty and have a fair number of spider webs, but bedding is clean. Fan and a/c rooms available, all with TV.

$$ Hotel Serena, Jln Marjuk 4-6, T022 420 4317. This is a good option for those wanting comfort, without being overly extravagant with the pennies. Clean, tiled rooms with a/c, hot water and cable TV are good value here. Wi-Fi access in the lobby. Recommended.

$ By Moritz, Jln Kebon Jati, Luxor Permai 35, T022 420 5788, bymoritz_info@yahoo.com. Things have improved in terms of cleanliness here in recent times, although the place is very quiet and decidedly downmarket. There is a maze-like assortment of very basic fan rooms, some with attached bathroom, also cheaper rooms with common bathroom. The best rooms are the 2 on the roof, with small garden, pleasant seating area and views over the roofs to the south. The downstairs communal area has an assortment of books, TV, simple restaurant and a couple of guitars, occasionally utilized by the friendly staff for yet another rendition of *Hotel California*.

🍴 Restaurants

Bandung *p43, map p45*
Local dishes including *gorengan* (a form of vegetable-based tempura) *bandrek* and *bajigur* (both drinks made of ginger

and sweetened coconut milk respectively) *pecel lele* (fried eels with a piquant sauce) and *comro* (made from cassava and tempe). There are also a large number of bakeries in Bandung, the best selection on Jln Kebon Kawang.

$$ Sapuldi, Jln Chihampelas 105. Open 0900-0000. This place is an oasis of calm off busy Chihampelas, with spacious trationally styled restaurant and a varied menu of Sundanese and regional Indonesian favourites. The best seats are the lesehan seats in the back garden around a fish-filled pond. Recommended.

$$ Momiji, Jln Braga 64, T022 420 3786. Open 1100-2200. Calm and relaxing Japanese restaurant with an extensive menu of sushi, *tempura*, *udon*, *tappanyaki* and *bento* boxes. This place is particularly popular with European and East Asian expats at the weekend.

$ Dapur Ku, Jln Lembong 12-18, T022 420 6612. Open 1000-2200. Popular place to try Sundanese cooking, with set meals, or a huge buffet-style selection to choose from. The staff speak good English and can help with deciphering the menu.

$ London Bakery, Jln Braga 37, T022 420 7351. Open 0800-2200. Good selection of coffees, teas, sandwiches and pasta dishes (small portions), with the *Jakarta Post* to linger over. There is an outdoor seating area, although the exhaust fumes are choking.

$ Maung Dodol, Jln Gatot Subroto 28, T022 731 8203. Though slightly out of town, this little eatery has an excellent selection of Sundanese set meals. The *sayur asem* is delicious and the *sambal* fiery.

$ Sederhana Bintaro, Jln Jendral Sudirman 111, T022 420 7733. Open 0800-2200. Fans of *nasi Padang* won't want to miss this sparkling restaurant, with an extensive menu of spicy Sumatran favourites and some excellent value set meals. The *sirsak* juice from here is delicious. They can deliver to hotels for free. Recommended.

$ The Kiosk, lining entrance to Braga City Walk, Jln Braga. A line of faux rustic *kaki* *lima* proffering some excellent value local cuisine in a clean setting. The *bebek van java* looks promising.

$ Warung Laos, Jln Prof Eyckman 2, T022 203 0516. Mon, Tue 1800-2330, Wed-Sun 1100-2330. Excellent little place just off Jln Cihampelas with pleasant upstairs seating area serving good pizzas, pastas, juices and soups. Recommended.

Chihampelas Walk (see Shopping) has a number of clean places (mostly **$**) to eat at in a/c comfort. There are plenty of places to choose from including **Gokana Teppan** (T022 204111), which serves bargain-priced Japanese set meals, and **Cing Wan** (T022 206 1001), which has a menu of Thai and Chinese dishes. Another mall, **Paris Van Java**, has an excellent selection of eateries including Peranakan (Straits Chinese), Japanese and Western cuisine. It is beautifully lit up at night and gets very busy

Jln Gardajati has a selection of Chinese restaurants. **Mei Hwa** and **Red Top** (open for lunch and dinner) are worth investigating.

Bakeries

Fa Fa Bapau, Jln Gardajati 63, T022 607008. Open 0800-2100. Has a fine selection of Chinese buns, filled with pork and spices, or sweet ones with red bean paste. head here for something a little different.

Kartika Sari, Jln Haji Akbar 4, T022 423 1355. Daily 0600-1900. A popular bakery that gets rammed with salivating customers at the weekend. They come for the signature *pisang molan* (pastries filled with banana and cheese), which fly off the shelf.

La Patisserie, in the **Grand Preanger** (see Where to stay). Open 0800-2100. Has some very naughty chocolate delights, cheesecake, and handy takeaway lasagne and pizza.

Foodstalls

Probably the best are down a tiny alley off Jln Bungsu, near the **Puri Nas Bakery** (open 1730 onwards). Stalls are also on Jln Merdeka, Jln Martadinata, Jln Diponegoro (near the RRI building), Jln Cikapundung

Barat and Jln Dalem Kaum, west of the Alun-alun Lor. Most are night stalls only.

🌙 Bars and clubs

Bandung *p43, map p45*
Bandung has a great array of bars, pubs and clubs, with good bands and atmosphere.

Jln Braga is a good place to start with a number of bars (many of the somewhat seedy variety), and gets lively in the evenings. Places worth checking out include **Roompoet**, **North Sea Bar**, and **Violet**. Bars open in the late afternoon and close around 0200.

Classic Rock Café, Jln Lembong 1, T022 420 7982. Open 1200-0200. A fun venue covered with rock memorabilia, which has brilliant guitar door handles. Local musicians come to play classic covers and Indonesian rock in the evenings to a lively crowd. Rock music can also be found at **The Rock Café Lounge and Club** on Jln Dr Junjuan 153.

Embassy Score, Cihampelas Walk 160, T022 206 1156. Daily 2200-0600. Renowned club that plays trance and techno to a cool crowd, and attracts some of the nation's best DJs.

🎭 Entertainment

Bandung *p43, map p45*
The entertainment schedule is very changeable in Bandung. It is imperative that you check at the tourist information office before you head anywhere.

Adu domba (ram fights)

Ram fights are held most Sundays at **Ranca Buni**, near Ledeng, north of the city on Jln Setiabudi. Get there by taking a Lembung bus to Ledung terminal; walk down Jln Sersan Bejuri then turn left; there will be many helpful locals around to ask if you get lost. Closer to town, *Adu domba* can be seen on the first Sunday of the month at **Baba Kansiliwangi**. This is within walking distance of the zoo, to the north of the city

Angklung (hand-held bamboo chimes)

Performances are held at **Pak Udjo's workshop**, Jln Padasuka 118 (8 km northeast of the town centre), 1530-1730, 80,000Rp. Take a Cicaheum colt and get off at the intersection with Jln Padasuka, near the Cicaheum bus station. Pak Udjo's workshop is a 7-min walk, on the right-hand side of the street.

Cinemas

Blitz Mulitplex, at Paris Van Java, Jln Sukajadi 137-139, T022 8206 3630. Shows all the latest English-language blockbusters, and has very comfy seats, all for between 20,000Rp to 35,000Rp. Recommended.

Cultural shows

Dago Teahouse (see page 46), open stage Sat evenings, free (buy a drink). Sundanese dance and alternative music performances.
Jln Naripan 7, dance rehearsals.
Rumentiang Siang, Jln Barangsiang 1 (near Jln A Yani), T022 423 3562. This is the place to go for performance of Jaipongan (Sundanese dance), epic *wayang golek* shows, *ketoprak* (traditional theatre).
STSI (Institute of Fine Arts), Jln Buah Batu, T022 731 4982. Performances and rehearsals of Sundanese dance, theatre and music.

O Shopping

Bandung *p43, map p45*

Art galleries Bandung is viewed as a centre for Indonesian arts and there are a number of galleries in town exhibiting work by promising young Indonesians. There are a few galleries along Jln Braga including: **Barli**, Jln Prof Dr Sutami 91, T022 201 1898, Mon-Sat 0900-1700, collection of traditional and contemporary art; **Bunga Art Gallery**, Jln Braga 41, T022 731 0960, daily 0900-1800; **Jalu Braga**, Jln Braga 29, daily 0700-2200; and **Taman Budya Jawa Barat**, Jln

Bukit Dago Selatan 53, T022 250 5364, Mon-Sat 0900-2200, Sundanese art, occasional performances.

Batik Batik Abstrak, Jln Tirtasari 9, T081 5628 1358. Funky and super-modern batik designs.

Books Branch of QB Books on Jln Setiabudi to the north of town. Daily 0900-2100. Good selection of English-language books and a relaxed café with Wi-Fi access.

Distros Taken from the Indonesian word *distribusi* (distribution), distros are a fashion phenomenon in Bandung that has spread elsewhere in Indonesia, notably to posh south Jakarta. These independent shops are run as cooperatives and act as distributing agents for local designers who do not have the means or desire to produce mass goods in a factory. The T-shirts and other clothing produced is therefore original and rare. Distros can be grungy places, with graffiti-covered walls and hard rock soundtracks, all adding to their underground charm. As with all things that are cool, there is some fear of distros becoming too mainstream, and losing the cooperative spirit that make them so popular. Bandung has over 200. If you're in the market for a cool T-shirt, check out the following distros, all on Jln Trunojoyo: **Blackjack, Screamous, Achtung** and **Cosmic.**

Handicrafts Pa Aming, Jln M Ramdhan 4; and **Pak Ruchiyat**, Jln Pangarang Bawah IV No 78/17B (behind No 20 in the alleyway). Both are workshops where you can also buy and the latter is reputed to sell perhaps the finest worked examples. **Pak Ruchiyat** has over 35 years' experience; note that prices are fixed. Shops along Jln Braga sell puppets. **Cupumanik**, Jln Haji Akbar, Mon-Sat 0900-1600. Collection of locally made masks, puppets and handicrafts. **Eddy Noor Gallery**, Jln Villa Bandung Indah, T022 707 1135. Beautiful painted glass exhibition by a local artist.

Shopping malls Chihampelas Walk, Jln Chihampelas 160, T022 206 1122. Brand-name goods in a clean a/c environment. Good for taking a breather from manic Jeans St shopping.

Supermarket Carrefour, Braga Walk, daily 1000-2200, is a good place to stock up on necessities. You can also find a few cafés and fast-food outlets here.

⚙ What to do

Bandung *p43, map p45*
Tour operators
Kangaroo Travel and Tours, Hotel Perdana Wisata, Jln Jebdral Sudirman 66-68, T022 420 0334.
Satriavi, Grand Hotel Preanger, Jln Asia Afrika 81, T022 420 3657, www.aerowisata.co.id.

Tours
The tourist office on Jln Asia Afrika will organize tours in and around town, as will many of the travel agents (depending on season and demand). Typical tours visit the Tangkuban Prahu crater and Ciater hot springs (5 hrs, US$40 per person), architecturally interesting buildings around town (3 hrs, US$12 per person) and an angklung music performance, plus traditional Sundanese dancing (3 hrs, US$10 per person).
By Moritz (see Where to stay, page 49) organize day trips to Mt Papandayan, with a guide leading visitors all over the mountain, and a bath in a sulphur spring. They also have trips to Ciwidey, to see the tea plantations, Cibuni crater and Danau Patenggang. All tours from By Moritz cost around US$45 per person, but prices are highly negotiable.

Walks
The Bandung tourist office has identified a number of walks in the city through the Central Business District (CBD), Chinatown and elsewhere. For maps and further information contact the tourist office – good background information on buildings and the city's history is available.

⊖ Transport

Bandung *p43, map p45*
Most roads in the centre of town are one-way. This, coupled with the dense traffic, makes it quite a struggle getting around town. Bandung must have more orange-suited traffic wardens than any other town on Java, ready to direct traffic dangerously (and collect their 300Rp *parkir*). Colts (Angkutan kota) charge 3000Rp for journeys around town and up to 5000Rp for longer journeys. They can be found at the station on Jln Kebonjati.

Air
Bandung's **airport** is 4 km from the city, T022 604 1313. Fixed price transport to town by taxi, US$7. AirAsia flies to **KL**, **Singapore**, **Denpasar**, **Medan** and **Pekanbaru**. Malaysian Airlines has flights to **KL** and **JB**. Merpati flies to **Batam**, **Yogyakarta**, **Surabaya**, **Denpasar** and **Kupang**. There are daily flights to **Jakarta** on **Garuda** and **Wings Air**. Sriwijaya flies to **Surabaya**. Susi Air flies daily to **Pangandaran** and **Jakarta** (**Halim**) in their tiny 12-seater Cessna.
   Airline offices Garuda, Jln Asia Afrika 118, T022 421 7747. Merpati, Jln Kebon Kawung 16, T022 4230 3180. Sirwaijaya, Jln Burangrang, T022 733 4026. Susi Air (book through Jakarta office: Susi Air Jakarta, BNI 46 Building 32nd floor, Jln Sudirman Kav I, T021 3929 726.

Bus
Local City buses go north–south or east–west; west on Jln Asia Afrika, east on Jln Kebonjati (beware that Nos 9 and 11 stop at 2100) south on Jln Otto Iskandarinata, north on Jln Astanaanyar, 3000Rp.

Long distance Bandung has 2 long-distance bus terminals: for destinations to the west is the **Leuwi Panjang** terminal, 5 km south of the city centre on Jln Soekarno-Hatta. Serves destinations including **Jakarta** (Kampung Rambutan terminal), **Bogor** and **Sumatra**. Terminal **Cicaheum** on Jln Jend A Yani (40,000Rp taxi ride from city centre) serves destinations to the east and north, including **Yogya**, **Solo**, **Surabaya**, **Garut**, There are also direct buses to **Pangandaran** (60,000Rp).

To avoid the hassle of going to the terminals, it is best to book bus tickets through **Pahala Kencana** (Jln Kebonjati, T022 42) or **Kramat Jati** (Jln Kebonjati (T022 420085). Both companies have buses departing from their offices to **Denpasar** (24 hrs, US$32), **Probolinggo** (19 hrs, US$30), **Surabaya** (19 hrs, US$17.50) **Yogya** and **Solo** (8-9 hrs, US$12.50).

Minibus Phone to make a booking, or get the hotel staff to do it for you, and pay when you have reached your destination. **4848**, T022 422 4848, has door-to-door services to **Jakarta** (US$10), and **Pangandaran** (US$8). Sarum Hari, T022 607 7065, also offers 2 daily connections with Pangandaran at 0600 and 1300 (US$8), **Deva Travel**, Jln Jend. A Ayani 810, T022 720 0679, offers 2 daily door-to-door services to **Bogor** (0400, 0900, US$8). Primajasa, T022 607 3992, has minibuses departing hourly from 0800-2100 from Bandung Super Mall to Jakarta's **Soekarno-Hatta** airport (3 hrs, US$9). Cipaganti, T022 426 4525, also offers this service as well as trips to various suburbs in the capital.

Car hire
Mulia Car Rental, Batununggal Indah 39, T081 201 5606, www.muliarental.com.
Total Car Rental, Jln Jajaway Dago Atas 12A, T022 8252 0044, www.rental.total.or.id.

Taxi
Taxis are notorious for rip-offs. The only company worth using is **Blue Bird**, T022 756 1234.

Train
The station is behind the bemo station, on Jln Stasion Barat and has a helpful information line with English-speaking staff (T022 426 6383). Regular connections with **Jakarta's** Jatinegara and Gambir stations. The best service is the **Parahiyangan** with 6 daily departures to **Gambir** taking 2½ hrs (*bisnis* US$3/*eksekutif* US$6). The Lodaya calls in at **Tasikmalaya**, Banjar (for **Pangandaran**), **Yogya** and **Solo** (*bisnis* US$11/*eksekutif* US$18). For **Surabaya**, hop on the daily **Argo Wilis** (*eksekutif* US$23).

◑ Directory

Bandung *p43, map p45*
Banks ATMs can be found along all commercial streets, particularly Jln Braga, Jln Cihampelas, Jln Jendral Sudirman and Jln Asia Afrika. **Money changers:** VIT Jln Cihampelas, in a small booth opposite Adventist Hospital. **Aneka Artha Mas**, Jln Naripan 43, T022 424 1204. **Medical services** Chemist: Ratu Farma, Jln Kebonjati 106, T022 439892. **Hospital:** Adventist Hospital, Jln Cihampelas 161, T022 203 4386. **Telephone** Wartel, Jln Asia Afrika (opposite Savoy Homann Hotel), for international calls and fax.

Pangandaran

Pangandaran is situated on the neck of a narrow isthmus and offers some of the best beaches on the south coast of Java. Originally a fishing village, many of the local people now derive their livelihoods from tourism. At weekends, during peak season, the town is crowded with Indonesian tourists; out of season, on weekdays, it is like a ghost town and hotel and losmen prices can be bargained down. The high season is June to September, the low season October to March.

On 17 July 2006, Pangandaran was hit by a tsunami. The tidal wave, at least 3 m high, devastated the coastal strip ploughing as far inland as 400 m and washing away hundreds of houses and businesses. Many locals have heartbreaking stories to tell and are trying hard to rebuild their lives, but there is still plenty of evidence of the disaster. The owner of Lotus Wisata, Lia Natalia, whose business was washed away, has an album of photos taken after the tsunami showing the immediate damage.

A visit to Pangandaran is highly recommended as a foil to the beaches of Bali and Thailand. It is a great chance to observe Javanese beach culture without the overload of tie dye and banana pancakes, and the surrounding countryside is truly superlative.

Note Look for the *Jalur Evakuasi* (Evacuation Route) signs around town in the unlikely event of another disaster occurring.

Beaches → *Phone code: 0265. For listings, see pages 55-58.*

① *Admission to the isthmus is 5000Rp.*

The best beach is on the west side of the isthmus and is named **West Beach** (Pantai Barat). Swimming is not recommended as currents are vicious. Look out for the red flags warning of dangerous areas. Locals seem to ignore the warning signs and there are lines of vendors offering body board rental (25,000Rp an hour) for those who fancy an exhilirating splash about. Souvenir shops line the beachfront and most accommodation is concentrated here. The east side of the isthmus, **East Beach** (Pantai Timur), is less developed; the water is often rough and swimming is poor, sometimes dangerous. Fishermen cast their nets from this shore and land their catches along the beach. Their colourful boats lining the shore are a lovely sight. The fish market is worth a visit in the mornings if you can stand the smell! The **PHKA tourist office** is on the edge of the park at the south end of the isthmus, near East Beach. Lia Natalia at **Lotus Wisata** speaks excellent English and is a good source of local information.

The promontory of the isthmus is the **Penanjung National Park** ① *0700-1730, 7500Rp, guides 100,000Rp for a tour lasting 4 hrs and worth the money,* only half of which is open to tourists. On both the east and west sides of the promontory are white-sand beaches. It is possible to walk the 10 km around the shoreline of the peninsula, or hike through the jungle that is said to support small populations of buffalo, deer, tapirs, civet cats, porcupines and hornbills, although how they tolerate the herds of tourists is a mystery. The Rafflesia flower can apparently be seen here in season. The park also has some limestone caves.

Around Pangandaran
Batu Karas ① *get here by hired motorbike or take a bemo to Cijulang, then hop on an ojek for the last 10 km to the beach from the main road,* is popular with surfers.

Green Canyon ⓘ *take a minibus from Pangandaran to Cijulang, and then an ojek from there, most hotels run tours to the canyon, which will also include a full day visit to local farming and craft industries; alternatively, visit the tourist information office for cheaper, good tours, starting at 150,000Rp per person*, is a very popular day trip. Boat hire is regulated and costs 80,000Rp per *prahu* (which seat up to eight people). Travelling upriver, the foliage becomes denser and the rocks close in, until you find yourself entering a canyon. After 15-20 minutes, the boat's path is blocked by rocks. There is a large plunge pool here, with swimming and rubber rings for hire. The best time to visit is during the week, as it gets crowded at weekends and holidays; a recommended trip.

Parigi Bay ⓘ *regular buses run from Pangandaran bus station on Jln Merdeka, ask specifically for a beach, eg Batu Karas, the bus doesn't go all the way – only to the bridge over the Green River (5000Rp); from here you need to hire a motorbike or hitch a lift*, is west of Pangandaran, and offers better and quieter beaches than the isthmus, namely **Batu Hiu**, **Batu Karas** and **Parigi**, and good water for surfing.

A worthwhile alternative to the bus trip back to Banjar is the much more enjoyable ferry journey from Kalipucang to Cilacap (see Transport, page 57). Local trips around the peninsula, stopping to swim or snorkel, can be bargained for with the local fishermen (around US$30). Trips to tiny white-sand islands (infrequently visited and uninhabited) off the peninsula cost about US$35 for a one-hour boat ride, and then you can stay on the island as long as you wish. A trip to **Nusakambangan** is available from Pangandaran (US$30). The island, once forbidden to tourists because of a high-security prison located there, has unspoilt beaches and forests. The prison is considered the highest security jail in the country and has played host to notables including Tommy Soeharto, poet and novelist Pramoedya Ananta Toer and the three Bali bombers – Imam Samudra, Amrozi, and Ali Gufron – who were executed here by firing squad in November 2008.

It's also possible to charter a boat between Kalipucang (Pangandaran's 'port') and Cilacap through the **Anakan Lagoon**, an 'inland' sea. A recommended four-hour journey and a gentle form of transport, the boat sails down the mangrove-clothed Tanduy River, stopping off in various fishing villages, before crossing the lagoon. The Tanduy River marks the border between West Java and Central Java. The last village before the ferry turns into the lagoon, **Majingklak**, is the easternmost village in West Java. The large island bordering the south of the lagoon and protecting it from the Indian Ocean, is **Kampangan Island**. In 1912, the Dutch depopulated the island, resettling three fishing villages, with the intention of making it a prison. The lagoon is one of Indonesia's largest areas of wetland and has a varied water bird population. For keen birdwatchers it is possible to jump ship at one of the fishing villages, sleep in a homestay, and then charter a boat to explore the lagoon early the next morning, before continuing the journey to Cilacap (or vice versa).➤➤ *See Transport, page 57.*

Pangandaran listings

For hotel and restaurant price codes and other relevant information, see pages 9-12.

● Where to stay

Pangandaran *p54*
Accommodation is concentrated on the west side of the isthmus – there are around 100 hotels and *losmen*. Rates can be bargained down substantially during low season (Oct-Mar) and weekdays. At Christmas and during Jul and Aug prices rise steeply. Many hotels and guesthouses rent out family rooms– usually 2 double rooms and living area.

$$$ Laut Biru, Jln Embah Jaga Lautan 17-18, T0265 639360, www.lautbiru.com. Handily located near a good stretch of beach and the entrance to the national park, this place has great facilities, comfortable rooms and good service. Pool. Substantial discounts available.

$$$ Nyuir Resort Hotel, Jln Bulak Laut, T0265 639349, www.nyiurresorthotel.com. Rooms here are overpriced and geared towards package tour groups. However, the hotel has all the trimmings of a resort with a pleasant garden, pool and restaurant.

$$ Adam's Homestay, Jln Bulak Laut, T0265 639396. Wonderful gardens, with ponds and small streams aplenty. Rooms are huge, and have fridge, a/c and TV. Pool. Recommended.

$$ Pondok Daun, Jln Bulak Laut 74, T0265 639788. Spacious clean rooms all with a/c, TV and outdoor bathroom, in a shady garden with small pool.

$$ Puri Alam, Jln Bulak Laut Depan Pasar Wisata, T0265 631699. The staff here don't speak English but are extraordinarily friendly and make every effort to ensure visitors feel at home. This hotel is covered in greenery further adding to its charms. Good-value spacious rooms, with TV and a/c. Breakfast not included. There is also a huge bungalow on site available for rental at weekends, which would suit a large group. Recommended.

$$-$ Sandaan, Jln Bulak Laut, T0265 639165. Wide variety of rooms, all of which are clean, and improve dramatically as prices rise. Standards have a/c and TV, but they face a brick wall. The more expensive de luxe rooms have a pleasant veranda and views of the pool.

$ Mini Tiga, Jln Bulak Laut, T0265 639436, kalmaja@yahoo.fr. This is prime backpacker territory and a great spot to meet up with fellow travellers and discuss the road ahead. The hotel feels a bit cramped, but has a pleasant café area, clean and simple fan rooms with attached bathroom. Recommended.

Restaurants

Pangandaran *p54*

There are innumerable places to eat, some of which are geared to Western tastes. Not surprisingly, seafood is by far the best bet.

$ Chez Mama Cilacap, Jln Kidang Pananjung, T0265 639098. Open 0730-2300. Excellent place for fresh seafood and breakfast. Also some Western standards. Recommended.

$ Eka Bamboo Café, Jln Bulak Laut, T0818 0974 0899. Open 0800-0100. Good for a cheap breakfast, a late-night beer or to sample some local cuisine including *nasi uduk*. This place has a reputation as a bit of a party place and is a good spot to socialise.

$ Only One Resto, Jln Bulak Laut, T0265 639969. Open 0700-2300. This comfortable and popular eatery has sea views, good fresh seafood, and tasty Indonesian cuisine.

$ Pasar Ikan, Jln Talanca. Open 0700-2000. If you only have one night in Pangandaran, this is the place to go. For seafood fans the *pasar ikan* is one of the best places in Java to get the catch of the day with its collection of clean restaurants serving up shark, lobster, jumbo prawns and fish accompanied by gargantuan portions of delicious *sambal kangkung* (water spinach fried with sambal). One of the more popular places is **Sari Melati** (T0265 639735). Recommended.

$ Patisserie, Jln Bulak Laut. Open 0700-2300. Pleasant spot to start the day with beach views, a decent menu of sandwiches and cakes and some Western standard dishes.

$ Restaurant Relax, Jln Bulak Laut 74, T0265 630377. Open 0800-2300. Run by a European woman, this place has delicious fresh brown bread, hard central European cheeses and offers a variety of Western and Indonesian dishes, excellent juices and lassis and some rather tasty cakes in a homely European café-style setting. Those in the mood for something substantial will find solace in the goulash. Recommended.

🍸 Bars and clubs

Pangandaran *p54*
Pangandaran isn't really a place to go wild, but on Sat nights the town comes alive and it is worth visiting one of the *dangdut* pubs that line the main road.
The Spot, at the **Surya Pesona**, see Where to stay. Open 2000-0100. Down a few bottles of *kratingdaeng* and dance with the local youths to ear-bleeding techno. There are occasional *dangdut* nights here for those in search of something a little more laid-back. Western visitors often congregate at **Only One Resto** or **Bamboo** for a drink and natter.

🛍 Shopping

Pangandaran *p54*
There is a large **Pasar Wisata** (tourist market) 0800-2100, which is mournfully empty on weekdays, selling cheap tourist trinkets. There is also a supermarket on Jln Merdeka, open 0800-2200.

🎯 What to do

Pangandaran *p54*
Tour operators
There are plenty of unlicensed guides wandering the streets and hanging out in cafés looking for business.

Tour agencies organize jungle, boat (fishing, snorkelling), home industry, village and other tours. Trips include a 6-hr visit to Green Canyon (US$15), a jungle tour (US$10) and many more. All tours include appropriate entrance fee, guide and lunch on longer excursions. Most hotels offer tours, and they can also be booked at **Lotus Wisata** (see below). Almost every hotel organizes trips to Yogya and Bandung, etc.

Lotus Wisata, Jln Bulak Laut 2, T0265 639635. Organizes local tours and transport to and from Pangandaran; recommended.

🚍 Transport

Pangandaran *p54*
400 km from Jakarta, 129 km from Bandung, 66 km from Banjar and 312 km from Yogya.

Air
Susi Air, www.susiair.com, has daily flights to **Bandung** and **Jakarta** (Halim). Book well in advance at travel agents around town or directly at their office on Jln Merdeka 31, T0265 639120.

Becak/bike/car/motorbike hire
Becaks and bicycle hire along the beach and from guesthouses, around US$4 per day.
Lotus Wisata, Jln Bulak Laut 2, T0265 639635. Rents motorbikes for around US$5 per day and cars for US$35 for 24 hrs, with a driver.

Boat
A private boat journey between **Kalipucan** (15 km from Pangandaran; take a local bus) and **Cilicap** takes 4 hrs. Approaching Cilacap is LP Nusa Kembangan, Indonesia's top security prison. The boat docks at **Sleko**, outside Cilacap. There is currently no public boat service running; chartering a boat costs US$50. See also page 55.

Bus
There are 2 stations on Jln Merdeka, north of the hotels and guesthouses (outside the main gates). Local bus connections tend to leave from the station at the eastern end of Jln Merdeka, not far from the main intersection before the gate, while express buses leave from the company terminal further west along Jln Merdeka. Regular buses link Pangandaran with **Banjar** (15,000Rp), from where there are frequent buses onward to **Jakarta** (7-10 hrs), **Bogor** (via **Ciawi**), **Bandung** (6 hrs), **Yogya** and **Solo**. Jakarta–Banjar buses leave Jakarta's Cililitan station every hour. There are also some direct connections with **Jakarta**

(8 hrs) and **Bandung**. Travel agents in town sell tickets for popular routes. For tickets to Bandung, head to the **Budimans** office at the bus terminal from where there are regular a/c buses (5-6 hrs, US$5).

Minibus An a/c door-to-door service can be booked from **Lotus Wisata** (see above) and most guesthouses in town. Daily departure to **Bandung** (daily at 0600, US$10) and 2 daily departures to **Yogyakarta** (departing 0600 and 0700 US$15). Be warned that this minibus service takes a lot longer than the train and stops at small villages and towns along the way to pick people up. Nevertheless, it's a scenic ride and if you're in no hurry, sit back and enjoy the views.

Train
No direct trains link Pangandaran with **Jakarta**, **Yogya**, **Bandung** or **Solo**. It is necessary to change in **Banjar**, a small town on the Bandung–Yogya road, and 66 km from Pangandaran. There are a number of cheap *losmen* over the railway bridge from the rail and bus stations in Banjar, for those who arrive too late to make a connection. The train and bus stations are 500 m apart; becaks wait to take travellers between them. Regular connections with **Jakarta** (1 daily, 10 hrs), **Bandung** (6 daily, 5 hrs, *eksekutif* US$19), **Yogya** (2 daily, 5 hrs, *eksekutif* US$18.50) and **Surabaya** to Banjar. Regular buses link Banjar with Pangandaran. Travel agents in Pangandaran sell package bus-train tickets that include pick up from hotel in Pangandaran and train ticket from Banjar. Packages cost around US$30 for an *eksekutif* train ticket to Yogya.

Directory

Pangandaran *p54*
Banks There is a BNI ATM on Jln Bulak Laut, opposite the Relax Restaurant. **Lotus Wisata** will change money. **Telephone** Telkom, Jln Kidang Penanjung, has an international phone service.

Yogyakarta

Yogyakarta (usually shortened to Yogya and pronounced 'Jogja') is the most popular tourist destination in Java. It is a convenient base from which to visit the greatest Buddhist monument in the world – Borobudur – and the equally impressive Hindu temples on the Prambanan Plain. The town itself also has a number of worthwhile attractions: the large walled area of the kraton, with the sultan's palace, the ruined water gardens or 'Taman Sari', and a colourful bird market. Yogya is arguably the cultural capital of Java, and certainly its many private colleges and university attest to its being the island's educational heart, which also accounts for the younger, relatively affluent individuals you will see in the city. For the tourist, it is also one of the best centres for shopping and offers a good range of tourist services, from excellent mid-range accommodation to well-run tour companies.

Yogya is situated at the foot of the volcano Gunung Merapi, which rises to a height of 2911 m, to the north of the city. This peak is viewed as life-giving, and is set in opposition to the sea, which is life-taking and situated to the south. The importance of orientation with relation to Gunung Merapi and the ocean is seen clearly in the structure of the kraton, or sultan's palace.

The May 2006 earthquake that virtually destroyed the town of Bantul (26 km to the south) and killed over 6000 people, badly affected many sights in the southern part of the city. The quake killed 27 people in Yogyakarta and damaged the Taman Sari, the Kraton Kerata Museum and the Museum Perjuangan.

In late 2010, Mount Merapi, the gorgeous volcano clearly visible from the city on a sunny day, erupted numerous times over the space of a month covering the city in fine white ash.

Major damage was done to the villages closer to the volcano with the displacement of over 350,000 people and the deaths of 353 people, many as a result of devastating pyroclastic flows. Flights in and out of the city were cancelled as the authorities declared the eruption the largest since 1870. Eruptions subsided and the alert status was downgraded to level 3. Tourists are now scuttling up the north side of the volcano once again.

Arriving in Yogyakarta → *Phone code: 0274.*

Getting there

Yogyakarta may not be in the top league of Javanese towns by population, but because it is such an important destination for tourists it is well connected. **Adisucipto International Airport**①*8 km east of town, T0274 486666*, is the nation's fourth busiest and has daily flights from Kuala Lumpur and Singapore (with **AirAsia**) and daily connections with destinations in Java and further afield. The train station is centrally situated on Jalan Pasar Kembang, and there are regular services to Jakarta's Gambir station (565 km), and east to Surabaya (327 km) and frequent departures to Solo. The Umbunharjo long-distance bus terminal is 4 km southeast of the city centre, at the intersection of Jalan Veteran and Jalan Kemerdekaan. Buses of all types depart for most towns in Java and beyond. Agents for tourist buses and minibuses can be found throughout the hotel and *losmen* areas of town and particularly on Jalan Sosrowijayan and Jalan Prawirotoman. ▶▶ *See Transport, page 74.*

Getting around

While Yogya is not a small town by any means, exploring the city on foot, or a combination of foot and becak, is not beyond the realms of possibility. Becaks can be chartered by the hour or by the trip. Town buses (pick up a route map from the tourist office), bemos and colts offer cheaper local transport options. The excellent **TransJogja** bus lines offer fast, clean and efficient transportation around town for a flat fee of 3000Rp. Routes can be found at www.transjogja.com/rute. Note that becak and bemo drivers have an unerring tendency to take their passengers on extended tours of shops and art galleries. Taxis can be chartered by the trip, or by the hour, half-day or day. Self-drive car and motorbike hire is readily available, as are bicycles.

Tourist information

Tourist information office ① *Jln Malioboro 14, T0274 566000, Mon-Thu, Sat 0800-1900, Fri 0800-1800*, offers free maps of the town and environs, information on cultural events, bus routes, etc. There is also a tourist office counter at the railway station and another at the airport.

Places in Yogyakarta → *For listings, see pages 67-75.*

Alun-alun Lor

Yogya's main street is Jalan Malioboro, which runs from north to south. At its south end, the street becomes Jalan Jend A Yani and then Jalan Trikora, which leads into the kraton and the grassed square known as the Alun-alun Lor. This square was the site of major events such as tiger and buffalo fights, which were staged here from 1769. A raised stand afforded the sultan and any visiting Dutch dignitaries a good view of the spectacle. The tiger was deemed to represent the foreigner and the buffalo, the Indonesian. Invariably, the buffalo would win the contest – often with some help – but the symbolism was lost on the Dutch. Nonetheless, the unperceptive Dutch still succeeded in dominating Yogya

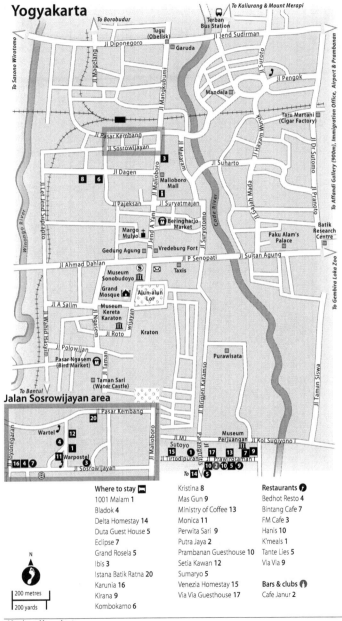

Yogyakarta

Jalan Sosrowijayan area

Where to stay 🛏

1001 Malam **1**
Bladok **4**
Delta Homestay **14**
Duta Guest House **5**
Eclipse **7**
Grand Rosela **5**
Ibis **3**
Istana Batik Ratna **20**
Karunia **16**
Kirana **9**
Kombokarno **6**

Kristina **8**
Mas Gun **9**
Ministry of Coffee **13**
Monica **11**
Perwita Sari **9**
Putra Jaya **2**
Prambanan Guesthouse **10**
Setia Kawan **12**
Sumaryo **5**
Venezia Homestay **15**
Via Via Guesthouse **17**

Restaurants 🍴

Bedhot Resto **4**
Bintang Cafe **7**
FM Cafe **3**
Hanis **10**
K'meals **1**
Tante Lies **5**
Via Via **9**

Bars & clubs 🍸

Cafe Janur **2**

and Indonesia. There are two sacred *waringin* trees (*Ficus benjamina*) in the centre of the square. The *waringin* represents the sky and the square fence or *waringin kurung* surrounding the trees, the earth with its four quarters. At the same time, the tree is said to symbolize chaotic nature, and the fence human order. If you see people blindly stumbling around, don't be alarmed. It's just the locals taking part in Masangin (*masuk antara dua beringin*), a game where they must walk between the two ficus trees blindfolded.

At the northwest edge of the Alun-alun Lor is the **Museum Sonobudoyo** ① *Tue-Sun 0800-1400, Fri 0800-1200, 7000Rp*. It was established in 1935 as a centre for Javanese culture, and the collection is housed, appropriately, within a traditional Javanese building. It contains a good selection of Indonesian art, largely Javanese, including a collection of *wayang* puppets, but also some Balinese woodcarvings. On the southwest side of the Alun-alun Lor is the **Grand Mosque**, built in Javanese style, with a wooden frame and a tiled roof.

The Kraton of Yogyakarta

The Kraton of Yogyakarta was one of three such palaces that came into existence when the kingdom of Mataram was partitioned after the Treaty of Giyanti was signed with the VOC in 1755. It has been described as a city within a city; it not only houses the sultan's palace, but also a maze of shops, markets and private homes supporting many thousands of people. This section only deals with the inner palace; the kraton actually extends much further, 'beginning' 1 km north at the far end of Jalan Malioboro.

The kraton was started in 1756 by the first sultan, Mangkubumi (who became Hamengkubuwono I in 1749), and finished almost 40 years later. The teak wood used to construct the palace came from the sacred forest of Karangkasem on Gunung Kidul. It is largely made up of *pendopo* or open pavilions, enclosed within interconnecting rectangular courtyards. The entire complex is surrounded by high white washed walls.

Facing the Alun-alun Lor is the **Pageleran** ① *Sat-Thu 0830-1330, Fri 0830-1230, 5000Rp*, a large open *pendopo*, originally employed as a waiting place for government officials. Today, this *pendopo* is used for traditional dance and theatrical performances. There are a number of further *pendopo* surrounding this one, containing mediocre displays of regal clothing. The very first classes of the newly created Gajah Mada University were held under these shaded pavilions. To the south of the Pageleran, up some steps, is the **Siti Inggil**, meaning 'high ground'. This is the spot where new sultans are crowned. Behind the Siti Inggil is the **Bronjonolo Gate**, which is kept closed.

The entrance to the main body of the palace is further south, down Jalan Rotowijayan, on the west side of the Pageleran complex. The first courtyard is the shaded **Kemangdungan** or **Keben**, with two small *pendopo*, where the *abdi dalem* or palace servants gather. The 'black' sand that covers most of the ground around the *pendopo* and other buildings in the kraton is from the beaches of the south coast. In this way, it is ensured that the Queen of the South Seas, Nyi Loro Kidul, with whom the sultan is believed to have intimate relations, is present throughout the palace.

The **Srimanganti** (meaning 'to wait for the king') **Gate** leads into a second, rather more impressive, courtyard with two *pendopo* facing each other; the **Srimanganti** to the right and the **Trajumas** to the left. The former was used to receive important guests, while the latter probably served as a court of law. The Srimanganti now contains gongs and other instruments that make up a *gamelan* orchestra. The Trajumas houses palanquins, litters and chairs, as well as a cage in which the sultan's children played. It is said that the children were placed in here, aged eight months, and given a selection of objects – pens, money, books. Whichever took their interest indicated their future careers.

The **Donapratopo Gate**, flanked by two *gupala* or *raksasa* statues to protect the palace from evil, leads into the heart of the palace where the sultan and his family had their private quarters. Notice the way that gateways never give direct access to courtyards; they were designed in this way to confuse spirits attempting to make their way into the complex.

Inside this gate, immediately on the right, is the sultan's office, the **Purwaretna**. Beyond it is the **Gedung Kuning**, an impressive yellow building which continues to be the sultan's private residence. Both are roped-off from the public.

The central and most impressive pavilion in the complex is the **Bangsal Kencono** ① *T0274 373721, Sat-Thu 0830-1330, Sun 0830-1230, admission 12,500Rp, camera 1000Rp extra, guides available with a donation, the palace can be partially closed on official ceremonial days*, or Golden Pavilion. The four teak pillars in the centre represent the four elements. On each is symbolized the three religions of Java: Hinduism (a red motif on the top of the columns), Buddhism (a golden design based on the lotus leaf) and Islam (black and gold letters of the Koran). Unfortunately, because the pavilion is roped off, it is difficult to see the pillars clearly. Behind the Golden Pavilion to the west is the **Bangsal Proboyekso**, which contains the armoury, and the **Gedung Keputrian**, the residence of the sultan's wives and children, both closed to the public. Immediately to the south of the Golden Pavilion is the **Bangsal Manis**, the dining room. **Kemakanan**, a *pendopo* to the south reached through a set of gates, is used for *wayang* performances at the end of Ramadan. To the east, through another gate (to the side of which is a large drum made from the wood of the jackfruit tree) there is another courtyard, the **Kesatrian**. The sultan's sons lived here. In the central *pendopo* of this courtyard there is another *gamelan* orchestra on display. Performances are held every Monday and Tuesday, 1000-1200 (the performance is included in the price of the entrance). At the east side of this courtyard is a collection of paintings, the best being by Raden Saleh, a 19th-century court painter who gained a reputation of sorts (and whose grave can be found in Bogor). The photographs of the sultans and their wives are more interesting. North of the Kesatrian is the **Gedung Kopo**, originally the hospital and now a museum housing gifts to the sultans.

Close to the palace, on Jalan Rotowijayan, is the **Museum Kereta Karaton** ① *Tue-Sun 0800-1600, 5000Rp plus 1000Rp for camera*, which houses the royal carriages.

Taman Sari and around

From the palace it is a five- to 10-minute walk to the Taman Sari. Walk south along Jalan Rotowijayan and turn left at the Dewi Srikandi Art Gallery. A number of batik painting galleries are down this road, which leads into Jalan Ngasem and then onto the **Pasar Ngasem** or bird market, an interesting place to wander. Song birds and turtle doves (*Genus Streptopelia*), are highly prized by the Javanese. It is sometimes said that wives take second place to a man's song bird and that they can cost as much as US$20,000.

By picking your way through the Pasar Ngasem it is possible to reach the **Taman Sari** ① *daily 0800-1530, 7000Rp,* which was known to the Dutch as the *waterkasteel* or 'Water Castle', as it is still called. This is a maze of underground passageways, ruins and pools, built as a pleasure garden by the first sultan, Mangkubumi, in 1765, at the same time as the kraton. Surrounded by high walls, it was the sultan's hideaway. He constructed three bathing pools – for his children, his *putri* (girls) and himself. A tower allowed the sultan to watch his 'girls' bathing and to summon them to his company. In addition, there were a series of underwater corridors and even a partly underwater mosque. It is these labyrinths that have led some historians to speculate that it was also built as a retreat in times of war. By climbing the stairs over the entrance gate it is possible to look over the surrounding *kampung*: this was originally an artificial lake, with a large colonnaded pavilion in the middle. Unfortunately, the gardens were damaged during the British attack on Yogya in 1812 and restoration programmes have been rather unsympathetic. It is difficult to imagine the gardens as they were – as a place of contemplation. Most visitors enter the water gardens from Jalan Taman, through the east gate, which leads into the bathing pool area or Umbul Binangun. This small section is the most complete area of the gardens, having been reconstructed in 1971. The gardens fell into disrepair following the death of Hamengkubuwono III, a process which was accelerated by a devastating earthquake in 1865. Much of the garden has no water in it now, which is disappointing.

To the southeast of the kraton and Taman Sari on Jalan Kol Sugiyono is the small **Museum Perjuangan** ① *Tue-Sun 0800-1600, admission by donation*, or the Struggle for Independence Museum. As the name suggests, this commemorates Indonesia's Declaration of Independence on 17 August 1945 and has a less than inspiring collection of historical artefacts. The museum suffered extensive damage during the earthquake of 2006.

Vredeburg Fort and around
① *Tue-Sun 0800-1600, 750Rp plus 3000Rp for camera.*
The Vredeburg Fort lies to the north of the kraton on the east side of Jalan Jend A Yani, near the intersection with Jalan P Senopati. It was built in 1765 by the Dutch as a military barracks. Restored in the late 1980s, the fort has lost what character it may have had. Now a museum, the fortress houses a series of dioramas depicting the history of Yogyakarta. Close by is the **March 1st Monument**, which commemorates the taking of Yogya from the Dutch in 1949 by a band of guerrillas led by (then) Colonel Suharto. The **Beringharjo Market** is set back from Jalan Jend A Yani on the same side of the street and just north of the Vredeburg Fort. A dimly lit mixed market, it is an interesting and colourful place to wander with fruit, vegetables, fish and meat, batik and household goods – all jumbled together and seemingly fighting for air. Locals warn that numerous pickpockets operate here. On the other side of Jalan Jend A Yani is **Margo Mulyo Church**, which dates from 1830.

Across the road from the fort is the **Gedung Agung**, built initially in 1823 and then rebuilt in 1869 after the devastating earthquake of 1865. It was the former home of the Dutch Resident in Yogya and is now a state guesthouse. Queen Elizabeth II of Great Britain, former Prime Minister Nehru of India and Queen Sirikit of Thailand have all stayed here. Between 1946 and 1949, President Sukarno lived in the Gedung Agung, while Yogya was the capital of an emerging independent Indonesia. South of the fort, on Jalan P Senopati, are three impressive **colonial buildings**, the General Post Office (1910), the Bank Indonesia and the Bank Negara Indonesia (1923).

Jalan Malioboro and Jalan Mangkubumi
North from the Vredeburg Fort, Jalan Jend A Yani becomes Jalan Malioboro; this is the tourist heart of Yogya, with shops, restaurants and a smattering of hotels. The town has the largest student population in Indonesia, and in the evenings they congregate along Jalan Malioboro – no doubt for intellectual discussions, as well as eating and music – and stay there till 0400. This has become known as the 'Malioboro culture'. At its north extension, Malioboro becomes Jalan Mangkubumi.

To the west of Jalan Mangkubumi in Tegalrejo is **Sasono Wirotomo**, or the **Diponegoro Museum** ① *Tue-Sun 0900-1300 (regulations state that foreign visitors need a special permit to enter the museum, granted only in Jakarta, ask at the tourist information office in Jakarta for further information)*, a house built on the site of Prince Diponegoro's residence, which was levelled by the Dutch in 1825. The museum contains the prince's memorabilia, including a collection of weapons. At the end of Jalan Malioboro is an **obelisk** or *tugu* that marks the north limit of the kraton. The original *tugu* was erected in 1755, but collapsed; the present structure dates from 1889. Aart van Beek, in his book *Life in the Javanese Kraton*, explains that this was: "the focal point for the Sultan who would sit at an elevated place near the entrance of the palace and meditate by aligning his eyes with the *tugu* and the 3000-m-high Merapi volcano behind, in the distance".

East of the centre

To the east of the town centre, on Jalan Sultan Agung, is **Paku Alam's Palace** ① *Tue, Thu and Sun 0930-1330, 7000Rp.* A small part of the palace in the East Wing is a museum. Further east still, on Jalan Kusumanegara, is the **Gembira Loka Zoo and Amusement Park** ① *daily 0800-1800, 8000Rp.* It contains a reasonable range of Indonesian animals, including the Komodo dragon, orang-utan, tiger and rhinoceros.

Kota Gede ① *admission by voluntary contribution, Fri 1300-1600 for the actual cemetery, but the other areas are open daily, get to the tombs and workshops by taxi or by town bus (bis kota) No 4 or 8 from Jln Jend Sudirman, No 11 from Umbunharjo terminal and No 14 from Jln Prawirotaman,* also known as Sar Gede, lies 5 km to the southeast of Yogya and was the capital of the 16th-century Mataram Kingdom. Nothing remains except for the **tombs** of the rulers of Mataram; in particular, Panembahan Senopati, the founder of the kingdom and his son Krapyak (the father of the famous Sultan Agung). Senopati's son-in-law, Ki Ageng Mangir, is also buried here, his tomb protruding into common ground as he was Senopati's foe. About 100 m from the cemetery is the Watu Gilang, a stone on which Senopati killed Ki Ageng Mangir by smashing his head against it. Walled gardens and ponds containing fish and a yellow turtle, have claimed magical powers ('several hundred years old') and add to the atmosphere. Like the tombs of Imogiri, visitors must wear traditional Javanese dress which can be hired at the entrance (500Rp). Kota Gede is better known for its **silver workshops** which date back to the 17th-century rule of Sultan Agung. Both traditional silver and black (oxydized) silverwork can be purchased.

Taru Martani ① *Mon-Fri 0730-1500, there are English-, Dutch- and German-speaking guides,* is a cigar factory on Jalan Kompil B Suprapto, on the east side of town, where visitors can watch the process of cigar manufacture.

Education capital

The **Indonesian Art Institute (ISI)** is based in Yogyakarta, with faculties of Fine Art, Dance and Music, which partly explains why so much art can be found around town. (The town is the best place to see *wayang* performances and traditional dance.) In recent years it has become a popular town for Indonesian artists to base themselves. On the northern edge of the city is Indonesia's oldest, and one of its most prestigious, universities: **Gadjah Mada University (UGM)**. It was 'founded' in December 1949, when Sultan Hamengkubuwono IX allowed students and their teachers to use the Siti Inggil within the kraton. The campus can be a stimulating place for a stroll, and on Sundays hundreds of students can be seen practising martial arts at the university boulevard between 0700 and 0900, giving the place a very Chinese feeling.

Around Yogyakarta → *For listings, see pages 67-75.*

Hindu and Buddhist monuments, including the largest Buddhist monument in the world, Borobudur (see page 76), the magnificent Hindu temples at Prambanan (see page 80) and the small Hindu temples on the Dieng Plateau can also all be visited on day trips.

Tombs of the Mataram sultans

ⓘ *Admission by donation. Agung's tomb is only open Mon 1000-1300, Fri 1330-1630 and Sun 1000-1330, although it is possible to climb up to the site at any time. Get there by bus or colt, 5000Rp. (Buses continue on to Parangtritis from here – see below.) It is a 1-km walk east to the foot of the stairs from Imogiri town (ask for the makam or cemetery). The bus journey is lovely, along a peaceful country road past paddy fields.*

Imogiri, 17 km to the south of Yoga, is the site of the tombs of the Mataram sultans, as well as the rulers of the Surakarta Kingdom. Perhaps the greatest Mataram king, Sultan Agung (reigned 1613-1646), is buried here. He built the cemetery in 1645, preparing a suitably magnificent site for his grave, on a hillside to the south of his court at Kartasura. It is said that he chose this site so that he had a view of the Queen of the South (the sea goddess Nyi Loro Kidul). To reach his **tomb** ⓘ *Sun and Mon 1000-1300, Fri 1300-1600, 1000Rp, directly in front at the top of the stairway,* and those of 23 other royal personages (Surakarta susuhunans to the left, Yogya sultans to the right), the visitor must stagger up 345 steps. Walk behind the tombs to the top of the hill for fine views of the surrounding countryside. Javanese dress, which can be hired at the site, is required to enter the mausoleums. The Yogyakartan equivalent of Chelsea pensioners, with turbans and krisses, make sure correct behaviour is observed at all times. A traditional ceremony involving the filling of four bronze water containers – known as *enceh* – is held in the Javanese month of Suro; the first month of the year (June). The containers are placed at the gates of the cemetery and are an expression of gratitude to God for the provision of water.

Parangtritis

ⓘ *Regular connections with Yogya's Umbunharjo bus terminal (10,000Rp), either via Kretek along the main road and over the Opak River, or via Imogiri and Celuk. Those staying on Jln Prawirotaman can simply head to Jln Parangritis and flag down any bus heading to Parangritis. To get to Jln Parangritis from town, jump on TransJogja bus 2A and alight at Jln Kol Sugiono. The longer, rougher, trip via Imogiri passes through beautiful rural scenery.*

Parangtritis is a small seaside resort 28 km south of Yogya. It is accessible on a day excursion, although there are a number of places to stay.

Jatijajar Caves

ⓘ *2000Rp, 7 km west of Gombong, turn left; the caves are 13 km off the main road, there are minibuses from Kebumen (50 km) and from Gombong. Gombong is accessible from Yogya, Cilacap and Semarang, among other towns.*

Jatijajar Caves are to be found in the side of a strange ridge of jagged hills, southwest of the small town of Gombong and 157 km west from Yogya. Outside the entrance is a large concrete dinosaur which acts as a spout for the underground spring (bathing pools here). Inside, there are stalactites and stalagmites, springs and theatrical statues of human beings and animals which apparently recount the history of the kingdom of Pahaharan.

Karang Bolong Beach, near to the Jatijajar Caves, is known as a site for collecting bird's nests for the soup of the same name.

Gunung Merapi

ⓘ *It is imperative to take warm clothing (temperatures near the summit can reach zero) and energizing food. Tour operators often fail to stress the need for this kit.*

Gunung Merapi, whose name means 'giving fire', lies 30 km north of Yogya and is possibly the best known of all Java's many volcanoes. It rises to a height of nearly 3000 m and can be seen from the city. Merapi erupted with devastating and fatal force in late 2010 killing over 350 people. Because the volcano is still very active, it is closely watched by Indonesia's Directorate of Vulcanology who have an observatory here. Its first recorded eruption was in AD 1006, when it killed the Hindu king Darmawangsa, covered the island of Java with ash and is believed by scholars to have contributed to the collapse of the Mataram Kingdom.

Merapi erupted in 2006 causing the evacuation of 17,000 people from its flanks. The 2006 eruption occurred just before the deadly earthquake that flattened Bantul, some 50 km to the southwest. The deadly 2010 eruption, the largest eruption since 1870, caused the evacuation of over 350,000 people and caused massive damage to the area.

Climbing Gunung Merapi Most people start from the village of **Selo** (on the north slope), from where it is a four-hour trek up and three hours down. The trail is easy to follow but is steep and narrow in places (especially towards the top, where parts are quite gruelling); robust walking shoes are strongly advised – this is not suitable for the casual stroller. The spectacular views from the summit are best in the morning (0600-0800), which means a very early start, but it's well worth the effort. To see dramatic fireholes, take the path off to the left, about 25 m from the summit. The route passes a ravine before reaching the fireholes – a 10-minute walk. Guides at Selo charge about 100,000Rp and will offer their houses for overnight stays. Tours are not recommended, as the guides urge the group to walk fast, and walking in a group in volcanic cinder can be dusty. At the time of research tourists were climbing from Selo but it is imperative to check the latest before attempting the climb.

Kaliurang → *For listings, see pages 67-75. Phone code: 0293.*

ⓘ *5000Rp admission fee payable at a booth upon entering Kaliurang.*

The mountain resort of **Kaliurang** is 28 km north of Yogya, on the southern slopes of Merapi at just under 1000 m. It is the only point from which you can climb part way up Gunung Merapi and get good views of the lava avalanches. There are facilities at the **Hutan Wisata** (see below) for tennis and swimming, and a **waterfall** ⓘ *admission 500Rp*, near the bus station. Good walks include a 2.5-km trek to Plawangan Seismological Station, with views of the smoking giant (best in the morning, until about 0900-1000). The 'base station' is filled with *warungs* and has an additional entrance charge of 500Rp per person. The Seismological Station and the road leading to it are periodically closed. If this is the case, there is an alternative 2-km walk from the bus station to a belvedere, which overlooks the lava flow resulting from Gunung Merapi's 1994 eruption. There are good views of the volcano on clear days.

Places in Kaliurang

The brilliant **Ullen Sentalu (Museum of Javanese Art and Culture)** ⓘ *T0274 895161, www. ullensentalu.com, Tue-Sun 0900-1530, US$5*, is a wonderful place to learn more about Javanese culture. The lovingly presented displays emphasise the different types of Javanese batik. **Direktorat Vulkanologi (Pos Pengamatan Gunung Merapi)** ⓘ *Jln Cendana 15, T0274 895209, daily 24 hrs*, is the observation centre for volcanic activity on Gunung Merapi, and the staff are happy for tourists to pop in an look at the seismograph and get information about the latest situation. There is a small exhibition with captions in Indonesian detailing recent eruptions, with some grim photographs showing just how dangerous this beautiful mountain can be. **Hutan Wisata (Forest Park)** ① *next to the bus terminal, daily 0800-1600, 500Rp*, is a small forested park that has a couple of decent strolls, allowing for some great views of Merapi.

Yogyakarta listings

For hotel and restaurant price codes and other relevant information, see pages 9-12.

🛏 Where to stay

Yogyakarta *p58, map p60*
Yogya's different accommodation categories tend to be grouped in particular areas of town. Most of the expensive international-style hotels are to be found either on Jln Malioboro, in the centre of town, or on the road east to the airport (Jln Jend Sudirman). The former are in a convenient position if visitors wish to explore the city on foot from their hotels. Many middle-priced guesthouses are concentrated on Jln Prawirotaman, to the south of the kraton, about 2 km from the city centre (a becak ride away). These are smallish private villas converted into hotels, some with just a handful of rooms, some with small swimming pools. On Jln Prawirotaman, a gaggle of restaurants, shops and tour companies have grown up to service the needs of those staying here. Finally, there is the budget accommodation, which is concentrated on and around Jln Pasar Kembang and Jln Sosrowijayan, close to the train station. There are tour companies, travel agents, restaurants, car and motorcycle hire outfits, bus booking companies, and currency exchange offices here. See www.yogyes.com for accommodation and special offers.

Jalan Marlioboro and Jalan Dagen
These centrally located hotels are geared towards domestic tourists, and are more upmarket than those available in the Sosrowijayan area, but not as good value as those in the Prawirotaman area.

$$$ Hotel Ibis, Jln Marlioboro, T0274 516974, www.ibishotel.com. Rooms at this 3-star chain hotel are spotless, comfortable and feature cable TV and minibar. More expensive rooms come with bath. The hotel has a spa, pool, fitness centre and restaurant.
$$ Hotel Kombokarno, Jln Dagen 39, T0274 515812. Clean a/c and fan rooms facing a central courtyard with fish pond. More expensive rooms have TV (local channels only), a/c and hot water. Friendly staff.
$$ Hotel Kristina, Jln Dagen 71A, T0274 512076. Popular new place with a good selection of rooms. The standard singles are good value with TV, a/c and hot water.

Jalan Sosrowijyan area
This is prime backpacker territory, with plenty of cheap *losmen*. The area has seen better days and, with accommodation along Jln Prawirotaman becoming markedly cheaper in recent years, this area has lost its edge. However, it is close to all the action on Jln Malioboro and within walking distance of the train station and the major sights.
$$ 1001 Malam Hotel, Sosrowijayan Wetan GT I/57, T0274 515087, www.1001malam hotel.com. Popular place with plenty of Javanese flourishes and pleasant garden to relax in after a hard day pounding the pavements. Each of the 16 rooms has a massive wall painting done by a local artist. Wi-Fi available. Tours organized. One of the better places in the neighbourhood.
$$ Istana Batik Ratna, Jln Pasar Kembang, T0274 587012, www.dianagrouphotel.com/ istanabatik. The slightly overpriced rooms here are clean and come with a/c, TV and Wi-Fi connection. Bathrooms are new, and the more expensive have baths. 10% discount in low season. Pool.

$$-$ Bladok Losmen, Jln Sosrowijayan 76, T0274 560452. Welcoming place with a good selection of rooms and a brilliant swimming pool with noisy waterfall, perfect for a back massage (they turn it off at 1700 for fear it will disturb guests). Cheaper rooms are small and have squat toilet, but the VIP rooms are huge, with a/c and TV. Breakfast not included. Recommended.

$ Hotel Karunia, Jln Sosrowijayan 78, T0274 566057. Rooms here are clean and spacious with some artwork on the walls. Cheaper rooms have shared bathroom.

$ Monica Hotel, Jln Sosrowijayan, Gang 2 192, T0274 580598. Simple, clean rooms (the more expensive with TV and a/c), set around a pleasant courtyard with a fountain that functions occasionally.

$ Setia Kawan, Jln Sosrowijayan, Gang 2 127, T0274 552271, www.bedhots.com. Down a small alley off the gang, this popular place is covererd in contemporary artwork and has a gallery attached. There's no escape from the art in the bedrooms, which have wonderfully painted walls. Light comes into some rooms through small windows in the ceiling. Rooms are small, but clean. Good homely atmosphere. Wi-Fi available.Recommended.

Jalan Prawirotaman area

A selection of clean and well-managed middle-range accommodation is to be found on Jln Prawirotaman, south of the kraton, making this the best area to stay in. The hotels are the best of their kind in Yogya. The area's single obvious disadvantage is that it is not very central, but the street has numerous restaurants, shops, travel agents, cultural shows and a couple of watering holes nearby.

$$$ Eclipse Hotel, Jln Prawirotaman 35, T0274 380976, www.eclipsehtl.com. This hotel is the slickest on the street with spotless modern rooms, private balcony with pool view, good daily breakfast and Wi-Fi access throughout. The hotel lacks a little character but makes up for that with its creature comforts.

$$ Duta Guest House, Jln Prawirotaman 1 26, T0274 372064, www.dutagardenhotel. com. This well-run hotel has sparkling a/c and fan rooms, with TV and attached bathroom with bath. Pool and fitness centre. Recommended.

$$ Grand Rosela Hotel, Jln Prawirotaman 28, T0274 419191. Recently renovated, this sprawling place has a selection of simple a/c rooms, with attached bath. The suite rooms at the back come with a spacious communal veranda with views of Merapi, and a long balcony behind with views of the hills to the south. There is also a good-sized pool here. This hotel is slightly overpriced given the competition along the street. However, prices seem to drop by 10-20% upon asking.

$$ Kirana, Jln Prawirotaman 1 45, T0274 376600. This place has undergone some loving renovations and is well decorated with Javanese furniture and antiques. Rooms are comfortable, have a/c and are sparkling clean. The rooms out the back near the small garden are peaceful, although have less light than those at the front. Discounts for long stays.

$$ Ministry Of Coffee, Jln Prawirotaman 1 15A, T0274 747 3828, www.ministryof coffee.com. The tastefully decorated and comfy rooms feature a/c, Wi-Fi and access to a library as well as all the tea and coffee you can manage. Private balconies. Reservations are advisable.

$$ Prambanan Guesthouse, Jln Prawirotaman 14, T0274 376167. Homely guesthouse with a selection of simple fan and a/c rooms kept spotlessly clean. The rooms on the 2nd floor have views over the pool towards Merapi – beautiful in the early morning. Staff are friendly and there is Wi-Fi access throughout.

$$ Venezia Homestay, Jln Tirtodipuran, T0274 374049, www.venezia-homestay. com. Located down a quiet residential street 5 mins' walk from Jln Prawirotaman, this friendly homestay offers some massive rooms in an opulent house. Friendly owners, Wi-Fi access and plenty of spaces to socialize in.

$ Delta Homestay, Jln Prawirotaman 2 597, T0274 747537, www.dutagardenhotel.com. Small, clean and basic fan and a/c rooms. Friendly staff. Pool.

$ Perwita Sari Hotel, Jln Prawirotaman 1 31, T0274 377592, perwitasariguesthouse@ yahoo.com. Popular, with gregarious staff. The fan and a/c rooms are a bit dark, but clean. More expensive rooms have hot water. Pool.

$ Via Via Guesthouse, Jln Prawirotaman Mg 3/514A, T0274 374748, www.viaviajogja. com. Located down a small alley off Jln Prawirotaman, this place has simple but clean rooms, each named after an Indonesian island and adorned with artistic photographs. Some of the rooms have outdoor bathrooms, seperated from the world by a double wall of bamboo, which some guests may find a turn off. Breakfast included, nice garden and free Wi-Fi access throughout.

Kaliurang *p66*
There are over 100 places to choose from in Kaliurang, so availabty is never a problem. Many places are used to groups, and sell blocks of rooms, rather than single rooms. It is possible to get a single room at all the places listed here.

$ Hotel Muria, Jln Astamulya, T0274 446 4257. Spacious, clean rooms with TV. Bathrooms have hot water, squat toilet and *mandi*. Fair value for money.

$ Vogel Hostel, Jln Astamulya 76, T0274 895208. There is plenty of charm at this laid-back hostel. The most backpacker savvy place in town, the rooms here are clean and simple. The bungalows at the foot of the garden are filled with bamboo furniture and have amazing views of Merapi early in the morning. Cheaper rooms in the main building have shared bathroom. There are plenty of magazines to browse, and good information about Merapi. Recommended.

🍴 Restaurants

Yogyakarta *p58, map p60*
Central Javanese cooking uses a lot of sugar, tapped from the *aren* palm which produces 'red' sugar. Typical dishes include *tape* (a sweet dish made from fermented cassava) and *ketan* (sticky rice). Yogya specialities include *ayam goreng* (fried chicken) and *gudeg* (rice, jackfruit, chicken and an egg cooked in a spicy coconut sauce). Head to the stalls outside the batik market on Jln Marlioboro for some good cheap Javanese fare.

Jalan Sosrowijayan area
$ Bedhot Resto, Jln Sosrowijayan, Gang 1 127, T0274 412452. Inviting atmosphere with plenty of artwork, world beats and a large menu of steaks and pastas with a good vegetarian selection. Recommended.

$ Bintang Café, Jln Sosrowijayan 54, T0274 912 7179. Open 0800-2400. Popular place serving good salads, milkshakes, pastas and Indonesian dishes.

$ FM Café, Jln Sosrowijayan 10, T0274 747 8270. Open 0600-0100. Good helpings of standard Western dishes and a few interesting Javanese options for the adventurous. Happy hour 1300-2000, when a large beer goes for 15,000Rp.

Jalan Prawirotaman area
$$ K Meal's, Jln Tirtodipuran 67, T0274 829 0097. French-owned bistro that has taken Yogya by storm with tables filled with gleefully chomping punters. Food stretches from delectable steak with mash to wood fired pizza. Recommended.

$ Café Janur, Jln Prawirotaman 1, T0818 0265 3488. Open 1000-2300. Dutch-owned eatery with plenty of outdoors seating, chilled beers and a range of Dutch food. The *krokets* and french fries with fresh mayonnaise are a sight for sore eyes.

$ Hani's, Jln Prawirotaman 1 14, T0274 669 2244, www.hanisbakery.com. Open 0800-2300. Good breakfasts with freshly made bread, salads and pasta dishes in a modern, comfortable setting. Free Wi-Fi access and the *Jakarta Post* to browse, make this a good spot to pass a few hours.

$ Ministry Of Coffee, Jln Prawirotaman 1 15A, T0274 747 3828, www.ministryof coffee.com. Open 0600-2300. A great place to pass time, with table games, free Wi-Fi access and coffee. The spice espresso shake is delicious, and British travellers will be glad to get their hands on the roast beef and mustard salad. The selection of sweets is naughty, with excellent chocolate mousse. Recommended.

$ Tante Lies, Jln Parangritis, T0274 386719. Open 0900-2200. Essentially an overgrown *warung*, the best choices here are the East Javanese dishes, but there are some pseudo-Western and Chinese choices too.

$ Via Via, Jln Prawirotaman 1 30, T0274 386557, www.viaviacafe.com. Open 0730-2300. This funky restaurant has walls festooned with contemporary art, branches in Senegal, Belgium and Argentina and fine music to accompany a meal. The menu features delicious salads, daily Indonesian specials, pastas and good ice cream. Part of the profits go to local charities.

There is also a food court on the 3rd floor of the **Matahari Mall** (1000-2100) offering good portions of clean, cheap local cuisine.

Kaliurang *p66*

$ Amboja, Jln Kaliurang Km 18.7, T0274 660 6904. Tue-Sun 1100-2100. Located 7 km down the road towards Yogya from Kaliurang, this place has its own organic herb garden and specializes in tasty Indonesian fare. The *ayam asam pedas* (chicken cooked in a spicy tamarind sauce) is particularly good. There is also a range of herb- and spice-infused teas and coffees. Recommended.

$ Beukenhof, part of the Ullen Sentalu Museum complex, T0274 895161. Tue-Sun 1300-2100. An absolute gem of a restaurant set in staggeringly attractive gardens with mysterious walls and plenty of leafy shade. The restaurant is set in a colonial villa with a

great tropical veranda. The European menu features classics such as *boeuf bourguignon* and pastas, and some Dutch dishes such as *hutspot met klapstuk* (mashed potatoes with beef and sausage in red wine sauce). Locally made Javanese chocolate bars available.

For cheap, simple travellers grub, try the restaurant at the **Vogel Hostel**. **Wisma Joyo** (see Where to stay) cooks up good Javanese fare.

🍸 Bars and clubs

Yogyakarta *p58, map p60*

Café Janur, see Restaurants. Run by Arnold Schwarzenegger-lookalike Wim, this place is popular with Dutch expats at the weekend and is a friendly place for a beer.

There are fun bars along Jln Parangritis, including **Made's**, **Rui's**, and the gay-friendly **Banana Café**.

Live music

Bintang Café, Jln Sosrowijayan 54, T0274 912 7179. Open 0800-2400. Yogyakarta's musical cognoscenti descend on this place on Fri and Sat nights for live reggae and rock 'n' roll with occasional performances by well-known Indonesian bands.

🎎 Festivals

Yogyakarta *p58, map p60*

Yogya is host to a number of colourful festivals.

End of Ramadan Grebeg Syawal (movable). A Muslim celebration, thanking Allah for the end of this month of fasting. The day before is **Lebaran Day**, when the festivities begin with children parading through the streets. The next day, the military do likewise around the town and then a tall tower of groceries is carried through the street and distributed to the people.

Apr/May Labuhan (movable – 26th day of 4th Javanese month Bakdomulud; also held in Feb and Jul). Offerings made to the South Sea Goddess, Nyi Loro Kidul. Especially colourful ceremony at Parangtritis, where offerings are floated on a bamboo palanquin and floated on the sea. Similar rituals are held on Mount Merapi and Mount Lawu.

Jun Tamplak Wajik (movable), ritual preparing of 'gunungan' or rice mounds in the kraton, to the accompaniment of *gamelan* and chanting to ward off evil spirits. **Grebeg Besar** (movable), a ceremony to celebrate the Muslim offering feast of Idul Adha. At 2000, the 'gunungan' of decorated rice is brought from the inner court of the kraton to the Grand Mosque, where it is blessed and distributed to the people.

Jul Siraman Pusaka (movable, 1st month of the Javanese year), ritual cleansing, when the sultan's heirlooms are cleaned. The water used is said to have magical powers. **Anniversary of Bantul** (20th), celebrated with a procession in Paseban Square, Bantul, south Yogyakarta.

Aug Kraton Festival (movable), range of events including ancient ritual ceremonies, cultural shows, craft stalls. **Turtle dove singing contest** (2nd week), a national contest for the Hamengkubuwono X trophy, held in the south Alun-alun from 0700. **Saparan Gamping** (movable), held in Ambarketawang Gamping village, 5 km west of Yogya. This ancient festival is held to ensure the safety of the village. Sacrifices are made of life-sized statues of a bride and groom, made of glutinous rice and filled with brown sugar syrup, symbolizing blood.

Sep Rebo Wekawan (2nd), held at the crossing of the Opak and the Gajah Wong rivers, where Sultan Agung is alleged to have met the Goddess Nyi Loro Kidul. **Sekaten** (movable – the 5th day of the Javanese month Mulud), a week-long festival honouring the Prophet Mohammad's birthday. The festival starts with a midnight procession of the royal servants (*abdi dalem*), carrying 2 sets of *gamelan* instruments from the kraton to the Grand Mosque. They are placed in

opposite ends of the building and played simultaneously. A fair is held before and during Sekatan in the Alun-alun Lor. **Tamplak Wajik** (5th day of Sekaten). Ritual preparation of 'gunungan' (see above), decorated with vegetables, eggs and cakes at the palace, to the accompaniment of a *gamelan* orchestra and chanting to ward off evil spirits. **Grebeg Mulud**, a religious festival celebrating the birthday of Mohammad, and the climax of Sekatan. Held on the last day of the festival (12th day of Mulud), it features a parade of the palace guard in the early morning, from the Kemandungan (in the kraton) to the Alun-alun Lor.

⏴ Entertainment

Yogyakarta *p58, map p60*
Up-to-date information on shows can be obtained from the tourist office, travel agents or from hotels. There is a wide choice of performances and venues, with something happening somewhere every night.

Batik art galleries
3 batik painters from Yogya have achieved an international reputation – Affandi, Amri Yahya and Sapto Hudoyo. The **Affandi Gallery** is at Jln Adisucipto 167 (town bus 8) on the banks of the Gajah Wong River. Daily 0900-1600. It lies next to the home of the Indonesian expressionist painter Affandi (1907-1990) and displays work by Affandi and his daughter, Kartika. The **Amri Gallery** is at Jln Gampingan 67 and **Sapto Hudoyo** has a studio on Jln Adisucipto, opposite the airport.

Batik lessons
Available at: **Batik Research Centre**, Jln Kusumanegara 2, plus a good exhibition; **Gapura Batik**, Jln Taman KP 3/177, T0274 377835 (phone to book), 3-day courses for US$35 including materials (near main entrance to Taman Sari); **Lucy Batik**, Jln Sosrowijayan Gang 1; **Via Via**, Jln Prawirotaman, runs day courses.

Gamelan

Performances at the kraton,
Mon-Thu 1000-1200.

Ketoprak

Traditional Javanese drama at the
auditorium of **RRI Studio Nusantara 2**,
Jln Gejayan 2030, twice a month
(see tourist board for details).

Modern art gallery

Cemeti, Jln Ngadisuryan 7A (near the
Taman Sari), has changing exhibits of
good contemporary Indonesian and
Western artists. Tue-Sun 0900-1500.

Ramayana

Open-air performances at **Prambanan**,
T0274 496408, held on 'moonlight nights'
May-Oct, starting at 1930 and year-round at
the **Trimurti Covered Theatre**, 1930-2130.
The story is told in 4 episodes over a period
of 4 consecutive evenings coinciding with
the climax during the full moon (outdoors
Jan-Apr, Nov-Dec only, indoors year round).
Tickets cost 75,000-200,000Rp, less at the
Trimurti. Most agencies in town sell tickets
at face value but add on 50,000Rp for
transport to and from Prambanan.There are
also performances at the **Purawisata Open
Theatre (THR)**, Jln Katamso, T0274 375705,
daily 2000-2130. Admission 160,000Rp (it's
worth it). Good buffet dinner served before
the performance (270,000Rp for the ticket
and the meal).

Wayang golek

At the kraton on Wed 0930-1330, 12,500Rp.

Wayang kulit

Performances held at the **Museum
Sonobudoyo**, Jln Trikora, daily 2000-2200,
20,000Rp; **Sasana Hinggil** (South Palace
Square-Alun-alun Selaton), every 2nd Sat
of the month, 2100-0500, 12,500Rp; **Gubug
Wayang-44**, Kadipaten Kulon, Kp 1/44, is
a *wayang kulit* puppet workshop run by
Olot Pardjono, who makes puppets for the

Museum Sonobudoyo. Ask at the museum
for information on when his workshop is
open and how to get there.

Wayang orang

At the kraton every Sun, 1000-1200.
Javanese poetry can be heard at the
kraton on Fri between 1000-1200.
Gamelan is performed at the kraton
on Mon and Tue 1000-1200.

O Shopping

Yogyakarta *p58, map p60*
Yogya offers an enormous variety of
Indonesian handicrafts, usually cheaper than
can be found in Jakarta. Avoid using a guide
or becak driver to take you to a shop, as you
will be charged more – their cut. There are
hustlers everywhere in Yogya; do not be
coerced into visiting an 'exhibition' – you
will be led down alleyways and forced to
purchase something you probably don't
want. It is important to bargain hard. The
main shopping street, Jln Malioboro, also
attracts more than its fair share of 'tricksters',
who maintain, for example, that their
exhibition of batik paintings is from Jakarta
and is in its last day, so prices are good –
don't believe a word of it. The west side
of Jln Malioboro is lined with stalls selling
batik, *wayang*, *topeng* and woven bags. Best
buys are modern batik designs, sarongs and
leather goods. However, the quality of some
items can be very poor – eg the batik shirts –
which may be difficult to see at night.

Batik Yogya is a centre for both batik
tulis and batik *cap* and it is widely available
in lengths (which can be made up into
garments) or as ready-made clothes. Many
of the shops call themselves cooperatives
and have a fixed price list, but it may still be
possible to bargain. There are a number of
shops along Jln Malioboro. Batik factories
are on Jln Tirtodipuran, south of the kraton,
where visitors can watch the cloth being
produced. Batik paintings are on sale

everywhere, with some of the cheapest available within the kraton walls.

Bookshops **Periplus**, inside Marlioboro Mall, Jln Marlioboro. Daily 0930-2100. With international newspapers, magazines, bestsellers and guidebooks. **Book Exchange Yogyakarta**, is a good place to swap books (added cost of around 20,000Rp per book). The best shops are in the Sosrowijayan area, notably **Mas** (Jln Sosrowijayan Gang 1, T0813 2842 0359, 0900-2200), and **Boomerang Bookshop** (Jln Sosrowijayan Gang 1, 0800-2100). There are a couple of second-hand bookshops along Jln Prawirotaman, although the selection of titles is quite poor.

Krisses **Kris Satria Gallery**, Rotowijyan 2/64, T0811 286743. Open 0800-1800. Interesting selection of kriss (a type of dagger). There are a couple of other places on Jln Prawirotaman 2.

Pottery Earthenware is produced in a number of specialist villages around Yogya. Best known is Kasongan, 7 km south of the city, which produces pots, vases and assorted kitchen utensils. Get there by bus towards Bantul; the village is 700 m off the main road.

Silverware In Kota Gede, to the southeast of the city (most shops are to be found along Jln Kemesan). 2 major workshops are: **MD Silver**, T0274 375063, and **Tom's Silver**, T0274 525416. Numerous shops on Jln Prawirotaman. Try making your own ring with **Via Via Tours**, Jln Prawirotaman, 50,000Rp with instruction, and take home your finished article.

Topeng masks Available from stalls along Jln Malioboro and near Taman Sari.

Wayang kulit and wayang golek
Available from roadside stalls along Jln Malioboro. They come in varying qualities. Hard bargaining recommended. **Putro**

Wayang, Kampek Ngadisuryan 1 172, T0274 386611, Sat-Thu 0900-1700, Fri 0900-1100, is a small puppet workshop where visitors can observe the creators at work. They have a small range of beautiful leather *wayang kulit* puppets, *wayang golek* puppets and masks.

☀ What to do

For visitors without their own transport, one way to see the sights around Yogya is to join a tour. Although it is comparatively easy to get around by public transport, it can mean waiting around. Yogya has many companies offering tours to the sights in and around the city, mainly centred on Jln Prawirotaman.

There are city tours to the kraton, Taman Sari, batik factories, *wayang* performances and Kota Gede silver workshops.

Also out of town tours to Prambanan (US$9, transport only), Borobudur (US$6, transport only), the Dieng Plateau (US$22), Kaliurang, Parangtritis, Solo and Candi Sukuh, Gedung Songo, Gunung Bromo and Gunung Merapi. Taxis can also be commissioned from US$35 for a full day. Check various companies to select the vehicle, time of departure and cost (tours on non-a/c buses are considerably cheaper). Becak drivers will often take visitors for a tour of the city, and know of some good off the beaten track places. Prices start at US$10 for 5 hrs. Watch out for hidden entrance charges either for yourself or for parking your car.

Yogyakarta *p58, map p60*
Tour operators
There are a number of companies around Jln Sosrowijayan and Jln Pasar Kembang, as well as Jln Prawirotaman, who will organize onward travel by *bis malam* and train. Many of the hotels offer similar services.
Annas, Jln Prawirotaman 7, T0274 386556. Ticketing, car and motorbike rental.
Intras Tour, Jln Malioboro 131, T0274 561972, info@intrastour.com. Recommended by the tourist office for ticketing.

Kartika Trekking, Jln Sosrowijyan 8, T0274 562016. Bus, plane and train ticketing as well as tours around the region and beyond.
Via Via, see Restaurants.
Offers excellent tours.
Vista Express, in Natour Garuda Hotel, Jln Malioboro, T0274 563074.
Yogya Rental, Jln Pasar Kembang 85-88, T0274 587648.

Kaliurang *p66*
Vogel Hostel, see Where to stay. Organizes sunrise walks up the flanks of Merapi to see the lava flows. Walks are led by guides that have a great understanding of local fauna, and plenty of stories to keep walkers enthralled. Depart at 0400, return at 0900, US$10 per person (minimum 2 people) including breakfast.

⊖ Transport

Yogyakarta *p58, map p60*
Air
Adisucipto Airport is 8 km east of town, along Jln Adisucipto (aka Jln Solo). Transport to town: TransJogja bus 1A runs to Jln Marlioboro from the airport (3000Rp) a taxi is 55,000Rp. (Taxi desk in Arrivals hall.) Domestic departure tax is 35,000Rp; international is 100,000Rp.

Daily connections with **Kuala Lumpur** and **Singapore** on AirAsia and 3 flights a week with Malaysian Airlines.

There are plenty of daily flights to **Jakarta** and **Denpasar**, **Bandung** and **Makassar**. Domestic airlines flying out of Yogyakarta include Garuda, Merpati, Batavia and Lion Air.

Airline offices Garuda, Hotel Inna, Jln Marlioboro, T0274 483706. Merpati, Jln AM Sangaiji, T0274 583478.

Becak
10,000-20,000Rp per trip. Bargaining hard is essential. Jln Prawirotaman to Jln Marlioboro and back should cost no more than 25,000Rp. Drivers are happy to wait for a few

hours. Beware of drivers who offer a very good price; they will almost certainly take you to batik or silverware shops.

Bicycle hire
Along Jln Pasar Kembang or Gang 1 or 2, and hotels on Jln Prawirotaman for approximately 20,000Rp per day.

Bus
Local TransJogja buses criss-cross the town (3000Rp); the tourist office sometimes has bus maps available. Minibuses leave from the Terban station on Jln C Simanjuntak, northeast of the train station.
Long distance Yogya is a transport hub and bus services are available to most places. As it is a popular tourist destination, there are also many a/c tourist buses and minibuses. Agents are concentrated in the hotel/*losmen* areas. The Umbunharjo bus station is 4 km southeast of the city centre, at the intersection of Jln Veteran and Jln Kemerdekaan. Fastest services are at night (*bis malam*). Check times at the bus station or at the tourist office on Jln Malioboro. Regular connections with **Jakarta** (9 hrs) and **Bandung** (6 hrs), as well as many other cities and towns. To get to **Solo** (1½-2 hrs), or north to **Semarang** (3½ hrs), it is better to take a local bus, (hail on the main roads). A/c buses along Jln Sosrowijayan (board bus here too) or from Jln Mangkubumi to, for example, **Jakarta** US$20, **Bandung** US$20, **Surabaya** US$15, **Malang** US$15, **Probolinggo**, US$17.50 and **Denpasar** US$25.

Car hire
Self-drive from **Annas** Jln Prawirotaman 7, T0274 386556. Vehicles are in good condition and vary from US$27 to US$38 per day depending on the size of the car; Yus T0852 9282 0222, yoes_pnd@yahoo.co.id, is a knowledgeable Yogya-based driver who drives tourists to Pangandaran and can offer tailor-made tours to most places in Java.

Colt

Offices on Jln Diponegoro, west of the Tugu Monument. Door-to-door minibus service offered. **Rahayu**, Jln Diponegoro 9, T0274 561322, is a reputable company. Seats are bookable and pick-up from hotels can be arranged. Regular connections with **Solo** US$2.50, **Jakarta** US$16 and **Surabaya** US$19. **Anna's Travel** on Jln Prawirotaman has a door-to-door service to **Pangandaran** (7-9 hrs, US$25).

Motorbike hire

Along Jln Pasar Kembang and at **Annas** (see above), 35,000-50,000Rp per day depending on bike size and condition. Check brakes, lights and horn before agreeing; bikes are sometimes poorly maintained.

Taxi

The great majority of taxis in the city are now metered. Flagfall and 1st km, 5000Rp. Taxis/cars can be chartered for the day from **Annas** (see above), or for longer trips to Borobudur or Prambanan. Taxis can be ordered, call **Ria Taxi**, T0274 586166, or **Progo Taxi**, T0274 621055.

Train

The railway station is on Jln Pasar Kembang. Regular connections with **Jakarta**'s Gambir station (8 hrs; the Gajayana night train leaves at 2345 and arrives at 0710). Costs depend on class of train (*eksekutif*, US$31.50). A useful connection is the **Fajar Utama Yogya**, which leaves at 0800 and pulls into Jakarta's Pasar Senen at 1601. 5 daily trains to **Bandung** (*eksekutif* US$21, 8 hrs), 7 daily trains to **Surabaya** (*eksekutif* US$16.50,7 hrs). There is 1 daily connection with **Solo** on the Prambanan Ekspress from 0535-1905 (9000Rp, 1hr).

To Bali via Gunung Bromo

A popular way to get to Bali includes a night in Cemoro Lawang, Gunung Bromo, before heading onto destinations in Bali including **Lovina** and **Denpasar**. A night's accommodation at the **Café Lava** is included. Prices start at US$32. Most travel agencies on Jln Sosrowijayan and Jln Prawirotaman sell this.

Kaliurang *p66*
Bus

There are regular buses from **Yogya**'s **Giwangan** bus terminal and colts from **Condong Catur** bus terminal (1½ hrs, 10,000Rp).

Directory

Yogyakarta *p58, map p60*
Banks There are many banks in Yogya, rates are good and most currencies and types of TC are entertained. Good rates are especially found along Jln Prawirotaman. Money changers next to the **Hotel Asia Afrika**, Jln Pasar Kembang 17 and on Jln Prawirotaman. ATMs on Jln Prawirorotaman and Jln Marlioboro, including inside Marlioboro Mall. **Emergencies** Police: Jln Utara, on city ring road, T0274 885494. Tourist police: Tourist Information, Jln Malioboro, T0274 566000, for reporting robberies and seeking general information. **Immigration office** Jln Adisucipto Km 10, T0274 486165 (out of town on the road to the airport, close to Ambarrukmo Palace Hotel). **Medical services** Hospitals: PKU Muhammadiyah, Jln KHKA Dahlan 14, T0274 512653. 24 On-Call Doctor, T0274 620091. **Telephone** Jln Yos Sudarso 9. Open daily, 24 hrs. IDD international calls.

Borobudur and around

The travel business is all too ready to attach a superlative to the most mundane of sights. However, even travellers of a less world-weary age had little doubt, after they set their eyes on this feast of stone, that they were witnessing one of the wonders of the world. The German traveller Johan Scheltema in his 1912 book Monumental Java, wrote that he felt the "fructifying touch of heaven; when tranquil love descends in waves of contentment, unspeakable satisfaction".

Borobudur → *Phone code: 0293. For listings, see pages 84-85.*

Arriving in Borobudur

ⓘ *T0293 788266, www.borobudurpark.co.id, daily 0600-1700, ticket office closes at 1630, (tourists must leave the temple by 1720), US$15, student US$8, video/camera free.*

The entry fee does not include a guide but the extra 75,000Rp fee is really worth it. In theory, visitors should wait for a group to accumulate and then be shown round by a guide, however, many people simply explore the *candi* on their own. There is an extra payment for those who wish to get into the temple at 0430, in time for the sunrise. This can be facilitated by the **Manohara Hotel** (see Where to stay, page 84). For guests of the hotel the additional fee is US$17.50, for non-guests it is US$32. Many consider this money well spent, as the temple is unusually quiet and watching the sun come up from here is quite magical.

The best time to visit is early morning before the coaches arrive, although even by 0600 there can be many people here. Some visitors suggest sunset is better as the view is not affected by mist (as it commonly is in the morning). Consider staying the night in Borobudur, to see the sun rise over the monument.

Background

Borobudur was built when the Sailendra Dynasty of Central Java was at the height of its military and artistic powers. Construction of the monument is said to have taken about 75 years, spanning four or five periods from the end of the eighth century to the middle of the ninth century. Consisting of a nine-tiered 'mountain' rising to 34.5 m, Borobudur is decorated with 5 km of superbly executed reliefs – some 1500 in all – ornamented with 500 statues of the Buddha, and constructed of 1,600,000 andesite stones.

The choice of site on the densely populated and fertile valleys of the Progo and Elo rivers seems to have been partially dictated by the need for a massive labour force. Every farmer owed the kings of Sailendra a certain number of days labour each year (labour tax) in return for the physical and spiritual protection of the ruler. Inscriptions from the ninth and tenth centuries indicate that there were several hundred villages in the vicinity of Borobudur. After the rice harvest, a massive labour force of farmers, slaves and others could be assembled to work on the monument. It is unlikely that they would have been resistant to working on the edifice – by so doing they would be accumulating merit and accelerating their progress towards nirvana.

Art historians have also made the point that the location of Borobudur, at the confluence of the Elo and Progo rivers, was probably meant to evoke, as Dumarçay says, "the most sacred confluence of all, that of the Ganga (Ganges) and the Yumna (Yamuna)", in India. Finally, the monument is also close to a hill, just north of Magelang, called Tidar. Although hardly on the scale of the volcanoes that ring the Kedu Plain, this hill – known as the 'Nail of Java' – lies at the geographic centre of Java and has legendary significance. It is said that it was only after Java, which was floating on the sea, had been nailed to the centre of the earth that it became inhabitable.

The design

The temple is made of grey andesite (a volcanic rock), which was not quarried but taken from river beds. Huge boulders are washed down volcano slopes during flood surges, and these were cut to size and transported to the building site. The blocks were linked by double dovetail clamps; no mortar was used. It is thought that the sculpture was done in situ, after the building work had been completed, then covered in stucco and probably painted.

The large base platform was added at a later date and remains something of an enigma. It actually hides a panel of reliefs, known as the 'hidden foot'. Some authorities believe that this series of reliefs was always meant to be hidden, because they depict earthly desires (true of a similar series of panels at Angkor Wat in Cambodia). Other art historians maintain that this is simply too elaborate an explanation and that the base was added as a buttress. Inherent design faults meant that even during initial construction, subsidence was probably already setting in. In 1885 these subterranean panels were uncovered to be photographed, and then covered up again to ensure the stability of the monument.

The monument was planned so that the pilgrim would approach it from the east, along a path that started at Candi Mendut (see page 79). Architecturally, it is horizontal in conception, and in this sense contrasts with the strong verticality of Prambanan. However, architectural values were of less importance than the sculpture, and in a sense the monument was just an easel for the reliefs. Consideration had to be made for the movement of people, and the width of the galleries was dictated by the size of the panel, which had to be seen at a glance. It is evident that some of the reliefs were conceived as narrative 'padding', ensuring that continuity of story line was achieved. To 'read' the panels, start from the east stairway, keeping the monument on your right. This clockwise circumambulation is known as *pradaksina*. It means that while the balustrade or outer reliefs are read from left to right, those on the main inner wall are viewed from right to left. The reliefs were carved so that they are visually more effective when observed in this way.

The symbolism of Borobudur

Symbolically, Borobudur is an embodiment of three concepts: it is, at the same time, a stupa, a replica of the cosmic mountain *Gunung Meru*, and a *mandala* (an instrument to assist meditation). Archaeologists, intent on interpreting the meaning of the monument, have had to contend with the fact that the structure was built over a number of periods spanning three-quarters of a century. As a result, new ideas were superimposed on older ones. In other words, it meant different things, to different people, at different periods.

Nonetheless, it is agreed that Borobudur represents the Buddhist transition from reality, through 10 psychological states, towards the ultimate condition of nirvana – spiritual enlightenment. Ascending the stupa, the pilgrim passes through these states by ascending through 10 levels. The lowest levels (including the hidden layer, of which a portion is visible at the southeast corner) depict the Sphere of Desire (*Kamadhatu*), describing the cause and effect of good and evil. Above this, the five lower quadrangular galleries, with their multitude of reliefs (put end to end they would measure 2.5 km), represent the Sphere of Form (*Rupadhatu*). These are in stark contrast to the bare upper circular terraces with their half-hidden Buddhas within perforated stupas, representing the Sphere of Formlessness (*Arupadhatu*) – nothingness or nirvana.

The reliefs and the statues of the Buddha

The inner (or retaining) wall of the first gallery is 3.5 m high and contains two series of reliefs, one above the other, each of 120 panels. The upper panels relate events in the historic Buddha's life – the *Lalitavistara* – from his birth to the sermon at Benares, while the lower depict his former lives, as told in the *Jataka* tales. The upper and lower reliefs on the balustrades (or outer wall) also relate Jataka stories as well as *Avadanas* – another Buddhist text, relating previous lives of the Bodhisattvas – in the northeast corner. After viewing this first series of reliefs, climb the east stairway – which was only used for ascending – to the next level. The retaining wall of the second gallery holds 128 panels in a single row 3 m high. This, along with the panels on the retaining walls and (some of the) balustrades of the third gallery, tells the story of Sudhana in search of the Highest Wisdom – one of the most important Buddhist texts, otherwise known as *Gandawyuha*. Finally, the retaining wall of the fourth terrace has 72 panels depicting the *Bhadratjari* – a conclusion to the story of Sudhana, during which he vows to follow in the footsteps of Bodhisattva Samantabhadra. In total there are 2700 panels – a prodigious artistic feat, not only in quantity, but also the consistently high quality of the carvings and their composition.

From these enclosed galleries, the monument opens out onto a series of unadorned circular terraces. On each are a number of small stupas (72 in all), diminishing in size upwards from the first to third terrace, pierced with lozenge-shaped openings, each containing a statue of the Buddha.

Including the Buddhas to be found in the niches opening outwards from the balustrades of the square terraces, there are a staggering 504 Buddha images. All are sculpted out of single blocks of stone. They are not representations of earthly beings who have reached nirvana, but transcendental saviours. The figures are strikingly simple, with a line delineating the edge of the robe, tightly-curled locks of hair, a top knot or *usnisa*, and an *urna* – the dot on the forehead. These last two features are distinctive bodily marks of the Buddha. On the square terraces, the symbolic gesture or mudra of the Buddha is different at each compass point: east-facing Buddhas are 'calling the earth to witness' or *bhumisparcamudra* (with right hand pointing down towards the earth); to the west, they are in an attitude of meditation or *dhyanamudra* (hands together in the lap, with palms facing upwards), to the south, they express charity or *varamudra* (right hand resting on the knee); and to the north, the Buddhas express dispelling fear or *abhayamudra* (with the right hand raised). On the upper circular terraces, all the Buddhas are in the same mudra. Each Buddha is slightly different, yet all retain a remarkable serenity.

The main central stupa on the summit contains two empty chambers. There has been some dispute as to whether they ever contained representations of the Buddha. Those who believe that they did not, argue that because this uppermost level denotes nirvana – nothingness – it would have been symbolically correct to have left them empty. For the pilgrim, these top levels were also designed to afford a chance to rest, before beginning the descent to the world of men. Any stairways except the east one could be used to descend.

The decline, fall and restoration of Borobudur

With the shift in power from Central to East Java in the 10th century, Borobudur was abandoned and its ruin hastened by earthquakes. In 1814, Thomas Stamford Raffles appointed HC Cornelis to undertake investigations into the condition of the monument. Minor restoration was carried out intermittently over the next 80 years, but it was not until 1907 that a major reconstruction programme commenced. This was placed under the leadership of Theo Van Erp, and under his guidance much of the top of the monument was dismantled and then rebuilt. Unfortunately, within 15 years the monument was deteriorating once again, and the combined effects of the world depression in the 1930s, the Japanese occupation in the Second World War and then the trauma of independence, meant that it was not until the early 1970s that a team of international archaeologists were able to investigate the state of Borobudur once more. To their horror, they discovered that the condition of the foundations had deteriorated so much that the entire monument was in danger of caving in. In response, UNESCO began a 10-year restoration programme. This comprised dismantling all the square terraces – involving the removal of approximately 1,000,000 pieces of stone. These were then cleaned, while a new concrete foundation was built, incorporating new water channels. The work was finally completed in 1983 and the monument reopened by President Suharto.

Museum
ⓘ *Free with entrance ticket to Borobudur, daily 0600-1700.*
There is a museum close to the monument, which houses an exhibition showing the restoration process undertaken by UNESCO, and some pieces found on site during the excavation and restoration process.

Candis around Borobudur

Candi Pawon ⓘ *daily 0600-1700, 5000Rp (admission fee includes admission to Candi Mendut, don't throw the ticket away)*, was probably built at the same time as Borobudur and is laid out with the same east–west orientation. It may have acted as an ante-room to Borobudur, catering to the worldly interests of pilgrims. Another theory is that it acted as a crematorium. Candi Pawon is also known as 'Candi Dapur', and both words mean kitchen. The unusually small windows may have been this size because they were designed as smoke outlets. The shrine was dedicated to Kuvera, the God of Fortune. The temple sits on a square base and has an empty chamber. The exterior has some fine reliefs of female figures within pillared frames – reminiscent of Indian carvings – while the roof bears tiers of stupas. Among the reliefs are *kalpataru* or wish-granting trees, their branches dripping with jewels, and surrounded by pots of money. Bearded dwarfs over the entrance pour out jewels from sacks. Insensitive and poor restoration at the beginning of the 20th century has made architectural interpretation rather difficult.

    Candi Mendut ⓘ *Sun-Mon 0600-1700, 5000Rp (admission fee includes admission to Candi Prawon, don't throw the ticket away)*, lies further east still and 3 km from Borobudur. It was built by King Indra in AD 800. It is believed the *candi* was linked to Borobudur by a paved walkway; pilgrims may have congregated at Mendut, rested or meditated at Pawon, and then proceeded to Borobudur. The building was rediscovered in 1836, when the site was being cleared for a coffee plantation. The main body of the building was restored by Van Erp at the beginning of this century, but the roof was left incomplete (it was probably a large stupa). The temple is raised on a high rectangular plinth and consists of a square cella containing three statues. The shrine is approached up a staircase, its balustrade decorated with reliefs depicting scenes from the *jataka* stories. The exterior is elaborately carved with a series of large relief panels of Bodhisattvas. One wall shows the four-armed Tara or Cunda, flanked by devotees, while another depicts Hariti, once a child-eating demon but here shown after her conversion to Buddhism, with children all around her. Atavaka, a flesh-eating ogre, is shown in this panel holding a child's hand and sitting on pots of gold. The standing male figure may be the Bodhisattva Avalokitesvara, whose consort is Cunda.

There are also illustrations of classical Indian morality tales – look out for the fable of the tortoise and the two ducks on the left-hand side – and scenes from Buddhist literature. The interior is very impressive. There were originally seven huge stone icons in the niches; three remain. These three were carved from single blocks of stone, which may explain why they have survived. The central Buddha is seated in the unusual European fashion and is flanked by his two reincarnations (Avalokitesvara and Vajrapani). Notice how the feet of both the attendant statues are black from touching by devotees. The images are seated on elaborate thrones backed against the walls but conceived in the round (similar in style to cave paintings found in western Deccan, India).

There are no architectural remains of another, Sivaite, monument called **Candi Banon**, which was once situated near Candi Pawon. Five large sculptures recovered from the site, all examples of the Central Javanese Period, are in the National Museum in Jakarta.

Prambanan Plain and around → *For listings, see pages 84-85.*

ⓘ *Daily 0600-1800, admission to complex US\$13, student US\$7. Guides will show you around, pointing out the various stories on the reliefs for US\$5. Audiovisual show runs for 30 mins, most languages available, 2000Rp.*

The Prambanan Plain was the centre of the powerful 10th-century Mataram Kingdom that vanquished the Sailendra Dynasty – the builders of Borobudur. At the height of its influence, Mataram encompassed both Central and East Java, together with Bali, Lombok, southwest Borneo and south Sulawesi. The magnificent temples that lie scattered over the Prambanan Plain – second only to Borobudur in size and artistic accomplishment – bear testament to the past glories of the kingdom. The village of Prambanan is little more than a way station, with a handful of *warungs*, a number of *losmen* and hotels, a market and a bus stop.

Getting there Take the road south before crossing the Opak River, towards Piyungan, for about 5 km. On the road, just over a bridge on the left-hand side, are steep stone stairs that climb 100 m to the summit of the plateau and to the kraton. Alternatively, it is possible to drive to the top; further on along the main road, a turning to the left leads to **Candi Banyunibo**, a small, attractive, restored Buddhist shrine dating from the ninth century. It is set in a well-kept garden and surrounded by cultivated land. Just before the *candi*, a narrow winding road, negotiable by car and motorbike, leads up to the plateau and Ratu Boko.

Places in Prambanan Plain

There are six major *candis* on the Prambanan Plain, each with its own artistic character, and all well worth visiting. The account below describes the temples from east to west, travelling from Prambanan village towards Yogya. The Prambanan temple group were restored by the Indonesian Archaeological Service and now stand in a neat, landscaped and well-planned historical park.

Candi Prambanan or **Candi Lara Jonggrang** (Slender Maiden) as it is also known, stands on open ground and can be clearly seen from the road in Prambanan village. This is the principal temple on the Prambanan Plain, and the greatest Hindu monument in Java. In scale, it is similar to Borobudur, the central tower rising almost vertically, over 45 m. Built between AD 900-930, Prambanan was the last great monument of the Central Javanese Period and, again like Borobudur, the architects were attempting to symbolically recreate the cosmic Gunung Meru.

Originally, there were 232 temples at this site. The plan was focused on a square court, with four gates and eight principal temples. The three largest *candis* are dedicated to Brahma (to the south), to Vishnu (to the north) and the central and tallest tower to Siva. They are sometimes known as Candi Siva, Candi Brahma and Candi Vishnu. Facing each is a smaller shrine, dedicated to each of these gods' 'mounts'.

Candi Siva was restored by the Dutch, after a 16th-century earthquake left much of the temple in ruins. It was conceived as a square cell, with portico projections on each face, the porticos being an integral part of the structure. The tower was constructed as six diminishing storeys, each ringed with small stupas, and the whole surmounted by a larger stupa. The tower stands on a plinth with four approach stairways, the largest to the east, each with gate towers imitating the main shrine and edged with similar shaped stupas. At the first level is an open gallery, with fine reliefs on the inside wall depicting the Javanese interpretation of the Hindu epic, the *Ramayana*. The story begins to the left of the east stairway and is read by walking clockwise – known as *pradaksina*. Look out for the *kalpataru* (wishing trees), with parrots above them and guardians in the shape of rabbits, monkeys and geese or *kinaras*. The story continues on the balustrade of Candi Brahma. Each stairway at Candi Siva leads up into four separate rooms. In the east room is a statue of Siva, to the south is the sage Agastya, behind him, to the west, is his son Ganesh, and to the north is his wife Durga. Durga is also sometimes known as Lara Jonggrang, or Slender Maiden, hence the alternative name for Prambanan – Candi Lara Jonggrang.

The name of this monument is linked to the legend of King Boko and his son Bandung Bondowoso. Bandung loved a princess, Lara Jonggrang, who rejected his advances until her father was defeated in battle by King Boko. To save her father's life, Princess Lara agreed to marry Prince Bandung, but only after he had built 1000 temples in a single night. Summoning an army of subterranean genies, Bandung was well on the way to meeting the target when Lara Jonggrang ordered her maids to begin pounding the day's rice. Thinking it was morning, the cocks crowed and the genies retreated back to their underground lair, leaving Bandung one short of his 1000 temples. In an understandable fit of pique he turned her to stone – and became the statue of Durga. For those leaving Yogya by air, there is a mural depicting the legend at Adisucipto Airport.

The two neighbouring *candis* dedicated to Vishnu and Brahma are smaller. They have only one room each and one staircase on the east side, but have equally fine reliefs running round the galleries. On **Candi Vishnu**, the reliefs tell the stories of Krishna, while those on the balustrade of **Candi Brahma** are a continuation of the Ramayana epic which begins on Candi Siva. On the exterior walls of all three shrines can be seen voluptuous *apsaris*. These heavenly nymphs try to seduce gods, ascetics and mortal men; they encourage ascetics to break their vows of chastity and are skilled in the arts.

Opposite these three shrines are the ruins of **three smaller temples**, recently renovated. Each is dedicated to the mount of a Hindu god: facing Candi Siva is Nandi the bull – Siva's mount; facing Candi Vishnu is (probably) Garuda, the mythical bird; and facing Candi Brahma (probably), Hamsa the goose. The magnificent statue of Nandi is the only mount that still survives.

This inner court is contained within a gated outer court. Between the walls are 224 smaller shrines – all miniature versions of the main shrine – further enclosed by a courtyard.

Candis near Candi Prambanan

From Candi Prambanan, it is possible to walk north to the ruined **Candi Lumbung**, under restoration, as well as **Candi Bubrah**. Together with Candi Sewu, they form a loose complex.

Candi Sewu (meaning 'a thousand temples') lies 1 km to the north of Candi Prambanan and was constructed over three periods from AD 778-810. At first, the building was probably a simple square cella, surrounded by four smaller temples, unconnected to the main shrine. Later, they were incorporated into the current cruciform plan, and the surrounding four rows of 240 smaller shrines were also built. These smaller shrines are all square in plan, with a portico in front. The central temple probably contained a bronze statue of the Buddha. The *candi* has been renovated. The complex is guarded by *raksasa* guardians brandishing clubs, placed here to protect the temple from evil spirits.

Two kilometres to the northeast of Candi Prambanan is **Candi Plaosan**, probably built around AD 835, to celebrate the marriage of a princess of the Buddhist Sailendra Dynasty to a member of the court of the Hindu Sanjaya Dynasty. Candi Plaosan consists of two central sanctuaries surrounded by 116 stupas and 58 smaller shrines. The two central shrines were built on two levels with six cellas. Each of the lower cellas may have housed a central bronze Buddha image, flanked by two stone Bodhisattvas (similar to Candi Mendut, page 79). Again, the shrines are guarded by *raksasa*. The monument is currently being restored.

About 2 km to the south of Prambanan village is **Candi Sojiwan**, another Buddhist temple, undergoing restoration.

The ruins of the late ninth-century **Kraton Ratu Boko** occupy a superb position on a plateau, 200 m above the Prambanan Plain, and cover an area of over 15 ha. They are quite clearly signposted off the main road (south), 2 km. Because this was probably a palace (hence the use of kraton in its name), it is thought that the site was chosen for its strong natural defensive position. The hill may also have been spiritually important. Little is known of the palace; it may have been a religious or a secular royal site – or perhaps both. Some authorities have even suggested it was merely a resting centre for pilgrims visiting nearby Prambanan. Inscriptions celebrate the victory of a ruler, and may be related to the supremacy of the (Hindu) Sanjaya Dynasty over the Buddhist Sailendras.

For the visitor, it is difficult to make sense of the ruins – it is a large site, spread out over the hillside and needs some exploring. From the car park area, walk up some steps and then for about 1 km through rice fields. The dominant restored triple ceremonial porch on two levels gives an idea of how impressive the palace must have been. To the north of the porch are the foundations of two buildings, one of which may have been a temple – possibly a cremation temple. Turn south and then east to reach the major part of the site. Many of the ruins here were probably Hindu shrines, and the stone bases held wooden pillars, which supported large *pendopo*, or open-sided pavilions. Beyond the palace was a series of pools and above the whole complex a series of caves.

Candis on the road west to Yogya

About 3 km west of Candi Prambanan and Prambanan village, on the north side of the main road towards Yogya, is **Candi Sari**. This square temple, built around AD 825, is one of the most unusual in the area, consisting of two storeys and with the appearance of a third. With three cellas on each of the two levels and porticos almost like windows, it strongly resembles a house. Interestingly, reliefs at both Borobudur and Prambanan depict buildings of similar design – probably built of wood rather than stone. Some art historians think that the inspiration for the design is derived from engravings on bronze Dongson drums. These were introduced into Indonesia from north Vietnam and date from between the second and fifth century BC. There is an example of just such a drum in the National Museum in Jakarta. It is thought that both the lower and the upper level cellas of the *candi* were used for worship, the latter being reached by a wooden stairway. The exterior is decorated with particularly accomplished carvings of goddesses, Bodhisattvas playing musical instruments, the female Buddhist deity Tara, and male naga-kings. Like Candi Kalasan, the stupas on the roof bear some resemblance to those at Borobudur. Inside there are three shrines, which would originally have housed Buddha images. Nothing remains of the outer buildings or surrounding walls, but it would have been of similar design to Candi Plaosan. The *candi* was restored by the Dutch in 1929 and like Candi Kalasan is surrounded by trees and houses.

A short distance further west, and on the opposite side of the road from Candi Sari, is **Candi Kalasan** – situated just off the road in the midst of rice fields. The temple dates from AD 778, making it one of the oldest *candis* on Java. It is a Buddhist temple dedicated to the Goddess Tara and is thought to have been built either to honour the marriage of a princess of the Sailendra Dynasty, or as the sepulchre for a Sailendra prince's consort. The monument is strongly vertical and built in the form of a Greek cross – contrasting sharply with the squat and square Candi Sambisari. In fact, the plan of the temple was probably altered 12 years after construction. Of the elaborately carved *kalamakaras* on the porticos projecting from each face, only the south example remains intact. They would have originally been carved roughly in stone and then coated with two layers of stucco, the second of which remained pliable just long enough for artists to carve the intricate designs. The four largest of the external niches are empty. The style of the reliefs is similar to Southeast Indian work of the same period. The roof was originally surmounted by a high circular stupa, mounted on an octagonal drum. Above the porticos are smaller stupas, rather similar in design to those at Borobudur. The only remaining Buddha images are to be found in niches towards the top of the structure. The building contains a mixture of Buddhist and Hindu cosmology – once again evidence of Java's religious syncretism. The main cella almost certainly contained a large bronze figure, as the pedestal has been found to have traces of metallic oxide. The side shrines would also have had statues in them, probably figures of the Buddha.

Another 5 km southwest from Candi Kalasan, towards Yogya, is the turn-off for **Candi Sambisari**, 2 km north of the main road. If travelling from Yogya, turn left at the Km 12.5 marker – about 9.5 km out of town. Candi Sambisari, named after the nearby village, sits 6.5 m below ground level, surrounded by a 2-m-high volcanic tuff wall. It has only recently been excavated from under layers of volcanic ash, having been discovered by a farmer in the 1960s. It is believed to have been buried by an eruption of Gunung Merapi during the 14th century and as a result is well preserved. The *candi* was probably built in the early ninth century, and if so, is one of the last temples to be built during the Mataram period. A central square shrine still contains its linga, indicating that this was a Hindu temple dedicated to Siva. There are also smaller boundary lingams surrounding the temple. On the raised gallery, there are fine carvings of Durga (north), Ganesh (east) and Agastya (south). Pillar bases on the terrace indicate that the entire *candi* was once covered by a wooden pavilion.

Borobudur and around listings

For hotel and restaurant price codes and other relevant information, see pages 9-12.

● Where to stay

Borobudur *p76*

Most people visit Borobudur as a day trip from Yogya. However, accommodation is quite well established here and can get fully booked over public holidays. Although large international hotels are attracted to the area, many budget hostels are in demand and, as a result, the standard is generally poor.

$$$$ Amanjiwo, 10-min drive and 30-min walk from Borobudur, T0293 788333, www.amanresorts.com. A gloriously opulent resort. The hotel faces Borobudur and offers early morning trips to the temple to see the sun rise; magical. 35 gorgeous suites set around the reception, each with a terraced area, shaded day bed and private pool. Facilities include restaurant, spa service, bar, library, art gallery and tennis centre. Offers free rental of good mountain bikes to explore the countryside. Exceptional quality of service.

$$$ Manohara Hotel, Borobudur Complex, T0293 788131, www.manoharaborobudur. com. Smart hotel set in well-manicured gardens, fantastic position, a/c rooms in a peaceful location are fairly good value. Guests do not automatically get access to Borobudur before the gates open at 0600 – there's an additional sunrise fee. There are stunning views of the sunrise and sunset over the temple. The room price includes the temple entrance fee.

$$-$ Lotus Guesthouse, Jln Madeng Kamulan 2, T0293 788281. This well-run establishment is a popular choice for backpackers, with fair rooms. The rooms are clean, but some have bars over the windows. Cheaper rooms have squat toilet and *mandi*. The owner is a great source of local knowledge and can arrange trips around the local area including rafting.

$$-$ Pondok Tingal Hostel, Jln Balaputradewa 32 (2 km from the temple towards Yogya), T0293 788145, www. pondoktingal.com. Traditional-style wooden building set around courtyard, clean smart rooms with bathroom, dorm beds also available, room rate includes breakfast.

$ Rajasa, Jln Badrawati 2, T0293 788276, ariswara_sutomo@yahoo.com. On the road to the Amanjiwa, this friendly hotel has gorgeous views of verdant rice paddies, and clean a/c and fan rooms with hot water.

Prambanan Plain and around *p80*

There are a number of *losmen* in Prambanan village. Few people stay here because the *candi*s are so easily accessible from either Solo or Yogya, but it may be worth doing so, to enjoy the sunrise and sunset.

$$$ Poeri Devata Resort Hotel, Taman Martani, T0274 496435. Very quiet setting offering lovely views of sunset and rise over Prambanan, separate cottages with fully equipped rooms and al fresco *mandi*. Pool, upstairs open restaurant with views. Recommended.

$$-$ Hotel Prambanan Indah, Jln Candi Sewi 8, T0274 497353. Simple hotel with a variety of rooms, ranging from hotel to dorm beds, all share the same facilities including pool.

● Restaurants

Borobudur *p76*

There are 2 restaurants within the complex, a number around the stall and car park area, and in Borobudur village, although the quality at most places is mediocre and they are poor value.

$$ Saraswati, Jln Pranudyawardini. Has a reasonable restaurant with good set meals.

$$-$ Rajasa, Jln Pranudyawardini. Open 0700-2200. Has a traveller-friendly menu of good curries, seafood dishes and vegetarian options. Recommended.

❀ Festivals

Borobudur *p76*
May Waicak (movable, usually during full moon), celebrates the birth and death of the historic Buddha. The procession starts at Candi Mendut and converges on Borobudur at about 0400, all the monks and nuns carry candles – an impressive sight. However, during daylight hours the area is mobbed with visitors making a visit more stressful than pleasurable.

❂ What to do

Borobudur *p76*
Cycling
The tour guides in Borobudur offer 2-hr guided rides around the surrounding countryside for 50,000Rp per person (minimum 5 people). Ask at the ticket office for more information.

Elephant treks
Organized through the Manahora Hotel (see Where to stay). 2½-hr treks through the surrounding area. Contact the hotel for further information.

Whitewater rafting
Run by Lotus Guesthouse (see Where to stay). 9 km of Grade II-III rafting down the Progo.

❂ Transport

Borobudur *p76*
Bicycle hire
From some *losmen*/guesthouses (eg Lotus Guesthouse). An excellent way to visit Candi Pawon and Candi Mendut.

Bus
Regular connections from Yogya's Jombor Bus Terminal in the northern part of the city or from the street 15,000Rp, 1-2 hrs (ask at your hotel to find out where the bus stops).

For those staying on Jln Prawirotaman, the best place is the corner of Jln Parangtritis and Jln May Jend Sutoyo. The buses run along Jln Sugiyono, Jln Sutoyo and Jln Haryono (1½-2 hrs). Note that the last bus back to Yogya leaves at 1700. Leave at 0500 to arrive early and avoid crowds. From the bus station in Borobudur, it is a 500-m walk to the monument. *Bis malam* (night) and *bis cepat* (express) tickets can be booked from the office opposite the market in the village. There are buses to Yogya, Jakarta, Bogor and Merak for those in a rush to get to Sumatra.

Taxi
This may be the best option for 3-4 people travelling together – cheaper than a hotel tour and without time restrictions. Hiring a taxi should cost around 225,000Rp from Yogya.

Prambanan Plain and around *p80*
In order to see the outlying *candis*, it is best to have some form of transport. If on a tour, enquire which *candis* are to be visited, or hire a taxi, minibus or motorbike from Yogya. Horse-drawn carts and minibuses wait at the bus station; they can be persuaded to drive visitors around.

Bus
Regular connections with Yogya on the excellent TransJogya system. Jump on bus 1A which passes the airport (3000Rp) from Jln Marlioboro (1 hr). First bus leaves at 0600 and then every 20 mins during daylight hours. Connections with Solo (1½ hrs).

❂ Directory

Borobudur *p76*
Banks There is a BNI ATM on Jln Medang Kamulan. **Telephone** Wartel, Jln Pramudyawardani (opposite the market).

Solo (Surakarta) and around

Situated between three of Java's highest volcanoes – Gunung Merapi (2911 m) and Gunung Merbabu (3142 m) to the west, and Gunung Lawu (3265 m) to the east – Surakarta, better known simply as 'Solo', is Central Java's second royal city. The kraton (palace) of the great ancient kingdom of Mataram was moved to Surakarta in the 1670s and the town remained the negara (capital) of the kingdom until 1755, when the VOC divided Mataram into three sultanates: two in Solo and one in Yogya. Although foreigners usually regard Yogya as Java's cultural heart, the Javanese often attach the sobriquet to Surakarta. Solo's motto is 'Berseri' – an acronym for Bersih, Sehat, Rapi, Indah (clean, healthy, neat, beautiful) – and the city has won several awards for being the cleanest in Indonesia.

Solo is more relaxed, smaller and much less touristy than Yogya and has wide tree-lined streets. There are bicycle lanes (on the main east–west road Jalan Slamet Riyadi) that are almost as busy as the main roads. Reflecting the bicycle-friendly character of Solo, many companies run cycling tours of the city. Solo has gained a reputation as a good place to shop; not only is it a centre for the sale of batik, with a large market specializing in nothing else, there is also an 'antiques' market that's worth visiting.

Arriving in Solo → *Phone code: 0271.*

Getting there

Solo's **Adisumarmo Airport** ① *T0271 780400*, is 10 km northwest of the city and there are connections with Singapore, Java and the outer islands. The **Balapan railway station**, just north of the city centre, has connections with Jakarta, Surabaya and points along the way including Yogya. The **Tirtonadi bus station** is 2 km north of the city centre, and has connections with many Javanese towns as well as destinations in Bali, Lombok and Sumatra. Book night and express bus tickets through hotels, *losmen* and at travel agencies. Local buses regularly leave Yogya for Solo (two hours). ➤➤ *See Transport, page 100.*

Getting around

Cycling is the best way to explore Solo; the city is more bicycle-friendly than just about any other Javanese town. Angkutans and town buses run along set routes. Becaks are useful for short local trips or for charter. It is also worth taking a becak to explore the streets to find some of the interesting colonial houses.

Tourist information

① *Jln Slamet Riyadi 275, next to the Museum Radya Pustaka, T0271 711435, daily 0800-1600.* The **tourist office** ① *supplies maps and has information on cultural events.* Staff speak English and are very helpful. Tourist information is also available at the bus station (very poor), the railway station and the airport.

Places in Solo → *For listings, see pages 95-106.*

Kraton Surakarta Hadiningrat

① *Mon-Thu 0900-1400, Sat-Sun 0900-1500, admission 8000Rp, 2000Rp for camera, all visitors are asked to wear a samir (a gold-and-red ribbon) as a mark of respect. Guide obligatory (they are the abdi dalem – palace servants).*

The **Kraton Surakarta Hadiningrat**, better known as the **Kasunanan Palace**, is the senior of the city's two kratons and the more impressive. It lies south of the main east–west road, Jalan Slamet Riyadi. Like the kraton in Yogya, the Kasunanan Palace faces north onto a square – the Alun-alun Lor – and follows the same basic design, consisting of a series of courtyards containing open-sided pavilions or *pendopo*. On the west side of the Alun-alun is the **Grand Mosque**, built by Pangkubuwono III in 1750, though substantially embellished since then.

Entering the Kasunanan Palace, the first *pendopo*, the **Pagelaran**, is original, dating from 1745, and is used for public ceremonies. This is where visiting government officials would wait for an audience with the Susuhunan. From here, stairs lead up to the **Siti Inggil** (High Place), the area traditionally used for enthronements. Like Borobudur and Prambanan, the Siti Inggil represents the cosmic mountain Meru, but on a micro-scale. On the Siti Inggil is a large *pendopo*. The fore section of this pavilion was rebuilt in 1915, but the square section towards the rear (known as the **Bangsal Witana**), with its umbrella-shaped roof, is 250 years old.

Visitors are not permitted to enter the main palace compound through the large **Kemandungan Gates**. They must walk back out of the first compound, over a road, past

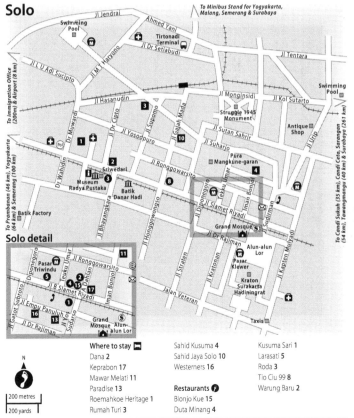

Solo

Where to stay 🛏
Dana **2**
Keprabon **17**
Mawar Melati **11**
Paradise **6**
Roemahkoe Heritage **1**
Rumah Turi **3**

Sahid Kusuma **4**
Sahid Jaya Solo **10**
Westerners **16**

Restaurants 🍴
Bionjo Kue **15**
Duta Minang **4**

Kusuma Sari **1**
Larasati **5**
Roda **3**
Tio Ciu 99 **8**
Warung Baru **2**

the private entrance to the prince's quarters and an area used to store the royal carriages, through a second gate, to an entrance at the east of the main compound. Near the second gate is a school; this was originally a private school for the royal children but was opened to children of commoners at the time of independence. Walk through one courtyard to reach the large central courtyard, known as the **Plataran**. This shaded area, with its floor of black sand from the south coast, contains the main palace buildings. Much of the prince's private residence was destroyed in a disastrous fire in 1985, but has subsequently been restored. An electrical fault was the alleged cause of the fire, although local belief is that the Susuhunan neglected his duties and provoked the anger of the Goddess Nyi Loro Kidul. Restoration was followed by extensive ceremonies to appease the goddess.

The three *pendopo* on the left are original and are used for *gamelan* performances. Behind them, along the walls of the courtyard, are palanquins once used for transporting princesses around the city. An octagonal tower, the **Panggung Songgobuwono**, survived the fire and was supposedly used by the Susuhunan to communicate with the Goddess Nyi Loro Kidul. Songgobuwono means 'Support of the Universe'.

The main *pendopo*, the **Sasana Sewaka**, is not original – it was restored in 1987 – although the Dutch iron pillars that support it, are. If members of the public are to have an audience with the sultan, they have to walk upon their knees across the *pendopo*: look out for the cleaners, who crouch to sweep the floor. It is used for four ceremonies a year and sacred dances are held here once a year. Behind this *pendopo* is the private residence of the prince, with the **kasatrian** (the sons' quarters) to the right and the **keputren** (the daughters' quarters) to the left. A concrete area to the left was the site of the **Dining Hall**, which burnt to the ground in the fire of 1985 and is awaiting restoration funds.

The guide leads visitors back to the first courtyard, where two sides of the square are a museum, containing an interesting collection of enthronement chairs, small bronze Hindu sculptures and three fine Dutch carriages which are 200-350 years old.

Pura Mangkunegaran

① *Daily 0900-1400, 10,000Rp, guide obligatory (about 1 hr),* gamelan *performances are held here. Dance and* gamelan *practice is held here every Wed at 1000 and worth seeing.*

The less impressive kraton, Pura Mangkunegaran at the north end of Jalan Diponegoro, is still lived in by the princely family that built it. In 1757, the rebel prince Mas Said established a new royal house here, crowning himself Mangkunegoro I. However, his power was never as great as the Susuhunan, and Mangkunegoro's deference to him is evident in the design of his palace, which faces south towards the Susuhunan's kraton. Much of the original structure has been restored. Built in traditional style, the layout is like other kratons, centred around a *pendopo*.

This central *pendopo* is the **Pendopo Agung** ① *Mon-Sat 0900-1400, Sun 0900-1300,* built in 1810 and one of the largest and most majestic in Java. Note how the ceiling is painted with cosmic symbols. Behind the central *pendopo* is the **Paringgitan,** a large room that houses, among other things, a good collection of antique jewellery and coins of the Majapahit and Mataram periods. In a corridor behind this room are a number of topeng masks. Voyeurs can peer through the windows into the private rooms of the present prince. Next to the ticket office are three fine carriages from London and Holland.

Around Jalan Slamet Riyadi

The small **Museum Radya Pustaka** ① *Tue-Thu 0900-1400, Fri-Sat 0800-1200, 10,000Rp,* is housed in an attractive building on the main road, Jalan Slamet Riyadi, next door to the tourist office. It contains a collection of *wayang kulit*, *topeng*, *gamelan* instruments, royal barge figureheads and some Hindu sculptures.

Next door to the museum is **Sriwedari** ① *daily 0800-2200, park entrance on a Sat is 1000Rp, Wayan orang performances Tue-Sat 2000-2200, 3000Rp*, an amusement park. It is also the home of one of the most famous Javanese classical dancing troupes, specializing in *wayang orang*. It is possible to go for a backstage visit to meet the artists and take photos (25,000Rp, ask at the tourist office).

Museum Batik Danar Hadi ① *Jln Slamet Riyadi 261, T0271 714253, daily 0900-1530, 25,000Rp (includes guide)*, introduces visitors to the different methods of batik making including wax stamping and handwaxing, and it is possible to see workers producing batik. There is also a display of antique batik and batik from around Asia. Five-day batik courses are available here, but a minimum of 15 people is needed.

Markets

There are several markets in Solo worth visiting. The antiques market, **Pasar Triwindu**, is situated off Jalan Diponegoro, on the right-hand side, walking towards the Pura Mangkunegaran. This is the only authentic flea market in Central Java and is a wonderful place to browse through the piles of goods. There are some good-quality antiques to be found, but time is needed to search them out. Bargaining is essential. **Pasar Klewer**, situated just beyond the west gate of the Alun-alun Lor near the kraton, is a batik-lover's paradise. It is filled with cloth and locally produced batik – a dazzling array of both *cap* and *tulis*. Prices are cheaper than the chain stores, but the market is very busy and first-time visitors may be persuaded into paying more than they should. It's best to go in the mornings, as it starts to wind down after lunch. Again, bargain hard. At the east side of the Alun-alun are a small number of shops and stalls selling fossils, carvings, krisses, puppets and masks. Don't expect to find anything of real quality, though.

Candi Sukuh

① *Daily 0700-1700, 10,000Rp. Take a bus from Solo's Tirtonadi station on Jln Jend A Yani to Karangpandan (41 km). Or pick up a bus on Jln Ir Sutami travelling east to Karangpandan. From Karangpandan, it is 12 km to Candi Sukuh. Most minibuses travel as far as Ngolrok, from where there are motorbike taxis up on the steep road to the top. From Candi Sukuh there is a well-worn stone path to the mountain resort of Tawangmangu, an easy 1½-2 hrs' hike.*

Candi Sukuh and Candi Ceto, two of the most unusual and stunningly positioned temples in Indonesia, lie to the east of Solo, on the west slopes of Gunung Lawu. Candi Sukuh stands at 910 m above sea level, and was probably built between 1434 and 1449 by the last king of the Majapahit Kingdom, Suhita. This enigmatic *candi* is situated in an area that had long been sacred and dedicated to ancestor-worship. The style is unlike any other temple in Java and has a close resemblance to South American Maya pyramid temples (which led archaeologists to believe, wrongly, that it was of an earlier date). It is built of laterite on three terraces, facing west. A path between narrow stone gates leads up from one terrace to the next, and steep stairs through the body of the main 'pyramid' to a flat summit. There are good views over terraced fields down to the plain below.

The first terrace is approached through a gate from the west, which would have been guarded by *dvarapalas* (temple guardians). The relief carvings on the gate are *candra sangkala*; the elements that make up the picture signify numbers which, in this instance, represent a date ('1359' is equivalent to AD 1437). On the path of the first terrace is a relief of a phallus and vulva: it is said that if a woman's clothes tear on passing this relief, it signifies excessive promiscuity and she must purify herself. The gate to the second terrace is guarded by two more *dvarapalas*. On the terrace are a number of carved stones, including a depiction of two blacksmiths, one standing (probably Ganesh) the other squatting, in front of which is a selection of the weapons they have forged. The third and most sacred terrace is approached through a third gate. There are a number of relief carvings scattered over the terrace. The figures of many are carved in *wayang* form with long arms, and the principal relief depicts the Sudamala story. This story is performed in places where bodies are cremated, in order to ward off curses or to expel evil spirits. Also on the third terrace are standing winged figures (Garuda), giant turtles representing the underworld (strangely similar to the turtle stelae of pagodas in North Vietnam), and carvings of Bima and Kalantaka. It is thought Bima was the most important god worshipped here. A Bima cult became popular among the Javanese elite in the 15th century.

The 'topless' pyramid itself has little decoration on it. It is thought that originally it must have been topped with a wooden structure. A carved phallus was found at the summit; it is now in the National Museum, Jakarta. Although Candi Sukuh is often called Java's 'erotic' temple, the erotic elements are not very prominent: a couple of oversized penises and little else.

Candi Ceto
ⓘ *Daily 0700-1700, 10,000Rp. From Karangpandan via Ngolrok there are minibuses to the village of Kadipekso; from Kadipekso it may be possible to hitch, or catch a motorcycle taxi, the final 2.5 km to the site. Alternatively walk; exhausting at this altitude. There are reportedly some direct bemos from Sukuh to Ceto, making this journey much easier. The easiest way to reach Ceto is to take a tour, see page 99.*

At 1500 m, Candi Ceto is considerably higher than Sukuh and lies 7 km to the north. Fewer people go here as it's harder to get to. It is possible to walk between the two *candis* (about four hours, no obvious trail, but worth it). It was built in 1470 and is the last temple to have been constructed during the Majapahit era. Candi Ceto shows close architectural affinities with the *pura* of Bali, where the Hindu traditions of Majapahit escaped the intrusion of Islam. Getting to the temple is an adventure in itself (although tours do run from Solo and Tawangmangu); the road passes tea estates, steeply terraced fields, and towards the end of the journey seems to climb almost vertically up the mountain. The road ends at the temple.

Candi Ceto is one of the most stunningly positioned temples in Southeast Asia. It has recently been restored and is set on 12 levels. Nine would originally have had narrow open gateways (like those at Sukuh), but only seven of these remain. Pairs of reconstructed wooden pavilions on stone platforms lie to each side of the pathway on the final series of terraces. There is some sculpture (occasionally phallic) and strange stone decorations are set into the ground – again, very reminiscent of Mayan reliefs. For the best views visit the *candi* in the early morning; clouds roll in from mid-morning.

Candi Jabung
ⓘ *Minibuses running east towards Sitabundo will stop at Candi Jabung. The village of Jabung is small and the* candi *rather poorly signposted; it's situated 500 m off the main road, a pleasant walk through fruit groves.*

Candi Jabung lies 26 km east of Probolinggo, about 5 km on from the coastal town of Kraksaan, in the small village of Jabung. It was completed in 1354 and unusually is circular (although the inner cella is square). It was a Buddhist shrine, built as a funerary temple for a Majapahit princess. The finial is now ruined but was probably in the form of a stupa. The *candi* is built of brick and was renovated in 1987 – as too was a smaller *candi* 20 m to the west of the main structure. The *candi* is notable for its finely carved *kala* head. Visitors should sign the visitors' book.

Gunung Bromo → *For listings, see pages 95-106. Phone code: 0335.*

This active volcano stands at 2329 m and is one of the most popular natural sights on Java, lying within the **Bromo-Tengger-Semeru National Park**. The park consists of a range of volcanic mountains, the highest of which (and Java's highest) is Gunung Semeru at 3676 m. Semeru is sometimes also called Gunung Mahameru ('Mountain above of the Hindu gods').

At the time of research Gunung Bromo was on high alert due to several eruptions starting in 2010. In 2011 an exclusion zone was set up, with authorities recommending that tourists go no closer than 2 km from the caldera. The resulting ash cloud reached heights of 5550 m and prompted several airlines to cancel flights into Bali for a few days. Check the latest with tour operators in Yogya and Bali before setting out for a trip up Bromo.

For many visitors to Indonesia, the trip to Bromo is their most memorable experience: seeing the sun bathe the crater in golden light, picking out the gulleys and ruts in the almost lunar landscape; sipping sweet *kopi manis* after a 0330 start; and feeling the warmth of the sun on your face as the day begins. No wonder the Tenggerese view this area as holy, feeling a need to propitiate the gods. It is hard not to leave feeling the divine hand has helped to mould this inspired landscape.

That's the good experience. But like most good things, there are those who are disappointed. In particular, you may find yourself surrounded by hundreds of other tourists (especially July to August) barking into mobile phones and shattering the calm. It is hard to feel the divine hand in such circumstances. The viewpoint at Gunung Pananjakan also suffers from the curse of over-popularity: it has become a popular stop for package tours from Surabaya. The buses even travel to the crater floor, making this area even more crowded at sunrise and entrenching further unsightly vehicle marks across the sea of sand.

Arriving in Gunung Bromo

The **National Park Information Booth** ① *Cemoro Lawang (near Bromo Permai I)*, has a range of photos and maps, and is a good place to gain some information before attempting Gunung Semeru. The best time to visit is during the dry months from May to November. Avoid Indonesian holidays.

Background

The local inhabitants of this area are the Tenggerese people, believed to be descended from the refugees of the Majapahit Kingdom, who fled their lands in AD 928 following the eruption of Gunung Merapi. They embrace the Hindu religion and are the only group of Hindus left on Java today.

Wildlife in the park includes wild pig, Timor deer, barking deer and leopards, as well as an abundance of flying squirrels. You are unlikely to see much wildlife in the Bromo-Tengger Park unless you manage to get off the beaten track and away from all the human and vehicular traffic. Perhaps the most distinctive tree is the cemara, which looks on first glance rather like the familiar conifer. It is, however, no relation and grows above 1400 m on the volcanic ash, where few other trees can establish themselves.

Reaching the crater

From Ngadisari via Probolinggo and Sukapura The easiest access to the park is from the north coast town of Probolinggo, via Sukapura and Ngadisari, and then to Cemoro Lawang on the edge of the caldera. The turning from Probolinggo is well signposted. The road starts in a dead straight line and begins to climb slowly through dense forested gulleys of dipherocarps. The road meanders, precariously at times, past fields of cabbage, onions and chillies. The route becomes steeper and steeper and only first gear seems feasible in the overladen minibuses. After Sukapura, the road becomes yet more precipitous. The National Park begins at the village of Ngadisari. The road narrows through here and continues up to Cemoro Lawang.

On arrival in Ngadisari, it is important to obtain a ticket (50,0000Rp per person) from the **PHKA (Forest Department of Indonesia) booth** ① *T0335 541038, open 24 hrs*, in order to visit the crater's edge. This is the national park entrance fee and the money is used to protect and develop the area. The trip to the caldera is usually undertaken in the early morning, in order to watch the sun rise over the volcanoes. To reach the summit for dawn, an early start from Ngadisari is essential, leaving no later than 0330. It is easiest to travel to Cemoro Lawang (from Ngadisari) on one of the six-seater jeeps, organized by guesthouses in Ngadisari. It takes 20 minutes by road from Ngadisari to the outer crater at Cemoro Lawang, and is another 3-km walk from here to the edge of the crater. Either take a pony (it should cost about 100,000Rp per pony for a 30-minute return trip) or walk for about one hour along a winding path marked by white concrete stakes, through a strange crater landscape of very fine grey sand, known as *Laut Pasir* (Sand Sea). Vegetables and other crops are grown in the sand, and it is surprising that it doesn't just get blown or washed away. It is also possible to walk the entire way, about 5.5 km, from Ngadisari (four to five hours). The final ascent is up 250 concrete steps to a precarious metre-wide ledge, with a vertical drop down into the crater. Aim to reach the summit for sunrise at about 0530. As this is their business, *losmen*-owners will wake visitors up in good time to make the crater edge by sunrise, and are used to arranging transport.

From Tosari via Pasuruan It is also possible to approach the summit from Tosari, on the north slopes of the mountain. The turn-off for Tosari is about 5 km out of Pasaruan, on the road to Probolinggo. Take a minibus from Pasuruan to Tosari (31 km). From Tosari, take an ojek the 3 km to **Wonokitri** (sometimes minibuses continue on to here). Both mountain villages have basic accommodation available. There is a **PHKA** office at Wonokitri, where it is necessary to pay the park entrance fee of 50,000Rp per person. Jeeps and ojeks are available here to take visitors all the way to the summit of Gunung Panajakan (275,000Rp for a jeep). For those who want to walk, it is 5 km from Wonokitri to Simpang Dingklik and then another 4 km up to the summit of Gunung Panajakan. From the summit, a path leads to Cemoro Lawang. Leave before 0400 to see the sunrise over the crater.

From Ngadas via Malang and Tumpang Visitors can also reach Bromo's summit from the west, via Malang, Tumpang and Ngadas. From Tumpang there are bemos to Gubugklakah, and from there it is a 12-km walk to Ngadas. From Ngadas it is a 2.5-km walk to the crater rim at Jemplang, and then another 12 km (three hours) across the crater floor to Bromo and Cemoro Lawang. At Jemplang it is also possible to branch off and climb Gunung Semeru (see below). This walk is much more of a trek and quite demanding, although easy enough for anyone with a reasonable level of fitness.

Equipment

Take warm clothing as it can be very cold before sunrise. A scarf to act as a mask to protect against the sulphurous vapour, and a torch to light the way, can also be useful. Avoid changing camera film at the summit; the thin dust can be harmful to the mechanism.

Trekking

There are several worthwhile treks in the Bromo-Tengger-Semeru National Park. Ask at your hotel/*losmen* for information and (in most cases) a map. It is possible to trek from **Cemoro Lawang** to **Ngadas**, or vice versa; from Ngadas, minibuses run down to Tumpang and from there to Malang. The trek takes four to six hours; guides are available, but the route is well marked. For the best view of Bromo, trek to **Gunung Penanjakan**, 6 km from Cemoro Lawang. This trek is well worth it if you are staying up in Cemera Lawang. The route is easy to follow but torches are a necessity, as is a degree of adventurous spirit. The trek takes about 1½ hours from Cemera, so it is best to leave before 0400 (ignore advice from hostels to leave by 0300, as that then entails a long, cold wait at the top). Take the road opposite the **Cemera Indah** and follow the winding track that turns to gravel and rock. There are white posts leading the way up but these are difficult to spot in the dark. The track is direct until you reach some steps leading up to the right; these steps can be hard to find, but the track comes to a halt and turns back on itself about 25 m after the steps. At the top of the steps a large concrete shelter has been built. This is a great place to watch the sunrise as it is not busy, and only those who have made the effort to walk will be there. Jeeps can be hired for a sunrise trip taking in both Gunung Bromo and Gunung Penanjakan for US$27.50 (to two locations) to US$45 (to four locations) for a group of six people, departing at 0400 and returning at 0830. Enquire at hotels. Alternatively, it is possible but not totally necessary to hire a guide for the walk up Gunung Penanjakan for around US$10-15. There is a **visitor centre** at Cemoro Lawang, not far from **Café Lava** with a range of photographs and maps. It's a good place to obtain information on Gunung Semeru, although it is rarely staffed.

Around Gunung Bromo → *For listings, see pages 95-106.*

Probolingo → *Phone code: 0335.*

Probolinggo is a commercial town that doubles as a Javanese holiday resort. The inhabitants are a mixture of Javanese and Madurese, and most foreign visitors only stop off here en route to Gunung Bromo. Probolinggo is noted for the grapes produced in the surrounding area, and in honour of the fruit the municipal authorities have created a giant bunch, out of concrete, on the main road into town from Pasaruan. It has earned Probolinggo a sobriquet *Kota Anggur* (Grape Town). More enjoyable still is the port, **Pelabuhan Probolinggo**, north from the town centre off Jalan KH Mansyur – about a 1.5-km walk. Brightly coloured boats from all over Indonesia dock, with their cargoes of mostly dry goods. The northern part of town, centred on Jalan Suroyo and the Alun-alun, is the administrative heart of Probolinggo; the portion further east on Jalan P Sudirman is the commercial heart, with the large **Pasar Barde** – a covered market. The **tourist office** faces the bus terminal. It is not a real tourist office, but an advice centre run by several tour companies. We have received complaints about the office and their business practices.

Gunung Semeru

Gunung Semeru, also known as Gunung Mahameru ('Seat of the Gods'), is Java's highest Gunungain and lies 13 km (as the crow flies) to the south of Gunung Bromo. This route is only suitable for more experienced climbers/trekkers; a guide and appropriate equipment are also necessary.

Climbing Gunung Semeru Gunung Semeru can be reached from Cemoro Lawang or, more easily, from Malang. If you also wish to visit Gunung Bromo as well as climb Gunung Semeru, then it is possible to trek four hours across the sea of sand. Guided all-inclusive treks up the the summit of Gunung Semeru start at US$180 for the two-day/one-night trek. Enquire at the **Cemara Indah Hotel.**

The approach from **Malang** starts with a 22-km bemo ride to **Tumpang**, from which it is a further 26-km (1½ hour) bemo ride to **Ngadas**, where *losmen* accommodation is available. A further 2.5 km from Ngadas is **Jemplang** village, which is the arrival point for trekkers coming across the sea of sand from Cemoro Lawang. **Ranu Pani** is 6 km further on, and this is where the PHPA post is located. For safety reasons, climbers must both check in and out at this post. It is possible to get a jeep as far as Ranu Pani, but any further and it's walking all the way to the summit (another 20 km).

Climbers usually spend one night at Ranu Pani, either camping or in **Pak Tasrip's Family Homestay** (**$**, T0334 84887), where there is a small restaurant, baggage storage and camping equipment for hire. From Ranopani, the next stop is **Ranu Kumbolo**. It takes three to four hours to walk the flat 10-km trail. Climbers may replenish their water supplies at the freshwater lake here. At Ranu Kumbolo, there is a camping area and resthouse with cooking facilities (free).

From Ranu Kumbolo, the climb continues to **Kalimati** (4.5 km), passing through savannah – a great area for bird spotting. There is a campsite at Kalimati and a fresh water supply at **Sumbermani** (30 minutes, following the edge of the forest). The next stop is **Arcopodo**, one hour away. This is a popular camping stop for the second night on the mountain. (Some of the soil is unstable.) The climb to the summit of Semeru has to be carefully timed, as toxic gas from the **Jonggring Saloko** crater is dangerously blown around later in the day. It is unsafe to be on the mountain after midday. The heat from the sun also makes the volcanic sand more difficult to walk on. This last climb should therefore commence between 0200 and 0300. From the summit, on a clear day, there is a fantastic view down into the crater, which emits clouds of steam every 10-15 minutes. Climbers are advised only to attempt Gunung Semeru during the dry season, as sand avalanches and high winds can be a real danger during the wet season. The temperature at the summit ranges from 0-4°C, so come prepared with warm clothing. For more information, enquire at the Malang **PHKA office**① *Jln Raden Intan 6, T0341 491820*, or at the information centre at Cemoro Lawang.

An interesting walk is to **Widodaren Cave**, halfway up **Gunung Kursi**. It is rarely visited by tourists, but is a regular worshipping site for the local Hindu Tenggerese. There is a spring at the back of the *gua*, which may explain why local people view the site as sacred. To avoid hours of endlessly traversing the sand sea in search of the path leading up to Widodaren, ask for further directions from the park rangers in the visitor's centre or even get them to guide you. It is a 1½-hour walk from Cemoro Lawang.

Madakaripura waterfall
① *The turn-off for the waterfall is on the main road up to Bromo from Probolinggo, just before Sukapura, hire an ojek or catch a bemo to Lumbang (1½ hrs' drive) after which it is a further 15-min ride to the waterfall.*

There are people on the approach to the 'air terju', who wait to lend visitors umbrellas to shield them from the water cascading down the narrow path through the hillside. Swimming is possible.

Solo (Surakarta) and around listings

For hotel and restaurant price codes and other
relevant information, see pages 9-12.

⊖ Where to stay

Solo *p86, map p87*
$$$$-$$$ Hotel Sahid Jaya Solo, Jln
Gajah Mada 82, T0271 644144, www.sahid
jayasolo.com. The outfits worn by some of
the staff here wouldn't look out of place
at a *Star Wars* convention. This 5-star hotel
has spotless rooms, that are well decorated
featuring TV and minibar. The hotel has a
pool and fitness centre with numerous bars
and restaurants. Discounts available.
$$$ Hotel Sahid Kusuma, Jln
Sugiyopranoto, T0271 646356, www.
sahidhotels.com. This hotel is resonant
with birdsong and makes for a quiet respite
from the busy streets. The standard rooms
are set in a dull block but are clean and
spacious. The marginally more expensive
cabana rooms have a pool view, TV, bath,
minibar and are good value. There is a pool,
bar, fitness centre and spa. Efficient staff.
Discounts available. Recommended.
$$$ Roemahkoe Heritage, Jln Dr
Radjiman 501, T0271 714024, www.
roemahkoe.com. Oustanding hotel in the
heart of the city. Those that want to revel
in olde world charm will love this hotel,
originally the pad of a wealthy batik trader.
The 16 rooms are comfortable, simple and
elegant with crisp white sheets on the
bed and access to a relaxing garden. Wi-Fi
available. Recommended.
$$$ Rumah Turi, Jln Srigading II No 12
Turisari, T0271 736606, www.rumah-turi.
com. Stylish place founded on green
principles not far from the town centre.
Rooms are comfy and have flatscreen
TV and internet access. Friendly staff
and a relaxed ambience make this a very
pleasant place to stay. Recommended.
$$$-$$ Hotel Dana, Jln Slamet Riyadi 286,
T0271 711976, www.hoteldanasolo.com. The

horrific concrete car park is in contrast with
the tasteful Javanese reception. The cheaper
rooms are dark and a little musty, but feature
a TV and clean bathroom. More expensive
rooms are brighter and well furnished.
Friendly staff, sizeable discounts available.
$ Hotel Keprabon, Jln Ahmad Dahlan 12,
T0271 632811. There is art deco style aplenty
here. Cheap rooms have dirty walls, TV;
pricier ones have a/c and hot water.
$ Istana Griya, Jln Ahmad Dahlan 22,
T0271 632667, www.istanagriya.tripod.
com. The most popular place in town for
budget travellers, this hotel has a friendly
atmosphere and offers lots of good local
information. All rooms only have windows
onto a dim corridor. Rooms are colourful,
and have attached Western bathrooms. The
more expensive rooms have cable TV and
hot water. Free tea and coffee all day. Bike
hire and internet access available.
$ Mawar Melati, Jln Imam Bonjol 54,
T0271 636434. The cheap fan rooms are
a little grungy and have dark bathroom
with squat toilet. Things improve drastically
as you climb the price range, with good-
value, clean, spacious rooms with a/c and
TV that are great value.
$ Paradise, Jln Empu Panuluh, T0271
652960. This rambling hotel oozes decrepit
charm, with antique lamps and old photos
of Solo's past. Rooms are shady, and
spacious and the a/c ones are surpisingly
cheap and feature a bath. There's plenty
of outdoor seating and a distinct lack of
guests. Tax not included in the room price.
$ The Westerners, Jln Empu Panuluh,
T0271 633106. In a friendly family
compound, this place has wholesome vibes.
Simple fan rooms and attached Western
bathrooms with cold-water shower.

Gunung Bromo *p91*
Ngadisari
$$-$ Yoschi's, Jln Wonokerto 1,
2 km before Ngadisari, T0335 541018,

www.yoschi.bromosurrounding.com.
Owner speaks good English. This is the
best place to stay, some rooms with hot
water and showers, attractively furnished
and designed with bamboo and *ikat*, the
cottages are excellent value, the restaurant
serves good dishes using local produce and
the *losmen* is a good source of information.
Highly recommended.

Sukapura
$$-$ Sangdimur Cottages, Desa Ngepung
Sukapura, T0335 581193. The location here is
not good for an early morning ascent of the
crater, but those who are lazing around the
Bromo area and don't like the cold nights will
enjoy the relative warmth. Rooms are large
and some have lovely views. It's worth paying
a bit more for the rooms with hot water.

Tosari
$$$ Bromo Cottages, T0343 571222.
Restaurant, hot water, tennis courts, views.

Cemoro Lawang
Hotels can be full during peak season (Jul-
Aug). All hostels have their own restaurants.
A good place to stay for early morning walks.
$$ Lava View Lodge, T0335 541009, www.
globaladventureindonesia.com. Pleasant
spacious rooms all come with TV, hot water
and a large buffet breakfast. The rooms are in
good shape and very clean. Recommended.
$$-$ Café Lava Hostel, T0335 541020,
www.globaladventureindonesia.com.
This well-run and friendly hotel has the
best-value rooms in town, with their
superior doubles with TV, hot water
and cosy beds trouncing all the other
competition. As you slide down the
price range, things get rather ordinary.
$$-$ Cemara Indah, T0335 541019, info@
bromotrail.com. The most popular place
for foreign visitors, the economy rooms are
characterless ice boxes, but the standard
rooms are fair value and have attached
bathroom and hot water. It is possible to
negotiate cheaper rates in low season.

$$-$ Hotel Bromo Permai, T0335 541021.
Usually packed with Indonesian tourists
and very busy at weekends. The cheapies
have shared bathroom and cold water
and are poor value. As you go up the price
range things improve with hot water, bath
and TV. Prices increase at the weekend. Tax
is not included.

Camping As the area is a national park,
it is possible to camp (40,000Rp). The site
is just before the Lava View Lodge, 20 m
from the lip of the crater. Ask the national
park information booth, close to the
Bromo Permai I, for more details and about
renting equipment. All visitors who wish to
camp must report to the PHKA post or the
Forestry Department, T0852 3236 7281.

Around Gunung Bromo *p93*
Probolinggo
Most people get in and out of Probolinggo
as quickly as possible, but there are a few
fair options in town.
$ Bromo Permai 2, Jln Panglima Sudirman
327, T0335 422256. This is the first port of
call for most tourists needing a place to
crash. Rooms are clean and spacious and
some come with an attractive garden view.
All the a/c and fan rooms have a Western
bathroom. The staff here are friendly, and can
help with booking train tickets. The reception
desk is open 24 hrs. Recommended.
$ Hotel Paramita, Jln Siaman 7, T0335
421535. Not far from the bus station and
tucked just off the busy main street, follow
the large signposts to find this hotel with
clean and spacious a/c and fan rooms.
$ Hotel Ratna, Jln Panglima Sudirman 16,
T0335 412597. Decent clean and large a/c
and fan rooms.

⍟ Restaurants

Solo *p86, map p87*
Solo is renowned as a good place to
eat and there is certainly no shortage of
restaurants and *warungs* to choose from.

Solo specialities include *nasi gudeg* (egg, beans, rice, vegetables and coconut sauce), *nasi liwet* (rice cooked in coconut milk and served with a vegetable) and *timlo* (embellished chicken broth). The Yogyanese speciality *gudeg* is also popular here. Most places are closed by 2130.

$$ O Solo Mio, Jln Slamet Riyadi, T0271 664785. Open 1030-2300. Set in a beautifully painted restored shophouse, this authentic Italian restaurant is the best place in town for pizza, pasta and has carafes of Australian red and white wine. There is a monthly special menu, live acoustic music on Thu-Sun and free Wi-Fi access. Recommended.

$ Duta Minang, Jln Slamet Riyadi 66, T0271 648449. 24 hrs. Great place to go for a fix of *nasi Padang*, with excellent *rendang* and plump *percedel* to satisfy a greedy appetite.

$ Kusuma Sari, Jln Slamet Riyadi 111, T0271 656400. Open 1000-2100. Popular place with generous helpings of ice cream, and Western fare with a distinctively Indonesian slant.

$ Larasati, Jln Slamet Riyadi 230, T0271 646600. Open 0800-1700. This delightful place serves up local treats such as *nasi asem asem* (beef in a sweet spicy sauce) and *nasi timlo* (chicken soup with vegetables and Javanese sausage) as well as Indonesian favourites such as *nasi goreng* and *gado gado*. Recommended.

$ Ramayana, Jln Imam Bonjol 49, T0271 646643. Open 0800-2100. Plenty of steaks, sizzling hot plates and Chinese and Indonesian favourites are offered. Popular with nearby office workers for lunch.

$ Roda, Jln Slamet Riyadi (next to Radya Pustaka Museum), T0271 734111. Inexpensive and delicious freshly made *dim sum*, and good selection of Chinese cuisine in a friendly outdoor setting.

$ Tio Ciu 99, Jln Slamet Riyadi 244, T0271 644361. Open 1000-2200. Good portions of Chinese favourites such as *Mapo tahu* (tofu in a spicy Sichuan pepper sauce), *sapi lada hitam* (beef in black pepper sauce) and *ayam kungpao* (chicken with chillies and peanuts).

$ Warung Baru, Jln Ahmad Dahlan, T0271 656369. Open 0700-2100. Friendly place with a huge menu of Western dishes, including some good sandwiches with home-made brown bread. This is also a good, clean place to try Javanese dishes including *nasi liwet ayam* and *nasi gudeg*.

Cafés and bakeries

Blonjo Kue, Jln Ahmad Dahlan 7, T0271 634727. 24 hrs. This a/c coffee shop is a great place to escape the heat, enjoy coffees and juices and indulge in cheesecake and their outrageous truffle cake. Recommended.

New Holland Bakery, Jln Slamet Riyadi 151, T0271 632452. Recommended by many locals as the best bakery in the city.

Purimas, Jln Yosodipuro 51, T0271 719120. Open 0700-2100, bakery with good range of well-priced Indonesian sweet breads and Western-style baked goodies.

Foodstalls

There are many *warungs* and food carts to be found around Solo, which vary enormously in quality; 3rd floor of **Matahari** deptartment store at Singosaren Plaza offers a variety of Indonesian food. Fans of *bakso* should try the excellent street stall **Mas Tris**, Jln Honggowongso (south from the intersection with Jln Slamet Riyadi). There's a night market at **Pujasari** (Sriwedari Park), next to the Radya Pustaka Museum on Jln Slamet Riyadi, with Indonesian favourites like *sate* and *nasi ranies*, along with Chinese dishes and seafood include grilled fish and squid. Carts set up along the north side of **Jln Slamet Riyadi** in the afternoon and evening and sell delicious snacks (*jajan* in Javanese). On the south side of town, near Nonongan, *sate* stalls set up in the evenings. There are also stalls near the train station on **Jln Monginsidi**. Jln Tuangku Umar comes alive in the evenings and is a great place to try local Javanese favourites such as *nasi liwet* and *nasi gudeg*. Other street food to keep an eye open for include *intip* (fried rice crust with Javanese sugar or spices and shaped like a bowl), *srabi notosuman* (rice flour pancakes topped with sweet rice and chocolate or banana) and *wedang jahe* (warm drink made with ginger).

Gunung Bromo *p91*

Most people eat in hotel restaurants (all $, 0730-2130). Food in Bromo is nothing exciting. The **Cemara Indah** has a row of picnic benches on the lip of the crater with spectacular views to accompany their good range of Indonesian and Western dishes. **Café Lava Hostel** serves up pastas, fresh juices and good sandwiches in a homely setting. **Hotel Bromo Permai** has an extensive range of Indonsian and Chinese dishes. Other than the hotels, **Warung Sejati**, T0335 541117, 0600-2200, has a range of cheap Indonesian and Javanese dishes.

🎵 Bars and clubs

Solo *p86, map p87*

Most of the hotels have bars that get quite busy at the weekend and close around 0100. **Saraswati Bar**, Jln Slamet Riyadi 272, T0271 724555, has live music Mon-Sat evenings. You can sing karaoke at **Madunggondo Bar** in the Hotel Sahid Kusuma (see Where to stay).

🎉 Festivals

Solo *p86, map p87*

Mar/Apr 2-week fair held in the Sriwedari **Amusement Park**. On the 1st day there's a procession from the King's Palace to Sriwedari, with stalls selling handicrafts.
Jun/Jul Kirab Pusaka Kraton (movable), a traditional ceremony held by the 2 kratons to celebrate the Javanese New Year. A procession of heirlooms, led by a sacred albino buffalo (the *Kyai Slamet*), starts at the Pura Mangkunegaran at 1900 and ends at the Kasunanan Palace at 2400. The ceremony is 250 years old, from the time of Sultan Agung.

Sep Sekaten or Gunungan (movable), a 2-week-long festival prior to Mohammad's birthday. The celebrations begin at midnight, with the procession of 2 sets of ancient and sacred *gamelan* instruments from the kraton to the Grand Mosque. A performance is given on these instruments and at the end of the 2 weeks they are taken back to the Kraton. A fair is held on the Alun-alun Lor in front of the mosque. The closing ceremony is known as *Grebeg Maulud*, when a rice mountain (*gunungan*) is cut up and distributed. The people believe that a small amount of *gunungan* brings prosperity and happiness.

Gunung Bromo *p91*

Feb Karo (movable, according to Tenggerese calendar), held in Ngadisari and Wonokitri to commemorate the creation of Man by Sang Hyang Widi. Tenggerese men perform dances to celebrate the event.
Dec Kasodo (movable, according to Tenggerese calendar). This ceremony is linked to a legend that relates how a princess and her husband pleaded with the gods of the mountain to give them children. Their request was heeded on the condition that their youngest child was sacrificed to the mountain. The couple had 25 children, then finally conceded to the gods' wishes. When the child was thrown into the abyss she chided her parents for not offering her sooner and requested that on the night of the full moon in the month of Kasado, offerings be made to the mountain. The ceremony reaches a climax with a midnight pilgrimage to the crater. Ritual sacrifices of animals and offerings of fruit and vegetables are thrown in to appease the gods.

🎭 Entertainment

Solo *p86, map p87*
Cinema

Multi-screen, the **Studio 123** in the Matahari department store screens some English-language films.

Gamelan
At the Pura Mangkunegaran on Sat 1000-1200 and accompanied by dance on Wed at 0900. Admission is included in the entrance fee to the palace. Also at Sahid Kasuma Hotel, daily 1700-2000.

Ketoprak
Traditional folk drama performances at the RRI, Jln Abdul Rahmna Salleh, T0271 641178, every 4th Tue of the month, 2000-2400.

Wayang kulit
RRI, every 3rd Tue and 3rd Sat of the month, from 0900 to 0500 the next morning.

Wayang orang
At the Sriwedari Amusement Park on Jln Slamet Riyadi, Mon-Sat 2000-2300, 3000Rp. Pura Mangkunegaran dancing practice, Wed 1000 until finished, free. STSI, T0271 647658, has dancing and *gamelan* practice starting at 0900 daily except Fri and Sun, free.

⊙ Shopping

Solo *p86, map p87*
Solo has much to offer the shopper, particularly batik and 'antique' curios.

Antiques Pasar Triwindu, off Jln Diponegoro (see page 89). Much of the merchandise is poor quality bric-a-brac, but the odd genuine bargain turns up. Bargaining is essential. There is also a good jumble of an antique shop on Jln Urip Sumoharjo, south of Jln Pantisari with some good things (including batik, stamps, old masks, carvings, Buddhas, etc) for those with the time to search).

Batik Classical and modern designs, both *tulis* and *cap*, can be found at the Pasar Klewer, situated just beyond the west gate of the Alun-alun Lor, near the kraton. Prices are cheaper than the chain stores, but the market is very busy and bargaining is essential. It is best to go in the mornings, as the market starts to wind down after lunch. Batik Danar Hadi, Jln Slamet Riyadi 261, T0271 714326, daily 0900-1530. Batik Keris, Jln Yos Sudarso 62, T0271 643292, Sun-Wed 0900-1900, Thu-Sat 0900-2000. Both these shops are great for browsing. Batik Keris has slightly the edge on everyday wearability, and some of their batik shirts are funky. All prices are fixed.

Handicrafts Bedoyo Srimpi, Jln Dr Soepomo (opposite Batik Srimpi); Pengrajin Wayang Kulit Saimono, Sogaten RT/02/RW XV, Pajang Laweyan Surakarta; Solo Art, made-to-order tables, chairs, picture frames and even doorstops, good prices, details in Warung Baru Restaurant; Sriwedari Amusement Park, Jln Slamet Riyadi; Usaha Pelajar, Jln Majapahit 6-10.

Krisses A fine example will cost thousands of dollars. These traditional knives can be bought at Keris Fauzan, Kampung Yosoroto RT 28/RW 82, Badran (Bpk Fauzan specializes in Keris production and sale), and also from the stalls at the eastern side of the Alun-alun Utara.

Markets Pasar Besar is on Jln Urip Sumoharjo and is the main market in Solo, excellent for fresh fruit and vegetables.

Supermarket In the basement of the Matahari department store, Jln Gatot Subroto, T0271 664711, 0930-2100.

⊙ What to do

Tour companies, *losmen* and hotels, as well as independent guides, all run cycling tours of Solo, trips to the kraton, batik and *gamelan* factories, *arak* distillers, Prambanan, Sangiran, Candi Sukuh, or to surrounding villages to see rural life and crafts. Prices vary considerably, but for city tours expect to pay around 70,000Rp, and for out-of-town tours around 1000,000Rp, depending on the distance covered. Highly recommended is Patrick at the Istana Griya and the guide from Warung Baru (see Restaurants) also gets good reports. Most tours are 0800-1400. Some *losmen* and homestays will run batik classes, for example the Istana Griya, 75,000Rp for a 5-hr lesson including materials.

Solo *p86, map p87*
Tour operators
Mandira Tours, Jln Gadah Mada 77, T0271 654558.
Miki Tours, Jln Yos Sudarso 17, T0271 665352.
Natratour, Jln Gadah Mada 86, T0271 634376, natra@indo.net.id.
Pesona Dunia Tour, Jln Ronggowarsito 82, T0271 651009.
Warung Baru, Jln Ahmad Dahlan 8. Really a restaurant, but this *warung* also runs highly recommended bicycle tours.

Gunung Bromo *p91*
There is an interesting 2-hr guided tour at the Gunung Bromo Volcanology Centre that teaches visitors about the seismic activity of Gunung Bromo. Tours can be booked at Bromo Permai Hotel, 75,000Rp per person.

Around Gunung Bromo *p93*
Probolinggo
Travel agents here are notorious for charging inflated prices for bus tickets. It seems that people are charged for a return ticket to Bromo and then find that the return vehicle fails to materialize. Avoid this is by only getting buses at the terminal and paying on the bus. Destinations are clearly signposted above the bus lanes on the roof. Queue here until the bus arrives.

⊖ Transport

Solo *p86, map p87*
Air
Solo's Adisumarmo Airport, T0271 780400, is 10 km northwest of the city. Taxis are available for the trip into town (50,000Rp); there is no easy public transport. There are daily flights to **Kuala Lumpur** with AirAsia (www.airasia.com). SilkAir (www.silkair.com) have expensive flights direct to Singapore. If you want to get to **Singapore** cheaply it is better to fly from Jakarta. Domestic flights are only to **Jakarta**. If you want to fly elsewhere, you will have to fly from Yogya.

Angkutan/becak/bicycle
Angkutan Ply fixed routes around town. The station is close to the intercity bus terminal at Gilingan. **Becak** For short trips around town, bargain hard. **Bicycle** Solo is more bicycle-friendly than just about any other city on Java; cycling is an excellent way to get around town. Hire is available from Istana Griya, Warung Baru and Westerners (see Where to stay). Daily rental is around 20,000Rp for a good mountain bike.

Bus
The Tirtonadi station, T0271 635097, is on Jln Jend A Yani, 2 km north of the city centre. Most bus companies have their offices on Jln Sutan Syahrir or Jln Urip Sumoharjo. Regular *ekonomi* connections with most cities, including **Jakarta**, **Bogor**, **Bandung**, **Malang** (9 hrs), **Surabaya** (6 hrs), **Semarang** and **Denpasar**. Night buses and express buses can be booked through most tour companies and many hotels and *losmen*. They run to most places in Java, and also to **Lovina**, **Lombok/Mataram** and, in Sumatra, to **Padang**, **Medan** and **Bukittinggi**. Companies including Java Baru, Jln Dr Setiabudi 20, T0271 652967.

Minibus The Gilingan minibus terminal is near to the main Tirtonadi bus terminal; regular a/c door-to-door connections with **Yogya**, US$3, 1½ hrs; **Denpasar**, US$21, 14 hrs; **Bandung**, US$18; and **Jakarta**, US$20. Tickets can be booked at most guesthouses. For **Gunung Bromo**, minibuses run to **Probolinggo** (8 hrs, US$17).

Train
Balapan station is on Jln Monginsidi, T0271
63222. A/c connections with **Jakarta**, 6 daily,
8-12 hrs. The most useful connection is the
overnight **Gajanya** departing at 2253 and
arriving in Jakarta at 0710 (*eksekutif* US$29).
The only a/c daytime connection with
Jakarta is on the **Argolawu** departing 0800
and arriving at Gambir at 1617 (*eksekutif*
US$24). If travelling to Jakarta, confirm which
station your train is heading to, as trains
travel to Gambir, Pasar Senen and Jakarta
Kota. Gambir station is the most convenient
for travellers. To **Surabaya**, 7 a/c trains
daily, 7 hrs. To **Bandung**, 5 daily a/c trains
(*eksekutif* US$252.50, 8 hrs. The **Prambanan
Ekspres** departs Solo 12 times a day for
Yogya (1 hr) from 0335 until 1853 (9000Rp).

Around Gunung Bromo *p93*
Probolinggo
Night buses from Bali usually arrive
just before sunrise. Travellers are often
deposited bleary-eyed at a travel agency
and subjected to the hard sell. Avoid this by
hopping in a yellow bemo going to the bus
terminal (3000Rp), where onward transport
can be easily organized independently.

Bemo It is possible to charter a bemo
cheaply, haggle for it. Bemos start running
at sunrise.

Bus All the bus destinations are written
up clearly at the terminal and it is best to
deal directly with the bus companies, rather
than the tourist office. The **Bayuangga**
bus terminal is on the west side of town,
about 5 km from the centre, on the road
up to Bromo. Bemos whisk bus passengers
into town (3000Rp). Regular connections
with **Surabaya**, 2 hrs, 25,000-30,000Rp,
Malang, 3 hrs, and **Banyuwangi**, 4 hrs,
50,000Rp. Night buses to **Denpasar**, 8 hrs,
at least 2 a day at 1200 and 1930, US$15,
economy buses are every hour. A/c buses
to **Singaraja** (for **Lovina**); **Jakarta**, US$24;

Denpasar, **Yogya** and **Solo**, US$10, are
available at regular times. Many buses to
Yogya and Solo go via **Surabaya**, adding
considerable time to the journey. Check
whether it's direct.

Minibus To **Cemoro Lawang**, 2 hrs,
25,000Rp, leave when full (10-15 people).
The 1st bus is scheduled to leave at 0700,
but there is often a long wait for it to fill up.
The last bus to Cemoro Lawang leaves at
1700. It is possible to charter a minibus for
the trip for 250,000Rp. Alternatively, hire
an ojek for upwards of 75,000Rp, not much
fun with a lot of luggage. If you arrive in
Probolinggo later than 1600 for **Gunung
Bromo**, the only option is to charter a
minibus or hire an ojek (around 75,000Rp).

Train The train station is on the main
square or Alun-alun, on Jln KH Mansyur,
regular *eksekutif* and *bisnis* connections
with **Surabaya** and **Banyuwangi**. There is a
direct economy-class train to **Yogyakarta**.

⊙ Directory

Solo *p86, map p87*
Banks There are plenty of ATMs along
Jln Slamet Riyadi. **Emergencies** Police
Station Jln Adisucipto 52, T0271 714352.
Immigration Jln Laksda Adisucipto 8,
T0271 712649. **Medical services** Hospital
Kasih Ibu, Jln Slamet Riyadi 404, T0271
744422, most doctors here speak English.
Telephone Jln Mayor Kusmanto 1
(24 hrs). **Wartel**, Jln Slamet Riyadi 275A (at
intersection with Jln Prof Dr Sutomo).

Gunung Bromo *p91*
Banks Guesthouses at Ngadisari and
Cemoro Lawang change money at poor
rates. There is a BNI ATM in Cemoro Lawang
that accepts Visa and MasterCard.

Around Gunung Bromo *p93*
Probolinggo
Telephone Wartel, Jln Jend A Yani.

Bali

Bali is the original magical isle. From the earliest years after its bloody incorporation into the expanding territories of the Dutch East Indies in the early 20th century, Westerners have been entranced by the heady combination of fabulous landscape and mesmerizing culture. Streams cascade down impossibly green mountainsides from sacred crater lakes, while dance dramas are performed to please the gods. Artists and the artistically inclined settled, worked and died amidst the rice fields and temples, reluctant to leave their Garden of Eden.

The advent of cheap air travel has brought increasing numbers of visitors, interested more in the attractions of the beach than of the temple and theatre. Today, hundreds of thousands of people visit Bali, many scarcely aware of the world beyond the sun lounger and the cocktail shaker. But while Bali may have changed – and the notion that the island is on the verge of being 'ruined' is a constant motif in writings about the island from the 1930s – the singular magic of the place has not been erased. As tourists continued to pour onto the island, the calm was shattered in October 2002 by bombings in Kuta blamed on Jemaah Islamiyah. Many people were killed, and for months afterwards tourists stayed away, damaging the island's economy. Just as plane-loads of sun seekers were starting to return, a second wave of bombings hit Kuta and Jimbaran in 2005 further decimating the island's reputation and economy. It has been a rough decade for the Balinese tourism industry, and some places continue to be affected by low numbers of visitors. However, tourists are again returning in droves, particularly tourists from emerging markets such as Russia and China, and the travel accommodation specialist Wotif.com revealed that Bali was Asia's most sought after destination, knocking off Singapore, which had previously held the number one spot for the past three years.

Arriving in Bali

Getting there

Denpasar's airport, **Ngurah Rai**, is very well connected with the rest of Indonesia with frequent flights throughout the country. The many flights to Mataram (Lombok) cost around US$45 and take only 30 minutes. Budget carriers flying into Bali include **Jetstar Asia** (www.jetstarasia.com) from Singapore, and **AirAsia** (www.airasia.com), which flies direct from Singapore, Bangkok, Kuala Lumpur and Darwin.

Getting around

The main form of the local transport is the bemo (a small van). Travel by bemo often requires several changes, especially in the south, and most trips are routed through Denpasar, where there are five different bemo terminals in different parts of town, serving different directions. It can be almost as cheap and a lot quicker to charter a bemo or catch the tourist shuttle bus. In recent years bemo services have been significantly pared back and with the fairly efficient and cheap tourist shuttle bus service, foreigners are a rare sight on a bemo. It is also worth noting that bemo services are less frequent in the afternoons, and away from tourist centres are almost non-existent after night-fall. **Note** Taxi/bemo drivers can be very pushy and find it hard to believe you may be happy to walk. Expect to be asked for double the correct fare. Always use registered bemos, which have yellow-and-black licence plates. For a list of the key bemo terminals around Denpasar, see Transport, page 105.

Denpasar

Once the royal capital of the princely kingdom of Badung, there is little evidence now of Denpasar's past. Situated in the south of the island, about 5 km from the coast, Bali's capital has grown in the past 10-15 years from a sleepy village to a bustling city with choked streets buzzing with the sound of waspish motorbikes. Today, the town has a population of over 450,000 and is Bali's main trade and transport hub, with its central business area centred around Jalan Gajah Mada. Puputan Square pays homage to the tragic end of the Rajah and his court; it is named after the 'battle to the death' – or puputan – against a force of Dutch soldiers in 1906.

Arriving in Denpasar → *Phone code: 0361.*

Getting there

Denpasar's **Ngurah Rai International Airport**ⓘ *24-hr airport information T0361 22238, flight information T0361 7571647, at the south end of the island, just south of Kuta,* is one of Indonesia's 'gateways', with regular international connections with Southeast Asian cities and beyond. It also has excellent domestic connections. International departure tax is 150,000Rp; domestic is 30,000Rp. A tourist office with a well-run hotel booking counter offers comprehensive details and prices of upmarket accommodation on Bali. Other facilities include money changers, ATMs, bars, restaurant, shops and taxi counter.

There are fixed-price taxis from the airport, starting at US$4.50; US$5 to Kuta 2; US$5.50 to Legian and US$6 to Seminyak; US$19.50 to Ubud; US$33.50 to Padangbai and US$33.50 to Candi Dasa. Alternatively, catch a cab just after it has dropped someone off at the International Departures area. This is a little cheeky, but the drivers use the meter and the cost of the drive to Kuta is around US$3.50. Some hardened souls walk all the way along the beach towards Tuban or Kuta.

Getting around

As Bali's capital, Denpasar is well connected with the rest of the island. No fewer than five terminals provide bemo services and minibuses run between the different terminals. Metered taxis are also abundant in Denpasar.

Tourist information

The **tourist office** ① *Jln Surapati 7, T0361 223602, Mon-Thu 0730-1530, Fri 0730-1300,* is not utilized very often, which is a shame given the eagerness of the staff. The office provides a free map, calendar of events and Bali brochure.

Places in Denpasar → *For listings, see pages 105-106.*

Denpasar is not particularly attractive and the major tourist attraction is easily found in the centre of town and is a focus for local hawkers. The **Museum Bali** ① *T0361 222680, Mon-Thu 0800-1500, Fri 0800-1230, Sat 0800-1500, 2000Rp, child 1000Rp,* was established in 1931 and is situated on the east side of Puputan Square. The entrance is on Jalan Mayor Wismu. The museum, built in 1910, mirrors the architecture of Balinese temples and palaces, and is contained within a series of attractive courtyards with well-kept gardens. The impressive collection of pre-historic artefacts, sculpture, masks, textiles, weaponry and contemporary arts and crafts was assembled with the help of Walter Spies, the German artist who made Bali his home. Labelling could be better and there is no guide. Nonetheless, it gives an impression of the breadth of the island's culture.

Next door to the museum is the new **Pura Jaganatha**, a temple dedicated to the Supreme God *Sang Hyang Widi Wasa*. The statue of a turtle and two nagas signify the foundation of the world. The complex is dominated by the *Padma Sana* or lotus throne, upon which the gods sit. The central courtyard is surrounded by a moat filled with water-lilies and the most enormous carp.

From an archaeological perspective, **Pura Masopahit** is the most important temple in Denpasar. The main gateway to the **pura** faces the main street, but the entrance is down a side road off the west end of Jalan Tabanan. The temple is one of the oldest in Bali, probably dating from the introduction of Javanese civilization from Majapahit in the 15th century, after which it is named. It was badly damaged during the 1917 earthquake, but has since been partly restored. Note the fine reconstructed split gate, with its massive figures of a giant and a garuda.

The **Taman Werdi Budaya Art Centre** ① *Jln Nusa Indah, Tue-Sun 0800-1700, free,* was established in 1973 to promote Balinese visual and performing arts. It contains an open-air auditorium, along with three art galleries. Arts and crafts are also sold here. Activity peaks during the annual **Bali Festival of Art**, held from mid-June for a month.

Denpasar listings

For hotel and restaurant price codes and other relevant information, see pages 9-12.

● Where to stay

Denpasar *p103*
Most people head to the beach areas in southern Bali, which are closer to the airport. Accommodation in Denpasar is geared more towards the domestic market and can get busy during holidays.
$$$ Inna Hotel, Jln Veteran 3, T0361 225681, www.innabali.com. Built in the 1930s, this was the first hotel on Bali. Its glory has somewhat faded, but pockets of charm remain. Clean rooms, pool and a garden.
$$ Adinda Hotel, Jln Karma 8, T0361 249435. The superior rooms are huge, bright and have bath and TV. Standard rooms are a little pokey, and have tiny windows. Garden.
$$ Hotel Taman Suci, Jln Imam Bonjol 45, T0361 484445, www.tamansuci.com. Near Tegal bemo station, with spacious clean rooms, TV and minibar. De luxe rooms have bath.

● Restaurants

Denpasar *p103*
Indonesian food dominates the scene. There is a collection of clean *warungs* outside the Inna Hotel selling Indonesian favourites.
$ Aseupan, Jln Tukad Unda 7, Renon, T0361 743 1501. Sundanese food served in clean, simple restaurant. Recommended.
$ Mie 88, Jln Sumatra. Good range of juices and local food. Noodles are the speciality.

● Shopping

Denpasar *p103*
Department stores Duta Plaza, Jln Dewi Sartika; Tiara Dewata and Matahari both have a wide range of goods. The former also has a public swimming pool.

● What to do

Language schools
IALF, Jln Raya Sesetan 190, T0361 225245, ialfbali@ialf.edu. Bahasa Indonesia courses mainly suited to expats. However, they have a 2-week homestay programme combining language studies with cultural studies for AUS$1120.

● Transport

Denpasar *p103*
As Denpasar is the transport hub of the island, it's easy to get to most of the main towns, beaches and sights from here.

Air
There are plenty of airline offices outside the Domestic Departures area of the airport, including **AirAsia** (T0804 133 3333, 0900-1700) **Garuda** (T0804 180 7807, 0600-0130), and **Merpati** (T0361 751011, 0600-1830) **Transnusa** (T0361 787 7555, 0600-1800).
   Airline offices Batavia, Jln Teuku Umar 208-210, T0361 254947; **Garuda**, Jln Sugianyar 5, T0361 254747; **Merpati**, Jln Melati 51, T0361 235358.

Bemo
Bemos travel between the main bemo terminals (6000Rp), criss-crossing town. It is also possible to charter these bemos. From the terminals, of which there are several, bemos travel to all of Bali's main towns: the **Ubung terminal**, north of town on Jln Cokroaminoto for trips to **West Bali**, **North Bali** and **Java**; **Tegal terminal**, west of town, near the intersection of Jln Imam Bonjol and Jln G Wilis, for journeys to **South Bali**; **Suci terminal**, near the intersection of Jln Diponegoro and Jln Hasanuddin, for **Benoa Port**; **Kereneng terminal**, at the east edge of town off Jln Kamboja (Jln Hayam Wuruk), for destinations around town and for **Sanur**; and **Batubulan terminal**,

east of town just before the village of Batubulan on the road to Gianyar, for buses running **East** and to **Central Bali**. **Tegal,** the bemo terminal for Kuta, used to be a thriving place with crowded bemos leaving regularly. Nowadays, however, it is a shadow of its former self and you might find yourself waiting around for a while before your bemo is ready to leave. Getting the correct fare can be a challenge. Ask one of the guys at the entrance to the station who record each departure. Fares from Tegal include **Kuta,** 10000Rp; and **Sanur,** 10000Rp. Beware of pickpockets on bemos.

Due to terrible traffic congestion, bemos have been banned from Jln Legian and the road from Kuta to Seminyak is mercifully free of them.

Bus
There are also bus connections with **Java** from the Ubung terminal, just north of Denpasar on Jln Cokroaminoto.

Express and night bus offices are concentrated near the intersection of Jln Diponegoro and Jln Hasanuddin; for example, **Safari Dharma Raya,** Jln Diponegoro 110, T0361 231206. Journey time and fares for night and express buses include: **Jakarta,** 24 hrs, US$35; **Solo,** 18 hrs, US$25; **Yogyakarta,** 18 hrs, US$25; and **Probolinggo,** 8 hrs US$15.

Car hire
Car hire can be arranged through hotels, or one of the rental agencies in town, for approximately US$11 per day. There are also private cars (with drivers) that can be chartered by the hour or day, or for specific journeys. Bargain hard, expect to pay about US$35-50 per day (car plus driver). Drivers can be found along Jln Legian with their constant offers of transport.

Motorbike hire
Arrange hire through travel agents, hotels or from operations on the street, from 50,000Rp per day.

Ojek
Motorbike taxis, the fastest way around town, are identified by the riders' red jackets (6000Rp min).

Taxi
Numerous un-metered cars can be chartered by the hour or day, or hired for specific journeys. Bargain hard. There are also some metered taxis; the best company to use is the blue **Bali Taxi,** T0361 701111. **Praja Bali Taxi,** pale blue taxis, also operate with meters and make no extra charge for call-out service, T0361 289090. Flag fall is 5000Rp.

Ⓘ Directory

Denpasar *p103*
Embassies and consulates For Indonesian embassies and consulates abroad and for foreign embassies in Indonesia, see http://embassy.goabroad.com. **Medical services** Emergency dental clinic: Jln Pattimura 19, T0361 222445. Hospitals: Sanglah Public Hospital, Jln Kesehatan Selatan 1, T0361 227911. Wangaya Hospital, Jln Kartini, T0361 222141; 24 hr on-call doctor and ambulance, Jln Cokroaminoto 28, T0361 426393. Main hospital with best emergency service. Some staff speak English. Bali's only decompression chamber for divers is located here. Bear in mind that medical facilities are not up to Western standards. For any serious medical problem, Singapore is the best place to go.

South Bali

Most visitors to Bali stay in one of the resorts at the south end of the island. Most famous is Kuta, the original backpackers' haven, together with its northern extension, Legian; both of these are fairly noisy, crowded, downmarket resorts. Much nicer is Seminyak, further north, which is still relatively rural. To the south of Kuta is Tuban, a town with many hotels and restaurants. Sanur is on Bali's east coast and offers largely mid-range accommodation, though some newer budget places to stay have opened. Serangan, or Turtle Island, is a short distance offshore.

Kuta and around → *For listings, see pages 112-125. Phone code: 0361.*

Kuta was the main port and arrival point for foreigners visiting south Bali for over 100 years, from early in the 18th century, until the airport at Denpasar usurped its role. The town prospered as a hub of the slave trade in the 1830s, attracting an international cross-section of undesirables.

Miguel Covarrubias wrote in 1937 that Kuta and Sanur were "small settlements of fishermen who brave the malarial coasts". It was not until the 1960s that large numbers of Western travellers 'discovered' Kuta. Since then, it has grown into a highly developed beach resort with a mind-boggling array of hotels, restaurants and shops. While Sanur is no longer a backpackers' haven, there are still many cheap *losmen* in Kuta as well as a growing number of mid- to high-range options. Central Kuta was decimated by the Bali bombings, and the area acted as a barometer for the island's suffering, with many businesses forced out of action. Things now are returning to normal, and bars such as the rebuilt **Paddies** (destroyed in the 2002 bombing) are pulling in big crowds of pleasure-hungry punters once more. Kuta's image as a beachside paradise was somewhat tarnished in 2011 when half the beach was closed to swimmers for a number of days due to contamination of the sea, which turned an English Channel pale brown due to all the dead plankton – a shocking shift away from its usual glassy blue.

Arriving in Kuta
Traffic in Kuta frequently comes to a standstill, despite the one-way system. The main street, containing most of Kuta's shops, is Jalan Legian, which runs north–south (traffic travels one-way south). Jalan Pantai meets Jalan Legian at 'Bemo Corner' and is the main east–west road to the south end of the beach (with traffic going one-way west). The beach road is northbound only. There is also a government **Tourist Information Office** ⓘ *Jl Bakungsari, T0361 756176, daily 0800-1300, 1500-1800.*

The town
Many people dislike Kuta. Other than the beach, it is not an attractive place. However, it does offer a wide range of consumerist and hedonist treats and people often find themselves staying here longer than expected. In the rainy season the drainage system is hopelessly inadequate, and some areas of Kuta, noticeably Jalan Legian, become flooded.

Since the Bali bombings, which slowed business down considerably in the area, tourists have increasingly complained of hassle from Javanese hawkers along Jalan Legian and Jalan Pantai Kuta who can get a little aggressive at times. There are also numerous women offering massage of a dubious nature on Jalan Legian. Pickpockets are less of a problem than they used to be, and children now swarm in packs selling friendship bracelets rather than rifling through your bag.

The beach

Kuta has a fine beach: a broad expanse of golden sand where local officials have taken reasonable steps to limit the persistence of hawkers. It is because of its accessibility that it is popular with surfers, although better waves can be found elsewhere. It is an excellent spot for beginners and recreational surfers. Boards can be hired on the beach and locals will offer insider knowledge of surf conditions. Strong and irregular currents can make swimming hazardous so look out for the warning notices and coloured flags that indicate which areas are safe for swimming on any particular day: red flags represent danger; yellow and red flags represent safe areas for swimming. The currents change daily and there are teams of lifeguards keeping an eye on proceedings who won't hesitate to blow their whistle if they see people straying into dangerous waters. There are allegations that levels of contamination in the sea are above internationally accepted safety levels, though many people swim with no apparent ill effects.

The sand is white to the south, but grey further north. The hawkers are less of a problem now they are forbidden to cross an invisible line that divides the beach. Sit on the half of the beach closest to the sea if you want to avoid hassle. The beach faces west, so is popular at sunset, which can be truly spectacular. Head to the stretch of beach between Legian and Seminyak for cheap beachside cafés offering icy beer and glorious sunset views. On a clear day and looking north it is possible to see Gunung Agung soaring to the heavens. Religious ceremonies sometimes take place on the beach and are fascinating to watch.

Legian → *Phone code: 0361*

It is hard to say where Kuta ends and Legian begins as the main shopping street, Jalan Legian, dominates both places. Like Kuta, Legian is a shopping haven. However, Legian is far more relaxed and less congested than Kuta and there are significantly fewer hawkers.

Seminyak → *Phone code: 0361*

This area to the north of Legian begins at Jalan Double Six and runs northwards into unspoilt ricefields. With a fabulous coastline, spectacular sunsets and views of the mountains of North Bali on a clear day, it is still relatively quiet compared to Kuta and Legian, but some long-term residents are complaining that the place has lost its charm in recent years and are selling up. In August, Seminyak's villas are filled with European holidaymakers. There is good surfing, but be warned: the sea here can be lethal. There are strong undercurrents and riptides. Lifeguards patrol the beach, which is wide, sandy and much less crowded, with a few mostly mid-range to upmarket hotels dotted along it. Jalan Pura Bagus Taruna is also known as Rum Jungle Road. Jalan Dhyana Pura is also known as Jalan Abimanyu.

Travelling north from Seminyak, you pass through **Petitenget** with its large temple made of white coral (covered in moss, so not looking white at all). Further north still, the village of **Batubelig** is in an undeveloped area, with a luxury hotel and a small guesthouse. This is a surfing rather than swimming beach. Unless you are a keen walker, you will probably need to hire a car if staying in this area.

Canggu

This area of coastline, only 20 minutes north of Legian, is slowly being developed and (at the moment) offers peace and rural tranquillity, traditional villages untouched by tourism, and frequent ceremonies and festivals at one of its many temples or on the beach.

Canggu district offers unspoilt, grey-sand beaches, with the possibility of excellent surfing (easy 1- to 2-m-high waves off left- and right-hand reef breaks), as well as

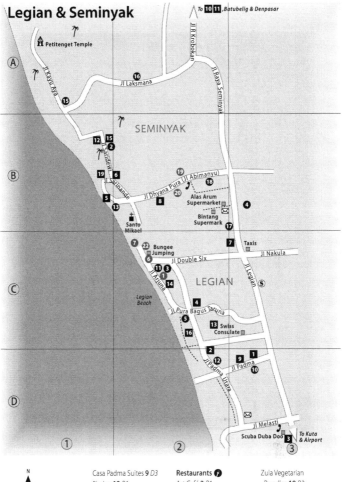

Legian & Seminyak

To **10 11**, Batubelig & Denpasar

Petitenget Temple

SEMINYAK

LEGIAN

Legian Beach

Santo Mikael

Bungee Jumping

Alas Arum Supermarket

Bintang Supermark

Taxis

Swiss Consulate

Scuba Duba Doo

To Kuta & Airport

N

300 metres

300 yards

Where to stay

All Seasons **2** D2
Anantara **5** B1
Balisani Suites **10** A2
Bali Sorgowi **3** D3
Batubelig Beach
  Bungalows **11** A2

Casa Padma Suites **9** D3
Elsyian **12** B1
Green Room **8** B2
Island Bali **13** C2
Le Jardin **6** B2
Lokha **1** D3
O-CE-N Bali **14** C2
Puri Cendana **15** B1
Puri Raja **16** C2
Sarinande Beach Inn **19** B1
Sinar Bali **4** C2
Sun Island **7** C3

Restaurants 🍽
Art Café **2** B1
Café Marzano **3** C2
Gado Gado **13** B2
Indonational **10** D3
Ku De Ta **15** A1
Lanai **11** C2
Pantarei **17** B3
Seaside **11** C2
Trattoria **16** A2
Unico **4** B3
Wali Warung **5** C2
Warung Yogya **12** D2

Zula Vegetarian
  Paradise **18** B2

Bars & clubs 🍸
Bush Telegraph Pub **19** B2
Cocoon **6** C2
Dejavu **1** C2
Double Six **22** C2
Sandpit **7** C2
Q Bar **20** B2

swimming. The following beaches are all part of Canggu: **Pererean**, **Banjartengah**, **Canggu**, **Tegal Gundul**, **Padang Linjong**, **Batu Bulong** and **Berewa**. The villages from which the beaches draw their names are inland and most offer simple homestays; just ask around. Local people are very friendly and helpful.

The drive to Canggu is very beautiful as you pass endless lush green paddy fields, coconut and banana palms, cows grazing, and the occasional picturesque, small village full of temples and shrines.

Berewa beach

A very peaceful location (the drive from Kuta takes about 30-45 minutes; as yet there is no coast road) with an unspoilt beach backing onto ricefields, friendly local people and few tourists. There are a few unpretentious restaurants hoping to attract tourists from the local hotels; outside the high season, these are usually only open for dinner. There are also a few small shops near the hotels. The main temple is **Pura Dang Khayangan**; there has been a temple here since the 16th century. **Note** Swimming in the sea here can be dangerous.

Sanur → *For listings, see pages 112-125. Phone code: 0361.*

The first of Bali's international resorts, Sanur falls midway between the elegant, upmarket Nusa Dua and the frenetic, youthful Kuta and is situated 6 km from Denpasar. Attracting a more sedate, middle-aged clientele, many on package tours, Sanur's attractions are its long golden beach, restaurants and shopping. This is also a centre for watersports with surfing, snorkelling by Serangan Island and diving. Noticeably more expensive than Kuta, hotels tend to be mid-range to upmarket, though there are some more reasonably priced small guesthouses. Nightlife here does not compare to that of Kuta, although there are plenty of good restaurants and a few fun bars. The road parallel to the beach is lined with money changers, tourist shops (selling clothing and jewellery), tour companies, car rental outlets and shipping agents.

Places in Sanur

The **Le Mayeur Museum** ① *Jln Hang Tuah, T0361 286201, Mon-Thu and Sat 0800-1500, Fri 0800-1200, 5000Rp, 2000Rp child*, is just to the north of the **Bali Beach Hotel** and is named after the famous Belgian artist Adrien Yean Le Mayeur, who arrived in Bali in 1932. He was immediately captivated by the culture and beauty of the island, made Sanur his home, married local beauty Ni Polok in 1935 and died in 1958. The museum contains his collection of local artefacts and some of Le Mayeur's work. The interior is dark and rather dilapidated, making the pieces difficult to view – a great shame because Le Mayeur's impressionistic works are full of tropical sunlight and colour. Le Mayeur's paintings were a great influence on a number of Balinese artists, including the highly regarded I Gusti Nyoman Nodya.

Temples made of coral are dotted along Sanur beach. The presence of primitive, pyramid-shaped structures at many of these temples suggests their origin dates back to pre-historic times. At the southern, south-facing end of Sanur beach is the **Pura Mertasari**, a small temple under a canopy of trees that is considered to harbour exceptionally powerful forces of black magic. The *odalan* festival of this temple falls at the most favoured time in the Balinese calendar, two weeks after the spring equinox. An unusual ritual trance dance, the *baris cina* (Chinese dance), is performed on the night of the festival. The dancers wear old Dutch army helmets and bayonets and the evening can end with a dramatically violent dance movement. A nearby village, **Singhi**, is home to the Black Barong, the most powerful Barong (masked figure) in Bali, made from the black feathers of a sacred rare bird.

Sanur

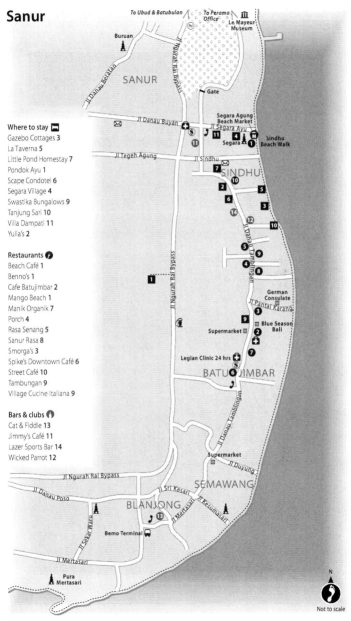

Where to stay 🛏
Gazebo Cottages **3**
La Taverna **5**
Little Pond Homestay **7**
Pondok Ayu **1**
Scape Condotel **6**
Segara Village **4**
Swastika Bungalows **9**
Tanjung Sari **10**
Villa Dampati **11**
Yulia's **2**

Restaurants 🍴
Beach Café **1**
Benno's **1**
Cafe Batujimbar **2**
Mango Beach **1**
Manik Organik **7**
Porch **4**
Rasa Senang **5**
Sanur Rasa **8**
Smorga's **3**
Spike's Downtown Café **6**
Street Café **10**
Tambungan **9**
Village Cucine Italiana **9**

Bars & clubs 🍸
Cat & Fiddle **13**
Jimmy's Café **11**
Lazer Sports Bar **14**
Wicked Parrot **12**

On a clear day there are fantastic views of several mountain ranges to the north, including Gunung Agung and Gunung Batur, especially beautiful at sunset and sunrise. There is a path running along the beach for the entire length of Sanur. The beach varies in width along its length and is at its best in front of the the **Tanjung Sari** and adjacent hotels, and at the southern end. There are several roads and tracks leading down to the beach from Jalan Danau Tamblingan along its length, including Jalan Pantai Karang, where the German consul is situated, and Jalan Segara Ayu.

Serangan Island

Serangan Island is also known as Turtle Island and is, unsurprisingly, famous for its turtles. They are caught in the surrounding sea, raised in pens, and then slaughtered for their meat – which explains why they are becoming rarer by the year. The formerly common green turtle is now said to be virtually extinct in the area.

The beaches on the east coast of the island are best, with offshore coral providing good snorkelling. One of Bali's most important coastal temples is the **Pura Sakenan** in Sakenan village, at the north end of the island. Pura Sakenan's *odalan* or **anniversary festival**, held at Kuningan (the 210th day of the Balinese calendar), is thought by many to be one of the best on Bali.

Arriving on Serangan Island
Boats can be chartered from Sanur. Jukungs, the brightly coloured fishing boats scattered along the beach, can be chartered by the hour (US$40) with a captain. Usually visitors leave from a jetty just south of Kampong Mesigit and 2 km southwest of Sanur; from here there are public boats to Serangan Island. Unfortunately tourists are often forced to charter a boat for far more; share if possible and bargain furiously. It is easier, and often just as cheap, to go on a tour. It is also possible to wade out to the island at low tide.

South Bali listings

For hotel and restaurant price codes and other relevant information, see pages 9-12.

🛏 Where to stay

Kuta *p107*
It's advisable to book accommodation during the peak periods of Jul and Aug and at Christmas and New Year, as hotels are often full. There are countless places to stay. Taxi drivers are often reluctant to drive down Poppies Gangs I and II. Except when the area is flooded during the rainy season, Poppies Gang II is driveable, so it is worth trying to find a driver who will drop you by your chosen accommodation. Prices include 21% government tax and breakfast unless stated.

$$$ Barong Hotel, Poppies Gang 2, T0361 751804, www.barongbalihotel. com. In the heart of the action on Poppies Gang 2, the a/c rooms here are clean and reasonably sized. The draw is the large pool with swim-up bar and massage service. Popular with familes.
$$$ Poppies I, Poppies Gang I, PO Box 3378, T0361 751059, www.poppiesbali.com. Running since 1973, tasteful Balinese-style a/c cottages set in beautifully landscaped gardens with pool. This peaceful and well-run hotel is very popular so book in advance.
$$ Fat Yogi Cottages and Restaurant Poppies Gang 1, T0361 751665, www.fat yogicottages.baliklik.com. Good selection of comfortable and spacious rooms some with a/c and hot water, pool. Staff can be surly.

$$ La Walon Hotel, Poppies Gang 1, T0361 757234, www.lawalonhotel.com. A spanking new exterior leads into an older wing with simple clean rooms with a/c and TV, or fan, with bathroom. Pool. Discounts available for stays of more than 1 week. Friendly staff.

$$-$ Tanjung Bali Inn, Poppies Gang 2, T0361 762990. Surrounding a swimming pool are 3 big Balinese-style buildings. Clean, large a/c and a fan rooms with dimly lit balcony and private bathroom. Very popular.

$ Kedin's 2, Gang Sorga (off Poppies Gang 1), T0361 763554. Fan rooms with private cold-water bathroom lead onto private veranda. Pool. Warm and friendly staff, popular and relaxing hotel. Recommended.

$ Mimpi Bungalows, Gang Sorga (just off Poppies Gang 1), T0361 751848, kumimpi@ yahoo.com.sg. Simple a/c and fan rooms with hot water. Pool.

Legian *p108, map p109*

There is less budget accommodation available in Legian, but mid-range accommodation is good value here.

$$$$ O-CE-N Bali by Outrigger, Jln Arjuna 88, T0361 737 4000, www.outrigger. com. Occupying a prime piece of land overlooking the beach, this top end hotel is ultra-stylish, with sleek modern rooms, sea-view pools and jacuzzi. Strictly for surfers leading a double life as investment bankers. Discounts available. Recommended.

$$$$-$$$ Hotel Puri Raja, Jln Padma Utara, T0361 755902, www.puriraja.com. Relaxing hotel of pools and verdant gardens with sparkling white tiled rooms and access to the beach. Those who are in a sporting mood can enjoy the table tennis table before leaping into the surf.

$$$ All Seasons, Jln Padma Utara, T0361 767688, www.allseasonslegian.com. Top choice for mid-range travellers, with a slightly cramped but well-equipped hotel offering 113 rooms with pool facing views and cheery clean rooms with all mod cons. Breakfast and Wi-Fi are chargeable. For the best rates, book online in advance. Free shuttle service to Kuta offered. Staff are excellent. Highly recommended.

$$$ Casa Padma Suites, Jln Padma, T0361 753073, www.casapadmasuites.com. Handy location for those keen to dive straight into the drinking and shopping action along Jln Padma, this hotel has large, clean rooms with cable TV and chargeable Wi-Fi access and slightly tatty furnishings. The deluxe rooms are cavernous and would suit a group travelling together. Bar, pool and massage service.

$$$ The Lokha, Jln Padma Utara, T0361 767601, www.thelokhalegian.com. Well-run hotel with 49 spacious, stylish rooms, some with baths. 2 spacious pools, café, massage service and Wi-Fi.

$$$-$$ The Island Bali, 18 Gang Abdi, Jln Padma Utara, T0361 762722, www.theisland hotelbali.com. Bali's first true flashpacker venue blows the cobwebs of standard backpacker hostels with smart dorms, swish but small loft rooms, Wi-Fi access and even an infinity pool and cinema. Recommended.

$$ Bali Sorgowi Hotel, Jln Legian, T0361 755266, www.balisorgowi.com. Down a quiet alley on the Kuta/Legian border this place is much touted on the internet, comfortable pool-facing a/c rooms with TV and fridge.

$$ Sinar Bali Jln Padma Utara, T0361 751404, www.hotelsinarbali.com. Tucked away down an alley, this quiet hotel offers clean, comfortable a/c rooms with TV and bathroom. Good-sized pool. Recommended.

Seminyak *p108, map p109*

Long a favoured haunt of expats, some of the accommodation in Seminyak is in bungalows and houses available to rent monthly or long term. Look for signs along the streets, notices in the *Wartel* on Jln Dhyanapura or the estate agents. For shorter stays most places are in the mid- to upper range with only a handful of budget options. Those looking for a bit of rustic peace and quiet away from the main drag should wander along Jln Sarinande and Jln Saridewi towards Jln Kayu Aya for a decent selection of quiet, upmarket villas and guesthouses.

$$$$ Anantara, Jln Abimanyu, T0361 737773, www.bali.anantara.com. Hotel offering unsurpassed views of the beach, the 59 gorgeous sea-view suites feature floor-to-ceiling windows, terrazzo tub, iPod dock and modern Balinese decor. 3 pools, including 1 infinity pool. 3 restaurants and a rooftop bar with DJs spinning chill out tunes as the sun sets. Free Wi-Fi access.

$$$$ The Elysian, Jln Saridewi 18, T0361 730999, www.theelysian.com. Beautiful place with 26 1-bedroom villas and private pool. Villas are ultra modern and come with all the hi-tech goodies necessary for computer addicts. Restaurant, massage service and even an a/c library. Significant discounts offered for online bookings.

$$$$ Le Jardin, Jln Sarinande 7, T0361 730165, www.lejardinvilla.com. A short stroll from the beach, 11 2- to 3-bedroom walled villas each with small private pool, dining room, kitchenette and small garden. The surrounding walls make each villa seem slightly cramped. Well-furnished rooms and friendly, professional staff. Facilities include gym, health spa and Wi-Fi.

$$$$ Sun Island, Jln Raya Seminyak, T0361 733779, www.sunislandboutiquevillas. com. 22 spacious and stylish villas with private walled garden. Each has private plunge pool, kitchenette and bath tub. Private butler, chef service and in-room spa treatments available.

$$$ Puri Cendana, Jln Camplung Tanduk just off Jln Abimanyu, T0361 732947, www.puricendanaresortbali.com. Homely place a short stroll from the beach offering comfortable and attractive Balinese-style rooms with cable TV and 4-poster beds. Wi-Fi is available in the lobby and around the pool.

$$$-$$ The Green Room, Jln Abimanyu 63B, T0361 731412, www.thegreenroombali. com. Follow the signs down a small lane off the main street. Sociable and popular

with young Europeans. De luxe a/c rooms, simple fan rooms, pool, and a covered decking area with plenty of cushions, hammocks and Robinson Crusoe style. Also has another relaxed place down in Canggu. Recommended.

$$ Sarinande Beach Inn, Jln Sarinande 15, T0361 730383, www.sarinandehotel. com. Cheerful, with friendly staff. Spotless comfortable rooms with minibar, private terrace and private hot-water bathroom. Pool and restaurant serving Asian and Western cuisine. Reservations are necessary. Discounts available for stays of more than 14 days. Recommended.

Batubelig

$$$$ Balisani Suites, Jln Batubelig, Kerobokan, T0361 730550, www.bali-sani. com. 126 rooms and suites in peaceful seaside location. Built in Balinese village style, attractively decorated. Swimming pool, 4 restaurants and bars. Free shuttle to Kuta and airport transfers.

$$$ Batubelig Beach Bungalows, Jln Batubelig 228, Kerobokan, T0361 30078. Attractively furnished thatched roof bungalows, with kitchen, large bedroom and bathroom, hot water, a/c, set in garden. Peaceful location 3 mins' walk to the beach. Breakfast not included. Longstay rates available. **Sastika Restaurant** on premises, very cheap and good value.

$$$ Intan Bali Village, PO Box 1089, Batubelig beach, T0361 752191. A/c, several restaurants, 2 pools, extensive sports facilities, large central block with some bungalow accommodation. Caters almost exclusively to tour groups, with little to attract the independent traveller.

Canggu *p108*
The scenic countryside around Canggu is dotted with private villas, many of which are for rent. There are also many hotels being constructed and the sight of dumper trucks rattling along the rutted roads is common.

$$$ Hotel Pisang Mas, Jln Tibu Peneng, Jln Pantai Berewa, T0361 786 8349. Walled complex featuring 3 beautifully furnished 1-bedroom cottages built above a pool. There is a kitchen and outdoor dining area to seat 8. Would suit a group. Dogs barking incessantly outside are tiresome. The owner lives in Legian so needs to be contacted in advance.

$$$ Legong Keraton Beach Hotel, Jln Pantai Berewa, T0361 730280, www. legongkeratonhotel.com. Facing the sea, this spacious but somewhat characterless hotel has a/c rooms with TV and balcony. Sea-view rooms have bath. Hotel offers free daily shuttle service to Kuta. Restaurant, pool and open-air bistro serving Western food. Bike hire.

$$$ Villa Senyum, Jln Pemelisan Agung Jln Pantai Berewa, T0361 7464915, www. villa-senyum.com. Clean tasteful cottages with TV and attached bath with private balcony in an outstandingly peaceful location. Pool and restaurant.

Sanur *p110, map p111*

Accommodation on Sanur is largely mid-to high-range, though there are a couple of decent budget guesthouses along Jln Danau Tamblingan, which offer fair value for money. For the best rates, book high-end hotels well in advance. Walk-in rates can be astronomical. Unless otherwise stated, all accommodation includes private bathroom and Western toilet.

$$$$ Segara Village, Jln Segara Ayu, T0361 288407, www.segaravillage.com. Sprawling complex divided into 5 villages over the 5 ha, this place is popular with European and Australian tour groups and has simple, clean rooms, though lack the mod cons of other hotels in this price range. However, with good restaurant, 3 pools, tennis courts and weekly outdoors cinema there is no reason to spend too much time in the room.

$$$$ Tanjung Sari, Jln Danau Tamblingan 41, T0361 288441, www.tandjungsarihotel. com. 26 bungalows set in atmospheric

grounds, each crafted in traditional Balinese style. Each bungalow is decorated differently and has different amenities – check first. Well-stocked library. Beachfront bar and restaurant. Recommended for a splurge.

$$$$ Villa Dampati, Jln Segara Ayu 8, T0361 288454, www.banyuning.com. 9 spacious 3-bedroom walled villas each with private garden and pool, internet access and a deep bathtub in immaculate bathroom.

$$$ Gazebo Cottages, Jln Danau Tamblingan 35, T0361 288212, www. baligazebo.com. 76 pleasant rooms in a range of styles. 3 smallish pools and large outdoor chess set, big, attractive Balinese-style gardens leading to the beach. Peaceful, friendly, reasonable value.

$$$ La Taverna, Jln Danau Tamblingan 29, PO Box 3040, T0361 288497, www. latavernahotel.com. Discounts available, restaurant (recommended), pool. 34 well-decorated rooms with safety box, attractive gardens leading down to the sea and not a particularly good beach. De luxe rooms have private pool and kitchenette. Broadband. *Legong* dance every Fri evening at 2030 in the restaurant.

$$$ Pondok Ayu, Jln Sekuta, Gang Pudak 3, T0361 284102, www.pondok.com.au. Australian-owned complex 15 mins' walk from the beach. There are 4 comfortable, homely rooms with TV and DVD player overlooking a small pool. The owner rents out her large suite when she is out of Bali. Free transport into town provided. Wi-Fi (chargeable) and decent breakfast provided. Good value. Book well in advance.

$$$ Scape Condotel, Jln Danau Tamblingan 80, T0361 281490, www.scapebali.com. Smart place just off the busy main drag with comfortable rooms facing a grassy garden and 22-m lap pool. Rooms feature a living room area with TV and DVD player. Free Wi-Fi throughout. Recommended.

$$$-$$ Swastika Bungalows, Jln Danau Tamblingan 128, T0361 288693, swastika@ indosat.net.id. 81 rooms. Standard rooms have funky outdoor bathrooms and are cosy and filled with Balinese character. The de luxe a/c rooms are huge, but have a lot less character. 2 pools, quiet location set back from road, 15 mins' walk from the beach, pleasant gardens, popular with families, central for shops and restaurants.

$$-$ Little Pond Homestay, Jln Danau Tamblingan 19, T0361 289902, www.ellora bali.com. Undoubtedly the best budget bet in town with sparkling fan and a/c rooms facing a lap pool. The more expensive rooms have TV. The comfy fan rooms are great value. Free Wi-Fi. Recommended.

$ Yulia's 1 Jln Danau Tamblingan 38, T0361 288089. The owner's prize-winning songbirds fill the shady gardens with tropical banter in this friendly and popular place with spacious fan and a/c rooms. The spacious fan rooms with private balcony on the 2nd floor of the building at the back are great value.

❼ Restaurants

Kuta p107

Most of the restaurants offer a range of food, including Indonesian and international cuisines. There is also a line of cheap *warungs* selling Indonesian favourites such as *nasi goreng* and *soto ayam* in the middle of Gang Ronta, joining Poppies 1 and 2.

$$$ Poppies, Poppies Gang 1, T0361 751059, www.poppiesbali.com. Open 0800-2300. In beautiful gardens, romantic **Poppies** is much favoured by couples. The menu offers a safe blend of good Indonesian and Western with dishes such as half-moon swordfish and delectable steaks. Serves famed Toraja coffee from Sulawesi. Reservations recommended.

$$ Kedai Tiga Nyonya, Jln Pantai Kuta 8-9, T0361 767218. Open 1000-2200. Delightfully furnished with gramophones and photos of the Straits Chinese community from the distant past, this top-rated eatery has a wide selection of Peranakan (Straits Chinese) fare with some Dutch flourishes (try the bitterballen).

Juices are good and staff attentive. Recommended.

$$ Kopi Pot (and the Lone Palm Bar), Jln Legian, T0361 752614. Managed by the same people who run **Poppies**, the menu here skips gracefully from Sumatran fish curries and beef satay cooked table-side to greek salads and some delectable Indonesian coffees. The **Lone Palm Bar** is a good place to pull up a bar stool, sink a beer and catch up on some sporting action after dinner.

$$ Kori, Poppies Gang 2, T0361 758605, www.korirestaurant.co.id. Open 1200-2400. Soft jazz and tinkling water features provide mellow vibes. Indonesian and Western fare is washed down with 2-for-1 on selected cocktails most nights.

$$ Maccaroni, Jln Legian 52, T0361 754662, info@maccaroniclub.com. Open 0900-0200. Sleekly designed for the hipper tourist, diners eat fusion food and Western and Asian favourites to mellow pre-club beats.

$$ TJ's, Poppies Lane 1, T0361 751093. Open 0900-2330. Well-established and cheery Mexican eatery serving large portions of *fajitas* and *chimminchangas* with an extensive tequila cocktail list.

$$ Un's Paradise Restaurant, Un's Lane (off Jln Pantai Kuta), T0361 752607. Open 1700-2400. The tables in the peaceful courtyard are a fine spot to sample some Balinese dishes such as *gulai babi* (pork stew), Balinese-style *sate*, and seafood such as the excellent potato-wrapped red snapper fillet. Also serves fair Western cuisine. Excellent service.

$$-$ Made's Warung, Jln Pantai Kuta, T0361 755297, www.madeswarung.com. Open 0900-2400. A bit quieter than it used to be, this Kuta institution has a mind-bogglingly long and rambling menu of Western and Indonesian fare. Homely ambience with friendly service.

$ Warung 96, Jln Benesari (off Poppies Gang 2), T0361 750557. Open 1000-2400. Excellent pizzas served from a wood-fired oven are the highlight of this laid-back place popular with those fresh from the beach. Friendly service.

$ Warung Indonesia, Gang Ronta (off Poppies Gang 2), T0361 739817. Open 0900-2300. Menu of bog standard Indonesian favourites such as *nasi goreng* and *pecel lele*. The real highlight here is the extensive *nai campur* selection where you choose a selection of dishes to accompany your rice. Superb fresh fruit juices, laid-back vibes and cool reggae after the sun goes down, though the staff seem to become strangely spaced out as the moon rises higher in the sky.

Legian *p108, map p109*

Warungs are scattered along the beach selling simple local fare and drinks.
$$ Café Marzano, Jln Double Six, T0361 874 4438. Good value authentic Italian fare including pizza, salad, pastas and delectable tiramisu. They'll deliver to hotels for those feeling little worse for wear after a night on the Bintangs.
$$ Lanai, Jln Pantai Arjuna 10, T0361 731305. Open 0800-2300. Sea views and an eclectic menu that features sushi, sashimi and Mexican food. Decent kids' menu.
$$ Seaside, Jln Pantai Arjuna 14, T0361 737140, www.seasidebali.com. Open 1100-2300. Stunning sunset views at this cool beachside eatery dishing up international cuisine. Daily special offers. Popular for sunset drinks accompanied by chilled-out tunes.
$$-$ Wali Warung, Jln Padma Utara 16, T0819 3620 1874. Friendly and popular spot offering Western and Indonesian favourites. The real reason to come here is to sample the *babi guling* (roasted pig) or the seafood platter, both of which are huge and need to be ordered a day in advance.
$ Indonational, Jln Padma Utara 17, T0361 759883, www.indonationalrestaurant.com. Open 0900-2300. Popular Australian-owned restaurant that totes its high levels of hygiene. Rammed with Aussies most days chomping through their lengthy menu of Western and pseudo-Asian fare; family-friendly ambience.
$ Warung Yogya, Jln Padma Utara 79, T0361 750835. Open 1000-2200. Tasty Javanese dishes in a friendly setting. Popular with Dutch visitors. The hearty *nasi campur* and *soto rawon* are worth sampling. Recommended.

Seminyak *p108, map p109*

Food is taken seriously in this part of the world, and a diverse selection of excellent cuisine can be found here. Restaurants are concentrated along Jln Abimanyu, Jln Raya Seminyak and Jln Laksmana
$$$ Gado Gado, Jln Abimanyu, T0361 736966. Open 0800-2300. Located on the beach, this eatery is popular for sundown drinks and good international fare. Some superb seafood dishes. There is an extensive list of pasta dishes and salads. Good service.
$$$ Ku De Ta, Jln Laksmana 9, T0361 736969, www.kudeta.net. Open 0700-0200. Possibly the coolest dining venue in Bali with expansive views, gorgeous contemporary decor and superb selection of music including live performances. Menu features tasty, fresh and light fusion cuisine. Well worth a visit, even if just for a sunset cocktail.
$$ Pantarei, Jln Raya Seminyak 17 A, T0361 732567, adonis@indosat.net. Open 1100-0100. Delicious Greek staples such as *dolmades* and *bourek* in this friendly and well-lit restaurant popular with couples and families.
$$ Trattoria, Jln Laksmana T0361 737082. Open 1000-2400. Popular and friendly Italian restaurant with a menu that changes daily.
$$ Unico, Jln Kunti 7, T0361 735931. Superb value authentic Italian cuisine with very reasonably priced good-quality house wines, and an Italian owner who used to make more than 150 pizzas a day in Italy. Recommended.
$ Art Café, Jln Sari Dewi, T0361 737671. You can just about forget all about Kuta here in this quiet and open setting. The restaurant

serves tasty sandwiches and healthy soups, has free Wi-Fi access and overlooks and calming lily-covered pond. The owner also has some good accommodation out the back (www.villakresna.com) for those who fall in love with the peace and quiet here.

$ Zula Vegetarian Paradise, Jln Abimanyu 5, T0361 731080. Serves up healthy treats such as pumpkin and ginger soup, amazingly wholesome falafel sandwiches and a range of zingy antioxidant drinks. Also a grocery attached that sells healthy products and has a noticeboard detailing local events. Recommended.

There is also a small family-run *warung* selling inexpensive grilled seafood on the beach in front of the **Dhyana Pura Hotel**.

Sanur *p110, map p111*

Sanur has a glut of eateries ranging from fine dining to cheap and cheerful backpacker cafés. The more expensive places are attached to the beachfront hotels. However, good food doesn't need to cost the earth and is readily available on the beach or along Jln Danau Tamblingan.

$$$ The Village Cucine Italiana, Jln Danau Temblingan 47, T0361 285025. Open 1100-2400. Italian food in a trendy lounge environment. The dishes are classic Italian and cover the range from meat, pasta and seafood. Good range of antipasti. Free unlimited broadband access.

$$-$ The Porch, Jln Danau Tamblingan 110, T0361 281682. Retro-styled place with friendly staff and long menu of Western treats like baked beans on toast and bangers and mash for homesick travellers. High tea, excellent sandwiches and extensive coffee menu keep this place busy. Free Wi-Fi. There's a small guesthouse out the back.

$$-$ Spikes Downtown Café, Jln Danau Tamblingan 174, T0361 28247. Unpretentious and friendly American diner themed eatery with extensive menu of burgers, Mexican favourites, milkshakes and apple pie with ice cream.

$$-$ Street Café, Jln Danau Tamblingan 21, T0361 289259. Open 0800-2300. Comfy and inviting café place with free book exchange, Wi-Fi, salad bar and menu of Turkish *pide* (similar to pizza), Balinese dishes and hearty breakfasts. Live music some nights.

$ Café Batujimbar, Jln Danau Tamblingan 75A, T0361 287374, www.cafebatujimbar. com. Open 0700-2230. Extremely popular, serving a crowd-pleasing mix of smoothies, toasted sandwiches and Indonesian favourites in a relaxed, modern setting. Recommended.

$ Manik Organik, Jln Danau Tamblingan 85, T0361 8553380. Australian-owned, this bright and cheery organic café sells a delicious range of healthy sandwiches, juices, curries and cakes (try the beetroot chocolate brownies) as well as organic beauty products. Nightly classes held in a room upstairs including belly dancing, meditation, yoga, tai chi and life drawing.

$ Rasa Senang, Jln Danau Tamblingan, T0361 289333. Promising Indonesian food with a Dutch touch, this friendly place offers a good selection of Indonesian and Balinese fare and 2 excellent value *rijstaffel* to choose from. The Indonesian burger served here is worth trying for its blend of flavours.

$ Smorga's, Jln Pantai Karang 2, T0361 289361. Open 0600-2100. Gourmet sandwiches with a range of fresh bread, coffees and gelato. Has the *Jakarta Post* to linger over. Good value and deservedly popular.

Sindhu Beach

There are plenty of places to choose from on Sindhu Beach.

$$-$ Beach Café, Sindhu Beach Walk, T0361 282875. Open 0900-2200. Good spot for a breakfast of eggs Benedict or even a full English with delightful views over to Nusa Penida. Good sandwiches, seafood and Mexican served throughout the day.

$$-$ Benno's, Sindhu Beach Walk, T0361 286638. Open 0700-2300. Long menu that is designed more to please a crowd of hungry Aussies rather than discerning gourmets. Good Aussie breakfast, Western favourites like chicken cordon bleu and some Indonesian favourites.

$$-$ Mango Beach, Sindhu Beach Walk, Open 0700-2300. Rasta-inspired place that offers live reggae after dark, and fair Western and Indonesian standards.

Cheap sunset beers and a simple menu of Indonesian dishes including excellent *ikan baker* (grilled fish) can be found at **Warunng Pantai Indah ($)** midway along the beach walk.

🎵 Bars and clubs

The Kuta to Seminyak belt has the most varied and certainly the wildest nightlife on Bali with venues for both the glamorous and the flip-flop crowd. Most of the bars are on Jln Legian. All these places are free for tourists, but locals often have to pay to enter. Generally speaking, as with hotels, the further north you are, the more glamorous the crowd.

Kuta *p107*
The Bounty, Jln Legian, T0361 752529. Open 2200-0600. Popular drinking hole akin to a UK highstreet club set on a recreated ship. Gets sweaty and raucous as the night progresses.
Eikon, Jln Legian 178, T0361 750701. Attracts a cool set of punters with DJs spinning varied tunes from house to hip hop. Happy hour 2100-2400. Well worth a visit.
Paddys, Jln Legian, T0361 758555, www.paddysclub.com. Open 1600-0300. Rebuilt after being destroyed in the 2002 bombings, and going from strength to strength. Plays commercial music much loved by the drunken hordes. 2-for-1 happy hour 1930-2300.
Sky Lounge, Jln Legian 61, T0361 755423. Open 24 hrs. Cocktails lovingly created at this popular spot, which is growing famous

for its 14-day vodka-infused martini. Serves tapas during the day and early evening. Ladies drink for free 2200-2400 on Sun.
Vi Ai Pi, Jln Legian 88, T0361 750425. Tapas bar by day and transforming itself into a sleek lounge bar by night. This is not a bad place to get away from the beer swilling crowds for a touch of glamour in the heart of Kuta.

Legian *p108, map p109*
Cocoon, Jln Double Six 66, T0361 731266, www.cocoon-beach.com. More of a beach club than a nightclub, **Cocoon** occupies a prime sunset spot overlooking the beach and attracts well-known DJs to play chilled beats to a discerning audience. On Sun mornings it is transformed into a kids' club with clowns, breakfast menu and pool activities.
Dejavu, Jln Pantai Arjuna 7, T0361 732777. Open 2100-0400. Stylish lounge bar with gorgeous sunset views, popular with the glamorous set. 2-for-1 happy hour 2100-2300.
Double Six Jln Arjuna, T0361 733067, www.doublesixclub.com. Daily 2200-0600. Free entrance Sun, Mon, Tue, 75,000Rp Wed, Thu, Fri, Sat (includes 1 drink). Top international and Indonesian DJs spin hard house at this trendy venue that starts to fill up after 0200.
The Sandpit, Jln Pantai Double Six. Beachside *warung* with good selection of drinks. Perfect positioning for a sunset beer.

Seminyak *p108, map p109*
Bush Telegraph Pub, Jln Abimanyu, T0361 723963. Open 1100-0200. Serves icy Aussie beers such as VB and Fosters and a range of grub from Australian steak to Asian staples.
Q Bar, Jln Abimanyu, T0361 730923. Open 1800-late. Popular gay bar with a golden stage area featuring live cabaret.

Sanur *p110, map p111*
Not known for its wild nightlife; evenings are fairly sedate in Sanur. There are a few small bars scattered along Jln Danau Toba that could make for an amusing pub crawl.

Cat & Fiddle, Jln Cemara, T0361 282218. Open 0730-0100. Live music, a good range of booze and British food at this British-owned pub popular with expats. Recommended.
Jimmy's Café, Jln Danau Toba. Popular Aussie watering hole with thrice weekly barbecues, cheap. Icy beer and sociable bar.
Lazer Sports Bar, Jln Danau Tamblingan 82, T0361 282840. Open 0900 until the last customer staggers home. Keep up-to-date with English football in this relaxed bar with cold beers and live music on some nights.
Wicked Parrot, Jln Danau Tamblingan.

Entertainment

Kuta *p107*
Kecak, legong, Ramayana dance and Balinese music; performances take place at many of the major hotels.

Shopping

Kuta *p107*
Kuta is one of the best places on Bali to shop for clothing; the quality is reasonable and designs are close to the latest Western fashions, with a strong Australian bias for bright colours and bold designs. There is a good range of children's clothes shops. Silver jewellery is also a good buy (although some of it is of inferior quality). Kuta also has a vast selection of 'tourist' trinkets and curios. Quality is poor to average. Almost all the hawkers and stallholders are from Java. They are unskilled workers who live in cardboard boxes. This has led to a rise in petty crime, and has sorely tried the tolerance of the Balinese.

Batik PitheCanThropus, Jln Pantai Kuta, T0361 761880. Open 0900-2230. Sells everything and anything possible containing elements of batik. Beautiful selection of stock making this the ideal place to pick up gifts to take back home.

Bookshops Periplus has a small but decent selection of books on Bali and Indonesia. Newspapers and the latest bestsellers are also available here. There is also a second-hand bookshop at the beach end of Poppies Gang 2 selling books in various languages.

Handicrafts Home Ide, Jln Legian, T0361 760014, homeide2006@yahoo.com. Open 0800-2300. Locally made accessories for the home. **Jonathan Gallery**, Jln Legian 109, T0361 754209. Open 0800-2300. Well-stocked with Balinese handicrafts including wood carvings, jewellery and *ikat*. Uluwatu, Jln Legian, T0361 751933, www.uluwatu. co.id. Open 0800-2200. This local venture sells handmade Balinese lace and elegant white cotton clothing.

Shopping mall Matahari, T0361 757588. Open 0930-2200. A popular alternative for those fed up of haggling to pick up a wide selection of tourist trinkets at fixed prices.

Silver Ratna Silver, Jln Legian 72, T0361 750566. Open 0900-1000. Sells attractive contemporary silver jewellery made on Bali by a local artist. It has 3 branches on Bali. Other silver shops are along Jln Pantai Kuta and Jln Legian.

Supermarket In Matahari, selling fresh fruit and daily necessities.

Surfing clothes Surf Clothes Star Surf, Jln Legian, T0361 756251, open 0900-2230, and **Bali Barrel**, Jln Legian, T0361 767238, open 0900-2230, are both huge stores selling brand label surf wear at reasonable prices.

Legian *p108, map p109*
Hammocks Carga, Jln Padma Utara, T0361 765275. Open 0800-2200. Hammock specialist, friendly owner, expansive collection. Prices start at US$20 for a simple *ikat* hammock.

Handicrafts 'Antiques' and Indonesian fabrics at the north end of Jln Legian.

Swimwear and sportswear Several good shops on Jln Legian and side streets.

Seminyak *p108, map p109*
Jln Raya Seminyak is lined with interesting little boutiques, and shopping here is decidedly more upmarket than in Kuta. Locally made clothes and lifestyle stores dominate.
Clothes Neko, Jln Raya Seminyak, T0813 3738 7719, neko@telkom.net. Open 0900-2100. Cotton clothes made by 2 Balinese ladies. Welcoming staff and reasonable prices.
Paul Ropp, Jln Raya Seminyak, T0361 734 2089. Open 0900-2100. Bright cotton clothes made of fabric sourced in India and designed and made in Bali.

Sanur *p110, map p111*
Shopping in Sanur is a breeze if you've just arrived from the tout-ridden pavements of Kuta. There is the usual tourist stuff, including a beachside market along Sidhu beach selling cheap T-shirts, sunglasses and hats, but also some art shops and galleries to peruse.

Antiques Gotta Antique Collection, Jln Danau Tamblingan, T0361 292188. Open 0900-2200. Stocks a variety of antiques from around the archipelago, with a focus on carvings and *ikat* from eastern Indonesia.

Batik Puri Suar, Jln Danau Toba 9, T0361 285572. Open 0900-2000. Sells a colourful selection of locally made Balinese batik and *kebaya*.

Supermarkets Hardy's Supermarket, Jln Danau Tamblingan 136. Daily 0800-2230. Has a cheap supermarket, an optician's and a **Periplus** bookshop, stocking paperbacks, guidebooks, trashy magazines and postcards. The Pantry, Jln Danau Tamblingan 75, T0361 281008. Open 0900-2100. This grocery sells a range of

Australian-produced goodies and has a good deli counter.

⚙ What to do

Major hotels often have tour companies that organize the usual range of tours: for example, to Lake Bratan (where waterskiing can be arranged); to Karangasem and Tenganan to visit a traditional Aga village; to Ubud; whitewater rafting on the Agung River; to the temples of Tanah Lot and Mengwi; to the Bali Barat National Park; and to Besakih Temple.

Kuta *p107*
Body and soul
Numerous masseurs – with little professional training – roam the beach and hassle tourists on Jln Legian; more skilled masseurs can be found at hotels or specialist clinics around Kuta. Jln Pantai Kuta has many aromatherapy and massage places.
Aroma Mimpi, Jln Pantai Kuta, Kuta Suci Arcade 12, T0361 762891. Open 0900-2400. Offers Balinese massage, body scrubs, facials and pedicures.
Dupa Spa, Jln Pantai Kuta 47, T0361 7953132. Open 0900-2400. 1-hr massage is 85,000Rp.

Diving
Aquamarine Diving, Jln Petitenget 2A, Kuta, T0361 738020, www.aquamarinediving.com. Owned and run by an Englishwoman, Annabel Thomas, a PADI instructor. It offers a personal service, uses Balinese Dive Masters who speak English (and Japanese) and has well-maintained equipment. PADI courses up to Dive Master can be provided in English, German, Spanish, French and Japanese. Dive safaris all over Bali and beyond are offered – check the website.

Surfing
Kuta is famous for its surfing, although the cognoscenti would now rather go elsewhere. Boards are available for rent on the beach at

around 50,000Rp per hr. Bodyboards can be rented for 30,000Rp per hr. The guys renting boards on the beach offer surf lessons at US$15 for 2 hrs. Bargain hard.

Quicksilver Surf School, on the beach in Legian, www.quiksilversurfschoolbali.com. Offers more of the same at similar costs.

Rip Curl School of Surf, Jln Arjuna, T0361 735858, www.ripcurlschoolofsurf.com. This school has various packages. 30-min lesson US$65. Kids' courses available starting at US$50.

Tubes, Poppies Gang 2, T0361 765726. Open 1000-0200. A popular meeting spot for surfers. The tide chart is posted outside and surfing trips to Java's **G-land**, www.g-land.com, can be boked here.

Tour operators
Amanda Tours, Jln Benesari 7, T0361 754090. One of the many tour operators offering full-day multi-stop tours to places tuch as Kintamani, Tanah Lot and Lovina. Also offers car rental. Prices are negotiable.

Bali Adventure Tours, Jln Tunjung Mekar, T0361 721480, www.baliadventuretours.com. An organized company owned by long-term Australian resident, offers rafting or kayaking trips, mountain biking, elephant riding in Taro or trekking, US$23-89, including pick-up from hotel, lunch and insurance.

MBA, Poppies Gang 1, T0361 757349, www.mba-sensational.com. This company has branches all over Kuta, and offers domestic flight bookings, horse riding, river rafting and more.

Perama, Jln Legian 39, T0361 751875, www.peramatour.com. Organizes shuttle buses all over the island and tours further afield to destinations such as Flores and Lombok. **Perama** consistently manages to offer significantly cheaper fares than other operators and is developing something of a monopoly on the budget market. Gives a discount to passengers who present a used **Perama** ticket for travel on shuttle buses on Bali.

Water attractions
Head to Tuban, a 5-min taxi ride to the south of Kuta for the following:

Bali Slingshot, Jln Kartika Plaza, T0361 758838, www.balislingshot.net. Open 1100-late. US$25 (including T-shirt) per person. This Australian-owned ride involves being shot up into the air at ridiculous speeds, and advises tourists to 'make sure ya wear ya brown jocks'.

Waterbom Park, Jln Kartika Plaza, T0361 755676, www.waterbom.com. Daily 0900-1800. Adult US$26, child (under 12) US$16 (some rides and activities cost extra). Within walking distance of Tuban hotels, over 600 m of water slides in 3.8 ha of landscaped tropical gardens. Other facilities include water volleyball, spa offering traditional massage, etc, gardens, restaurant, lockers and towels for hire (children under 12 must be accompanied by an adult).

Legian *p108, map p109*
Bungee jumping
AJ Hackett at Double Six Club, Jln Arjuna, T0361 752658, www.ajhackett.com/bali. Mon-Fri 1200-2000, Sat and Sun 0029 until 0600. The 45-m leap of faith can be made towering above the raving masses at this popular nightspot. The price of US$99 includes a T-shirt, certificate and hotel pick-up. For US$199, if you feel it is necessary, you can be set on fire and then jump.

Diving and surfing
Scuba Duba Doo, Jln Legian 367, T0361 761798, www.divecenter bali.com. Dive centre and school that runs 4-day Open Water courses for US$375, and dive safaris to various locations around Bali, including Nusa Penida and Menjangan Island.

Surfboards and bodyboards can be rented on the beach for 50,000Rp and 30,000Rp per hr, respectively.

Seminyak *p108, map p109*
Body and soul
Putri Bali, Jln Raya Seminyak 13, T0361
736852. Open 0900-2000. Javanese *mandi
lulur* scrub treatment where the body is
exfoliated using spices such as turmeric and
ginger and then bathed in a milk moisturiser.
Other local beauty treatments available here
include Balinese *boreh* wrap and a coconut
scrub technique imported from Sulawesi.
2-hr packages start at US$17.50.

Surfing
Surfboards and bodyboards are available
for rent on the beach. Bargain hard.

Canggu *p108*
Horse riding
Canggu Tua, T0361 747 0644. A 2-hr ride
including lunch costs US$50.
Tarukan Equestrian Centre, Jln Nelayan 29.

Sanur *p110, map p111*
Body and soul
Massages are also available at the beach.
Bali Usada Meditation Center, By Pass
NgurahRai 23, T0361 289209, www.bali
meditation.com. Courses in meditation.
Jamu Traditional Spa, Jln Danau Tamblingan
41, T0361 286595. Open 0900-2100.

Cruises
Bali Hai, Benoa Harbour, T0361 720331,
www.balihaicruises.com. Packages to Nusa
Lembongan from Benoa. Trips include the
Reef Cruise on the company's purpose-built
pontoon just off Lembongan. The *Aristocrat
Cruise* is on a luxury catamaran and includes
snorkelling, and use of the facilities at a
Lembongan beach club for the day (both
US$98 adult/US$66 child).

Dance
Tandjung Sari Hotel offers Balinese dance
lessons for children Fri and Sun 1500-1700.

Diving
Blue Season Bali, Jln Danau Tamblingan
69, T0361 270852, www.baliocean.com.
A 5-star IDC centre offering PADI scuba-dive
courses, and a variety of other courses such
as Rescue Diver and Night Diver. Also offers
trips to Nusa Penida and Nusa Lembongan
and Tulamben.

Mountain biking
Sobek, Jln Tirta Ening 9, T0361 287059,
www.balisobek.com. Trips down the
mountainside from Gunung Batur to Ubud
with guide, buffet lunch and insurance;
US$79 adult, US$52 children (7-15).

Surfing
The reef here has one of the world's best
right-hand breaks, but it is only on for
about 28 days a year. It's best in the wet
season Oct-Apr, and is possible with any
tide depending on the size and direction
of the swell. Beware of strong currents and
riptides in high winds. To the north of Sanur,
the right-hand break in front of the **Grand
Bali Beach Hotel** is a fast 4-5 m with some
good barrels, but is best on a mid- or high-
tide and needs a large swell. Opposite the
Tanjung Sari Hotel at high tide, there is the
possibility of a long, fast wall. For the biggest
waves, hire a jukung to take you out to the
channel opposite the **Bali Hyatt**, very good
right handers on an incoming tide.

Tour operators
Asian Trails, Jln By Pass Ngurah Rai 260,
T0361 285771, www.asiantrails.info.
Arranges hotels, flights and tours.
Nick Tours, Jln Danau Tamblingan
(opposite Gazebo Hotel), T0361 287792,
www.nicktours.com. Variety of tours offered
from elephant trekking, swimming with
dolphins and jeep safaris. Can help arrange
visits to places outside Bali including to
Komodo and Flores.
Perama, Warung Pojok, Jln Hang Tuah 39,
T0361 287594. Island-wide shuttle bus.

Sobek, Jln Tirta Ening 9, T0361 287059, www.balisobek.com. Arranges birdwatching and sporting activities.

Watersports
Equipment is available from the bigger hotels or on the beach at Sindhu beach walk. Typical prices per person: jet ski US$25 per 15 mins; canoe US$5 per person per hr. **White Water Rafting Sobek**, www.bali sobek.com, down Grade III rapids on Telaga Waju including professional guides, safety equipment and buffet lunch. US$79 adult, US$52 child (7-15).

⊖ Transport

Kuta *p107*
Kuta is the centre of **Perama** operations, Jln Legian 39, T0361 751551, in southern Bali and can arrange onwards transport to most Balinese destinations and beyond on their tourist shuttle buses. Prices include 4 daily connections to **Sanur** (US$2.50), 4 to **Ubud** (US$5), 1 to **Lovina** (US$12.50) and 3 to both **Candidasa** and **Padangbai** (US$6). They also go daily (1000) to the **Gili Islands** for US$35. A fast boat connection from Serangan Harbour departs to **Nusa Lembongan** daily at 0630 (200,000Rp to Lembongan). **Blue Water Express** (T0361 895 1082, www.bluewater-express. com) departs daily for Nusa Lembongan (30 mins, 325,000Rp) and the **Gili Islands** (2 hrs, 690,000Rp) from Serangan Harbour. Free pick-up from hotels in southern Bali included in the price.

Legian *p108, map p109*
Car/motorbike hire
Sudarsana, Jln Padma Utara, T0361 755916. Open 0800-1800. Cars from US$16.50 per day (plus US$11 per day for a driver). Motorbikes US$5.50 per day.

Shuttle
To most tourist destinations on the island; shop around for best price. Perama is a

good place to start. **Taxi** 40,000Rp to airport. The best metered taxi company is blue **Bali Taxi**, T0361 701111.

Canggu *p108*
To reach Canggu you will need your own transport. Follow the main road north from Legian until you pick up signs for Canggu. The beach signposted 'Canggu Beach' is in fact Pererean Beach. To reach Canggu Beach, turn left at the T-junction in Canggu village and keep going to the beach. The 25-min drive in a hired car should not cost more than 60,000Rp from the Kuta/Legian area.

Sanur *p110, map p111*
Air
Sumanindo Graha Wisata, Jln Danau Tamblingan, T0261 288570. Open 0800-1900. Domestic and international ticketing.

Bemo
Short hops within Sanur cost 5000Rp. There are connections on green bemos with **Denpasar**'s Kreneng terminal and on blue bemos with Tegal terminal (both 7000Rp).

Bicycle hire
25,000Rp a day.

Boat
Perama has a daily service to the surfer's and diver's mecca of **Nusa Lembongan** leaving at 1030 (1½ hrs) from the jetty at the north of town for US$12.50. Public boat leaves at 0800 and costs US$4. Ticket booth at beach end of Jln Hang Tuah. **Lembongan Fast Cruises**, Jln Hang Tuah, T0361 285522, www.scoot cruise.com. 4 sailings per day (0930, 1130, 1330, 1600), 30-min trip. US$50/US$30 for adult return/one way, US$43/25 child (13-16) return/one way and US$34/US$22 child (3-12) return/one way. Price includes pick-up and drop service. This company also offers daily connections to the Gili Island (Trawangan and Air) daily at 0930 via Nusa Lembongan (3 hrs, stopover at no extra cost permitted) US$125/US65

adult return/one way, US$85/US$45 child return/one way.

Car/motorbike hire
A1 Rental, (Jln Danau Toba, T0361 284287, offers cars at US$16.50 per day and motorbikes at US$6 per day.

Shuttle
Perama (see above) has 4 daily to **Ubud** (US$4), 5 daily to **Kuta** (US$2.50), and 3 daily to **Padangbai** (US$6).

Taxi
Most hotels will arrange airport transfer/pick-up and will charge the same, or more, than taxis (40,000Rp). A metered trip from one end of Sanur to the other is around 15,000Rp.

⊕ Directory

Kuta p107
Banks Money changers on Jln Legian. Very few, if any, are licensed, and most are masters of sleight of hand and deception: take a calculator with you and count your money *very* carefully. **Embassies and consulates** For Indonesian embassies and consulates abroad and

for foreign embassies in Indonesia, see http://embassy.goabroad.com. **Medical services** International SOS Bali, Jln Ngurah Rai By Pass, T0361 710505, sos.bali@internationalsos.com. **Legian** Clinic, Gang Benasari, T0361 758503.

Legian p108, map p109
Banks Money can be changed in many places along Jln Padma Utara and Jln Legian. **Medical services** Padma Clinic, Jln Padma Utara 517, T0361 761484.

Seminyak p108, map p109
Banks Money changers and ATMs on Jl Raya Seminyak. **Medical services** Pharmacy: Apotek Taiga Farma, Jln Raya Seminyak, T0361 730877, open daily 24 hrs. Clinic: Rahayu Clinic, Jln Adimanyu, T0361 774960.

Sanur p110, map p111
Embassies and consulates For Indonesian embassies and consulates abroad and and for foreign embassies in Indonesia, see http://embassy.goabroad.com. **Medical facilities** Dentist: Dr Alfiana Akinah, Jln Sri Kesari 17. Doctor: Bali Beach Hotel, daily 0800-1200. **Police** Jln Ngurah Rai, T0361 288597.

Ubud and around

Ubud is a rather dispersed community, spread over hills and valleys with deep forested ravines and terraced ricefields. For many tourists, Ubud has become the cultural heart of Bali, with its numerous artists' studios and galleries as well as a plentiful supply of shops selling clothes, jewellery and woodcarving. Unfortunately, the town has succumbed to tourism in the last few years, with a considerable amount of development.

During the rainy season Ubud gets more rain than the coastal resorts and can be very wet and much cooler.

Arriving in Ubud → *Phone code: 0361.*

Getting there
Public bemos stop at the central market, at the point where Jalan Wanasa Wana (Monkey Forest Road) meets Jalan Raya, in the centre of Ubud. **Perama** ① *Jln Hanoman, T0361 96316*, which runs shuttle buses to the main tourist destinations, has a busy depot 15 minutes'

walk away from the centre of town. Buses won't drop passengers off at accommodation. Arrivals are greeted with a small army of touts offering accommodation and transport. Public bemos run from Ubud to Batubalan for connections south including to Kuta and Sanur; Gianyar for connections east to Padangbai and Candi Dasa; and north to Singaraga and Louina and Kintaman. Perama also runs regular shuttles to the airport.

The **Bina Wisata tourist office**ⓘ *Jln Raya Ubud (opposite the Puri Saren), open 0800-2000*, is good for information on daily performances and walks in the Ubud area, but otherwise not very helpful.

Places in Ubud → *For listings, see pages 130-136.*

Much of the charm and beauty of Ubud lies in the natural landscape. There are few official sights in the town itself – in contrast to the surrounding area (see page 128). The **Museum Puri Lukisan** ⓘ *in the centre of Ubud, T0361 975136, www.mpl-ubud.com, 0900-1700, 40,000Rp*, contains examples of 20th-century Balinese painting and carving and that of Europeans who have lived here.

Antonio Blanco ⓘ *T0361 975502, daily 0900-1800, 50,000Rp, walk west on the main road and over a ravine past Murnis Warung – the house is immediately on the left-hand side of the road at the end of the old suspension bridge*, is a Western artist who settled in Ubud has turned his home into a gallery. The house is in a stunning position, perched on the side of a hill, but the collection is disappointing. Blanco – unlike Spies and Bonnet – has had no influence on the style of local artists.

The **Museum Neka** ⓘ *1.5 km from town, up the hill past Blanco's house, daily 0900-1700, 40,000Rp*, consists of six Balinese-style buildings each containing a good collection of traditional and contemporary Balinese and Javanese painting, as well as work by foreign artists who have lived in or visited Bali. There is a good art bookshop here and a good restaurant with views over the ravine.

ARMA (Agung Rai Museum of Art) ⓘ *Jln Pengosekan, T0361 976659, www.arma museum.com, daily 0900-1800, 40,000Rp*, has a fascinating permanent exhibition of paintings by Balinese, Indonesian and foreign artists who spent time in Bali. It is the only place on Bali that exhibits the delightful work of Walter Spies, as well as famed Javanese artist Raden Saleh. Classical *kamasan* (paintings on tree bark) are displayed here, alongside works by the Balinese masters and temporary exhibitions featuring local photographers and artists. The centre is also the venue for numerous cultural performances, and, more interestingly, for workshops on topics as diverse as Balinese dance, Hinduism in Bali, modernity in Bali and woodcarving. Recommended.

The **Bali Botanic Gardens**ⓘ *Jln Kutuh Kaja, T0361 780 3904, www.botanicgardenbali. com, daily 0800-1800, 50,000Rp*, are 320-400 m above sea level and contain an impressive collection of ferns, palms, bamboo and other tropical trees. The garden is crisscrossed with pathways in a ravine. The garden also houses Bali's first maze, an Islamic garden and three teak *joglos* (Javanese traditional house) where simple food is served. **Threads of Life**ⓘ *Jln Kajeng 24, T0361 972187, www.threadsoflife.com, daily 1000-1900*, a member of the Fairtrade Organization, is a textile centre that provides an opportunity to learn about *ikat* and batik in Indonesia. There is a two-hour introduction course detailing the textiles and differences between hand-spun and commercial threads, essential if you are to purchase a pricey piece of *ikat*. The gallery has examples of *ikat* from Bali, Flores, Sumba, Sulawesi and Timor, showing the different regional motifs and contemporary uses. Talks on Tuesday (Introduction to Textiles of Indonesia – 150,000Rp for one to two people) and

Wednesday (Textiles and their place in Indonesian Culture – 280,000Rp for one to four people). Register in advance.

At the south end of Jalan Monkey Forest is the **Sacred Monkey Forest Sanctuary** ① *daily 0830-1800, 20,000Rp, child 10,000Rp*, which is overrun with cheeky monkeys. An attractive walk through the forest leads to the **Pura Dalem Agung Padangtegal**, a Temple of the Dead. Back in town on Jalan Raya Ubud, opposite Jalan Monkey Forest, is the **Puri Saren**, with richly carved gateways and courtyards. West of here behind the Lotus Café is the **Pura Saraswati**, with a pretty rectangular pond in front of it. **Note** Do not enter the forest

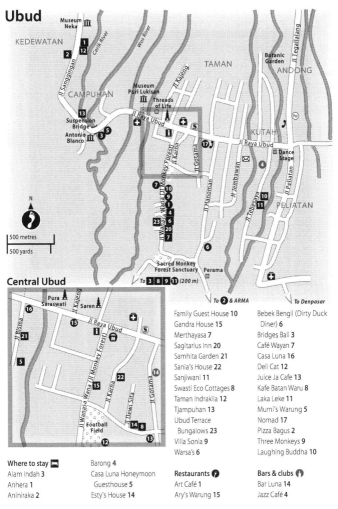

Ubud

Where to stay		Restaurants	Bars & clubs
Alam Indah 3	Barong 4		
Anhera 1	Casa Luna Honeymoon	Art Café 1	Bar Luna 14
Aniniraka 2	Guesthouse 5	Ary's Warung 15	Jazz Café 4
	Esty's House 14		

Family Guest House 10
Gandra House 15
Merthayasa 7
Sagitarius Inn 20
Samhita Garden 21
Sania's House 22
Sanjiwani 11
Swasti Eco Cottages 8
Taman Indrakila 12
Tjampuhan 13
Ubud Terrace
  Bungalows 23
Villa Sonia 9
Warsa's 6

Bebek Bengil (Dirty Duck
  Diner) 6
Bridges Bali 3
Café Wayan 7
Casa Luna 16
Deli Cat 12
Juice Ja Cafe 13
Kafe Batan Waru 8
Laka Leke 11
Murni's Warung 5
Nomad 17
Pizza Bagus 2
Three Monkeys 9
Laughing Buddha 10

with food – these monkeys have been known to bite. You will only have 48 hours to get to Jakarta for a rabies injection.

The **Ubud Writers Festival**, www.ubudwritersfestival.com, held annually in October, attracts literary notables from Asia and beyond to participate in discussions on culture, society, politics and religion from a literary perspective. Workshops are held throughout the festival on travel writing, novel writing and short story writing. There are also cultural workshops held for those who wish to deepen their knowledge of all things Balinese.

Around Ubud

There are villages beyond Ubud that remain unspoilt and it is worth exploring the surrounding countryside, either on foot or by bicycle. Around Ubud, particularly to the north in the vicinity of Tampaksiring, and to the east near Pejeng and Gianyar, is perhaps the greatest concentration of temples in Bali. The most detailed and accurate guide to these *pura* is AJ Bernet Kempers's *Monumental Bali* (Periplus: Berkeley and Singapore, 1991). **Sangeh** and the **Pura Bukit Sari** are two temples about 25 km west of Ubud, but easier to reach via Mengwi.

Goa Gajah ① *15,000Rp, dress: sarong, a short ride by bemo from Ubud or from the Batubulan terminal outside Denpasar; alternatively, join a tour.* 'Elephant Cave', lies about 4 km east of Ubud, via Peliatan, on the right-hand side of the road and just before Bedulu. The caves are hard to miss as there is a large car park, with an imposing line of stall holders catering for the numerous coach trips. The complex is on the side of a hill overlooking the Petanu River, down a flight of steps. Hewn out of the rock, the entrance to the cave has been carved to resemble the mouth of a demon and is surrounded by additional carvings of animals, plants, rocks and monsters. The name of the complex is thought to have been given by the first visitors who mistakenly thought that the demon was an elephant. The small, dimly lit, T-shaped cave is man-made and is reached by a narrow passage whose entrance is the demon's mouth. It contains 15 niches carved out of the rock. Those on the main passageway are long enough to lead archaeologists to speculate that they were sleeping chambers. At the end of one of the arms of the 'T' is a four-armed statue of Ganesh, and on the other, a collection of *lingams*.

The **bathing pools** next to the caves are more interesting. These were discovered in the mid-1950s by the Dutch archaeologist JC Krijgsman, who excavated the area in front of the cave on information provided by local people. He found stone steps and eventually uncovered two bathing pools (probably one for men and the other for women). Stone carvings of the legs of three figures were uncovered in each of the two pools. These seemed to have been cut from the rock at the same time that the pools were dug. Water spouts from the urns, held by the nymphs, into the two pools.

Stairs lead down from the cave and pool area to some meditation niches, with two small statues of the Buddha in an attitude of meditation. The remains of an enormous relief were also found in 1931, depicting several stupas. To get there, walk down from the cave and bathing pools, through fields, and over a bridge. The complex is thought to date from the 11th century.

Yeh Pulu ① *350 m off the main Ubud–Gianyar road just south of the Tampaksiring turning, signposted to Bendung Bedaulu, bemos from Ubud will drop passengers at the turning; it is an easy walk from there to the site, dress: sarong and sash (for hire at site), it is probably possible to visit this site at any time, as there are no entrance gates, 60000Rp,* is 2 km east of Goa Gajah, beautifully set amongst terraced ricefields, and a short walk along a paved path from the end of the road. This is a peaceful place, free from crowds and hawkers. It is also the location of the local bath house. Yeh Pulu is one of the oldest holy places in Bali, dating from the 14th or 15th century. Cut into the rock are 20 m of vigorous carvings depicting village life, intermingled with Hindu and Balinese gods: figures carrying poles, men on horseback, Krishna saluting, wild animals and vegetation. Originally these would have been plastered over – and perhaps painted – although almost all of the plaster has since weathered away. A small cell cut into the rock at the south end of the reliefs is thought to have been the abode of a hermit – who probably helped to maintain the carvings. Until 1937 when the site was renovated, water from the overhanging paddy fields washed over the carvings causing significant erosion. There is also a small bathing pool here. An old lady looks after the small shrine to Ganesh and ensures a donation is placed there.

On the road north from Bedulu, Gianyar Regency contains a number of important archaeological sites, the majority located near **Pejeng**, 4 km east of Ubud. This sacred area, inhabited since the Bronze Age, contains over 40 temples as well as massive stone statues, carvings, sarcophagi, Buddhist sanctuaries, bathing sites and bronze artefacts. A number of artefacts have been removed to museums as far afield as Amsterdam, but many have remained *in situ*, beside rivers, in paddy fields or in nearby temples. Pejeng was once the centre of a great kingdom which flourished between the ninth and 14th centuries, before falling to the Majapahit. These days it is home to many Brahmin families.

The small, poorly labelled, **Purbakala Archaeological Museum**, consisting largely of a collection of sarcophagi, neolithic tools and Hindu relics, is 400 m north of Bedulu. About 200 m further north still is the **Pura Kebo Edan** ⓘ *admission by donation, dress: sarong*, or 'Mad Bull Temple', a rather ramshackle and ill-kept temple. Among the monumental weathered stone figures in the courtyard is a statue of Bima dancing on a corpse, its eyes open, protected under a wooden pavilion. The figure – sometimes known as the 'Pejeng Giant' – is renowned for its 'miraculous' penis, pierced with a peg or pin (used to stimulate women during intercourse, a feature of sexual relations across the region).

Pura Pusering Jagat (the 'Navel of the World' Temple) is 50 m off the main road, a short distance north from Kebo Edan. **Pura Panataran Sasih** ⓘ *admission by donation, dress: sarong, bemo from Ubud or from the Batubulan terminal outside Denpasar*, lies another 250 m north in Pejeng and is thought to date from the ninth or 10th century. This temple was the original navel *pura* of the old Pejeng Kingdom. The entrance is flanked by a pair of fine stone elephants. Walk through impressive split gates to see the '**Moon of Pejeng**' (*sasih* means 'moon'). It is housed in a raised pavilion towards the back of the compound and is supposedly the largest bronze kettledrum in the world. In Balinese folklore, the drum is supposed to have been one of the wheels of the chariot that carries the moon across the night sky. The wheel fell to earth and was kept (still glowing with an inner fire) in the temple. It is said that one night a man climbed into the tower and urinated on the drum, extinguishing its inner fire, and paid for the desecration with his life. Visitors should on no account try to climb the tower for a better look at the drum. The drum is believed to date from the third century BC, although no-one is absolutely sure – certainly, it has been housed here for centuries. It may be a Dongson drum from Vietnam or it may be a later example produced elsewhere. The fine decoration on this incomparable piece of bronze work was first recorded – in a series of brilliantly accurate drawings – by the artist WOJ Nieuwenkamp in 1906 (although it was mentioned in a book by the blind chronicler GE Rumphius, published in 1705). A collection of 11th-century stone carvings are also to be found here.

Gunung Kawi ⓘ *6000Rp, dress: sash or sarong required, to get there catch a connection at Denpasar's Batubulan terminal or from Ubud to Tampaksiring, it is about a 3-km walk from* here, passing Tirta Empul (see below), although bemos also make the journey to the temple site, the 'Mountain of the Poets', is one of the most impressive, and unusual, temples in Bali. A steep rock stairway with high sides leads down to the bottom of a humid, tree-filled, ravine. At the bottom lies the temple. The whole complex was literally hewn out of the rock during the 11th century, when it was thought to have been created as the burial temple for King Anak Wungsu and his wives, who probably threw themselves on his funeral pyre. You descend 315 steps to a massive rock archway, and from there to the nine tombs which face each other on either side of the Pakerisan River. These two rows of *candis*, four on the south side and five on the north, were cut out of the rock. It is believed that the five on the north bank of the river were for the king and his four wives, while the four on the south bank may have been for four concubines. They resemble temples and are the earliest traces of a style of architecture that became popular in Java in the following centuries. As such they may represent the precursor to the Balinese *meru*.

East of the five *candis*, on the far side of the river, is a cloister of various courtyards and rooms, also carved out of the rock. They were created for the Buddhist priests who lived here (visitors are asked to remove their shoes before entering). Still farther away, on the other side of the river, is the so-called 'tenth tomb'. The local people call this tomb 'The Priest's House'. The 10th tomb is, in all likelihood, a monastery and consists of a courtyard encircled by niches. To get to the 10th tomb take the path across the paddy fields, that runs from the rock-hewn gateway that leads down into the gorge; it is about a 1-km walk. There is accommodation close by in Tampaksiring, which also has a number of good jewellery workshops.

Tirta Empul ① *2 km north of Tampaksiring, 1 km on from Mount Kawi, 6000Rp, to get there take a bemo from Denpasar's Batubulan terminal or Ubud towards Tampaksiring, the temple is 2 km north of the town centre; either walk or catch a bemo, from here it is a 1-km walk to Gunung Kawi (see above),* one of the holiest sights on Bali and is a popular pilgrimage stop, evident by the maze of trinket stalls. Tirta Empul is built on the site of a holy spring, which is said to have magical healing powers. In the past, *barong* masks were bathed here to infuse them with supernatural powers during the dance. Originally constructed in AD 960, during the reign of Raja Candra Bayasingha, the temple is divided into three courtyards and has been extensively restored with little of the original structure remaining – just a few stone fragments. The outer courtyard contains two long pools fed by around 30 water spouts, each of which has a particular function – for example, there is one for spiritual purification. The holy springs bubble up in the inner courtyard. During the **Galungan** festival, sacred *barong* dance masks are brought here to be bathed in holy water.

Ubud and around listings

For hotel and restaurant price codes and other relevant information, see pages 9-12.

● Where to stay

Ubud *p125, map p127*
Ubud has a great choice of good-value, clean and mostly high-quality accommodation, in often romantic and well-designed bungalows. Except in the more expensive

hotels, breakfast is included in the rates. Cheaper accommodation often involves staying in a family compound providing a unique opportunity to watch the daily goings on of a Balinese family. Discounts of up to 30% available at expensive places in the low season. Book ahead in peak seasons. Those with a bit more cash to splash are advised to choose one of the places slightly outside town. These are generally far better value and often offer free shuttle service to and from town.

$$$$ Barong, Jln Monkey Forest, T0361 971758, www.barong-resort.com. A thatched reception filled with local antiques leads into a shady garden hosting 11 rooms. Tastefully decorated, in modern Balinese style, rooms have bathroom with sunken bath. De luxe rooms with private pool. Spa and 2 pools. Discounts available.

$$$ Casa Luna Honeymoon Gueshouse, Jln Bisma, T0361 977409, www.casaluna bali.com. Delightful selection of Balinese style rooms with 4-poster beds and spacious bathrooms and just on the edge of town. Good for a spot of romancing. Excellent breakfast included in the price. Recommended.

$$$ Samhita Garden, Jln Bisma, T0361 975443, www.samhitagarden.com. Far enough away from the town centre to escape the madness and calls for transport, yet close enough to be able to pop along to see a performance and have a decent meal every night, the **Samhita** offers spotless a/c rooms facing an inviting pool and well-tended garden. Spacious bathrooms.

$$ Sagitarius Inn, Jln Monkey Forest. The spacious open gardens are filled with an abundance of water features. Accommodation is in simple cottages with veranda. Pool.

$$-$ Merthayasa, Jln Monkey Forest, T0361 974176. Down towards the forest end of Jln Monkey Forest, this popular place has simple, functional clean fan rooms and some spacious comfortable a/c rooms, all facing a pool.

$$-$ Sania's House, Jln Karna 7, T0361 975535, sania_house@yahoo.com. Balinese cottages on a quiet street. A/c and fan rooms with comfy bed and clean bathroom. Popular.

$$-$ Ubud Terrace Bungalows, Jln Monkey Forest, T0361 975690, ubud_terrace@ yahoo.com. Situated in a quiet, verdant grove, a/c and fan rooms

with attractive decor including Balinese-style 4-poster bed. Hot water, upstairs rooms have good sunset views. Pool. Recommended.

$ Esty's House, Jln Dewi Sita, T0361 980571. 6 well-maintained rooms with fan in quiet area, large and clean bathrooms. Recommended.

$ Gandra House, Jln Karna 8, T0361 976529. Good-value, simple clean fan rooms with veranda and hot water in friendly compound.

$ Warsa's, Jln Monkey Forest, T0361 971548, www.baliya.com/warsabungalow. Good location slap bang in the heart of the action, a/c and fan rooms here are very simple and cleanish. Bathrooms feature hot water, shower and *mandi*.

Nyuh Kuning Village

This small village just behind the Monkey Forest is home to ashrams, meditation centres and some excellent mid-range accommodation. Most places offer free shuttle service back and forth into town, or else it's a half-hour walk into the heart of town. There is a path skirting the Monkey Forest that is used by motorbikes and can be used by people staying at hotels in the village in order to avoid paying the forest admission fee everytime one wants to go home from town.

$$$ Alam Indah, T0361 974629, www. alamindahbali.com. This attractive and well-managed hotel offers Balinese-style rooms in verdant gardens, with some rooms offering stunning views over a riverine valley. Staff are friendly and great with kids making this an excellent choice for families. Excellent breakfast and afternoon tea, pool with attractive views and Wi-Fi access in some rooms. Recommended.

$$$ Swasti Cottages, T0361 974079, www.baliswasti.com. Peaceful place with organic garden producing some delcious veggies served in the restaurant, salt water pool and comfortable rooms. Very popular and well run. Recommended.

$$$ Villa Sonia, T0361 971307, www.soniahotel.com. Sonia's is a quiet spot offering comfortable accommodation in a variety of cottages set in a garden with a natural spring water pool.

West of Ubud Centre
The hotels to the west of Ubud offer breath-taking views and are often set among the rice paddies. However, they are a fair walk into town. Hotels are generally of high standard, and this is reflected in the prices.
$$$$ Anhera Jln Raya Sanggingan 168, T0361 977843, www.anherahotelbali.com. 8 rooms each designed to reflect one of the major Indonesian islands, some more tasteful than others. Spacious and comfortable rooms, with CD player and minibar. Obscenely large bathrooms feature jacuzzi with beautiful views of the rice terraces. 2 pools. Restaurant and spa facilities. Big discounts available.
$$$$-$$$ Tjampuhan, Jln Raya Campuhan, T0361 975368, www.tjampuhan-bali.com. Built in 1928 for the guests of the Royal Prince of Ubud, this charming hotel offers 67 well-decorated Balinese-style a/c and fan bungalows set on the side of a lush valley. The pool here is filled with spring water.
$$$ Aniniraka, Jln Raya Sanggingan, T0361 975213, www.aniniraka.com. 11 rooms surrounded by bright green rice paddies. Each of the large rooms has a kitchenette, dining area, spacious sleeping area and bathroom with sunken bath. Other facilities include a sauna and pool. 20% discounts available.
$$ Taman Indrakila, Jln Raya Sanggingan, T0361 975017, www.tamanindrakila.com. The view across the Sungai Cerik Valley is amazing, and is the main reason to stay here. 10 bungalows with Balinese-style 4-poster bed and balcony. Worn furniture, but reasonable value given the location. Wi-Fi access.

East of Ubud Centre
The streets lying to the east of the village centre are leafy and quiet, and are lined with Balinese family compounds. Jln Tebesaya and Jln Jembawan have a lot of good-value guesthouse accommodation.
$$ Family Guest House, Jln Tebesaya 39, T0361 974054, familyhouse@telkom.net. Spacious, well-decorated fan rooms with huge private balcony overlooking the forest, good value. Bath. Breakfast includes home-made brown bread.
$$ Sanjiwani, Jln Tebesaya 41, T0361 973205, www.sanjiwani.com. Clean fan rooms with hot water in a friendly and peaceful family compound. Residents can use the kitchen.

⑦ Restaurants

Ubud *p125, map p127*
Food in Ubud is good, particularly international. Most restaurants serve a mixture of Balinese, Indonesian and international dishes.
$$$ Ary's Warung, Jln Ubud Raya, T0361 975053. Open 0900-2400. Classy eatery serving up Asian and fusion cuisine and cocktails in a modern lounge-style setting. The *sake* and soya grilled salmon is worth investigating.
$$ Bebek Bengil (Dirty Duck Diner), Jln Hanoman, T0361 975489. Open 0900-2200. A renowned spot for Balinese duck dishes such as crispy fried duck, in a lovely setting that stretches out to the rice paddies behind. Popular.
$$ Bridges Bali, Jln Raya Campuhan, T0361 970095, www.bridgesbali.com. Located near the Blanco Museum, this smart place offers excellent contemporary fare, good wine selection and makes for a sound choice for those staying in this part of town.
$$ Café Wayan and Bakery, Jln Monkey Forest, T0361 975447. Open 0800-2300. Ubud favourite with its long menu of Balinese and international dishes and lip-smacking cakes. The restaurant offers

some garden seating. Head here on Sunday evenings for the Balinese buffet extravaganza with over 20 dishes to sample.

$$ Casa Luna, Jln Raya Ubud, T0361 977409, www.casalunabali.com. Open 0800-2300. Brunch here is scrumptious with a wide choice of Western favourites including a superb eggs Benedict. Throughout the day the kitchen produces excellent Balinese and Mediterranean fare in an elegant breezy setting with a green paddyfield view. Highly recommended.

$$ Kafe Batan Waru, Jln Dewi Sita, T0361 977528. Attractive eatery with colonial-era botanical drawings and old Indonesian city maps covering the walls. The food is excellent and this place offers possibly the best place in Ubud to try regional Indonesian cuisines such as *ayam rica rica* (from Sulawesi), *sayur belado* (from Sumatra) and *ayam taliwang* (Bali). Sun night is satay festival night with variety of satay to try. Good cocktail menu. Highly recommended.

$$ Laka Leke, Nyuh Kuning Village, T0361 977565, www.lakaleke.com. Fair international and Indonesian fare here, with excellent service on the edge of the rice paddies which are delightfully illuminated by lanterns after sunset. The real reason to come here is to see the dance performances (4 nights a week). Check the website for schedule.

$$ Laughing Buddha, Jln Monkey Forest, T0361 970928. Open 0900-0000. Small but attractive place offering contemporary Asian dishes, tapas and some Mediterranean fare and good range of devilish cocktails to accompany their live music evenings on Mon, Thu and Sat. Free Wi-Fi. 2-for-1 happy hour 1600-1900.

$$ Murni's Warung, Jln Raya Campuhan, T0361 975233, www.murnis.com. Open 0900-2100. Long menu of Western and Indonesian dishes. The Balinese food is worth trying, particularly the *betutu ayam* (chicken slow cooked in local spices for 8 hrs).

$ Art Kafe, Jln Monkey Forest, T0361 970910. Homely spot with pastel walls, scatter cushions, book and excange and free Wi-Fi, this is a pleasant spot to pass and hour or 2. Menu features Indonesian and Balinese dishes, though the owner claims the real crowd pleasers are the Mexican items. Live music 3 nights a week.

$ Deli Cat, Jln Monkey Forest, by the football pitch, T0361 971284. Open 0900-2400. Very good value, proffers tasty sausages and cheeses from around the world, chunky sandwiches, and hearty fish and meat main courses. The owner, from Iceland, has set the place up with sociable long benches, so expect interesting conversation while you get stuck into your bratwurst. Recommended.

$ Juice Ja Café, Jln Dewi Sita, T0361 971056. Open 0730-2200. Laid-back organic café serving good range of fruit juices, salads and tasty bagels with delightful toppings such as kalamata olive cream cheese. The health cocktails here are very popular. There is also a noticeboard detailing interesting local events.

$ Nomad, Jln Ubud Raya 35, T0361 977169, www.nomad-bali.com. Open 0900-2200. Popular for its fantastic selection of fresh pasta dishes, soups, juices and salads. Good range of teas from around the world. Nice upbeat atmosphere.

$ Pizza Bagus, Jln Pengosekan, T0361 978520, www.pizzabagus.com. Open 0830-2230. Popular Italian place serving the best pizza in Ubud, along with fine pasta and salads. There is a deli attached that makes sandwiches and sells cheeses, hams and German chocolate biscuits. The weekly organic farmers market is held here on Sat 0930-1400. Recommended.

$ Three Monkeys, Jln Monkey Forest, T0361 974830. Open 0700-2300. Popular place with a great menu of fresh pastas, salads and some scrumptious and unorthodox desserts. Also Javanese chocolate bars on sale. The breezy rice field out the back is a big plus.

🄽 Bars and clubs

Ubud *p125, map p127*
Ubud isn't exactly a centre of hedonism and most places shut around 0100. However, there are a few spots for an evening drink.
Bar Luna, Jln Goutama, T0361 971832. Open 0800-2300. Relaxed and friendly spot claiming to be the home of the town's intellectual elite. Thu night is Literary Night and offers the chance for a bit of lively banter.
Jazz Café, Jln Sukma, T0361 976594, www.jazzcafebali.com. Open Tue-Sun until 0100. Atmospheric surroundings make this a relaxed place for a drink or meal (cheap), with enticing menu and good live music. Free pick up service from **Laughing Buddha Bar** or hotels around Ubud offered.

🄴 Entertainment

Ubud *p125, map p127*
Art
Ubud has perhaps the greatest concentration of artists in Indonesia, exceeding even Yogya. Many will allow visitors to watch them at work in the hope that they will then buy their work. The **Pengosekan Community of Artists** is on Jln Bima.

Dance and cultural performances
Ubud has the most accessible cultural performances in Bali, with nightly events at various locations scattered around town, and in villages around Ubud. Transport is usually included in the cost of the ticket if the venue is outside Ubud. Performances start around 1930 and last for 2 hrs, but this varies so check beforehand. Tickets cost between US$5 and US$16.50 and are available from Ubud Tourist Information on Jln Ubud Raya, or at the venue. Go to the tourist office to check performance and venue. Recommended dances are the legong dance, the barong dance and the *kecak* dance. The **Puri Saren** on Jln Raya Ubud is a convenient and charming venue.

🄾 Shopping

Ubud *p125, map p127*
Art Ubud painters have a distinctive style, using bright colours and the depiction of natural and village scenes. There is a large selection of paintings in the town and galleries are concentrated along the east section of Jln Raya Ubud. It is possible to visit the artists in their homes; enquire at the galleries. **Macan Tidur**, Jln Monkey Forest, T0361 977121, www.macan-tidur-textiles.com. Excellent selection of stylishly presented ethnographica. **Nikini Art**, Jln Monkey Forest, T0361 973354. Open 0800-2200. Has a fascinating range of *ikat*, carvings and silver from Timor.
Tegun Folk Art Galeri, Jln Hanoman 44, T0361 970581. Daily 0800-2100. The overwhelming collection of eye-catching art and crafts from across the archipelago is well worth a browse. The owner is very friendly and has excellent English.

Bookshops **Ganesha Bookshop**, Jln Raya Ubud, T0361 970320. Fair selection of new and second-hand tomes, some maps, postcards and stationery. **Periplus**, Jln Monkey Forest. Open 0900-2200. Postcards, newspapers and a good selection of Indonesia-related books.

Textiles **Kuno Kuno Textile Gallery**, Jln Monkey Forest, T0361 973239. Open 1000-1900. Has decent quality *ikat* and batik.

Woodcarving Concentrated on the Peliatan road out of town. The so-called 'duck man' of Ubud (Ngurah Umum) is to be found on the road to Goa Gajah, with a selection of wooden fruits and birds. Recommended shop near the **Bamboo Restaurant**, off Jln Monkey Forest, facing the football field.

🕐 What to do

Ubud *p125, map p127*

Ubud has turned into something of an 'alternative' centre, and there is plenty to do here. Many people come to learn something, while others enjoy pottering about the countryside on 2 wheels.

Body and soul

Iman Spa, Jln Sri Wedari 8, T0812 3600 9610, www.imanspa.com. Open 1000-2100. Treatments include Balinese *boreh* and Javanese *mandi lulur*. Packages start at US$12.
The Yoga Barn, Jln Pengoseken, T0361 970992, www.theyogabarn.com. Classes start at US$10. This well-regarded centre offers an assortment of yoga, meditation and t'ai chi classes daily, in a relaxed and green setting at the edge of town.

Birdwatching

The **Bali Bird Club**, www.balibirdwalk. com, sets off on walks around the Ubud countryside, on trails that differ according to the season. Birds that can be spotted include the Java kingfisher, bar-winged prinia, the black-winged starling and other birds endemic to Indonesia. The sociable 3½-hr walks leave from the **Beggar's Bush Pub** at 0900 on Tue, Fri, Sat and Sun. The price of US$37 includes lunch and water along the trail. Other rambles can be organized in demand; check the website.

Bike tours

Bali Eco, T0361 975557, www.balieco cycling.com. Small-group tours which start with breakfast overlooking Gunung Batur and then cruise downhill through villages to Ubud for 2½ hrs. Includes a walk around a coffee plantation, visit to a temple and decent Balinese buffet lunch in a family compound. US$36 per person (US$25 for children under 12), including hotel pick-up and drop off. Recommended.

Cooking

Casa Luna Cooking School, Jln Bisma, T0361 977409, www.casalunabali.com. Run by the owner of **Casa Luna** restaurant Janet de Neefe, this school offers the chance to explore the spices and kitchen myths of Bali. Each lesson concludes with a Balinese meal and cooking notes to take home. Different menu each day. Each lesson is around 4 hrs. US$30 per person. Recommended.
Ibu Wayan Cooking Classesl, T0361 975447. Ibu Wayan and her daughter Wayan Metri provide Balinese cooking classes for groups and have a list of the food to be learned each day. The 2-hr lessons are followed by lunch or dinner. Morning or afternoon lessons US$35 per person. Phone ahead to reserve. Small groups. Classes held at **Laka Leke** restaurant in Nyuh Kuning village.
Nomad's Organic Farm. Owner Nyoman throws open the gates of his organic farm in the village on Baturiti on Sun and Wed for an explanation of the different methods of organic farming and a lunch of salad made from vegetables chosen by the visitors. Enquire at **Nomad** restaurant (see Restaurants).

Tour operators

Perama, Jln Hanoman, T0361 973316.

⊖ Transport

Ubud *p125, map p127*
Bemo

These leave from the Pasar Ubud in the centre of town, at the junction of Jln Monkey Forest and Jln Raya Ubud; regular connections with **Denpasar**'s Batubulan terminal (Brown – 8000Rp), Gianyar (Green – 8000Rp). **Perama** has 5 daily departures to **Kuta**/airport (US$5), 5 departures to **Sanur** (US$4), 1 daily to **Lovina** (US$12.50), 3 departures to **Padangbai** (US$5) and 1 daily further afield to **Senggigi** from (US$15) and the

Gili Islands (US$35). A ride to the airport or Kuta in a taxi costs arounds US$20.

Bicycle hire
Bicycles are the best way to get about (apart from walking); there are several hire places on Jln Monkey Forest, US$2.50 per day.

Car hire
Hire shops on Jln Monkey Forest, US$15 per day plus insurance for Suzuki 'jeep'; US$20 per day for larger Toyota Kijang.

Motorbike hire
Several outfits on Jln Monkey Forest, from US$7 per day.

⊙ Directory

Ubud *p125, map p127*
Banks Numerous money changers will change cash and TCs and offer rates similar to banks. **Medical services** Clinic: Taruna Medical Centre, Jln Monkey Forest, T0361 781 1818, 24 hrs. Pharmacy: Apotek Mertasari, Jln Monkey Forest, T0361 972351, 0900-2130. **Police** Jln Andong, T0361 975316.

Gianyar to Gunung Batur via Bangli

East of Ubud is the royal town of Gianyar. Some 15 km north of Gianyar, at the foot of Gunung Batur, is another former royal capital, Bangli, with its impressive Kehen Temple. A further 20 km leads up the slopes of Gunung Batur to the crater's edge – one of the most popular excursions in Bali. Along the rim of the caldera are the mountain towns of Penelokan and Kintamani, and the important temples of Batur and Tegen Koripan. From Penelokan, a road winds down into the caldera and along the west edge of Danau Batur. It is possible to trek from here up the active cone of Gunung Batur (1710 m), which thrusts up through a barren landscape of lava flows. North from Penulisan, the road twists and turns for 36 km down the north slopes of the volcano, reaching the narrow coastal strip at the town of Kubutambahan.

Gianyar → *For listings, see pages 141-142. Phone code: 0361.*

Gianyar is the former capital of the kingdom of Gianyar and in the centre, on Jalan Ngurah Rai, is the **Agung Gianyar Palace**, surrounded by attractive red-brick walls. At the turn of the century, the Regency of Gianyar formed an alliance with the Dutch in order to protect itself from its warring neighbours. As a result, the royal palace was spared the ravages and destruction, culminating in *puputan*, that befell other royal palaces in South Bali during the Dutch invasion. The rulers of Gianyar were allowed a far greater degree of autonomy than other Rajas; this allowed them to consolidate their wealth and importance, resulting in the regency's current prosperity and the preservation of the royal palace. It is not normally open to the public but the owner, Ide Anak Agung Gede Agung, a former politician and the Raja of Gianyar, does let visitors look around his house if you ask him. The bemo station is five minutes' walk to the west of the palace, also on Jalan Ngurah Rai.

Traditionally regarded as Bali's weaving centre, there is only a limited amount of cloth on sale these days. There is accommodation at **Agung Gianyar Palace Guesthouse ($$$)**, within the palace walls.

Bangli → *For listings, see pages 141-142. Phone code: 0366.*

Bangli, the former capital of a mountain principality, is a peaceful, rather beautiful town, well maintained and spread out. Set in a rich farming area in the hills, there is much to enjoy about the surrounding scenery, especially the captivating views of the volcanic area to the north including Gunung Agung and Gunung Batur. Both the town itself and the countryside around afford many opportunities for pleasant walks. The area claims to have the best climate on Bali and the air is cooler than on the coast. Despite these attractions, Bangli is not on the main tourist routes and is all the more charming for that.

Tourist information

The **Bangli Government Tourism Office** ① *Jln Brigjen Ngurah Rai 24, T0366 91537, Mon-Sat 0700-1400*, is very friendly and helpful, but little English is spoken and they are not really geared up for foreigners. A free booklet and map are available.

Background

Balinese believe that Bangli is the haunt of *leyaks* (witches who practise black magic). In Bali, misfortune or illness is frequently attributed to *leyaks*, who often intervene on behalf of an enemy. In order to overcome this the Balinese visit a *balian* (a shaman or healer), who often has knowledge of the occult. As a result of the presence of *leyak* in the area, Bangli has a reputation for the quality of its *balian*, with suppliants arriving from all over the island, dressed in their ceremonial dress and bearing elaborate offerings. The people of Bangli are also the butt of jokes throughout Bali, as Bangli is the site of the island's only mental hospital, built by the Dutch.

Places in Bangli

There is a **market** every three days in the centre of town. Locally grown crops include cloves, coffee, tobacco, vanilla, citrus fruit, rice, cabbages, corn and sweet potatoes; some of which are exported. Bangli lies close to the dividing line between wet-rice and dry-rice cultivation.

Most people come to Bangli to visit the **Pura Kehen** ① *6000Rp per person for a car, on the back road to Besakih and Penelokan, outside there are stalls selling snacks and sarongs*, one of Bali's more impressive temples and one of the most beautiful, set on a wooded hillside about 2 km to the north of the town centre. The *pura* was probably founded in the 13th century. There is some dispute over the true origin of the temple, because inscriptions within the compound have been dated to the ninth century. It is the second largest on Bali and the state temple of Bangli regency. Elephants flank the imposing entrance, leading up to three terraced courtyards, through finely carved and ornamented gateways decorated with myriad demons. The lower courtyard is dominated by a wonderful 400-year-old *waringin* tree (*Ficus benjamina*), with a monk's cell built high up in the branches. It is here that performances are held to honour the gods. The middle courtyard houses the offertory shrines, while the top courtyard contains an 11-tiered *meru* with a carved wood and stone base. The elaborate woodwork here is being beautifully restored and repainted by craftsmen. In the wall below, guides will point out the old Chinese plates cemented into it. Curiously, some of these depict rural England, with a watermill and mail coach drawn by four horses. Every three years in November (Rabu Kliwon Shinta in the Balinese calendar), at the time of the full moon (*purnama*), a major ceremony, **Ngusabha**, is held at the temple.

The **Sasana Budaya Arts Centre** stages performances of traditional and modern drama, music and dance, as well as art and cultural exhibitions. It is one of the largest cultural centres on Bali, located about 100 m from the Pura Kehen. Ask at the tourist office for information on performances. Bangli is particularly noted for its dance performances. Bangli also has one of the largest *gamelan* orchestras on Bali, captured from the ruler of Semarapura by the Dutch, who gave it to Bangli.

In the centre of town is the **royal palace**, which houses eight branches of the former royal family. Built about 150 years ago and largely restored by the present descendants, the most important section is the Puri Denpasar where the last ruler of Bangli lived until his death almost 40 years ago. The temple of the royal ancestors is situated on the northwest side, diagonally opposite the **Artha Sastra Inn**; important ceremonies are still held here.

There is an impressive **Bale Kulkul** in the centre of town, three storeys high and supported on columns made of coconut palm wood; it is about 100 years old. There are in fact two *kulkul*, *kulkul lanang* which is male, and *kulkul wadon* which is female. In times past the *kulkul* was sounded to summon the people, or act as an alarm warning of impending danger. The people of Bangli consider these *kulkul* to be sacred, and they are used during important temple festivals.

At the other end of town, the **Pura Dalem Penjungekan** (Temple of the Dead) is also worth a visit. The stone reliefs vividly depict the fate of sinners as they suffer in hell; hanging suspended with flames licking at their feet, being castrated, at the mercy of knife-wielding demons, being impaled or having their heads split open. The carvings are based on the story of Bima on his journey to rescue the souls of his parents from hell. The destructive 'Rangda' features extensively. In the centre there is a new shrine depicting tales of Siwa, Durga and Ganesh. The temple is in a parkland setting with possibilities for walks.

Around Bangli

There are a number of pleasant places to visit, including **Bukit Demulih** ① *walk or take a bemo bound for Tampaksiring, get off after about 3 km, take the narrow, paved road south for 1 km to Demulih village*, at an altitude of about 300 m. This small, pretty village has some well-carved temples, and a *kulkul* tower by the *bale banjar*. From here the villagers will show you the track up the hill, at the top of which is a small temple; on the way you pass a sacred waterfall. If you walk along the ridge you will come to other temples and fine views over the whole of South Bali.

A pleasant walk east of Bangli leads to **Sibembunut. Bukit Jati**, near Guliang about 2 km south of Bunutin, is another hill to climb for splendid views and scenic walks.

Sidan, just north of the main Gianyar–Semarapura road, 10 km south of Bangli, is notable for its **Pura Dalem** ① *6000Rp, car park opposite the temple, and a stage where dance performances sometimes take place*, which has some of the most vivid, spine-chilling depictions of the torture and punishment that awaits wrong-doers in hell. The carvings show people having their heads squashed, boiled or merely chopped off, and the wicked and evil widow Rangda dismembering and squashing babies.

Gunung Batur → *For listings, see pages 141-142.*

The spectacular landscape of Gunung Batur is one of the most visited inland areas on Bali. Despite the hawkers, bustle and general commercialization, it still makes a worthwhile trip. The huge crater – 20 km in diameter – contains within it **Danau Batur** and the active **Gunung Batur** (1710 m), with buckled lava flows on its slopes. The view at dawn from the summit is stunning. Although these days Gunung Batur is less destructive than Gunung Agung, it is the most active volcano on Bali having erupted 20 times during the past 200 years. Danau Batur in the centre of the caldera is considered sacred.

Trekking

A steep road winds down the crater side, and then through the lava boulders and along the west shore of Danau Batur. There are hot springs here and paths up the sides of Gunung Batur, through the area's extraordinary landscape. Treks begin either from **Purajati** or **Toya Bungkah** (there are four-, five- or six-hour treks), or around the lake (guides are available from the **Lake View Cottages** in Toya Bungkah). Aim to leave Toya Bungkah at about 0330. After reaching the summit it is possible to hike westwards along the caldera rim, though this hike is not for the faint-hearted as the ridge is extremely narrow in places with steep drops on both sides. The cinder track passes several of the most active craters, lava flows and fumaroles. In the north and east of the caldera the landscape is quite different. The rich volcanic soil, undisturbed by recent lava flows, supports productive agriculture. The vulcanology institute on the rim of the caldera monitors daily seismic activity.

Trunyan

Boats can be hired from the village of **Kedisan** on the south shore of Danau Batur (be prepared for the unpleasant, hard-line sales people here) or from Toya Bungkah, to visit the traditional Bali Aga village of Trunyan and its cemetery close by at **Kuban**, on the east side of the lake.

The Bali Aga are the original inhabitants of Bali, pre-dating the arrival of the Majapahit; records show that the area has been inhabited since at least the eighth century. Trunyan's customs are different from Tenganan – but these differences can only be noted during festival time, which tend to be rather closed affairs. Despite its beautiful setting beside Danau Batur with Mount Abang rising dramatically in the background, a visit can be disappointing. Most people come to visit the cemetery to view the traditional way of disposing of corpses. Like the Parsees of India, corpses are left out to rot and be eaten by birds rather than being buried or cremated. It is claimed that the smell of rotting corpses is dissipated by the fragrance of the sacred banyan tree. The idea behind this custom is that the souls of the dead are carried up towards heaven by the birds; this flight to heaven propitiates the gods and results in improved prospects for the souls in their reincarnation in the next life. The corpses are laid out on enclosed bamboo rafts, but very likely all you will see is bones and skulls. The cemetery is only accessible by boat; make sure you pay at the end of your journey, otherwise the boatman may demand extra money for the return journey. The villagers are unfriendly and among the most aggressive on Bali; with a long tradition of begging for rice from other parts of the island as they were unable to grow their own. They now beg or demand money from tourists.

Penelokan and Kintamani

On the west rim of the crater are two villages, Penelokan and Kintamani. Large-scale restaurants here cater for the tour group hordes. The area is also overrun with hawkers selling batik and woodcarvings.

Penelokan is perched on the edge of the crater and its name means 'place to look'. About 5 km north of here, following the crater rim, is the rather drab town of **Kintamani**, which is a centre of orange and passionfruit cultivation. The town's superb position overlooking the crater makes up for its drabness. Ask locally for advice on the best walks in the area and for a guide for the more dangerous routes up to the crater rim.

Pura Batur

Just south of Kintamani is Pura Batur, spectacularly positioned on the side of the crater. This is the new temple built as a replacement for the original Pura Batur, which was engulfed by lava in 1926. Although the temple is new and therefore not of great historical significance, it is in fact the second most important temple in Bali after Pura Besakih. As Stephen Lansing explains in his book *Priests and Programmers* (1991), the Goddess of the Crater Lake is honoured here and symbolically the temple controls water for all the island's irrigation systems. Ultimately, therefore, it controls the livelihoods of the majority of the population. A nine-tiered meru honours the goddess and unlike other temples it is open 24 hours a day. A virgin priestess still selects 24 boys as priests, who remain tied as servants of the temple for the rest of their lives.

Pura Tegeh Koripan

ⓘ *Daily, 6000Rp, catch a bemo running north and get off at Penulisan.*
Pura Tegeh Koripan is the last place on the crater rim, on the main road 200 m north of Penulisan. Steep stairs (333 in all) lead up to the temple, which stands at a height of over 1700 m above sea level next to a broadcasting mast. The temple contains a number of weathered statues, thought to be portraits of royalty. They are dated between 1011 and 1335. Artistically they are surprising because they seem to anticipate later Majapahit works. The whole place is run-down at the moment, though there are some signs that repairs are being attempted.

Alternative routes from Ubud to Gunung Batur

If you have your own transport and are starting from Ubud, you can turn left at the end of Ubud's main street and take the back road heading north. This leads through an almost continuous ribbon of craft villages, mainly specializing in woodcarving, with pieces ranging in size from chains of monkeys to full size doors and 2-m-high *garudas*. There are good bargains to be found in this area off the main tourist track. Follow the road through **Petulu**, **Sapat** and **Tegalalong**, and continue northwards. The road, its surface not too good in places, climbs steadily through rice paddies and then more open countryside where cows and goats graze, before eventually arriving at the crater rim – 500 m west of Penelokan.

The area around Gunung Batur is considered very sacred and comprises numerous temples, small pretty villages and countryside consisting of rice fields littered with volcanic debris. There are several rugged backroutes from Ubud through this region. One of the most interesting villages is **Sebatu**, northeast of Ubud near Pura Mount Kawi, reached via a small road leading east from the northern end of **Pujung Kelod**. This village has a number of temples and is renowned for the refined quality of its dance troupe, its *gamelan* orchestra and its woodcarving. The dance troupe has revived several unusual traditional dances including the *telek* dance and makes regular appearances overseas. **Pura Gunung Kawi** is a water temple with well-maintained shrines and pavilions, a pool fed by an underground spring and open air public bathing.

From Gunung Batur to the north coast

From Penulisan, the main road runs down to the north coast, which it joins at **Kubutambahan**. It is a long descent as the road twists down the steep hillsides, and there are many hairpin bends.

If exploring the northeast coast, a very pleasant alternative is to take the minor road that turns directly north, just short of a small village called **Dusa**. The turning is not well signed – ask to make sure you are on the right road.

This is a steep descent but the road is well made and quiet. It follows ridges down from the crater of Gunung Batur, with steep drops into ravines on either side. The route passes through clove plantations and small friendly villages, with stupendous views to the north over the sea. Behind, the tree-covered slopes lead back up to the crater.

The road eventually joins the coast road near Tegakula. Turn left, northwest, for Singaraja and Lovina, and right, southeast, for the road to Amlapura.

Gianyar to Gunung Batur via Bangli listings

For hotel and restaurant price codes and other relevant information, see pages 9-12.

🛏 Where to stay

Bangli *p137*
$$-$ Artha Sastra Inn, Jln Merdeka 5, T0366 91179. Offers 14 rooms. Located in the inner court of the royal palace with plenty of atmosphere, although don't expect anything too grand. This is the place to stay in Bangli. The more expensive rooms are clean, simple, with private bathroom and Western toilet; cheaper rooms have shared *mandis* with squat toilets. Restaurant (**$**).
$ Catur Aduyana Homestay, Jln Lettu Lila 2, T0366 91244. Clean and pleasant homestay located 1 km to the south of the town centre. 7 rooms: 3 with private *mandi*, squat toilet, 4 with shared *mandi*, squat toilet. Breakfast of tea/coffee and bread included. Friendly owner speaks no English.
$ Losmen Dharma Putra. A good, friendly, family-run *losmen*, price includes breakfast.

Gunung Batur *p138*
$$ The Art Centre (or *Balai Seni*), Toya Bungkah. Quite old but still good.
$ Under the Volcano, Toya Bungkah, T081 3386 0081. Clean rooms, friendly management, good restaurant.

Penelokan *p139*
$$$ Lakeview Hotel, Jln Raya Penelokan, T0361 728790 (Bali office), www.indo.com/hotels/lakeview. Basic, comfortable and with good views all the way to Lombok. Good online discounts available

$$ Gunawan Losmen. Clean, private bathroom, fantastic position.

Kintamani *p139*
$$ Hotel Surya, Jln Kedisan, T0366 51139, www.suryahotel.com. In a great position, comfortable rooms.
$$ Losmen Sasaka. Stunning views.
$$ Puri Astina. Large clean rooms.

🍴 Restaurants

Bangli *p137*
There are *warungs* beside the bemo station in the centre of town, and a good night market opposite the **Artha Sastra Inn,** with the usual staple Indonesian/Balinese stall food including noodles, rice, *nasi campur*, *sate*, etc. Near the **Catur Aduyana Homestay**, opposite *Yunika*, is a clean **Rumah Makan**. Foodstalls near the Pura Kehan sell simple snacks.

🎭 Entertainment

Gianyar *p136*
At 1900 every Mon and Thu, a cultural show including dinner is staged at the **Agung Gianyar Palace**, T0361 93943/51654.

⚙ What to do

Perama has a guided trek starting at 0300 from Pura Jati, on the edge of Danau Batur and reaching the peak in time for sunrise. US$60 per person (minimum 2 people), including transfers to and from Kuta, Ubud and Sanur. Or, you can arrange your own trek from Toya Bungka, using a local guide.

It should cost around US$40-50 for a 4- to 5-hr trek to the summit and back. Bargain hard. The guides will find you. This can be annoying, and makes the prospect of the hassle-free **Perama** package look enticing.

Gianyar *p136*
Mountain biking
Sobek Expeditions, T0361 287059, www.balisobek.com. Organizes rides down into the volcano on the 'Batur Trail'. US$79 adult, US$52 chid.

⊖ Transport

Gianyar *p136*
Bemo
Regular connections with **Denpasar**'s Batubulan terminal.

Bus
To **Semmarapura** (25 mins), **Padangbai** (50 mins) and **Candi Dasi** (1 hr 10 mins).

Bangli *p137*
Bemo
Many (but not all) bemos are 'colour coded'. Bemos run throughout the day, and most places are accessible by bemo if you are prepared to wait and do some walking. There are services between: **Denpasar**'s Batubulan terminal, many connect through to **Singaraja**; the market in **Gianyar** (these bemos are usually blue); and **Semarapura**.

Blue bemos wait at the Bangli intersection on the main road between Gianyar and Semarapura at Peteluan; so it's easy to change bemos here. The road climbs steadily up to Bangli with good views to the south. Generally, orange bemos run from Bangli to **Kintamani**. To **Rendang** they are generally black or brown and white. Bemos also run between to **Besakih** and to **Amlapura**. All fairly regularly from 0600-1700; fewer in the afternoon. The road from Bangli to Rendang is good but winding, with little traffic; it is also pretty with ravines, streams and overhead viaducts made of bamboo and concrete.

Trunyan *p139*
Bemo
From **Denpasar**'s Batubulan terminal to **Bangli** and then another to **Penelokan**. Some bemos drive down into the crater to **Kedisan** and **Toya Bungkah**.

Bus
Regular coach services from **Denpasar** (2-3 hrs).

❶ Directory

Bangli *p137*
Medical services General Hospital, Jln Kusuma Yudha 27, T0366 91020. Pharmacy: Apotik Kurnia Farma, Jln Kusuma Yudha, and in Toko Obat Rhizoma, Jln Bridjen Ngurah Rai.

Pura Besakih and Gunung Agung

The holiest and most important temple on Bali is Pura Besakih, situated on the slopes of Bali's sacred Gunung Agung. Twinned with Gunung Batur to the northwest, Agung is the highest mountain on the island, rising to 3140 m. It is easiest to approach Besakih by taking the road north from Semarapura, a distance of 22 km. However, there are also two east–west roads, linking the Semapura route to Besakih with Bangli in the west and Amlapura in the east. Although little public transport uses these routes, they are among the most beautiful drives in Bali, through verdant terraced rice paddies.

Pura Besakih

Pura Besakih is a complex of 22 *puras* that lie scattered over the south slopes of Gunung Agung, at an altitude of about 950 m. Of these, the largest and most important is the Pura Penataran Agung, the Mother Temple of Bali. It is here that every Balinese can come to worship – although in the past it was reserved for the royal families of Semarapura, Karangkasem and Bangli. The other 21 temples that sprawl across the slopes of Gunung Agung surrounding the Mother Temple are linked to particular clans. **Gunung Agung** last erupted in 1963, killing 2000 people. The area has been sacred for several centuries.

The **Pura Penataran Agung**, which most visitors refer to as Pura Besakih, is dedicated to Siva and is of great antiquity.

Arriving in Pura Besakih

The site is open daily from 0800 until sunset and entrance costs 10000Rp plus 1000Rp for a camera. There is another ticket office on the climb up the hill where you have to sign in and are invited to make a further donation (ignore the vast sums that are claimed to have been donated). Guides are available for around 25,000Rp. The best time to visit is early in the morning, before the tour groups arrive.

Getting there

Besakih is 22 km from Semarapura and 60 km from Denpasar, with regular minibus services from both. From Denpasar catch a bemo from the Batubulan terminal to Semarapura, and then get a connection on to Besakih (via Rendang). However, bemos are irregular for this final leg of the journey and it makes more sense to charter a bemo for the entire trip, or rent a car or motorbike (chartering a bemo makes good sense in a group).

Temple layout

From the entrance gate, it is a 10-minute walk up to the temple. Although you can walk up and around the sides of the temple, the courtyards are only open to worshippers. It is the position of this *pura* that makes it special: there are views to the waters of the Lombok Strait.

Pura Besakih consists of three distinct sections. The entrance to the forecourt is through a *candi bentar* or split gate, immediately in front of which – unusually for Bali – is a *bale pegat*, which symbolizes the cutting of the material from the heavenly worlds. Also here is the *bale kulkul*, a pavilion for the wooden split gongs. At the far end of this first courtyard are two *bale mundar-mandir* or *bale ongkara*.

Entering the central courtyard, almost directly in front of the gateway, is the *bale pewerdayan*. This is the spot where the priests recite the sacred texts. On the left-hand wall is the *pegongan*, a pavilion where a *gamelan* orchestra plays during ceremonies. Along the opposite (right-hand) side of the courtyard is the large *bale agung*, where meetings of the Besakih village are held. The small *panggungan* or altar, in front and at the near end of the *bale agung*, is used to present offerings. The similar *bale pepelik* at the far end is the altar used to present offerings to the Hindu trinity – Vishnu, Brahma and Siva. These gods descend and assemble in the larger *sanggar agung*, which lies in front of the *bale pepelik*.

From the central courtyard, a steep stone stairway leads to the upper section, which is arranged into four terraces. The first of these in the inner courtyard is split into an east (right) and west (left) half. To the right are two large *merus*; the *meru* with the seven-tiered roof is dedicated to the god Ratu Geng, while the 11-tiered *meru* is dedicated to Ratu Mas. The three-tiered *kehen meru* is used to store the temple treasures. On the left-hand side is a row of four *merus* and two stone altars. The tallest *meru*, with seven tiers, is dedicated to Ida Batara Tulus Sadewa. Up some steps, on the second terrace, is another 11-tiered *meru*, this one dedicated to Ratu Sunar ing Jagat (Lord Light of the World). There are also a number of *bale* here; the *bale* in a separate enclosure to the left is dedicated to Sira Empu, the patron god of blacksmiths. Up to the third terrace is a further 11-tiered *meru*, dedicated to Batara Wisesa. On the final terrace are two *gedongs* – covered buildings enclosed on all four sides – dedicated to the god of Gunung Agung.

At the back of the complex there is a path leading to three other major *puras*: **Gelap** (200 m), **Pengubengan** (2.5 km) and **Tirta** (2 km). There are over 20 temples on these terraced slopes, dedicated to every Hindu god in the pantheon.

Festivals

Seventy festivals are held around Pura Besakih each year, with every shrine having its own festival. The two most important festivals are occasional ceremonies: the **Panca Wali Krama** is held every 10 years, while the **Eka Dasa Rudra** is held only once every 100 years and lasts for two months. Two **Eka Dasa Rudra** festivals have been held this century. In March or April is the movable festival of **Nyepi** (on the full moon of 10th lunar month), the Balinese Saka new year, a month-long festival attended by thousands of people from all over Bali.

Gunung Agung

Gunung Agung is Bali's tallest and most sacred mountain, home of the Hindu gods and dwelling place of the ancestral spirits, it dominates the spiritual and physical life of the island. All directions on Bali are given in relation to this much revered mountain. Toward the mountain is called '*kaja*', away from the mountain is '*kelod*'. This is the site of the most important of the nine directional temples. Water from its sacred springs is the holiest and most sought after for temple rites. According to local legend, the god Pasupati created the mountain by dividing Mount Mahmeru, centre of the Hindu universe, in two – making Gunung Agung and Gunung Batur.

Standing 3014 m high, at its summit is a crater about 500 m in width. In 1969, after lying dormant for more than 600 years, the volcano erupted causing massive destruction; over 1600 people died in the eruption, a further 500 in the aftermath and 9000 were made homeless. Even today the scars left by the destruction are visible in the shape of lava flows and ravines. Much was read into the fact that the eruption took place at the time of Bali's greatest religious festival, **Eka Dasa Rudra** (see above). One theory is that the mountain erupted because the priests were pressured into holding the ceremony before due time, to coincide with an important tourism convention that was taking place on Bali.

Climbing Gunung Agung

Gunung Agung is a sacred mountain, so access is restricted during religious ceremonies, particularly in March and April. The arduous climb should only be attempted during the dry season, May to October; even then conditions on the summit can be quite different from the coast. There are several routes up Gunung Agung, but the two most popular depart from Besakih and Selat. You should be well prepared; the mountain is cold at night and you will need warm clothes, water, food, a good torch and decent footwear. You will also need a guide, and should aim to reach the summit before 0700 to witness the spectacular sunrise.

From Besakih The route takes you to the summit, providing the best views in all directions. The longer of the two ascents, this climb takes about six hours, with another four to five hours for the demanding descent. You start out in forest, but once you reach the open mountain it becomes extremely steep. The tourist office at Besakih hires guides (about US$60 per person, including temple offerings) and can arrange accommodation.

From Selat This route reaches a point about 100 m below the summit, which obscures all-round views. However, the climb only takes three to four hours; aim to set off by 0330. From Selat, take the road to Pura Pasar Agung, then climb through forest before reaching the bare mountain. Guides can be arranged in Muncan, Tirtagangga or Selat. A recommended guide is **I Ketut Uriada**, a teacher who lives in Muncan; he can be contacted at his shop in that village, T0812 364 6426. Costs start at about US$50, which includes temple contributions and registering with the local police. In Selat ask the police about guides, they should be able to advise. In Tirtagangga ask at your accommodation; rates here tend to be around US$50 per person, which should include transport. There is accommodation in Selat, or your guide may arrange cheaper lodgings at his home. **Perama** ① *T0361 751875 in Kuta, T0361 973316 in Ubud*, offers a one-night two-day trek up Gunung Agung including visits to Kamasan, Kertagosa and Sideman, where the climb begins at 0100. The four-hour trek arrives in time for sunrise on the summit. Transfers to and from Kuta, Ubud and Sanur are included in the price (US$100 per person – minimum two people).

East Bali, Karangasem and the north coast

The greatest of the former principalities of Bali is Semarapura (formerly Klungkung), and its capital still has a number of sights that hint at its former glory. It is worth driving east of here into the Regency of Karangasem: to the ancient Bali Aga village of Tenganan, 3 km outside Candi Dasa, then inland and northeast to Amlapura (Karangkasem), with its royal palace, then 7 km north to the royal bathing pools of Tirtagangga. From here the road continues north, following the coast all the way to Singaraja (almost 100 km from Amlapura). The drive is very beautiful, passing black-sand beaches and coconut groves.

An area of great beauty dominated by Gunung Agung (3140 m), Bali's highest and most sacred volcano, Karangasem is one of the most traditional parts of Bali and one of the most rewarding areas to explore. During the 17th and 18th centuries, Karangasem was the most powerful kingdom on Bali. Its sphere of influence extended to western Lombok, and the cross-cultural exchanges that resulted endure to this day. During the 19th century, the regency cooperated with the Dutch, thus ensuring its continued prosperity.

The massive eruption of Gunung Agung in 1963 devastated much of the regency and traces of the lava flows can still be seen along the northeast coast, particularly north of Tulamben.

Arriving in East Bali, Karangasem and the north coast

Getting there
By bus Buses run most frequently in the morning starting early (from 0500 or 0600), and continue until about 1700. Buses from Denpasar (Batubulan terminal) run to Semarapura

(1¼ hours), Padangbai (one hour 50 minutes) and Candi Dasa (two hours 10 minutes). There are also regular bus connections from Gianyar.

Several companies run tourist shuttle buses linking Padangbai, Candi Dasa, Tirtagangga and Tulemben with Ubud, Kuta, Sanur (and Nusa Lembongan by boat), Kintamani, Lovina, Bedugul and Air Sanih; as well as Mataram, Bangsal, the Gili Islands, Kuta Lombok and Tetebatu on Lombok. One of the best is **Perama**, with offices in all the above places; allow three hours to get to Denpasar airport from Candi Dasa.

Note All times are approximate and can vary enormously depending on traffic conditions from Denpasar, particularly on the main road from Semarapura to Denpasar.

By boat From Padangbai there is a 24-hour ferry service (leaving every two hours) to Lembar port on Lombok (four to five hours). There is also a fast ferry service direct from Padangbai to the Gili Islands off Lombok.

Getting around

While you can reach most of these villages by public bemo, it is better to hire a car. There are many scenic backroads that climb up into the hills, offering spectacular views when the weather is fine. Be warned that some of these minor roads are in dreadful condition with numerous huge potholes. The road leading up from Perasi through Timbrah and Bungaya to Bebandem is especially scenic and potholed. A much better road with outstanding views leads west from Amlapura to Rendang. From Rendang you can continue on up to Pura Besakih.

Semarapura and around → For listings, see pages 151-161. Phone code: 0366.

The **Puri Semarapura** was the symbolic heart of the kingdom of Semarapura. All that remains of this palace on Jalan Untung Surapati are the gardens and two buildings; the rest was destroyed in 1908 by the Dutch during their advance on the capital and the ensuing *puputan*. The **Kherta Ghosa** (Hall of Justice), built in the 18th century by Ida Dewa Agung Jambe, was formerly the supreme court of the Kingdom of Semarapura. It is famous for its ceiling murals painted in traditional, *wayang* style, with illustrations of heaven (towards the top) and hell (on the lower panels). As a court, the paintings represent the punishment that awaits a criminal in the afterlife. The murals have been repainted several times this century. Miguel Covarrubias describes the nature of traditional justice in Bali in the following terms:

"A trial must be conducted with the greatest dignity and restraint. There are rules for the language employed, the behaviour of the participants, and the payment of trial expenses ... On the appointed day the plaintiff and the defendant must appear properly dressed, with their witnesses and their cases and declarations carefully written down ... When the case has been thoroughly stated, the witnesses have testified and the evidence has been produced, the judges study the statements and go into deliberation among themselves until they reach a decision. Besides the witnesses and the material evidence, special attention is paid to the physical reaction of the participants during the trial, such as nervousness, change of colour in the face, or hard breathing."

The Kherta Ghosa was transformed into a Western court by the Dutch in 1908, when they added the carved seats, as they found sitting on mats too uncomfortable. It is said – although the story sounds rather dubious – that one of the Rajahs of Semarapura used the Kherta Ghosa as a watch tower. He would look over the town and when his eyes alighted on a particularly attractive woman going to the temple to make offerings, he would order his guards to fetch her and add the unsuspecting maid to his collection of wives.

Adjoining the Kherta Ghosa is the **Bale Kambangg** (Floating Pavilion), originally built in the 18th century, but extensively restored since then. Like the Kherta Ghosa, the ceiling is painted with murals; these date from 1942.

Further along the same road, just past a school, is the attractive **Taman Gili** ① *6000Rp*, also built in the 18th century. This consists of a series of open courtyards with finely carved stonework, in the centre of which is a floating pavilion surrounded by a lotus-filled moat.

To the east of the main crossroads in the centre of town – behind the shop fronts – is a bustling **market**, held here every three days and considered by many to be the best market on Bali, and also a large monument commemorating the *puputan*.

Kamasan village

Four kilometres southeast of Semarapura is an important arts centre where artists still practise the classical *wayang*-style of painting. Most of the artist families live in the Banjar Sangging area of town. Artists from this village painted the original ceiling in the Kerta Gosa in Semarapura in the 18th century, as well as the recent restoration, using the muted natural colours (reds, blacks, blues, greens and ochres) typical of this school.

Goa Lawah

① *Take a bemo heading for Padangbai or Candi Dasa.*

Goa Lawah, (Bat Cave), is one of the state temples of Semarapura, with tunnels that are reputed to lead as far as Pura Besakih. The temple is overrun by bats and their smells.

Kusamba

Boats leave for **Nusa Penida** and **Nusa Lembongan** from the fishing village of Kusamba, 8 km southeast from Semarapura. On the beach are huts and shallow troughs used in salt production. The fishing fleet consists of hundreds of brightly painted outrigger craft with triangular sails, which operate in the Lombok Strait (similar to the *lis-alis* of Madura). They are fast and manoeuvrable, and can make way in even the lightest breezes.

Tirtagangga

① *6000Rp adult.*

Seven kilometres northwest of Semarapura is the site of the royal bathing pools of Tirtagangga. The pools are set on a beautiful position on the side of a hill, overlooking terraced rice fields. The complex is composed of various pools (some of which can be swum in; enquire at the entrance gate) fed by mountain springs, with water spouting from fountains and animals carved from stone. It is popular with locals as well as foreign visitors, and is a peaceful spot to relax during the week, although those seeking tranquillity are advised not to visit at weekends when the place is overrun with domestic tourists. There are a couple of places to stay, and a few restaurants.

Amed → *Phone code: 0363.*

For peace and quiet, this area on the east coast, north of Tirtagangga, has much to offer. The drive from Culik via Amed to **Lipah Beach** is quite spectacular, especially on the return journey, with Gunung Agung forming a magnificent backdrop to the coastal scenery. Numerous coves and headlands, with colourful fishing boats, complete the vista and offer endless possibilities for walks and picnics. The area became popular because of the good snorkelling and diving available here, the reef is just 10 m from the beach with some good coral and a variety of fish. Amed is developing slowly with new guesthouses, hotels, restaurants and dive centres opening every year, some with spectacular hillside locations and stunning views of Gunung Agung. At present much of the accommodation lies beyond Amed on the stretch from Jemeluk to Bunutan.

The area called Amed is in fact a 15-km stretch from Culik to Selang village, encompassing the villages of **Amed**, **Cemeluk** (also spelt Jemeluk), **Bunutan** and **Selang**. At present the first accommodation you come to is 5.7 km from Culik. If you go during the dry season you can watch the local men making salt; they also work year round as fishermen, setting off at 0500 and returning about 1000, and then going out again at 1500. It is possible to go out with them. As there is no irrigation system, farming is mainly done in the wet season when the men raise crops of peanuts, corn, pumpkin and beans, on the steeply sloping hillside inland from the road, to sell in the market at Amlapura. In dry spells, all the water needed for the crops is carried by the women up the steep slope, three times a day; a back-breaking chore. Most of the land is communally owned by the local Banjar.

Padangbai → *For listings, see pages 151-161. Phone code: 0363.*

Padangbai has a beautiful setting, overlooking a crescent-shaped bay with golden sand beach, colourful *jukung* (fishing boats) and surrounded by verdant hills. This is the port for ferries to Lombok and boats to Nusa Penida, and is a hive of excitement when ferries arrive and depart. It is one of the best deep-water harbours in Bali. There are beaches on either side of the town. Walking south from the pier and bus station, follow the road until you come to a tatty sign on the left indicating the rough, steep path that leads up and over the hill to **Pantai Cecil** (400 m). This is a beautiful, white-sand beach, the perfect setting for a quiet swim or evening stroll. There are two beachside *warungs*. Unfortunately, the once-verdant hills behind the beach have been consumed by a development of luxury villas. The beach maintains its beauty, but the ambience is nowhere near as relaxed as it was. The walk over the headland has good views of the town and hills beyond.

Padangbai to Candi Dasa

For many people Bali is at its best and most rewarding away from the tourist centres. Along the road leading from Padangbai to Candi Dasa there are several hotels and bungalow-style accommodation, which offer peace and quiet in secluded settings with beautiful sea views. Breakfast is included in the price except at the luxury hotels.

Manggis and Balina Beach Balina Beach lies midway between Padangbai and Candi Dasa (approximately 4 km from the latter) adjacent to the village of Buitan, which runs this tourist development as a cooperative for the benefit of the villagers. It is a slightly scruffy black-sand beach with a definite tourist feel to it. **Sengkidu** village and beach 2 km further east have more charm. Sometimes there are strong currents.

The village of **Buitan** has a public telephone, several small *warungs* and shops; the road to the beach and the accommodation is signposted. Perhaps the highlight of this village is the large advertisement promoting the advantages of artificial insemination in pig breeding. The village of **Manggis**, inland and to the west of Buitan, is known locally for its associations with black magic; it is said to be the haunt of *leyaks*, witches with supernatural powers. There is a road from here leading up to **Putung**, 6 km away, with spectacular views over the Lombok Strait.

Candi Dasa is smaller, more intimate and offers better value for money than the main resorts of Bali. It is also an excellent base from which to explore the sights of East Bali.

The gold- and black-sand beach has been badly eroded and beach lovers will be disappointed. However, the government is pouring in money to create a new man-made beach at the western end of the development to try and regain some of the area's undoubted lost glory.

Candi Dasa gets its name from the **temple** on the hill overlooking the main road and the freshwater lagoon; the ancient relics in this temple indicate that there has been a village on this site since the 11th century.

Traditionally fishermen in these parts have gone out fishing each day from 0400 until 0800, and again from about 1430 until 1800. Although most people on Bali fear the sea as a place of evil spirits and a potential source of disaster, those who live near the sea and earn their living from it consider it a holy place and worship such sea gods as Baruna. The boats they use, *jukung*, are made from locally grown wood and bamboo, which is cut according to traditional practice. The day chosen for cutting down the tree must be deemed favourable by the gods to whom prayers and offerings are then made, and a sapling is planted to replace it. Carved from a single tree trunk without using nails and with bamboo outriders to give it stability, the finished boat will be gaily coloured with the characteristic large eyes that enable it to see where the fish lurk. The design has not changed for thousands of years; it is very stable due to the low centre of gravity created by the way the sail is fastened. These days there are fewer fish to catch and many fishermen take tourists out snorkelling. *Jukungs* cost about US$40 to hire for a couple of hours.

In the rice field by the road to Tenganan are two ingenious **bird-scaring devices**, operated by a man sitting in a thatched hut. One is a metre-long bamboo pole with plastic bags and strips of bamboo; when the man pulls on the attached rope, the pole swings round, causing the bamboo strips to make a clacking noise and the plastic bags to flutter. The other consists of two 4-m-long bamboo poles that are hinged at one end, with flags and plastic bags attached; when the attached rope is pulled, the two poles swing round with flags and plastic bags waving.

Tenganan

ⓘ *Admission to the village is by donation, vehicles prohibited. It is possible to walk the 3 km from Candi Dasa; take the road heading north, 1 km to the west of Candi Dasa – it ends at the village. Alternatively, walk or catch a bemo heading west towards Semarapura, get off at the turning 1 km west of Candi Dasa and catch an ojek up to the village. Tours to Tenganan are also arranged by the bigger hotels and the tour agents on the main road. Bemos run past the turn-off for the village from Denpasar's Batubulan terminal.*

This village is reputed to be the oldest on Bali, and is a village of the Bali Aga, the island's original inhabitants before the Hindu invasion almost 1000 years ago. The walled community consists of a number of longhouses, rice barns, shrines, pavilions and a large village meeting hall, all arranged in accordance with traditional beliefs. Membership of the village is exclusive and until recently visitors were actively discouraged. The inhabitants have to have been born here and marry within the village; anyone who violates the rules is banished to a neighbouring community. Despite the studied maintenance of a traditional way of life, the inhabitants of Tenganan have decided to embrace the tourist industry. It is in fact a very wealthy village, deriving income not only from tourism but also from a large area of communally owned and worked rice paddies and dryland fields.

Tenganan is one of the last villages to produce the unusual **double ikat** or *geringsing*, where both the warp and the weft are tie-dyed, and great skill is needed to align and then weave the two into the desired pattern. The cloth is woven on body-tension (back-strap) looms with a continuous warp; colours used are dark rust, brown and purple, although newer pieces suffer from fading due to the use of inferior dyes. Motifs are floral and geometric, and designs are constrained to about 20 traditional forms. It is said that one piece of cloth takes about five years to complete and only six families still understand the process. **Note** Much of the cloth for sale in the village does not originate from Tenganan.

About 13 km southwest of Candi Dasa is the temple and cave of **Goa Lawah**, see page 147.

Around Candi Dasa

The town and palace of **Amlapura** is within easy reach of Candi Dasa. Three small islands with coral reefs are to be found 30 minutes by boat from Candi Dasa. They make a good day trip for snorkelling or diving. Samuh village cooperative keeps goats on the largest of these islands, called **Nusa Kambing (Goat Island)** ① *most hotels and losmen will arrange a boat for the day*. Every six months the goats are transported back to the mainland by boat. Quite a sight if you are lucky enough to witness it.

Sengkidu village → *Phone code: 0366.*

West of Candi Dasa (2 km) is an authentic Balinese village as yet unravaged by tourism. The pretty backstreets lead down to the sea and beach. Surrounded by coconut groves and tropical trees, Sengkidu offers an attractive alternative to Candi Dasa. The village itself has a number of shops, fruit stalls and a temple where festivals are celebrated; foreigners are welcome to participate if they observe temple etiquette and wear the appropriate dress, otherwise they can watch.

Lovina → *For listings, see pages 151-161. Phone code: 0362.*

Lovina, an 8-km stretch of grey sand, is the name given to an area that begins 7 km west of Singaraja and includes six villages. From east to west they are **Pemaron**, **Tukad Mungga**, **Anturan**, **Kalibukbuk**, **Kaliasem** and **Temukus**, all merging into each other. Lovina is one of the larger beach resorts on Bali and caters to all ages and price groups, from backpackers to package tour-oriented clientele. Kalibukbuk is the heart of Lovina, the busiest, most developed part, with the greatest number of tourist facilities and nightlife. Lying 1 km to the east of Kalibukbuk, **Banyualit** has a number of peaceful hotels scattered along the shoreline. There are also a couple of hotels slightly inland here, some of which are fair value.

Recent times have been hard on Lovina, with tourist arrivals a mere trickle of what they were a few years ago. Local residents blame the bomb attacks in Bali for the low numbers, and many lament the tough competition they face in gaining customers. For visitors, the upside of this situation is the great deals that can be had at empty hotels. Lovina has a relaxed pace of life and the inhabitants are friendly and welcoming. It's a great place to linger and make a local friend or two.

The beach

The beach itself is quite narrow in places and the grey/black sand is not the prettiest, but the waters are calm, so swimming is very safe and there is reasonable snorkelling on the reef just offshore. The beach is interspersed with streams running into the sea, where some villagers wash in the evening. Several areas are the preserve of local fishermen whose dogs can be menacing if you are out for a walk, particularly in the evening. Hawkers are not as bad as they used to be but can still be a nuisance, and it seems as if the entire resort is on commission for the much-touted dolphin trips.

The most popular outing is an early morning boat trip to see the **dolphins** cavorting off the coast; there are two schools of dolphin that regularly swim there. In the Kalibukbuk area the fishermen run a cooperative that fixes the number of people in each boat and the price, currently 75,000Rp; snorkelling is not included in the price. If you book through your hotel you will pay more for the convenience, but the price may include refreshments and the opportunity to go snorkelling afterwards. Boats set off at about 0600 and the tour usually lasts 1½ hours. Bear in mind that there is no shade on the boats. People have mixed reactions to the experience. If yours is the first boat to reach the dolphin area then you may be rewarded with 12 dolphins leaping and playing, but as other boats arrive the dolphins may be chased away. It is worth bearing in mind that around Lombok, and further east, dolphins can often be seen leaping out of the water alongside ferries and boats.

Around Lovina
About 5 km to the west of Lovina there are waterfalls at the village of **Labuhan Haji**, and a Buddhist monastery near the village of **Banjar Tegeha**, nearby which there are **hot springs** ① *6000Rp adult, drivers will offer to take tourists there and back again for 150,000Rp, but this can easily be bargained down to 50,000Rp.* The cleanliness of some of the pools is dubious. Make sure you bathe in one that has a fast flow of water running into it. To the south there are cool highland areas with **lakes** and **botanical gardens** in the area surrounding Bedugul and Gunung Batur; it can be very wet here except at the height of the dry season. To the east is **Singaraja**, the capital of the district, and beyond Singaraja there are interesting temples and other cultural sites, and the *gamelan* village of **Sawan**.

East Bali, Karangasem and the north coast listings

For hotel and restaurant price codes and other relevant information, see pages 9-12.

🛏 Where to stay

Tirtagangga *p147*
$$$$ Tirta Ayu, in the grounds of the water garden, T0363 22503, www.hoteltirta gangga.com. 4 comfortable a/c cottages with bathroom featuring sunken bath and shower with water spouting from a demonic head. Free access to the bathing pools in the water garden.
$ Dhangin Taman Inn, T0363 22059. With a garden overlooking the water gardens, this place has whacky bright tiling and psychedelic ponds. Cleanish rooms, fair value.

Amed *p147*
All accommodation is along the coastal road, and spread out over 11 km. The greatest concentration of places is from Jemeluk to Bunutan. Price codes reflect low season. Many places double their rates in high season; always negotiate as prices quoted are far too high. Most places have a restaurant but quality varies wildly.
$$$$ Apa Kabar Villas, T0363 23492, www.apakabarvillas.com. Beautifully decorated cottages with spacious bathrooms containing fish pond and bath, rooms here can accommodate up to 4 people. The hotel is next to the beach and has a pool, full spa service and a top-notch restaurant. Discounts available.
$$$ Anda Amed, T0363 23498, www.andaamedresort.com. This hotel injects a bit of glamour to Amed's lodging choices with contemporary design, a sleek pool and a Moorish terrace area. Online discounts.
$$$ Puri Wisata Resort and Spa, T0363 23523, www.diveamed.com. Right down on

the beach, the a/c rooms here are big, some with private terrace looking out on the sea. Some rooms are located in a block at the back and have no view at all. There is a pool, dive centre (see What to do, page 158) and full spa service.

$$$ Santai, T0363 23487, www.santaibali. com. The 10 thatched a/c cottages, with enough space to sleep 4, are tastefully decorated and have a verdant outdoor bathroom. The hotel has a pool, and is right on the beach. You can rent (expensive) bikes here.

$$$-$$ Waeni's, T0363 23515, www. baliwaenis.com. Perched high on a headland, these cottages have stunning views of the sea and the surrounding hills; Gunung Agung can be seen clearly in the mornings, wrapped in cloud. The rooms are comfortable and have a great outdoors lounging area with bed and hammock. Service is friendly and the restaurant serves some great Balinese food. Recommended.

$$ Prema Liong, T0363 23486, www.bali-amed.com. The low-season prices for the 4 thatched cottages here are good value. Cottages are set in a lush garden on the hillside, and the sea can just about be seen through the foliage. They have spacious verandas with plenty of lounging potential. Average restaurant. Recommended.

$$ Wawa Wewe 2, T0363 23506, www. bali-wawawewe.com/en. On the beach, with a pool. Wide selection of rooms, including a well-furnished family room with space for 4 with sea view. Occasional performances of local dances and *gamelan* music. Book exchange. Restaurant serving excellent local and Western cuisine and play area.

Padangbai *p148*

The most attractive rooms are in town but the best location is to the north along the bay, where rooms and bungalows are surrounded by gardens and coconut groves and are quieter. You won't find the luxury of Ubud or Seminyak here, but there is a lot of simple, good-value accommodation.

$$$$-$$$ Bloo Lagoon, Jln Silayukti, T0363 41211, www.bloolagoon.com. Built on eco/green principles, this top-end joint is connected to the rest of town by a small paved road and offers gorgeous views from its cottages of the harbour or north towards Candidasa. Rooms are mostly fan cooled and a/c is chargeable in some rooms. Delicious daily breakfast and decent lap pool to work off any excess calories.

$$ Mustika Sari Hotel, Jln Silayukti, T0363 21540. www.mustikasaribeach.com. The hotel is set in pleasant gardens and has a pool and massage service. Rooms are large, clean and have a/c, TV, and bathroom with a bath. Sizeable discounts available.

$$ Puri Rai, Jln Silayuktil 7, T0363 41385, www.puriraihotel.com. The 30 a/c and fan rooms here are spacious, and clean with TV and fridge. Pool. Good value in this price range.

$ Billabong, Jln Silayukti, T0363 41399. The free breakfasts are good, and the simple rattan-walled bungalows are acceptable, but not as good value as the standard bungalows, some of which have a sea view.

$ Pondok Serangan Inn, 2 Jln Silayukti, T0363 41425. Friendly and quiet place with spacious fan and a/c rooms with hot water. The communal veranda on the 2nd floor has great view over the rooftops of the town and the boats in the bay. Recommended.

$ Pondok Wisata Parta, Jln Silayukti, Gang Tongkol 7, T0363 41475. Next door to the Dharma, the rooms are of a similar standard, although the locks on the doors and windows could do with being replaced. You can just about see the sea through a gap in the buildings in front.

$ Topi Inn, Jln Silayukti 99, T0363 41424, www.topiinn.nl. The 5 rooms here are average and quite dark, and with the smaller ones, guests have to use a communal bathroom. Nevertheless there is a great common veranda with a hammock and cushions scattered around, and sea views, making this the most social place to stay in Padangbai. Breakfast is not included in the price. The larger rooms with attached bathroom are often full, so it might be worth reserving in advance.

Padangbai to Candi Dasa *p148*
$$$$ Alila Manggis, Buitan, T0363 41011, www.alilahotels.com/manggis. Luxury hotel with 54 stylish rooms looking out onto a delightful coconut grove, and the ocean beyond. The hotel employs stunning use of lighting, which creates a soothing effect in the evenings. Cooking and diving courses offered. Pool. Good discounts available for online booking.
$$$$ Amankila, outside Candi Dasa near the village of Manggis, T0363 41333, www.amanresorts.com. One of the renowned **Aman** group of hotels, in an outstanding location spread out over the hillside with stunning sea views. Designed with simple elegance to create a calming and peaceful milieu. With only 35 guest pavilions and 3 vast swimming pools on different levels of the hill, it is easy to imagine you are the only guest in residence.
$$$ Matahari Beach Bungalows, Buitan, Manggis, postal address: PO Box 287, Denpasar 80001, T0363 41008/41009. Signposted from the main road, follow a steep path down the hill for about 50 m. Beautiful secluded setting in a large coconut grove beside the sea, with a beach suitable for swimming though occasionally there is a current. 11 fairly attractive bungalows and rooms, very clean, some large family rooms, several of the cheapest rooms have a shared ceiling so your neighbours will probably hear your every movement. Ketut, the owner, speaks good English and is very helpful and knowledgeable about Bali.
$$ Ampel Bungalows, Manggis Beach, 6 km from Candi Dasa, just off the main road, T0363 41209. A peaceful, rural setting overlooking rice paddies and the sea. 4 simple, very clean bungalows, with private *mandi*, signposted from the main road shortly after the **Amankila Hotel**.

Candi Dasa *p149*
There are plenty of accommodation choices in Candi Dasa (almost too many), although as the number of tourists has fallen, the upkeep of many of the places seems to have declined. Still, there are some good bargains to be had, and some stunning sea views. Most of the accommodation is on the seaward side of Jln Raya Candi Dasa. At the eastern end of Candi Dasa, where the main road bends to the left, a small road (Jln Banjar Samuh) leads off on the right, lined with accommodation on the seaward side. Known as **Samuh village**, this slightly rural area is perhaps the most attractive place to stay. Most places include breakfast in their rates. Most hotels with swimming pools allow non-residents to use their pools for a small charge.
$$$$ Villa Sassoon, Jln Puri Bagus, T0363 41511, www.villasasoon.com. Perfect for those seeking a little romance, the spacious, private villa compounds have 2 en suite cottages and a further cottage with living room and kitchen area. The buildings face a central pool and outdoor lounging area. It's all very sleek and modern. Good discounts available for stays of more than 7 days.
$$$$-$$$ The Watergarden, Jln Raya Candi Dasa, T0363 41540, www.watergardenhotel.com. The beautiful, lush tropical gardens are filled with a variety of water features, and the private cottages have koi-filled lily ponds around the veranda. Rooms are spacious, spotless and quiet. There are good mountain views between the abundant foliage. This place is popular with foreign couples seeking a Balinese-style wedding. Pool, bar. Recommended. Discounts available.
$$$ Alam Asmara, Jln Raya Candi Dasa, T0363 41929, www.alamasmara.com. Small fish-filled streams line the pathways in this new resort that offers elegant cottages with high ceilings and outdoor bathroom. Bedrooms have a safe and TV (no international channels). There is a resident Dive Master and a variety of diving

courses are offered. Pool, access to the sea and full spa service. Discounts available.

$$$-$$ The Grand Natia Bungalows, Jln Raya Candi Dasa, T0363 42007, www.indo.com/hotels/grand_natia. A path lined on both sides with koi-filled streams surrounds the 12 a/c cottages. The more expensive cottages have sea views from outside, but not from the bedrooms themselves. Cottages are tastefully decorated, and have a fridge. Pool.

$$$-$ Puri Oka, Jln Puri Bagus, T0363 41092. Large selection of rooms, some of which are vastly better value than the others. Cheap fan rooms are clean but have no hot water. Some of the a/c rooms need to be redecorated, but others, such as the sea-view rooms, feature TV, DVD player, outdoor bathroom and are tastefully decorated. The star is the spacious suite on the 2nd floor with plenty of light and a private terrace overlooking the sea. Pool.

$$ Dasa Wana, Jln Raya Candi Dasa, T0363 41444. Variety of bungalows, with living room, kitchen and bathroom with bath. Some bungalows are much better furnished than others, so ask to see a selection. This place is not on the seaward side of the main road, but has great views of the mountains behind. Pool.

$$ Geringsering, Jln Raya Candi Dasa, T0363 41084. The 4 a/c rooms here are huge, 2 of which have lovely sea views and are filled with the sound of the surf. Room have mosquito nets. Tax not included in the price.

$$ Ida's Homestay, Jln Raya Candi Dasa, T0363 41096, jsidas@aol.com. An anomaly in Candi Dasa's accommodation choice in that it is set in a spacious palm grove, with the cottages being a minor feature of the property. Ida Ayu Srihati, the owner, has an extensive collection of Indonesian antiques that can be found littering the grounds; there's even an entire rice barn from Madura transplanted here. The gardens lead down to a small beach and a decking area overlooking the sea. There are 5 simple fan cottages, which are often full. Things

are kept rustic, with a cow wandering the grove, chickens running free and hot water provided on demand rather than on tap. Book in advance. Recommended.

$$-$ Iguana Bungalows, Jln Raya Candi Dasa, T0363 41973, iguana_cafe_bali@yahoo. com. The dense tropical garden contains a/c and fan bungalows that are clean, but look slightly worn, particularly the bathrooms. Some rooms have great sea views. Pool.

$$-$ Seaside Cottages, Jln Raya Candi Dasa, T0363 41629, www.balibeachfront-cottages.com. Set in pleasant tropical gardens leading down to the sea, with a good selection of bungalows. The small fan rooms have a single bed, but are clean and have attached bathroom. The larger bungalows have a/c and some have wonderful sea views. Tax and breakfast are not included in the price. Massage and salon services available.

$ Agung Bungalows, Jln Raya Candi Dasa, T0363 41535. Cheap, clean fan-only rattan-walled bungalows, some have excellent sea views (ask for the rooms at the front of the property). There's an enticing strip of beach here. Recommended.

Sengkidu village p150

$$$ Candi Beach Cottage, reservations: PO Box 3308, Denpasar 80033, T0363 41234, www.candibeachbali.com. Luxury hotel set in large, scenic tropical gardens, in a quiet location beside sea with access to beach, offering everything you would expect from a hotel in this class, popular with tour groups.

$$ Dwi Utama, T0363 41053. Offers 6 very clean rooms, with fan, private bathroom, beachside restaurant (cheap), access to good, small beach, well-tended, small garden, peaceful, good value.

$$ Nusa Indah Bungalows, Sengkidu, signposted and reached via a separate track to the left of the temple. Set in a peaceful location beside the sea, amid coconut groves and rice paddies, 7 clean, simple bungalows with fan, access to small, rocky beach, beachside restaurant (**$**).

$$ Pondok Bananas (Pisang), T0363 41065. Family-run, 4 spotless rooms. Bungalows set in a large coconut grove beside the sea with access to beach, very peaceful and secluded.

$$ Puri Amarta (Amarta Beach Bungalows), T0363 41230. 10 bungalows set in large, attractive gardens beside the sea and beach, well run and very popular, liable to be full even off season, restaurant (**$**) beside sea.

Lovina *p150*

Mosquitoes can be a problem, not all bungalows provide nets. The central area of Kalibukbuk has the greatest concentration of accommodation, the widest choice of restaurants and nightlife, and most of the tourist facilities; however, it is becoming built up. Some of the side roads to the east in the Anturan area offer more attractive and peaceful surroundings.

Kalibukbuk

$$-$ Bayu Kartika Beach Resort, Jln Ketapang, T0362 41055, www.bayukartika resort.com. Lots of space in this 2-ha resort and featuring (so the owner claims) the largest pool in Lovina. Many rooms face the sea, but are a little faded. The more expensive rooms have an open-air bathroom. Interestingly, there is a monitor lizard pond. Popular.

$$-$ Nirwana Seaside Cottages, Jln Bina Ria, T0362 41288, www.nirwanaseaside.com. Set in huge, pleasant gardens, this hotel has a range of a/c and fan rooms, some with sea view. The clean de luxe rooms, feature bath and a pleasant veranda, but the 2-storey bungalows with fan represent better value and come with a sea view. Pool.

$$-$ Puri Bali Cottages, Jln Ketapang, T0362 41485, www.puribalilovina.com. Selection of a/c and fan rooms in a garden. Rooms are large and have hot water, but are a little decrepit. Cheaper ones come with a mosquito net. Pool and basketball area for those who fancy shooting some hoops under the tropical sun.

$$-$ Rini, Jln Ketapang, T0362 41386, www.rinihotel.homepage.dk. In a large compound with a saltwater swimming pool, this hotel has an excellent selection of well-designed a/c and fan rooms, some of which are cavernous, with equally large balconies. The largest rooms are the upstairs fan rooms in the 2-storey buildings and have nice sunset views. Friendly staff. Recommended.

$$-$ Villa Jaya, Jln Ketapang, T0362 700 1238. 100 m down a path off Jln Ketapang. New hotel with cosy fan and a/c rooms. Pool and views of the surrounding rice fields.

Banyualit

This area is much quieter, but offers the usual range of facilities, including internet cafés, cheap restaurants and provision stores.

$$$ Banyualit Spa and Resort, Jln Banyualit, T0362 41789, www.banyualit. com. Range of rooms set in a lush garden. A/c rooms are clean and have TV, but are a little cramped and dark. The fan rooms, with rattan walls are very simple and hugely overpriced. Full spa service with a host of friendly staff. Pool.

$$-$ Suma, Jln Banyualit, T0362 41566, www.sumahotel.com. The staff are very welcoming at this hotel with clean and comfortable a/c and fan rooms. Pool and spa.

$ Ray Beach Inn, Jln Banyualit, T0362 41088. Cheap, clean fan rooms and spa service.

Beachfront

$$$$-$$$ Sunari (formerly Sol Lovina), Jln Raya Lovina, T0362 41775, www.sunari. com. A full range of facilities is available in this hotel including spa and gym. Rooms are spacious and the more expensive have private garden and a plunge pool. Business doesn't seem too brisk here. 50% discounts available.

$$$ Aneka, Jln Raya Lovina, T0362 41121, www.aneka-lovina.com. This popular resort has 59 a/c rooms that are clean, well decorated and comfortable. The resort has a pool near the beach, fitness centre and offers Balinese dance lessons. Discounts available.

Tirtagangga *p147*
There are a few choices, mainly around the water garden.

$$ Tirta Ayu, (see Where to stay) is the best restaurant here, with sublime views and serving fair international cuisine.

$ Gangga Café, T0363 22041. Open 0700-2200. Cheap eatery near the entrance to the gardens, serves delicious home-made yoghurt, curries and Balinese food.

Amed *p147*
Many people choose to eat in the restaurants attached to their hotel. However, there are a handful of eateries along the road.

$$ Pazzo, T0828 368 5498. Open 1000-2300. Pasta, pizza and the usual Western fare alongside a fair selection of Indonesian dishes. **Pazzo** doubles as a popular bar with a choice of wines and cocktails, live music, pool and Balinese dancing.

$$ Wawa Wewe 1, 400 m down the road (away from Amed) from the hotel of the same name, T0363 23506. Open 0800-2200. This friendly restaurant has a good selection of international food and Balinese cuisine.

$ Ari's Warung, T0852 3788 2015, open 0900-2100, and **Café C'est Bon**, T0852 3482 66778, open 0900-2200. Both these small places look a little forlorn with a distinct lack of custom. This is a shame as they are both good places to try the catch of the day with tasty Balinese sauces. Both have sea views, and **Ari's Warung** offers free transport to and from the restaurant.

Padangbai *p148*
When you're a limp stone's throw to the sea, the seafood is going to be good, as is the case in Padangbai. It is quite common to see women walking around with large freshly caught yellow fin tuna thrown over their shoulder. Many of the hotels have restaurants, and there are numerous restaurants along the shoreline serving up the usual Indonesian and Western dishes.

There are a lot of cheap *warungs* around the port and on Jln Pelabuhan Padangbai.

$$ Topi Inn (see Where to stay). Open 0730-2300. The best place to eat in Padangbai, with an extensive menu of fresh seafood, vegetarian dishes, great salads and delights such as a delicious cheese platter with olives. The staff are friendly and the restaurant is deservedly popular. You can refill your used water bottle here with fresh drinking water for 1000Rp.

$ Café Papa John, Jln Segara. Open 0700-2200. Good spot to watch the world go by and see boats pulling in to the bay. The delicious fish kebabs are served in a tangy spicy sauce.

$ Depot Segara, Jln Segara, T0363 41443. Open 0800-2200. Friendly staff and an acoustic guitar propped up the in the corner point to good times at this relaxed eatery offering a range of Balinese food and fresh seafood. The fish *sate* is super and freshly made each morning. There is also the usual range of sandwiches, burgers and good chilled lassis.

Candi Dasa *p149*
There are a variety of well-priced restaurants dotted along the main road with similar menus; seafood is the best bet. Most restaurants cater to perceived European tastes, which can be disappointing for anyone who likes Indonesian food. Many of the hotels have restaurants, often with sea views. The following are also recommended though quality and ingredients can vary enormously from day to day; you might have a delicious meal one day, order the exact same dish the next day and be disappointed.

$$ Candi Dasa Café, Jln Raya Candi Dasa, T0363 41107. Open 0800-2300. Clean and comfortable restaurant, Balinese fare and *rijstafel*. Delicious icy ginger ale.

$$ Ganesha, Jln Raya Candi Dasa, T0813 3811 2898. Good-value set meals, plenty of fresh seafood, and suckling pig at this friendly good-value eatery, which has *legong* and mask dance performances nightly at 1930.

$$ Kubu Bali, Jln Raya Candi Dasa, T0363 41532. Specializes in seafood with fish, lobster and crab dishes cooked a variety of ways. Some standard international dishes.

$$ Toke, Jln Raya Candi Dasa, T0363 41991. Open 1100-2300. Known for its Indian cuisine, this is the place in Candi Dasa to get good mushroom *masala*, *naan* and *aloo gobi*. There's an extensive list of cocktails, and an excellent range of Western food. The kitchen here is open, so diners can watch their dinner being prepared.

$$ The Watergarden, Jln Raya Candi Dasa, T0363 41540. Open 0700-2300. Excellent array of fresh seafood, including delicious *ikan pepes* and grilled *mahi mahi* glazed with soy sauce, available in this peaceful setting of lily ponds and fountains. Also international favourites and plenty of salads, as well as Dom Pérignon champagne for those in the mood to really push the boat out. Good service. Recommended.

$ Raja's, Jln Raya Candi Dasa, T0363 42034. Open 0800-2200. This well-established roadside restaurant with pool table and an extensive selection of DVDs, has a good menu of set meals, including an Indian menu offering Goan curries and an interesting pork and banana curry. Happy hour 1700-1900.

$ Srijati, Jln Raya Candi Dasa. Open 0700-2100. Rustic and cheap venue to grab a lunch of *nasi goreng* or *opor ayam*. Also a fair number of authentic Balinese dishes.

Lovina *p150*

Lovina offers a great chance to tuck into some good, fresh seafood with excellent Balinese sauces, although there are plenty of places serving reasonable Western fare. There is also a line of *kaki-lima* and small *warungs* selling cheap *bakso*, *nasi goreng*, *roti bakar* and some Balinese street food on Jln Raya Lovina, near the traffic lights at the end of Jln Ketupang. It opens when the sun sets.

$$ Bali Apik, Jln Bina Ria, T0362 41050. Open 0800-2300. Slow staff, but a good range of vegetarian dishes and a good seafood menu that includes tasty tuna fish *sate*.

$$ Barcelona, Jln Ketupang, T0362 41894. Open 0900-2300. Popular family-run place, one of the better places to try Balinese food in Lovina. The *pepes babi guling* (grilled pork cooked in a banana leaf) and *sate pelecing* (fish *sate* with Balinese sauce) are excellent.

$$ Jasmine Kitchen, Jln Bina Ria, T0362 41565, jasminekitchen@beeb.net. Open 1130-2230. The cheery owner serves up good Thai favourites such as tom yum soup, steamed fish in a lime, lemongrass and coriander dressing and some delicious home-made cakes to the sound of the sitar in a relaxed setting. The specials are worth investigating.

$$ Kakatua, Jln Bina Ria, T0362 41144. Open 0800-2300. The water features make this restaurant a mellow place, serving Burmese fishballs, home-made cakes and baked fish.

$ Bakery Lovina, Jln Raya Lovina, T0362 42225. Open 0730-2130. This mini-market selling a range of cheeses, meats, wines and tinned Western food for the local expat community also makes excellent sandwiches, fresh bread and cakes.

$ Khi Khi, Jln Raya Lovina, T0362 41548. Open 1000-2200. Excellent-value seafood sets that allow a choice of fish, Balinese *bumbu* (dressing) a Chinese-style sauce, and a large bowl of rice. The restaurant is simple and unfussy and has an open kitchen.

$ Spunky's, on the beach near the **Aneka Hotel**, T0813 373 6509. Open 1300-2400. Owned by an Englishman, this is the place for homesick British tourists to get a long overdue helping of ham or sausage and egg. Also daily seafood specials. An unbeatable location – select one of the many cocktails on offer and watch the sun go down.

⊙ Bars and clubs

Padangbai *p148*

Babylon Bar and Kinky Reggae Bar on Jln Silyakuti open in the afternoon and serve booze until late.

Zen Inn, Jln Segara, T0819 3309 2012.
Open 0700-2300. Serves pies with mash
and gravy, and rocks until almost 2400
with live music and a video screen in a
comfortable and friendly pub-like setting.

Lovina *p150*

Many of the places on Jln Bina Ria offer
all-day happy hour in an attempt to lure
customers, but don't expect sophisticated
nightlife. Head to ZiGiZ Bar on Jln Bina Ria
for live acoustic music, cocktails and cable
TV showing live sporting events.

ⓔ Entertainment

Candi Dasa *p149*

Balinese dance performances are staged
nightly at various restaurants in town,
though are nowhere near Ubud quality.

Ⓞ Shopping

Semarapura and around *p146*

Textiles Although good examples are
hard to find, Semarapura is the centre
of the production of royal *songket* cloth,
traditionally silk but today more often
synthetic. The cloth is worn for ceremonial
occasions and characteristically features
floral designs, geometric patterns, *wayang*
figures and animals. It takes 2 months to
weave a good piece.

Padangbai *p148*

Books Wayan's Bookstore, Jln Penataran
Agung, T0819 1615 3587. Open 0800-1800.
On the way up to Pantai Cecil, down a small
lane on the right-hand side. Huge sign on
the roof in red letters. Has the best selection
of second-hand books in Padangbai. Also
offers rental and exchange services.

Candi Dasa *p149*

Books The best place is the Candi
Dasa Bookstore, which has a reasonable
selection of books on Bali and Indonesia as
well as second-hand books, magazines and

newspapers. The lady who runs it speaks
excellent English.

Crafts Geringsing, Jln Raya Candi Dasa,
T0363 41084, open 0900-1800, sells double
ikat cloth from Tenganan and other Balinese
arts and crafts. **Lenia**, Jln Raya Candi Dasa
T0363 41759, open 1000-2000, a good place
to see *ata* baskets, which are made from a
locally grown vine much more durable than
rattan. Water resistant, it is claimed these
baskets can last for up to 100 years. There
is also a small selection of Sumba blankets
and other quality crafts. **Nusantara**, Jln Raya
Candi Dasa, open 0900-2100, is also a good
place to pick up locally made handicrafts.

Groceries Asri, fixed-price store for film,
food and medicine.

Tailor The lady who runs the Candi Dasa
Bookstore is also a tailor.

ⓞ What to do

Amed *p147*
Body and soul

A Spa, T0813 3823 8846, open 1000-1900.
Lots on offer, including an Indonesian
massage, US$18 for 1 hr, and a 90-min
calming back treatment, US$26. Roaming
masseuses pop into hotels throughout the
day clutching comments from satisfied
customers looking for business. Bargain hard.

Diving and snorkelling

The reef in Amed is very close to the
beach, and the resorts are not far from
the *USAT Liberty* wreck at Tulamben.
Snorkelling gear can be hired from
hotels or stalls along the road for
between 30,000Rp and 40,000Rp per day.
ECO Dive Bali, T0363 23482, www.ecodive
bali.com. Offers dives at Tulamben (US$95
for 2 dives), and in locations in Amed.
Also runs a variety of courses including
the Open Water course for US$375.

Puri Wirata Dive Centre, T0363 23523. Slightly cheaper; for dives at Tulamben, at the nearby Japanese wreck. Open Water course also offered.

Padangbai *p148*
Diving and snorkelling
Diving is a popular activity in Padangbai, with numerous operators along Jln Silayukti. Dives can be taken in waters around Padangbai, at nearby **Gili Biaha** with its shark cave, and further afield at the wreck of the *USAT Liberty Bell* at Tulamben. Marine life that can be seen includes the giant tuna, napoleon wrasse, sea turtles and sharks. You can pick up a snorkel set along the seafront for 30,000Rp (though you'll have to bargain) and find reasonable snorkelling at the **Blue Lagoon Beach** over the headland at the east end of the town.
Geko Dive, Jln Silayukti, T0363 41516, www.gekodive.com. This professional company offers PADI Open Water courses for US$400, Rescue Diver for US$350. Also runs a Discover Scuba session for diving novices in their pool for US$75.
OK Divers, Jln Silayukti, T0363 41790, www.divingbali.cz. A popular Czech outfit that offers 2 dives for US$70, the PADI Open Water course for US$470, and Rescue Diver for US$470.

Workshops
Topi Inn (see Where to stay) has workshops on a wide variety of topics including Balinese woodcarving, coconut tree climbing, batik and *ikat* weaving. You can also join discussions on Balinese Hinduism.

Candi Dasa *p149*
Diving and snorkelling
Boat hire and snorkelling trips to Nusa Lembongan (US$40) can be organized through **Beli Made Tam**, T0818 551752, on the beach near the Puri Bali Hotel. He also offers snorkelling trips to White Sand Beach (3 hrs including equipment US$35). You can rent snorkelling equipment from him for 30,000Rp for 2 hrs.

Sub Ocean Bali, Jln Raya Candi Dasa, T0363 41411, www.suboceanbali.com. 5-star PADI dive centre offering trips to Nusa Penida, Tulamben and Gili Mimpang. They also rent snorkelling equipment

Lovina *p150*
Boats and fishing
Tours are organized by the larger hotels, tour and dive companies and *losmen* for 75,000Rp an hr per person. The wonderfully named **Captain Ketut Bonanza** (T0813 3822 1175) has excellent English and can regale customers with tales of tiger sharks and sea snakes.

Body and soul
Araminth Spa, Jln Ketapang, T0362 41901. Open 0900-1900. Variety of treatments available including facials (US$9.20), ayurvedic massage (US$25) and Indonesian treatments such *as mandi lulur* and *mandi rempah* (spice bath).
Bali Samadhi Spa, Jln Ketapang, T08133 855 8260, www.bali samadhi.com. Open 0900-1800. Similar to Araminth Spa.

Cooking
Putu's Home Cooking, T08122 856 3705. Includes a trip to the local market and instruction in cooking 7 Balinese dishes followed by a local feast. Lesson lasts 4-5 hrs, US$20 per person.

Diving and snorkelling
Average snorkelling just off the beach. Snorkel hire 20,000Rp for 1 hr or 100,000Rp an hr with a boat and captain; better marine life at Menjangan Island (with **Spice Dive**, below). Equipment available from boat owners and dive shops, not all of equal quality.
Spice Dive, Jln Bina Ria, T0362 41305, www.balispicedive.com. The waters around Lovina are not particularly special for diving, so this highly regarded dive centre offers a variety of diving courses and trips to nearby diving locations such as Pulau Menjangan and Tulamben as well as Zen Beach for

muck diving. Introduction dives cost US$60, and a PADI Open Water course costs US$350. Rescue Diver, Dive Master and many other courses are also offered.

Swimming and watersports
Most big hotels will let non-residents use the pool for between 10,000Rp and 20,000Rp if you look presentable.
Spunky's, on the beach in Banyualit (see Restaurants). Rents jet skis for US$70 per hr, surf bikes for US$10 per hr, canoes for US$5 per hr, and catamarans for US$20 per hr.

Trekking
Trekking in the area around Sambangan village can be organized through **Putu Puspa**, T0815 5857 7404 and includes walks through rice fields, and waterfalls and visits to meditation caves for US$15 (short trek) to US$30 for a longer trek.

⊖ Transport

Semarapura and around p146
Bemo
Connections with **Denpasar**'s Batubulan terminal and points east – **Besakih**, **Amlapura**, **Candi Dasa**.

Boat
Kusamba, from where there are boats to **Nusa Penida**.

Tirtagangga p147
Bemos
Connect Tirtagangga with **Semarapura** and **Singaraja** (for connections with Lovina).

Shuttles
2 daily to/from **Padangbai**, US$12.50.

Amed p147
Bemo
From **Semarapura** catch a bemo heading north to **Culik** (22,000Rp) and **Singaraja**. Change bemos at Culik; until 1200 there are a limited number of bright red bemos

running along the coast east to **Amed** and **Lipah**, after 1200 you can catch an ojek or try and hitch a lift, otherwise it is a long walk.

Car
45 mins from **Candi Dasa**.

Padangbai p148
Bemo
Padangbai is 2.5 km off the main coastal road; connections with **Denpasar**'s Batubulan terminal, **Candi Dasa** and **Amlapura**. Blue bemos run to **Semarapura**, 18,000Rp, and orange bemos run to **Amlapura**, 18,000Rp.

Boat
Ferries for Lembar on **Lombok** leave around the clock daily, every 1½ hrs, and take 4-5 hrs depending on the seas, 35,000Rp adult, 22,000Rp child, adult plus motorbike 92,000Rp (includes 1 or 2 passengers). The busiest departure is 0800, which is fine if one of the 2 large fairly modern ferries is doing that sailing; otherwise try to get on as early as possible to secure a decent seat. To the **Gili Islands**, the fastest way is using Gili Cat (Padangbai agent: Jln Silayukti, T0363 41441, www.gilicat.com). Their boats leave Padangbai daily at 1130 and sail to **Gili Trawangan** in 1½ hrs, US$66 one-way, US$120 for a return. Equally direct, but taking longer is the **Perama** boat, which leaves Padangbai at 1330 and arrives on Gili Trawangan 4 hrs later, US$30. Aggressive porters at the ferry terminal can be a real pain. They try and grab your luggage, carry it on board and then charge an outrageous amount. If you need help to carry your belongings, negotiate a fair price beforehand. 10000Rp per piece should cover it.

Bus
From the bus station you can catch long-distance buses, west to **Java** and east to **Sumbawa** and **Lombok**.

Shuttles
Perama office: Jln Pelabuhan Padangbai, T0363 41419. Daily connections to **Kuta** and **Ngurah Rai Airport**, 3 daily, US$6, **Ubud**, 3 daily, US$5, **Candi Dasa**, 3 daily, US$2.50 (sometimes the Perama shuttle to Candi Dasa does not run due to lack of customers and it will be necessary to jump on the orange bemo to Amlapura, 18,000Rp or hire a bemo, US$6). To **Lovina**, 1 daily (via Ubud), US$15, **Senggigi**, 2 daily, US$10 and **Mataram**, 2 daily, US$10.

Candi Dasa *p149*
Bemo
Regular connections with **Denpasar**'s Batubulan terminal (2 hrs 10 mins), **Amlapura** and **Semarapura**.

Bicycle hire
From **Srijati** (see Restaurants) for 20,000Rp a day.

Car/motorbike hire
From hotels, *losmen* and from shops along the main road.

Shuttles
Can be found at the western end of Jln Raya Candi Dasa, T0363 41114. To **Kuta** and **Ngurah Rai Airport**, 3 daily, US$6. **Ubud**, 3 daily, US$5. **Lovina**, 1 daily, US$15 via Ubud. **Padangbai**, 3 daily, US$2.50. Also to **Amed**, 2 daily, US$12.50, 2 people minimum. It's just as easy to hire an ojek for the ride costing around US$10, including a stop in **Tirtagangga** (30 mins). If you want to go to Lombok, they will shuttle you first to the office in Padangbai.

Lovina *p150*
Bus
From **Denpasar**'s Ubung terminal, catch an express bus to **Singaraja**, 1½-2 hrs, from where there are regular buses to Lovina. There are also regular buses and minibuses from **Gilimanuk**, taking the north coast route, 1½ hrs (buses from Java will drop passengers off at Gilimanuk to catch a connection to Lovina – sometimes included in the cost of the ferry and bus ticket). Buses to Gilimanuk for the ferry to Java cost US$3. To **Java** jump on a Singaraja–Java bus as it passes along Jln Raya Lovina. Tickets need to be booked a day in advance and can be bought in several places in Kalibukbuk. To **Jakarta**, US$35, to **Yogyakarta**, US$27, **Surabaya**, US$14, and **Probolinggo** (for Gunung Bromo) is US$13.

Car/motorbike/bicycle hire
From several places around town for US$11/US$4/US$2 per day.

Shuttles
Perama shuttles to **Kuta**, 1 daily, US$10. To **Ubud**, 1 daily, US$10. To **Padangbai**, 1 daily, US$15. To **Candi Dasa**, 1 daily, US$15. Look around town for other shuttle bus prices, as Lovina is the one place **Perama** doesn't seem to have the monopoly; on arrival in Lovina, **Perama** takes passengers to their office in Anturan for a lunch of *nasi goreng*, while touts hover around offering accommodation. After beating off the touts, you get back on the **Perama** bus and are taken to your hotel.

ℹ Directory

Padangbai *p148*
Banks Money changers along Jln Segara and Jln Silayukti. **Immigration** Jln Penataran Agung. **Police** Jln Pelabuhan Padangbai, T0363 41388.

Candi Dasa *p149*
Banks There are plenty of money changers along Jln Raya Candi Dasa, although rates are variable.

Lovina *p150*
Banks On the main road. There is a BCA ATM on Jln Raya Lovina. **Medical services** Pharmacy, Jln Raya.

Lombok to East Nusa Tenggara

Lombok has been earmarked for tourist development for decades, on the pretext that it is in a position to emulate Bali's success. Whether the development plans will ever come to fruition is another matter and for the time being it remains a relatively quiet alternative to Bali, although considerably busier and more developed than the islands to the east. The number of visitors to Lombok is generally dependent on the numbers visiting Bali, and since the bombs, tourism in Lombok has very much taken a beating. While there are a number of first-class hotels along the beaches away from these tourist areas, Lombok is still 'traditional' and foreigners are a comparative novelty. It is also a poor island; the famines of the Dutch period and the 1960s remain very much in the collective consciousness.

Most visitors to Lombok stay on Senggigi Beach, on the west coast and just north of the capital Mataram, or on the Gilis, a small group of islands north of Senggigi. However, the south coast, around Kuta, with its beautiful sandy bays set between rocky outcrops, is more dramatic, and significantly less developed. There is a reasonable surfaced road to Kuta and some good accommodation once you get there, including one international-class hotel (but be aware that plans are afoot to continue this tourist development). There are also a handful of towns inland with accommodation. While Lombok has gradually expanded over the years, with the exception of the Gili Islands, it has not yet exploded onto the tourist scene – which, of course, is why some people prefer it to Bali.

Arriving in Lombok

Getting there

Carriers flying to Lombok include **SilkAir** (T0370 633987, www.silkair.com), flying from Singapore four times weekly, and **Merpati** (T0370 621111), flying from Kuala Lumpur, Malaysia. **Garuda** and **Malaysian Airlines** also codeshare a route from Kuala Lumpur, via Jakarta. Internal carriers linking the Indonesian islands include **Lion Air** (T0370 663444, www.lionair.co.id), **Garuda** (T0370 646846, www.garuda-indonesia.com), **Merpati** and **Batavia Air** (T0370 648998, www.batavia-air.co.id).

Airport information Lombok's new international airport ① **Tanak Awu, Kabupaten Lombok Tengah**, Bandara Internasional Lombok, was opened in late 2011, to replace the smaller Selaparang Mataram Airport. The new airport is in central southern Lombok, 40 km south of Mataram near the small city of Praya. There are DAMRI scheduled bus services to Mataram and Senggigi. It is possible to pick up a VOA (visa on arrival) at the airport. There is a money changer, information office and hotel booking counters. There are metered taxis from the airport to various destinations, bemos and a public bus to Mataram and Senggigi. International departure tax is 100,000Rp. Domestic tax is 30,000Rp.

Getting around

Lombok's main artery is the excellent road running east from Mataram to Labuhan Lombok and good paved roads to Lembar, Praya, Kuta and to Bangsal in the north. Most of Lombok's roads are paved, but the secondary roads are not well maintained and car travel can be slow and uncomfortable, plus there are hazards of potholes and random rocks.

Bemos and colts are the main forms of transport and a good cheap way to get around the island and, unlike Bali, frequent changes of bemo are not necessary to get from A to B.

Perama ① *Jln Pejanggik 66, Mataram, T0370 635928*, operates shuttle buses from Bali to Lombok, offers tours and transport within Lombok, and provides onwards transport to Flores via Komodo.

Cidomos are a two-wheeled horse-drawn cart. In the west, cidomos are steadily being replaced by motorbikes and bemos, but in the less developed central and east they remain the main mode of local transport and are more elaborate, with brightly coloured carts and ponies decked out with pompoms and bells.

West coast Lombok

Senggigi Beach stretches over 8 km from Batulayar to Mangsit. The road from Mataram to Bangsal winds through impressive tropical forest in the foothills of Mount Rinjani. Travelling further north along the coast from Mangsit, the road reaches Bangsal, the 'port' for boats to the Gilis. Senggigi is the most developed tourist area on Lombok, with a range of hotels. The beaches here – and they extend over several kilometres – are picturesque and the backdrop of mountains and fabulous sunsets adds to the ambience.

The Gili Islands are becoming increasingly expensive and are no longer primarily geared to backpackers. There are no vehicles and there really isn't much more to do beyond sunbathing, swimming, snorkelling, walking, drinking and generally relaxing.

Senggigi lies 12 km north of Mataram on the west coast. The beach overlooks the famous Lombok Strait, which the English naturalist Alfred Russel Wallace postulated divided the Asian and Australasian zoological realms. The sacred Mount Agung on Bali can usually be seen shimmering in the distance. While Senggigi village supports the main concentration of shops, bars, restaurants and tour companies, hotels and bungalows stretch along the coast and the road for several kilometres, from **Batulayar Beach** in the south, to **Batubolong**, **Senggigi** and **Mangsit** beaches to the north. Mangsit is quieter and less developed.

Many visitors express disappointment with Senggigi Beach itself, which is rather tatty and not very attractive. The town's downfall as a destination has been meteoric. It never reached the status of Bali's main resorts and instead plunged dramatically in the wake of the Bali bombings: pavements are overgrown, rubbish lies strewn about, businesses are shutting at an alarming rate and hotels lie derelict. The increasingly easy connections with the Gili islands from Bali mean that fewer and fewer tourists ever make it to the mainland. Senggigi has many hotels catering largely for the package tour trade, and they are not always particularly well managed or maintained. Their rates are highly negotiable off season. Many of the best guesthouses on Lombok are Balinese owned, and as prices on Bali rise inexorably, they no longer seem as overpriced as they once did.

Further north, this area becomes more beautiful and peaceful, with unspoilt, windswept beaches and lovely views across the Lombok Strait to Mount Agung on Bali and superb sunsets. They are currently free of the hawkers that so mar a visit to Senggigi itself.

Places in Senggigi

About 2 km south of Senggigi, on a headland, is the **Batubolong Temple**. Unremarkable artistically (particularly when compared with the temples of Bali), it is named after a rock with a hole in it (*Batu Bolong* or 'Hollow Rock') found here. Tourists come to watch the sun set over Bali; devotees come to watch it set over the sacred Mount Agung.

Each evening an informal **beach market** sets up on the beach in front of the **Senggigi Beach Hotel**; vendors lay out their wares: textiles, T-shirts, woodcarvings and 'antiques'. Heavy bargaining is required – these people really know how to sell.

Tours: Lombok to Flores via Komodo by boat

Indonesian life is inextricably linked with the vast amount of water that surrounds the myriad islands, and it is definitely worth spending some time on a boat while you're in the country. There are a couple of companies that offer boat trips from Lombok to **Labuanbajo** (Flores) via **Komodo Island**. The tours usually sail across the top of Sumbawa, stopping at Pulau Satonda for some snorkelling before continuing to Komodo and finally the port of Labuanbajo (Flores). Most trips last three days and two nights, and it is undoubtedly one of the most convenient ways of seeing the Komodo dragon. For many, is the highlight of a trip to Indonesia. It is wonderful to fall asleep on deck to the sound of the sea and wake up with the sunrise, gliding past desolate islands and distant coastlines. However, these boats can get packed with tourists, and as the old adage goes, a boat gets smaller each day you spend on it. The seas in this area can be highly unpredictable, and sailing in a seaworthy vessel in crucial. It makes sense to research the trip you wish to undertake thoroughly, and if the boat is going to be packed with other tourists, will the trip be enjoyable? **Perama** offers three-day/two-night trips starting at US$200 for a place on the deck, and US$260 for a cabin room. All meals are provided, though don't expect too much. (The first meal on board is usually quite lavish, but they go quickly downhill from there – stock up on crackers and snacks.) The trip to Labuanbajo departs every six days. The return trip from Labuanbajo takes lasts two days and one night and sails via **Rinca**, another place to see Komodo dragons, and costs US$130 for deck and US$180 for a cabin. There are plenty of good snorkelling stops on the tour. Both trips can be combined for a five-day/four-night epic, where both Komodo and Rinca are visited costing US$300 for deck class and US$400 for a cabin.

Bangsal → For listings, see pages 165-168. Phone code: 0370.

The coast road north from Senggigi is slow, steeply switchbacking over headlands and past some attractive beaches and a colony of monkeys. There is some surf on this part of the coast, mainly reef breaks, surfed by the locals on wooden boards.

Bangsal is just off the main road from Pemenang, and is little more than a tiny fishing village. However, as it is also the departure point for the Gilis, there are a couple of restaurants here that double up as tourist information centres, a ferry booking office, a money changer and a diving company. Vehicles stop around 300 m short of the harbour, and it is necessary to walk or charter a cidomo (7000Rp) to the ticket office. The harbour area is a tatty little place, full of scam artists who will surround travellers and try numerous tricks to extract money. These guys are a real headache. Ignore them, and head to the ticket office to buy your ticket to the island of your choice. Boats leave when they are full, and there is an announcement telling passengers when their boat is ready to depart. Boats to Gili Trawangan fill up the quickest, followed by boats to Gili Air, which has a large local population. Boats to Gili Meno can take some time to fill up. The fare to Gili Trawangan is 10000Rp, Gili Meno 9000Rp and Gili Air 8000Rp. Those that don't want to wait around can charter a boat at for around 185,000Rp to Gili Tranwangan, 165,000Rp to Gili Meno and 145,000Rp to Gili Air.

West coast Lombok listings

For hotel and restaurant price codes and other relevant information, see pages 9-12.

⊜ Where to stay

Senggigi *p164*
All the hotels and guesthouses are easily accessible by bemo from Mataram. The better hotels have generators for when the mains power fails, which it does quite often. Many of the cheaper hotels in Senggigi are poorly maintained, but the hotels in Batu Balong, 1 km from the centre are well-managed and popular and have access to a decent stretch of beach.
$$$$ Senggigi Beach Hotel, Jln Pantai Senggigi, T0370 693210, www.senggigi beach.aerowisata.com. Set in 12 ha of gardens, with tennis courts, spa, a huge chess board, and numerous bars and

restaurants. Rooms are in comfortable a/c cottages with cable TV. The more expensive bungalows have a sea view.
$$$ Mascot Beach Resort, Jln Raya Senggigi, T0370 693365, mascot@telkom. net. Large selection of cottages in a large beachfront garden. More expensive ones have sea view. Rooms are simple and clean, and the more money you spend, the more space you get (and a bath thrown in). Discounts available. Recommended.
$$$ Sunset Cottages, Jln Raya Senggigi, T0370 692020, www.sunsethouse-lombok. com. 4 spacious rooms set in a block in a large garden, this place has effusive staff and access to the beach for splendid sunset views over the strait to Bali. Rooms are large and spotless, with cable TV and a veranda with sea view. Recommended.

$$$ Windy Beach Cottages, Mangsit, T0370 693191, www.windybeach.com. 14 attractive traditional-style thatched bungalows with fan and newly renovated private bathroom with shower/bath. Set in large gardens with an infinity pool amidst a coconut grove beside the sea, restaurant (**$**) offering good Indonesian, Chinese and Western food and a bar perfect for sunset drinks. Well managed. Recommended.

$$ Batu Bolong Cottages, Jln Raya Senggigi, T0370 693198. Well-managed hotel with a wide selection of cottages that straddle the busy road. Cheaper fan rooms have TV and are spacious and comfortable with a veranda facing the attractive garden. Somewhat tatty bathrooms. More expensive rooms have a/c and are closer to the beach.

$$ The Beach Club, Jln Raya Senggigi, T0370 693637, www.thebeachclublombok. com. Well-furnished a/c rooms with semi-open bathroom and veranda overlooking the beach. Cheaper backpacker rooms available, with communal area with TV and DVD player. Pool, popular bar, happy hour 1700-1900. One of Senggigi's better choices in this range. Recommended.

$$ Café Wayan, Jln Raya Senggigi, T0370 693098, www.alamindahbali.com. This Balinese-owned place has 4 spacious rooms with bathroom with bath. The ambience is laid-back and friendly.

❼ Restaurants

Senggigi p164
There are not many independent restaurants on Senggigi – most eating places are attached to hotels. Independent restaurants are struggling. Many places offer free transport.

$$ Café Alberto, Jln Raya Senggigi, T0370 693039. Open 0900-2400. Good Italian food served on the seafront. Pizzas, pastas and seafood dishes dominate the menu. The cocktail list is extensive, and the view makes this an ideal spot for a

sunset drink. They have a van that cruises the streets in the evening offering to drive people to the restaurant.

$$ Café Bumbu, Jln Raya Senggigi, T0370 692236. Open 0900-2300. Friendly. Offers fine Thai curries and salads, and has a great selection of Asian food, with some excellent deserts. Recommended.

$$ Square, Senggigi Square Blk B-10, T0370 693688, www.squarelombok.com. Open 1100-2400. Senggigi's concession to sophisticated dining, **Square** bills itself as a lounge restaurant, and has a decent wine list, good seafood and plenty of steaks to get your teeth into. They have a monthly cellar party – for US$30 you can drink as much wine and eat as many tapas dishes as you can handle.

$$ Ye Jeon Korean Restaurant, Senggigi Plaza, T0370 693059. Open 0930-2100. This Korean-owned eatery serves authentic Korean favourites such as *bibimbap* and *bulgogi*. The set meals are good value and filling.

$ Café Wayang, on the main road in Senggigi, T0370 693098. A branch of the one in Ubud, Bali, this building has character (complete with a family of mice in the rafters), but slow service.

$ Gelateria, Senggigi Plaza A1-04. Open 1000-1900. Perfect for a cheap lunch, offering lots of good Indonesian staples, including *bakso*, *nasi goreng*, and *mie goreng*. Also serves good coffee and home-made gelato to the strains of modern Indonesian rock music.

❼ Entertainment

Senggigi p164
If you really want to party, it would be better to wait until you get to the hedonist pleasures of Gili Trawangan, however, there are a couple of options in Senggigi.
Papaya Café, Jln Raya Senggigi, T0370 693616. Open1000-0100. Live music, serves pizza and steak and icy beer.

There are a few late-night options on Senggigi Square including **Gosip Discotique**

(T0819 1734 1437, until 0400), which features 'super sexy dancers live', and the nearby **Club 69** (T0370 692211, 1300-0400), with private karaoke rooms and a disco.

O Shopping

Senggigi *p164*
Senggigi Jaya, on the main road. Has everything from food to T-shirts, film and gifts at reasonable prices. There are a few boutique/craft shops that are less prone to haggling than the old-school vendors.

O What to do

Senggigi *p164*
Cycling
Lombok Biking Tour, Jln Raya Senggigi, T0370 692164, www.lombokbiking.com. Open 0830-1930. Seeing the countryside of Lombok on 2 wheels is highly recommended, and this outfit has a selection of half-day trips to Lengsar, Pusuk Pass, and southern Lombok, as well as a surprise ride of the day. Costs vary between US$13-35 depending on length.

Diving and snorkelling
Dream Divers, Jln Raya Senggigi, T0370 692047, www.dreamdivers.com. Dive trips to the Gilis and Nusa Penida and Tulamben in Bali, as well as trips to the waters of southern Lombok where hammerhead sharks can be seen. Each dive costs US$38. Also offers daily snorkelling trips to the Gilis with their dive boats for US$20.

Tour operators
Bidy Tour, Jln Raya Senggigi, T0370 693521. Full-day fishing trips. International and domestic flight ticketing.
Perama, Jln Raya Senggigi, T0370 693007.

Trekking
Perama, Jln Raya Senggigi, T0370 693007. All-inclusive treks to Rinjani's summit, leaving from Senggigi at 0500. Treks cost between

US$250 and US$300 depending on the number of nights. Minimum of 2 people.
Rinjani Trekking Club, Jln Raya Senggigi, T0370 693202, www.anaklombok.com. Senggigi is a good place to plan your ascent of Gunung Rinjani, and this place offers a variety of trips. Their 2-day trip to the summit costs US$200, the same as their 3-day trip. All costs include guide service, accommodation, transfers and food. Recommended.

⊖ Transport

Senggigi *p164*
Bemo
Bemos wait on Jln Salah Singkar in Ampenan to pick up fares for Senggigi Beach and north to **Mangsit**. Regular bemos link **Ampenan** with **Mataram**, **Cakranegara** and the main **Cakra** bemo terminal between 0600 and 1800, 5000Rp. From one end of Senggigi to the other costs 1500Rp. **Perama** has an office here (see Tour operators) and runs a bus service geared to travellers. Shuttles include **Kuta Lombok** for US$12.50, **Padangbai**, 1 daily, US$30, **Kuta** and **Nguarah Rai Airport**, 1 daily, US$35, and **Ubud**, 1 daily, US$35.

Boat
Dream Divers (see What to do) are the Senggigi agent for **Gili Cat**, which has a fast ferry (1½ hrs) to **Padangbai** for US$69.

Car hire and motorbike hire
Cars cost US$15 per day; motorbikes US$5.

Taxi
Blue Bird Taxi (also known here as Lombok Taksi) T0370 627000.

Bangsal *p165*
Bemo
Regular connections from **Mataram** or the Bertais terminal in **Cakranegara**; take a bemo heading for Tanjung or Bayan. Bemos stop at the junction at Pemenang, take a dokar

the last 1 km to the coast. From Pelabuhan Lombok there are no direct bemos; either charter one (US$15) or catch a bemo to the Bertais terminal in Cakranegara and then another travelling to Bayan/Tanjung. From the port of Lembar, it is easiest to club together and charter a bemo to Bangsal.

Bus
Perama Tour has regular connections with **Lembar**, as well as all-in bus/ferry tickets to most destinationss in **Bali** (**Kuta**, **Sanur**, **Ubud**, **Lovina** and **Candi Dasa**).

❶ Directory

Senggigi *p164*
Banks Senggigi Beach Hotel has a bank on site with exchange facilities for non-residents. Money changer at the Pacific Supermarket. ATMs can be found along Jln Raya Senggigi. **Medical services** Klinik Risa, Jln Pejanggik 115, Cakranegara, T0370 625560. 24 hrs emergency room, full hospital facilities. **Police** Tourist police: Jln Raya Senggigi, T0370 632733.

Gili Islands

The three tropical island idylls that make up the Gili Islands lie off Lombok's northwest coast, 20-45 minutes by boat from Bangsal. They are now a well-established fixture on the southeast Asian trail. Known as the 'Gilis' or the 'Gili Islands' by many travellers, this only means 'the Islands' in Sasak. Most locals have accepted this Western corruption of their language and will understand where you want to go. Be extra careful swimming here as there are very strong currents between the islands.

Arriving in the Gili Islands → *Phone code: 0370.*

With the development of Bali into an international tourist resort, many backpackers have moved east and the Gilis are the most popular of the various alternatives. This is already straining the islands' limited sewerage and water infrastructures, and a walk into the interior of Gili Trawangan will reveal large amounts of rubbish strewn about. During the peak months between June and August, Gili Trawangan becomes particularly crowded and it is advisable to book accommodation in advance.

The attraction of the Gilis resides in their golden sand beaches and the best snorkelling and diving off Lombok – for the amateur the experience is breathtaking. However, the coral does not compare with locations such as Flores and Alor: large sections are dead or damaged (because of dynamite fishing and the effects of El Nino, which raised the temperature of the water). Gili Meno and Gili Air are very quiet, and there is little to do except sunbathe, snorkel, swim, or dive. Gili Trawangan has the same attractions, but has also developed a reputation for its raucous nightlife, the most vibrant in Lombok, and it is the most popular of the islands, particularly with backpackers.

There is no police presence on any of the islands. In the event of anything untoward happening, contact the island's *kepala desa* – the village head (guesthouses or any of the dive centres should be able to point you in the right direction).

Getting there
Regular boats from Bangsal (see page 165) to the Gilis wait until about 20 people have congregated for the trip to the islands. Boats can also be chartered for the journey, 45 minutes to Gili Trawangan, 30 minutes to Gili Meno, 20 minutes to Gili Air. In the morning

there is rarely a long wait, but in the afternoon people have had to wait several hours. An alternative is to buy a combined bus-and-boat ticket with one of the shuttle bus companies.

Several dive centres around town have boats going directly from Teluk Nare to the Gilis. Enquire around town. This avoids the port of Bangsal. Enquire at the **Perama** office in Senggigi. There are various alternatives. It's also possible to charter a boat from Senggigi for around US$30. Within Lombok there are services from Mataram to the Gilis and from Senggigi to the Gilis. (From Senggigi, some of the dive centres operate boats throughout the day.) One of the more popular ways to get to the Gilis from Bali is the **Perama** ferry from Padangbai, which takes four hours and calls in at all three islands. This costs US$30 and departs at 1330. The cheapest way is to take the slow ferry to Lembar, a shuttle bus to Bangsal and then a public boat to the Gili of your choice. This takes seven to eight hours, and the ferry departs at 0900, and costs US$15 – enquire at tourist offices in Padangbai. **Gili Cat** (www.gilicat.com) has a fast service from Gili Trawangan to Padangbai (Jalan Silayukti, T0363 41441, 1½ hours, US$69) departing at 1130. **Bluewater Express** (www.bwsbali.com) runs fast ferries from Serangan Harbour in southern Bali. **Scoot Cruises** (www.scootcruise.com) runs a similar service from Sanur via Nusa Lembongan. Check their websites for latest schedule and prices.

Getting around

The islands are small enough to walk around. Even Gili Trawangan, the largest of the three, is little more than 2 km from end to end. Gili Air and Gili Trawangan are great for cycling with good tracks. Cidomo are the main form of transport used by locals for carrying goods; some offer round-island trips costing around 50,000Rp, although costs are very negotiable. There is a shuttle service between the islands, with tickets that can be bought at the ticket office at the harbour of each island Boats leave Gili Meno for Gili Trawangan at 0815 and 1520, from Gili Meno to Gili Air at 0950 and 1620. From Gili Air to Gili Meno at 0830 and 1500 and from Gili Air to Gili Trawangan at 0830 and 1500. There are departures from Gili Trawangan to Gili Meno at 0930 and 1600 and to Gili Air at 0930 and 1600. Fares for shorter hops (neighbouring islands) start at 18,000Rp, from Gili Air to Gili Trawangan, the most expensive trip, the fare is 25,000Rp.

Gili Trawangan → *For listings, see pages 172-178.*

The largest of the three islands – and the furthest west from Bangsal – is Gili Trawangan (Dragon Island). It is the most interesting island because of its hill in the centre; there are several trails to the summit and excellent views over to Mount Rinjani on Lombok from the top. In the opposite direction, you can watch the sun set over Mount Agung on Bali.

There is a coastal path around the island, which takes about 2½ hours to walk. Originally a penal colony, it now supports the greatest number of tourist bungalows. These are mostly concentrated along its east coast, as are a number of restaurants (serving good seafood) and bars. For lone travellers seeking company, this is the best island. But Gili Trawangan is in danger of ruining itself (like so many other tropical island idylls in the region). Indeed, for some it already has. The most developed area is brash, loud and over-developed, but the island is large enough to offer peace and tranquillity as well. Gili Air and Gili Meno are quieter.

The most luxurious accommodation is found in the developed southeast area of the island behind the restaurants; locals already refer to it being like Kuta, although this is an exaggeration. Here you can find well-equipped air-conditioned bungalows with cable TV and personal chefs; unfortunately you lose the peace and beauty associated with a small, relatively undeveloped island, as the accommodation is hidden behind the noisy restaurants away from the beach. To find a quiet tropical paradise, visitors have to accept more basic facilities at the outer edges of the developed areas, particularly the north and northeastern strip of coast, which remains accessible. Here guests can hear the waves lapping against the shore and the birds singing, watch stuning sunrises and sunsets from their verandas and believe they are in paradise. Room rates triple at some of the more upmarket places in the high season. Even off-peak rooms can become scarce, so it is worth arriving on the island early. The cheapest accommodation can be found away from the beach, along the lanes in the village. Gili Trawangan offers the best choice of restaurants of the three Gilis, and many people consider that it has the best snorkelling. Snorkelling is good off the east shore, particularly at the point where the shelf drops away near **Horizontal** and at the north end of the beach.

Gili Islands

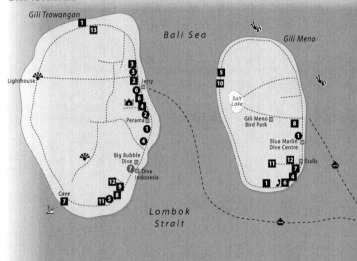

N

500 metres

500 yards

Inland from the tourist strip is the original village where life goes on almost as usual, a world apart from the tourists and therefore interesting to stroll through. Further inland there are scattered farms among the coconut groves that dominate the interior, and some pleasant walks to be had.

Safety Given the conservative nature of Lombok, women should abstain from topless sunbathing. There have been plenty of reports of women being hassled by local men, and it is not wise to set off on long walks alone in the dark. Also, single women should keep an eye on their drinks in bars, to make sure nothing is slipped in. It is unlikely that this would happen, but not unheard of.

Gili Meno → *For listings, see pages 172-178.*

Gili Meno (Snake Island), between Trawangan and Air, is the smallest of the islands, and also the quietest and least developed. The local residents are very friendly, and after half a day on the island most will know your name and where you stay. The disadvantage of staying on Gili Meno is that the hawker to tourist ratio is very high, so expect plenty of visits from trinket sellers (often the same ones repeatedly).

The snorkelling off Gili Meno – especially off the northeast coast – is considered by some to be better than Trawangan, with growths of rare blue coral. There is a path running round the island; a walk of one to 1½ hours. The salt lake in the northeast of the island provides a breeding ground for mosquitoes. Accommodation on Gili Meno tends to be more expensive than on the other two islands. Some of the guesthouse owners live on Lombok, and these bungalows are run by lads who are poorly paid and consequently have little motivation. However, the views from the many bungalows that face the sea are beautiful, especially towards the east and Mount Rinjani.

Gili Meno Bird Park

ⓘ *T0361 287727, www.balipvbgroup.com, 0800-1700, 50,000Rp adult, 25,000Rp child, follow the signposted path near the harbour through the middle of the island, it's a 10-min walk.*

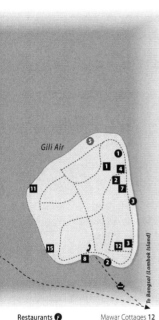

Gili Air

Restaurants ⑦
Rust Warung **1**

Gili Air
Where to stay ▭
Abdi Fantastik **4**
Coconut Cottages &
 Frangipani Restaurant **2**
Gili Air Santay &
 Restaurant **7**
Gili Indah **8**
Lucky's **15**
Matahari **11**
Mawar Cottages **12**
Sejuk Cottages **1**
Sunrise Cottages **3**

Restaurants ⑦
Blue Marlin
 & Dive Centre **1**
Go Go Cafe **2**
Green Café **3**

Bars & clubs ①
Space Bar **5**

To Bangsal (Lombok Island)

The 2500-sq-m aviary contains over 300 species of birds, and offers interactive feeding times and guided tours. There are also komodo dragons, kangaroos and plenty of turtles. This makes for a nice break from the monotony of beaches for kids, and the **Cavern Bar**, filled with Beatles memorabilia, is a good spot for mums and dads to take a break.

Gili Air → *For listings, see pages 172-178.*

Gili Air (Turtle Island) is the easternmost island, lying closest to Bangsal. It has the largest local population, with a village of around 400 families in the centre of the island. The island takes about an hour to walk around. As the local population is Muslim, visitors should avoid topless sunbathing. Despite the number of bungalows, it remains a peaceful place to stay. Snorkelling is quite good off the island. When leaving your accommodation take sensible precautions and make sure you lock both the door to the bathroom and the front door. As most bathrooms have no roofs, a favoured way for thieves to gain entry is over the bathroom wall and into your room via the bathroom door.

Gili Islands listings

For hotel and restaurant price codes and other relevant information, see pages 9-12.

⊖ Where to stay

In the past few years, many foreigners have invested in the Gilis, resulting in a wide range of accommodation options. Many bungalows are being upgraded. Of the more basic ones there is often little difference – they tend to charge the same rates, and the huts are similar in design and size, attractively built out of local materials, in a local style, mostly raised on stilts. Mosquitoes can be a problem at certain times of year and mosquito nets are routinely provided. The most luxurious bungalows fall into our **$$$$** category. Friendliness and the cleanliness of the *mandis* tends to be the deciding factor at the basic bungalows. The higher the price, the more likely tax and service charge will be extra, and the less likely breakfast will be included. During the peak months Jun-Aug it can be difficult to get a room, so arrive early in the day. Tips on where to stay from travellers are probably your best bet. The coastal strip on the easten side of each island is the most developed. Peace, solitude and outrageous sunsets can be found on the western side of each island. Unless otherwise stated, all bungalows have private bathrooms with shower. Fresh-water resources are scarce on the islands so water in the bathrooms can often be saline, as it is taken from wells. However, some places offer fresh-water showers. All prices quoted here are low season. Expect them to double during the high season.

Gili Trawangan *p169, map p170*
$$$$ Kelapa Kecil, T0812 375 6003, www.kelapavillas.com. Sleek and stylish but lacking island grace, the 3 a/c rooms here are popular, and have great sea views. Small pool.
$$$$ Villa Ombak, T0370 642336, www.hotelombak.com. Selection of 60 rooms, some in beautiful *lumbung*-style cottages set in well-tended gardens. The water here is saline, although they provide a jar of fresh water for guests to use to rinse off any residue after showering. These a/c rooms have large open bathroom, TV, and the more expensive *lumbung* cottages have a downstairs living area, and balcony with loungers. Full spa service, restaurant, pool and diving centre.
$$$$-$$$ Tir Na Nog, T0370 639463, www.tirnanogbar.com. 10 comfortable

and spacious a/c rooms with hot water set behind the popular bar. There is also a 2 bedroom villa available with small pool.

$$$$-$$ The Beach House, T0370 642352, www.beachhousegilit.com. This Australian-owned hotel is going from strength to strength, with its 12 bungalows and 3 villas currently being added to. The cheaper a/c rooms are comfortable, and have private terrace and cable TV. However, it's the villas here that are a steal, offering privacy and featuring fresh-water plunge pool, kitchenette, cable TV and space for 4 in tastefully decorated rooms. Consistently booked out well in advance, so reservations are essential. Fresh-water swimming pool. Recommended.

$$$ Alam Gili, T0370 630 466, www.alam indahbali.com. Set on the quiet northern shore, and near some good snorkelling, the Alam Gili is a well-managed establishment with cool, breezy Balinese-style bungalows with sea views and access to a salt-water jungle pool. This is a good retreat from the more hedonistic central strip. Those in need of some action can get into 'town' in around 20 mins on a cidomo.

$$$ Dream Village, T0370 664 4373. www.dreamvillagetrawangan.it. The 5 large a/c bungalows have cable TV and fine sunrise views, but are a little overpriced. There are 6 Balinese-style rooms. Reservations necessary.

$$$ Sama Sama Bungalows, T0812 376 3650, www.thesamasama.com. 4 a/c *lumbung* bungalows with high ceilings and tasteful decor. There is a bar in front playing live acoustic music, which the friendly owner insists stops at 0100.

$$ Blue Beach Cottage, T0370 263846. Located next to Trawangan's finest stretch of beach, the stylish a/c bungalows have huge bathrooms, high ceilings and mosquito nets. The staff are very friendly.

$$ Good Heart, T0370 663 0239, goodheart-trawangan@hotmail.com. No relation to the bungalows on Gili Meno, the comfortable a/c *lumbung* cottages are

a stone's throw from the beach, with cool outdoor bathroom and good views from the private balcony. Rooms have cable TV, fridge and safety box.

$$ Snapper Bungalows, T0370 624417, www.beachhousegilit.com/snapper_bungalows.html. Located just behind Wrap a Snapper fish n' chip shop, the Snapper has a decent selection of fan and a/c rooms with outdoor terrace. Guests can also use the swimming pool and facilities at the Beach House Resort.

$ Coral Beach 2, T0370 639946. Well located at the quiet northern end of the island, and near good snorkelling, the rooms here are simple and quite clean. There is a restaurant attached serving good pizza and icy drinks.

$ Melati Bungalows, T0852 3952 1697. This laid-back place has 4 simple fan rooms with friendly staff.

$ Pondok Maulana, T0817 574 6118, www.pondokmaulana.bravehost.com. 4 spotless rooms, with large veranda. Popular.

$ Sunset Cottages T0812 378 5290. Simple bungalows with 2 beds, mosquito nets, hammocks on balconies. Situated on the western side of the island, taking advantage of the splendid sunsets featuring Mount Agung on Bali as a breathtaking backdrop. Very peaceful. It's about a 40-min walk into 'town' for other restaurants and shopping, or take a cidomo (if you can find one).

$Trawangan Cottages, T0370 623582. Also in the village, lodgings here are popular and convenient for the bars along the main strip. Rooms are clean.

$ Warna Homestay, T0370 623859. 7 clean and comfortable rooms with plenty of light.

Gili Meno *p171, map p170*

$$$ Villa Nautilus, T0370 642143, www.villanautilus.com. Beautifully designed private cottages facing the sea, with outside terrace, some with sea views. The room has a living area, and the large bed is on a raised platform, with good quality fabrics used for bedding and curtains.

$$$-$$ Gazebo, T0370 635795. Set in forest, with its own stretch of beach with loungers, the well spaced out cottages look dreary from the outside, yet internally are spacious, well furnished and tastefully decorated with Indonesian artefacts. There is a small pool next the to the beach.

$$$-$$ Kontiki, T0370 632824. Used by tourists on **Perama** tours, near the beach, with large and clean rooms. The staff are a great source of local information and very friendly. Some rooms have fresh water shower and space to sleep 3 people.

$$$-$ The Sunset Gecko, T0815 766418, www.thesunsetgecko.com. This Japanese-owned place blows all the Meno competition out of the water with its innovative eco-friendly ideals, unconventional communal washbasins, outdoor showers and toilets (very clean and secure) and comfortable accommodation in thatched bungalows. There is a 2-storey house with amazing views of Gili Trawangan and Gunung Agung from its terrace at sunset, that is often booked for weeks at a time. If you want the house, it is necessary to reserve well in advance. Good snorkelling offshore. Recommended.

$$ Biru Meno, T08133 975 8968, www.biru meno.com. At the southern end of the main beach strip, the 8 bungalows here are set in a very tranquil location and seem rather underused. Fan rooms have sea view.

$$ Goodheart, T0813 3655 6976. Located on the western side of the island, the 5 2-storey *lumbung* cottages have precipitous stairs leading up to a simple bedroom. Access to the bathroom is through a trapdoor in the bedroom floor. A great beachside *berguga* (seating pavilion) to watch the sunset.

$$ Mallia's Child, T0370 622007, www.gili meno-mallias.com. These bungalows are right on the beach with excellent views over to Gili Air and Lombok. Rooms are clean, though a little small. Tax not included in the price. Slightly overpriced. Rates fall with a little gentle negotiation.

$$ Mimpi Manis, T0817 997 9579. Very spacious thatched bungalows with large balcony and hammock set in a large garden. Rooms come with a Bahasa Indonesia coursebook so guests can mingle with the locals better. Fresh-water shower. Breakfast and tax are not included in the price.

$$ Tao Kombo, T0812 372 2174, www.tao-kombo.com/uk/presentation.htm. Away from the beach in a forest clearing, there is plenty of birdsong here. The *lumbung* bungalows are filled with light, and have high ceilings. The location is very peaceful, and the hotel offers lots of boardgames and a book exchange. Recommended.

Gili Air *p172, map p170*

To make the most of this 'paradise' island it's best to stay in one of the bungalows dotted around the coast within sound and sight of the sea. There's also accommodation inland from the point where the boats land on the south coast, but this does not offer sea views.

$$$-$$ Coconut Cottages, T0370 635365, www.coconuts-giliair.com. Owned by a friendly Glasgow native and her husband, the 7 a/c and fan rooms here are great value, with well-designed interiors and huge bathrooms. The beds are king size, and there are reading lights. Recommended.

$$ Hotel Gili Indah, T0370 637328. Comfortable fan and a/c rooms with sea views close to the harbour and handy for quiet walks on the island's west.

$$ Lucky's, on the west side of the island, T0819 3316 0613, about a 15-min walk to the harbour. This friendly place doesn't get as much business as it ought to, given the marvellous sunset views and quiet vibes on offer. Fan and a/c rooms.

$$ Sejuk Cottages, T0370 636461, www. sejukcottages.com. Down a path off the eastern side of the island, this hotel has a good selection of clean bungalows with spacious verandas. The more expensive feature TV and a/c.

$$ Sunrise Cottages, T0370 642370. Set in a garden so parched that walking through it makes you feel thirsty. This hotel has a good, wide selection of rooms and the choice ones are often full. The 2-storey *lumbung* have an outdoor lounge area downstairs and an outdoor bathroom.

$$-$ Gili Air Santay, T0818 0375 8695, www.giliair-santay.com. Has a loyal following of regular Gili Air visitors, lured by the efficient Austrian management and simple yet comfortable bungalows. There are no locks on some of the bathroom doors.

$ Abdi Fantastik, T0370 622179. Simple bungalows with room for 3 people. All have sea view. Friendly staff. Good swimming and snorkelling offshore.

$ Matahari, 25-min walk from the harbour along the western coastal path. For serious seekers of isolation only, this simple place on the west coast is a great spot to leave the world behind, chat with local fishermen and watch clouds drift by. The owners can prepare decent Indonesian meals.

$ Mawar Cottages, T0813 6225 3995. These guys will probably meet you off the boat and try to entice you to stay at their lodgings, which are set away from the beach in a quiet garden. This is definite backpacker territory and an acoustic guitar looms ominously on the wall of the large communal area. All rooms with mosquito net and fan, although cheaper rooms feature squat toilet.

🍴 Restaurants

The choice of food is best on Gili Trawangan. A number of restaurants serving excellent seafood, particularly fish; the specials board will tell you the day's fresh catch. There are basic provision shops on all the islands selling snacks and some fresh fruit.

Gili Trawangan *p169, map p170*
$$ The Beach House, T0370 642352, www. beachhousegili.com. Open 24 hrs. Popular beachfront eatery serving fish kebabs, pies and quiches, home-made soups and some

Indonesian dishes. Fresh seafood is laid out around 1800 and diners pick their choice.

$$ Blue Marlin, T0370 632424. Open 0800-2300. Extremely popular place with good portions of Western food, fresh seafood and a decent vegetarian menu.

$$ Horizontal, T0878 63039727. Open 0800-2300. An attempt at Seminyak style, which looks a little faded during daytime, but comes into its own as the sunsets. Good range of fare including pan-fried fillet of white snapper, Japanese tuna rolls, Thai curries and banoffee pie.

$$ Pesona, T0370 6607233, www.pesona resort.com. Open 0800-2300. The owners are of Indian origin and you will find the best veg and non-veg Indian grub in the Gilis here. The *masala dosa* adds a few southern Indian vibes to the proceedings. It doubles up as a sheesha bar at night, where you can puff away on apple tobacco.

$$ Scallywags, T0370 631945. Open 0800-2300. Beautifully designed restaurant, with some seating on the beach. The menu features delights such warm goat's cheese salad, Basque tapas dishes and plenty of fresh seafood. Good wine selection.

$$ Tir Na Nog, T0370 639463, www.tirna nogbar.com. Open 0800-2300. Popular for pizza, steak-and-Guiness pie and with a decent vegetarian selection.

$$ Wrap A Snapper, T0370 624217. Open 0800-2200. Australian-owned, serving up fish 'n' chips, battered snacks and fish burgers, plus some healthy options! Will deliver food to diners to the beach for 5000Rp.

$ Coco, T0813 5353 5737. Open 0700-1800. Ideal spot for a light lunch, this small and efficient café prepares baguettes with tasty fillings such as roasted vegetables and feta cheese. The small salad menu is dreamy, with offerings like spicy smoked marlin salad. Good coffee selection. Recommended.

Gili Meno *p171, map p170*
The gourmet scene in Gili Meno is very quiet with eating mainly restricted to hotel

restaurants, which can be highly variable in quality. Places close when the last patron leaves, which can be early.

$$ Villa Nautilus, T0370 642124. Open 0700-2100. Good salads and pasta on offer with friendly service. Does a rather doughy wood-fired pizza smothered in cheese, if that's your thing.

$$-$ Good Heart, T0813 3655 6976. Open 0700-2100. Fresh seafood including barracuda, tuna, snapper and some vegetarian dishes such as tofu curry. There is a good cocktail list.

$$-$ Rust Warung, T0370 642324. Open 0700-2100. Cheap sandwiches, soups and local favourites, but really comes alive at night when the local boys lay out the fresh fish for patrons to choose. There's a good atmosphere and many diners linger after eating to enjoy the cool breeze and a Bintang.

$ Mallia's Child, T0370 622007. Open 0700-2100. Cheap Indonesian fare, reasonable Thai curries and home-made soup.

$ Sunset Gecko, T0815 766418. Open 0700-2100. Local Sasak cuisine, some Western food and a delicious vegetarian red curry.

Gili Air *p172, map p170*
Many restaurants cater primarily to Western tastes and the 'Indonesian' food is often disappointingly bland.

$$ Blue Marlin, T0370 634387. Hungry divers head here for good-quality Western food served in large portions.

$$ Frangipani (see Where to stay), T0370 635365. Open 0800-2200. Lots of tasty Indonesian, international and some Sasak cuisine served in a friendly, clean setting.

$$-$ Gili Air Santay, T0818 0375 8695. Open 0700-2200. Excellent array of Thai dishes and other Asian favourites served from a spotless kitchen. This laid-back place is deservedly popular and social.

$ Go Go Café, T0817 570 8337. Open 0700-2400. Not far from the harbour, this breezy eatery dishes up fair Indonesian staples, pizza and pasta dishes. Slow service.

$ Green Café, T0818 365954. Open 0800-2300. This beachside joint is a good place to sample some Sasak cuisine, such as *urap urap* (vegetables in a coconut sauce). Also prepares fresh seafood dishes and has a lovely home-made yoghurt. Movies are often shown in the evenings.

🎵 Bars and clubs

Gili Trawangan *p169, map p170*
There is plenty of nocturnal action available, with local boys competing with foreigners for the attention of female visitors. Many places have a designated party night that goes on until the wee hours. Be careful of the magic mushroom milkshakes on sale in many places, they can be very strong and Lombok is a long way from home.

Horizontal, T0878 6303 9727. Open 0700-0200. Cool lounge setting, plenty of drinks deals and chilled house music by the beach.

Rudy's Bar, T0370 642311. Open 0800-0200. Popular with the backpacking set, this is the place to get feral, with plenty of reggae and house, happy hour 1500-2200.

Sama Sama, T0812 376 3650. Open 1900-0100. This friendly bar has chilled acoustic music in a mellow setting close to the beach.

Tir Na Nog, T0370 639463. Open 0700-0200 except Wed 0700-sunrise. This Irish theme bar is cavernous, and caters for every whim, to the point where it almost becomes overwhelming. There is a darts board, table football, scattering of *beruga* with small TV and DVD player with an extensive film library, huge TV showing live football and a DJ spinning tunes nightly from 2100. Has a weekly party on Wed nights.

Gili Air *p172, map p170*
Most people are here to relax rather than get wild, so the beachfront restaurants double up as bars in the evening, and can be a great way to meet people. **Gili Air Santay** (see Restaurants) is recommended.

Space Bar, T0812 378 7254. Open 0700-2300 except Wed 0700-sunrise. Harking back to mid-1990s Goa trance days, the walls of this small bar are festooned with fluorescent paintings of dolphins leaping from the sea and naughty-looking mushrooms. The Wed night party comes with a complete DJ line up until sunrise. Happy hour is 1700-1900.

🎭 Entertainment

Gili Trawangan *p169, map p170*
Beautiful Life, open 1000-2400. On the busy southeastern coastal strip, this place offers movies in a darkened outdoor cinema, and personal movie booths on the beach side of the road where you can select a film from their library. You must buy some food or a drink to watch a film.

⚙ What to do

Gili Islands *p168, map p170*
Body and soul
Massage is available at many guesthouses and hotels on all 3 islands. Gili Trawangan has a few spa and massage places including **Villa Ombak**, T0370 642336, which has the most comprehensive spa and massage service.

Cycling
Gili Air and Gili Trawangan make superb places to get lost along island tracks, or follow the coastal paths for stunning views and peace and quiet. Bikes can be rented on Gili Air for 30,000Rp a day, and on Gili Trawangan for 35,000Rp a day.

Diving and snorkelling
While the diving here may not be quite as good as that in some other parts of Indonesia, it is ideal for less experienced divers as many of the dives are no deeper than 18 m and the waters are calm. Best diving conditions are late Apr-Aug. Good diving spots include **Shark Point** with white-and-black tipped reef sharks, sea snakes and turtles; **Meno Wall**, famed for

turtles and nudibranches; and Air Slope, with its population of ghost pipe fish, frog fish and leaf scorpion fish. The dive centres on all 3 islands have formed an association to monitor control of diving on the islands, and protection of the reefs. Prices are the same at all schools, so as to maintain high standards and safety. Example costs are US$35 for a guided fun dive (must be certified diver), PADI Open Water US$350, Advanced Open Water US$275, Discover Scuba US$60, and Dive Master US$650, with unlimited dives over a 1-month period.
Big Bubble Dive, T0370 625020, www.big bubblediving.com. Has courses in numerous European languages, and is highly regarded.
Blue Marlin, T0812 376 6496, www.blue marlindive.com. Has dive schools on all 3 islands, and offers a free pool try-out for anyone interested in diving at their centres in Gili Trawangan and Gili Air. On Trawangan.

Snorkels and fins can be hired for 25,000Rp from many of the *losmen* or vendors along the beach. The snorkelling off Gili Trawangan is marginally the best; be careful off Gili Meno, as the tide is strong and the water is shallow, and it is easy to get swept onto the coral. Many agencies on all 3 islands offer snorkelling trips around all 3 islands in a glass-bottomed boat for 80,000-100,000Rp. This trip is highly recommended.

Fishing
Night fishing can be organized from several places on Gili Air. Try **Abdi Fantastik** (see Where to stay), which has speargun fishing trips from 1800-2200, costing US40 per person.

Kayaking
Kayaking Alberto, the owner of Dream Village, T0370 664 4373, rents out sea kayaks for 45,000Rp per day.

Tour operators
Perama, T0370 638514, has their own office near the harbour on Gili Trawangan. On Gili Meno they can be found at the **Kontiki**

Hotel, T0370 632824, and on Gili Air at the Hotel Gili Indah, T0370 637328.

⊖ Transport

Gili Islands *p168, map p170*
Don't purchase bus tickets to Senggigi or other Lombok destinations on the islands, they are more expensive. You can purchase a ticket on a shuttle bus to Senggigi or Mataram at Bangsal for 40,000Rp. The shuttle bus touts will find you when you get off the boat. Be firm in your bargaining.

Boat
Public boats from the islands to **Bangsal** leave when full, except for Giili Meno, which has 2 sailings a day to Bangsal at 0800 and 1400 approximately; buy your ticket at the harbour. For onward connections to **Bali**, arrive at the ticket booth by 0730. At Bangsal you can also book through to Bali with one of the shuttle bus companies. The 'Island Hopping' boat makes 2 round trips a day connecting the islands.

To **Bali**, Perama has bus-boat ticket combination tickets. The direct **Perama** boat to **Padangbai** departs at 0700 and costs US$30. Also has connections to other destinations in Bali. **Gili Cat**, www.gilicat. com, sails direct from Gili Trawangan to **Padangbai** in 1½ hrs for 1100, US$69. **Bluewater Express** (www.bwsbali.com) sails directly to Serangan Harbour in southern Bali (US$69) **and Scoot Cruises** sail directly to Sanur (US$65). Check websites for schedules.

⊙ Directory

Gili Islands *p168, map p170*
Banks It is best to change money before leaving the mainland as rates are more expensive on the islands. There are money changers on all 3 islands. **Medical services** There is a small clinic on Gili Meno near the Bird Park. On Gili Trawangan there is a good clinic at Villa Ombak, T0370 642336. The doctor visits from the mainland on Tue, Thu and Sat.

Northwest coast and Mount Rinjani

Following the coast north from Pemenang and Bangsal, the road passes the turn-off for Sir each (about 2 km north of Pemenang). This northwest coast is little touched by tourism and there are several 'traditional' villages where the more adventurous tour companies take visitors. The best-known of these is Bayan, at the foot of Mount Rinjani's northern slopes and about 50 km from Pemenang. Mount Rinjani, rising to 3726 m, dominates north Lombok.

Northwest coast → *For listings, see pages 180-181.*

Siri Beach
Siri beach is down a dirt track – to the left are coconut plantations – and reaches the deserted, long, narrow strip of soft, white sand on a headland looking across to Gili Air. Take all food and drink: there are no facilities here. This is worth a visit to get away from the crowds. To get there, take a bemo running north from Pemanang; the walk to the beach is about 2 km from the road.

Bayan
This is a traditional Sasak village and the birthplace of Lombok's unique Muslim 'schism' – *Islam Waktu Telu*. There is a mosque here that is believed to be 300 years old. The village is the jumping-off point for climbs up Mount Rinjani (see below). There is no accommodation.

Mount Rinjani → *For listings, see pages 180-181.*

Visitors who have made the effort invariably say that the highlight of their stay on Lombok was climbing Mount Rinjani. The views from the summit on a clear day are simply breathtaking. The ascent requires three days (although some keen climbers try to do it in two). Be warned that the summit is often wreathed in cloud, and views down to the blue-green lake within the caldera are also often obscured by a layer of cloud that lies trapped in the enormous crater.

Mount Rinjani is the second-highest mountain in Indonesia outside Irian Jaya – rising to an altitude of 3726 m. The volcano is still active but last erupted some time ago – in 1901, although in 1997 rumblings left dust raining for a week. The mountain, and a considerable area of land surrounding the mountain totalling some 400 sq km, has been gazetted as a national park.

The climb
There are two routes up Mount Rinjani. The easier and more convenient begins about 2 km to the west of the village of Bayan, on the way to Anyer. The track leads upwards from the road to the small settlement of **Batu Koq** and from there, 1 km on, to another village, **Senaru**. Tents, equipment and guides or porters can be hired in either of these two settlements (ask at the *losmen*); accommodation is available. It is recommended that trekkers check in at the conservation office in Senaru before beginning the ascent. A guide is not essential as the trail is well marked from Senaru to the crater rim; however, suitable climbing gear is required. From Senaru, the trek to the summit takes about two days, or 10 hours solid climbing. On the trek up, the path passes through stands of teak and mahogany, then into pine forest and lichin. There are stunning views from the lip of the crater down to the beautiful blue-green and mineral rich lake, **Segara Anak** (Child of the Sea), below. A third day is needed to walk down into the caldera. The caldera is 8 km long by 5 km wide.

On the east side of the lake is **Mount Baru** (New Mountain), an active cone within a cone that rose out of the lake in 1942. It can be reached by boat and the climb to Mount Baru's summit, through a wasteland of volcanic debris, is rewarded with a view into this secondary crater. Along the base of the main crater are numerous hot springs including **Goa Susu** (Milk Cave – so called because of its colour), which are reputed to have spectacular healing powers. Bathing in them is a good way to round off a tiring descent.

An alternative and more difficult route up the mountain – but some climbers claim it is more interesting – is via **Sembalun Lawang**, **Sembalun Bumbung** or **Sapit** on the mountain's eastern slopes. This alternative route is less well marked. A guide is recommended to show climbers the route to the second rim. There is accommodation here and guides are also available, but there is a shortage of equipment for hire. There is food available to buy for the trek but the range is not as good as in Senaru. To get to Sembalun Bumbung, take a bus from Labuhan Lombok. The climb to the crater takes about nine hours. For ambitious climbers who intend to reach the true summit of Mount Rinjani – rather than just the caldera – this is the better of the two routes. **Note** In the past, some embassies in Jakarta have advised visitors not to climb Mount Rinjani because of fears of violent theft. However, no one going up, nor the guides, seemed concerned or particularly aware of any great problems. Nonetheless, check before beginning the climb.

It's also possible to do a **round trip**, taking in both sides of the mountain. Each side of Rinjani offers its own character and a recommended alternative is to climb up the eastern flank and down the western. To do this, go to Senaru to rent equipment and buy supplies (the choice is best here), return to Anyer or Bayan and take a bemo or ojek to Sembalun Lawang. (Start early, bemos to Sembalun Lawang are rare after 1600.) Hire a guide and porter in Sembalun Lawang and stay the night. The next day the guide can show the route to the second rim (six to seven hours); from here, the climb to the summit (three to four hours) and then down into the caldera (three hours), and from there up to the first rim and back down to Senaru (six to seven hours), is well marked and the guide is not needed.

Best time to climb The best time is from May to November, during the dry season, when it is less likely to be cloudy. Do not attempt the climb during the rainy season as the trail can be treacherous. The climb, though not technically difficult, is arduous and climbers should be in reasonable physical condition. **Recommended equipment**: water, sweater and coat, foam camping roll, sleeping bag, tough walking shoes, food/supplies, firewood (there is increasing evidence of climbers chopping down trees within this national park in order to light a fire). *Please* take all your litter with you. **Note** Some climbers have complained of the poor quality of equipment hired in Senaru; check it carefully. A tent and/or sleeping bag hired for the guide would be greatly appreciated; it's cold on the mountain.

There is a US$16.50 admission fee to the Gunung Rinjani National Park, that needs to be paid at either the **Rinjani Trekking Club** ① *T0868 1210 4132, www.rinjanitrekkingclub. com*, in Senaru, or at the **Rinjani Information Centre** in Sembalun Lawang. This is normally included in the price of a trek package, but make sure before you sign off. You can also rent any necessary equipment at these places. Treks can be arranged in Senaru through the **Rinjani Trekking Club**, or through one of the local guides. A reasonable package including guide fee and entrance fee would be around US$150-200 for a two-day/one-night ascent and up to US$300 for a longer four-day/three-night trek. Package rates fall in the low season. Treks can also be arranged in Senggigi with the reputable **Rinjani Trekking Club** (see What to do, page 167). Their prices are very reasonable and are all-inclusive. Alternatively, you can book treks up Gunung Rinjani at any of the Perama offices. They have a variety of treks that depart from **Senggigi**, see page 167.

Northwest coast and Mount Rinjani listings

For hotel and restaurant price codes and other relevant information, see pages 9-12.

◐ Where to stay

Mount Rinjani *p179*
It is possible to stay at Batu Koq and Senaru, as well as at Sembalun Lawang if making the climb from the east. Senaru has the best selection of *losmen* (basic, all **$$-$**) and new ones seem to open almost every month.
Bale Bayan Guesthouse, T0817 579 2943. Near the mountain, clean and friendly, the owner speaks reasonable English and German. Recommended.
Batu Koq Pondok, Segara Anak, T0817 575 4551. Has been recommended.

Price includes breakfast and supper; some exquisite views.
Pondok Gunung Baru, T0819 3312 8229. 5 clean rooms. Good trekking information.
Pondok Senaru, T0868 1210 4141. Clean, well run, big restaurant, ice-cold *mandi*.
Rinjani Trekking Club, contact their Senggigi office, T0370 693860, and **Emy Homestay**. Both have simple lodging.

✤ Festivals

Mount Rinjani *p179*
Dec In the 2nd week of Dec, the **Pakelem**, offering feast is held on Segara Anak to ask for God's blessings.

Mount Rinjani *p179*
Tours
The most convenient way to climb Rinjani is by booking a place on a tour. Several tour operators in Senggigi (see page 167) and on the Gilis organize climbs (US$150-250 all in). Tours are also available from *losmen* at various villages.

⊖ **Transport**

Bayan *p179*
Bemo
Connections with the Bertais terminal in Cakranegara. From Bayan bemos run up to Batu Koq. Bemos also run east from here along the very scenic coastal road to Labuhan Lombok. From the looks of surprise it is clear that few *orang putih* make this (long) journey.

Mount Rinjani *p179*
Bemo
For the more usual north route, take a bemo from the **Bertais** terminal to Bayan, and then a 2nd bemo from Bayan to Senaru. Alternatively, walk from Bayan. For the east route, take a bemo from Labuhan Lombok to Sembalun Bumbung.

Taxi
A taxi from Bangsal to Senaru should cost about US$16.

Kuta Beach and around

Kuta beach, also sometimes known as Putri Nyale beach, is situated among some of the most spectacular coastal scenery on Lombok; rocky outcrops and cliff faces give way to sheltered sandy bays, ideal for swimming and surfing.

Kuta Beach and around → *For listings, see pages 183-185. Phone code: 0370.*

Kuta itself has a stretch of sand on Lombok's south coast, in a bay with a little fishing village at its head. There is a substantial fishing fleet of sailing boats with brightly decorated dugout hulls and outriggers. There are no 'sights' other than the Sasak villages about 20 minutes' drive inland, beside the main Mataram to Kuta road.

The beach is the focal point of a strange annual festival, called the **Bau Nyale**, when thousands of seaworms come to the surface of the sea. Local people flock here to witness the event, and it is becoming quite a popular tourist attraction. See Festivals, page 184.

Still a relatively quiet place to stay, there is a good road linking it to Mataram with regular shuttle bus connections.

At present the roads beyond Kuta are poor. The coast road continues east from Kuta past some magnificent, white sandy bays. After 2 km a potholed tarmac road turns off to **Seger Beach**, one of the beaches where the Nyale fish come ashore.

Further on again by 4 km, past low-lying swampy land, is the fine gold-sand beach at **Tanjung Aan**, set in a horseshoe-shaped bay; it is good for swimming, though there are stones and coral about 10 m out. Despite its distance from any development there are stalls, and hawkers materialize as soon as any foreigners appear. **Note** There is no shade on any of these beaches, just basic scrub. The track bends round to the south and ends at **Gerupak (Desert) Point**.

There are many walks in the area: climb the hill immediately to the west of Kuta for spectacular views over the south coast. The **Seger Hills**, 2 km to the east, have numerous farm trails and a small cemetery; near Seger Beach is a rocky promontory with more superb views, especially at sunset.

There are several good surfing beaches. The best are: **Are Guling**, **Mawi**, **Mawun** and **Selong Blanak**. **Gerupak (Desert Point)** is rated as one of the best surf spots in the world outside Hawaii. Kuta was originally 'discovered' by surfers.

Traditional villages that can be visited include: **Sade** and **Rembitan**, 9 km north of Kuta just off the main Mataram road, 20 minutes' drive.

Safety There is an 'honoured' tradition of inter-village theft in these parts. A thief from one village gained prestige by successfully stealing from other villages. Be very careful if out walking after dark. Take extra precautions to safeguard money and valuables. However, all over Lombok local neighbourhood watch-style groups have formed, and will get your stolen goods back within the day. Hence crime has decreased considerably.

West of Kuta

There is now a sealed road running west of Kuta as far as Selong Blanak. Along the way there are several good beaches, all fairly deserted. The occasional bemo runs to Selong Blanak from Praya. Twenty minutes' drive (10 km) west of Kuta is **Mawan Beach**. A perfect horseshoe-shaped bay with a golden sand beach, a large tree and two bamboo shelters (called *garuga*) and several coconut palms offering some protection from the sun. Good for swimming, very protected though the sea bed slopes steeply near the shore. The road west climbs steeply out of Kuta, with spectacular views of the south coast and mist-covered hills in the rainy season. Further west near Selong Blanak are more good gold-sand beaches at **Mawi** and **Rowok**. Mawi in particular offers good surfing. The road continues to the fishing village of **Selong Blanak**, with its wide, sandy bay and accommodation a little inland. Few travellers make the trip further west to **Pengantap**, **Sepi** and **Blongas**; the last of which has good surfing, snorkelling and diving, though be wary of sharks. From Sepi the poor road heads inland via Sekatong to the port of **Lembar**. All roads deteriorate west of Pengantap and should probably be avoided in the wet season. There are some bemos, though most people get here by private or chartered transport. The better accommodation offers free transport to Tanjung Aan Beach to the east and Mawan Beach to the west.

East of Kuta

Shortly before Tanjung Aan the road forks; taking the left fork, northeast, the road passes through Sereneng en route to **Awang**, 18 km from Kuta. The right fork goes to **Gerupak** about 9 km east of Kuta. From here there are boats across Gumbang Bay to **Bumgang** for about US$5.50. From Bumgang there is a path north which connects with the road to Awang. The villagers in this area make their living from fishing and seaweed farming and will hire out boats for about US$25 a day. A few bemos travel these routes and their numbers are slowly increasing, but the best way to see the area is with your own transport.

From Awang, boats can be chartered across the bay to Ekas for about US$12 return. **Ekas** has good surfing and snorkelling. There are spectacular views from the cliffs overlooking Awang Bay on both sides, particularly from Ekas. It is possible but time-consuming to reach Ekas by public bemo: from Praya, catch a bemo bound for Tanjung Luar and Gubukdalem, get off just before Keruak at the turning south to Jerowaru and wait for a bemo going to Ekas, which is en route to Kaliantan in the southwest corner of the peninsula.

Kuta beach and around listings

For hotel and restaurant price codes and other relevant information, see pages 9-12.

🛏 Where to stay

Kuta Beach *p181*
Accommodation options have improved as Kuta's profile as a destination rises. The new airport in central Lombok has made will make Kuta a much easier destination to reach, and will bring in greater investment. Many of the older established hotels here have struggled with maintenance and are slowly becoming faded. However, in recognition of this, their prices have dropped considerably, and it is possible to find some excellent value accommodation. Many of the popular budget surfer hotels are strung out along the beachside road.
$$$ Ken's Hotel, Jln Raya Kuta, T0370 655057. This new hotel caters mainly for Japanese surfers, and the owner is very knowledgeable about the area. The a/c rooms are large and clean, with TV and fridge. The more expensive suites are enormous and have 2 bathrooms. Service here is very efficient, and the kitchen serves up a couple of good Japanese dishes. There is a small but stylish pool and sunbathing area, with showers. Recommended.
$$$-$$ Matahari Inn, Jln Pantai Kuta, T0370 655000. Beautiful gardens, with plenty of lush greenery and Buddha statues reclining and meditating on plinths. Faded rooms, the cheaper ones are musty, dark and charmless. Things improve as you go up the price range. Pool.
$$ Kuta Indah, Jln Pantai Kuta, T0370 653781. This place was built with grand ideas in mind, but lack of custom has forced the owners to slash rates considerably. The a/c and fan rooms are good value, and the pool is extremely inviting.
$$-$ Surfer's Inn, Jln Pantai Kuta, T0370 655582, www.lombok-surfersinn.com. Very

popular with a nice pool and lounging area. Rooms are very simple and fairly large. Can arrange surfing lessons.
$ Anda, Jln Pantai Kuta, T0370 654836. Packed with chest-thumping surfers glued to the TV watching waves, this place definitely caters to a niche market, and is obviously succeeding. Rooms are bare and simple.
$ Mimpi Manis Homestay, Desa Mong, T0818 369950, www.mimpimanis.com. It's a shame there aren't more lodgings like this in Indonesia, with extraordinarily friendly staff, good grub, a couple of choice volumes on the bookshelf, and a genuine homestay atmosphere. There are 2 rooms and a house on offer here, all of which are clean and come with TV and DVD player (there is a large library of films to choose from). It's 2 km inland, but the staff will drop you at the beach, and it is a cheap ojek ride back. Excellent value. Highly recommended.
$ Segare Anak, Jln Pantai Kuta, T0370 654846. The cheaper bungalows are wobbling on their stilts, but the slightly more expensive concrete rooms at the back are huge and clean and the bathrooms have a bath. Pool and badminton.

🍴 Restaurants

Kuta Beach *p181*
Most places in Kuta have almost identical menus, and the town is certainly no gourmet paradise. Nevertheless, it's easy to fill the belly for less than many places in Lombok, but cast your eyes over the cleanliness of a place before choosing to eat there. There are an awful lot of flies and rubbish around.
    Most of the hotels offer food, although the kitchens usually close earlier than the restaurants. Ken's Hotel (**$$**) whips up a few Japanese dishes, as well as some Indonesian and international favourites; **Mimpi Manis ($)** does a great *nasi campur*.

Be careful of the *warungs* on the beach, some tourists have reported cases of food poisoning after eating in them.

$ Bong's Café, Jln Pantai Kuta, T0819 1611 5552. Open 0800-2300. Friendly place serving wood-fired pizza, sandwiches and lots of good Indonesian fare. Surf films shown.

$ Cherry Café, Jln Pantai Kuta, T0878 6516 8341. Open 0800-2300. Lots of local options and a good salad menu, friendly Balinese.

$ Ketapang Café, Jln Pantai Kuta, T0370 655194. Open 0800-2100. This popular restaurant has a seaview and a menu favouring those starved of carbs, with good burgers, pizza and pasta dishes dominating.

$ Riviera Café, Jln Pantai Kuta. Open 0730-2300. A large and diverse menu in a spartan but friendly café near the **Matahari Hotel**. All the usual suspects are on offer here plus a few interesting local dishes such as *ayam taliwang* and *nasi begibung*. Happy hour 1800-2000.

$ Seger Reef, Jln Pantai Kuta, T0370 655528. Open 0800-2200. Lots of Indonesian food and pizza.

$ The Shore Bar, next door to **Seger Reef**. Open 0800-2400. Good, fresh seafood.

🎵 Bars and clubs

Kuta Beach *p181*
Nightlife is pretty thin on the ground. **The Shore Bar** (see Restaurants) is the place to be on Fri nights with live music, lots of surfers and local boys and even the occasional female. **Riviera Café** (see Restaurants) has live acoustic music on Wed and Fri evenings during the high season. Cultural shows are put on from time to time at the hotels.

✴ Festivals

Kuta Beach *p181*
Feb/Mar (19th day of the 10th month of the Sasak lunar calendar) **Nyale ceremony**, thousands of mysterious sea worms called Nyale fish (*Eunice viridis*) 'hatch' on the reef

and rise to the surface of the sea off Kuta. According to the legend of Putri Nyale, the episode is linked to the beautiful Princess Nyale, who drowned herself here after failing to choose between a bevy of eligible men. The worms are supposed to represent her hair, and celebrations are held each year to mark her death. Traditionally, this was a time for young people to find a partner for marriage, and it is still an occasion when the usual strictures controlling contact between the sexes are eased. The worms are scooped from the sea and eaten.

🛍 Shopping

Kuta Beach *p181*
Local shops along the beachfront sell basics, including fruit, at reasonable prices. An endless stream of young children offer locally woven sarongs of variable quality, T-shirts and fruit. The pineapples here are delicious, as are the green bananas (to tell green bananas from unripe yellow bananas just squeeze; the ripe green bananas will feel soft). Kuta has its market on Sat.

⏱ What to do

Kuta Beach *p181*
Cycling
There are a couple of bikes for rent at **Mimpi Manis** (see Where to stay) for 25,000Rp per day.

Fishing
Mimpi Manis (see Where to stay) offers the chance to go out with a local fisherman in his *perahu* to catch some fish and take it back to the hotel for a feast. Price is per boat rather than per person, and represents a good deal compared to fishing trips at many other places on Lombok (whole day US$80).

Surfing
Many people come to Kuta to surf. Boards, lessons, boat travel, repairs and nightly videos of the biggest tubes and breaks in

the world are on offer at the **Kimen Surf Shop**, T0370 655064.

⊖ Transport

Kuta Beach *p181*
Bemo
Public bemo to **Praya** from the bemo stop several times a day, about 8000Rp, 1 hr, from there you can catch a bemo to **Bertais**, 30 mins. Public bemos also connect Kuta with **Labuan Lombok** (for ferries to **Sumbawa**). Most people opt for the shuttle option (below), which is far less hassle.

Bemo services are increasing and more villages are coming on line, especially along the coast roads east and west of Kuta. Best to hire your own transport, though be aware that roads are bumpy. You can hire a car with driver, but self-drive is recommended here; the local drivers have limited skills for the most part. Mataram to Kuta is just over 1 hr, depending on traffic.

Motorbikes
Available to hire, often at very reasonable prices, eg 40,000Rp per day. Ask at your accommodation.

Ojek
It's easy to charter an ojek to **Senggigi** or **Mataram** for US$14 (1½ hrs) and stop to see the weaving village of Sukarara on the way. There are usually some fascinating local markets you can stop at along the way back, if you leave early enough. Ask your driver.

Shuttles
Daily **Perama** shuttles to **Mataram** and **Senggigi** leave at 0700 (US$12.50) for connections to **Bali** and the **Gilis**, the **Perama** office is in the Segara Anak Hotel.

Flores and around

Flores stretches over 350 km from east to west, but at most only 70 km from north to south. It is one of the most beautiful islands in the Lesser Sundas. Mountainous, with steep-sided valleys cut through by fast-flowing rivers, dense forests and open savannah landscapes, Flores embraces a wide range of ecological zones. One of the local names for the island is Nusa Nipa or 'Serpent Island', because of its shape.

Arriving in Flores
Overland transport on Flores, 375 km in length, is neither quick nor comfortable. The Trans-Flores Highway is quite bearable, though travelling on it once is usually enough for most people. The road twists and turns through breathtaking scenery for more than 700 km. The Highway stretches from Labuanbajo in the east to Larantuka in the west.

Labuanbajo → *For listings, see pages 187-190. Phone code: 0385.*

Labuanbajo, or Bajo, is really just an overgrown fishing village. However, it marks the beginning of Eastern Indonesia, with Melanesian features and culture starting to dominate, and Christianity becoming the major religion (often blended with fascinating animist elements), with wonderful tropical churches and friendly nuns in the streets. The views of the harbour and surrounding islands are beautiful, making this one of Indonesia's most alluring harbour towns. There are some reasonable beaches, with excellent offshore snorkelling. It is also an excellent base from which to explore Komodo and Rinca, or to join a boat tour via the reserve and other islands on the way to Lombok. The town is stretched out along one road that runs from the dock, along the seashore, and then south towards Ruteng. **Pramuka Hill**, behind the town, offers good views over the bay, especially at sunset.

Tourist information is available from the **PHKA information booth** ① *on the main street, opposite Gardena Hotel*. It can also provide information on Komodo and Rinca.

Around Labuanbajo

Waicicu Beach lies 15 minutes by boat north of town and offers good snorkelling and diving. One-day trips to the islands **Bidadari** and **Sabobo** can be arranged through hotels or tour operators (on the main road), US$55 per boat for return boat ride. There is good snorkelling in clear waters, and you will potentially have the island to yourself.

Overnight stays on **Seraya Island**, sleeping in bungalows on stilts, can be arranged through **Gardena Hotel** (see Where to stay, page 187).

Komodo → *For listings, see pages 187-190.*

The principal reason people come to Komodo is to see the illustrious Komodo dragon. However, there is more to the reserve than giant lizards and the islands has good trekking, swimming and snorkelling. The park covers 59,000 ha, and is made up not just of Komodo Island, but also Rinca and a number of other surrounding islets. The highest peak on this rugged spot is Mount Satalibo (735 m).

Arriving in Komodo

It is necessary to charter a boat from Labuanbajo (visit the Komodo Park offices in Labuanbajo for advice), or join a tour to get to the island. The rich and famous arrive direct by helicopter.

Komodo National Park

① *www.komodonationalpark.org. The island is a national park and visitors must register and buy an entrance ticket (US$15 plus US$4.50 valid for 3 days) on arrival at Loh Liang on Komodo, or Loh Buaya on Rinca. The Park HQ at Loh Liang consists of an office, information centre, 4 bungalows, a souvenir shop, church and mosque, and a restaurant.*
After the luxuriant vegetation of Bali, Komodo can come as a bit of a shock – at least during the dry season. The islands of the Komodo archipelago are dry and rainfall is highly seasonal. For much of the year, therefore, the grasslands are burnt to dust and interspersed with drought-resistant savannah trees such as the distinctive lontar palm. In contrast the seas are highly productive, so there is good snorkelling, particularly off **Pantai Merah** and **Pulau Lasa**, a small island near Komodo village. The iridescent blue of the water, set against the dull brown of the islands, provides a striking backdrop. However, this image of Komodo as barren is transformed during the short wet season, when rainfall encourages rapid growth and the formerly parched landscape becomes green and lush.

Despite the other attractions of Komodo, it is still the **dragons** that steal the show. They are easily seen, with Timor deer (their chief natural prey) wandering among them. Other wildlife includes land crabs, wild pigs, black drongos, white-bellied sea eagles, and cockatoos, evidence that this is part of the Australasian faunal world. Monkeys are absent.

Walks

The most accessible viewing spot is the dry river bed at **Banu Nggulung**, 30 minutes' walk (2 km) from the accommodation at Loh Liang. Guides can take you there for a small fee, depending on the size of your group (30,000Rp per person). **Note** Visitors are only allowed to walk alone along marked trails. Those wishing to hike off the trails, and see the dragons in a more natural setting, must hire a guide. This is not just to generate income for the wardens; there have been fatalities. For around US$10 per person (but highly negotiable) a guide can take you to **Poreng Valley**, a 7-km walk from the PHKA office. There is a reasonably good chance of spotting a dragon and even if you don't, you will see plenty of other wildlife. There is a short 30-minute walk along the beach from Loh Liang bungalows to the stilt village of **Kampong Komodo**, which can be done without a guide. **Mount Ara** can be climbed in less than two hours (8.5 km to the summit)

Rinca Island → *For listings, see pages 187-190.*

Arriving in Rinca Island
Some boats travelling from Lombok to Flores stop off here. Ask about chartering a boat at the **Princess office**① *Jln Kasimo 3, T0385 41744*. Rinca Island can also be reached from Komodo.

Wildlife
Rinca Island has a wider range of wildlife than Komodo, including wild horses, water buffaloes and dragons, and has the added advantage of fewer tourists. Only very simple food is available, so take your own snacks. It is more likely that you will go as part of an organized tour (arranged in Labuanbajo or Lombok) and therefore you will be catered for. Rinca is fast gaining popularity over Komodo and recent visitors have been highly complimentary about trips there.

Flores and around listings

For hotel and restaurant price codes and other relevant information, see pages 9-12.

🛏 Where to stay

Labuanbajo *p185*
Accommodation in Labuanbajo is generally poor value for money, particularly when compared with Bali and Lombok.
$$$$ Jayakarta Suites, T021 649 0101, www.jayakartahotelresorts.com. Standing somewhat at odds with the overall ambience of the town and its environs is this smart, modern hotel with comfy a/c overlooking the bay. Tennis courts, pools, bar and even a volleyball court to stretch the muscles before heading out to explore
$$ Chez Felix Hotel, T0385 41032. Set in spacious grounds on a hill above the town. The restaurant here has fine views. This is a peaceful place to stay, and all the rooms are tiled, clean and fairly spacious, although they face each other. The beds in the cheaper rooms are a little wobbly.

$$ Golo Hilltop, T0385 41337, www.golo hilltop.com. Located up a dirt track to the north of the town, the views at sunset from here are amazing. The more expensive rooms are comfortable, well decorated and have fan and a/c and Wi-Fi access.
$$ Hotel Wisata, Jln Soekarno Hatta, T0385 41020. Indonesian-style hotel, with huge clean rooms, toilets that almost flush and friendly staff. The rooms face each other, so be prepared for some eyeballing.
$$-$ Gardena, Jln Yos Sudarso, T0385 41258. Simple bungalows perched on the hillside overlooking the harbour, have great views but are in dire need of some maintenance. This is the most popular hotel in town, and is a nice retreat from the dusty main strip. Bathrooms have a mixture of squat and Western toilets (without seats or flush). Tourists have reported things going missing from their verandas and rooms. The hotel has a safety box. Often full.
$ Bajo Beach Hotel, T0385 41008. This hotel takes the overspill from the Gardena.

It's a rambling place with friendly, if somewhat eccentric staff. The simple tiled rooms have mosquito net, and bathroom with toilet (no flush), *mandi* and shower. Also rents snorkel equipment.

Seraya Island
$$-$ Seraya Island Bungalows, T0385 41258, www.serayaisland.com. 12 very simple bungalows on a lovely beach with superb snorkelling nearby. Many visitors struggle to leave this place. There is a 2-night minimum stay, and transport there and back costs 50,000Rp. Contact the **Gardena** to book.

Sape
Sape is used as an overnight stop by travellers that have taken a leisurely trip across Sumbawa, and missed the early morning ferry connection to Flores (see page 190).
$ Losmen Mutiara, right by port entrance, T0374 71337. Clean simple rooms, more expensive with a/c. Few places to eat nearby.

Komodo *p186*
It is very rare for people to stay the night on Komodo nowadays. If you wish to do so, contact the PHKA office in Labuanbajo beforehand. The only accommodation on Komodo is in the **PHKA bungalows ($)** at Loh Liang, which has a capacity of about 40. They are simple but clean bungalows in a beautiful bay. Electricity from 1800 to 2200. Bedding consists of mattresses on the floor. During the peak season Jul-Sep, visitors must sleep in the dining room. Some rooms have their own *mandi* for no extra cost. Rooms are not great, but it is worth staying on the island. The cafeteria is basic and rather overpriced.

Camping There is also a campground at Loh Liang.

Rinca Island *p187*
Most people visit Rinca on a day-trip rather than staying the night.
$ PHKA bungalows, Loh Buaya. Basic accommodation, these stilted wooden

cabins are the haunts of various rodent and insect populations, so be prepared.

🍴 Restaurants

Labuanbajo *p185*
Most of the hotels have a restaurant, but quality varies enormously. There is a huge number of *nasi Padang* places in Labuanbajo. Poke your head behind the lace curtain to check the freshness first.
$$ The Lounge, T0385 41962. Open 0800-2300. With a breezy harbour view, this relaxing place has a limited menu of Western food featuring fair burritos, feta salad and home-made ciabatta bread. Films are shown here occasionally and the staff are very friendly and keen to practise their English.
$ Gardena, Jln Yos Sudarso, T0385 41258. Open 0730-2200. The most popular travellers' hangout in town, with great views, enormous fish hot plates and cheap salads. This is a very social spot, and a great place to meet other people in order to form a group for a trip to Komodo, or the island's interior.
$ Matahari, T0385 41008. Open 0800-2200. Cheap pasta, seafood and soup with a wonderful view of the harbour.

🎵 Bars and clubs

Labuanbajo *p185*
Paradise Bar, T0385 41533. Open 24 hrs. Up a dirt track on the north side of the town, on the way to the **Golo Hilltop**, this is the place for connoisseurs of fine sunsets and cold beer. The views are truly beautiful. Sat night is when the bar comes alive, as locals and tourists head here in droves to listen to live acoustic and reggae music.

🛍 Shopping

Labuanbajo *p185*
Between 0630 and 0900, multiple stalls set up along the main road selling vegetables. The usual shops can be found. There is a small choice of sarongs and woven cloth; and

a good shop for wooden carvings, including some rather gruesome masks. Hawkers linger at the entrance to the **Gardena**, with strings of pearls, and dragon carvings.

⚙ What to do

Labuanbajo *p185*
Tour operators
There are a few tour operators offering boat trips as well as inland tours. Labuanbajo is the jumping-off point for journeys into the interior and there are companies offering breakneck 3-day tours of Flores. However, Flores is an island rich in natural beauty and cultural heritage and deserves more time to be spent on it. It is easy enough to organize independent travel around the island.
Lestari Jaya, at entrance to **Gardena Hotel**, T0852 3900 5498. Offers 4-day/3-night boat tours to Bangsal (Lombok), stopping at Komodo, Rinca and Pulau Moyo and Pulau Satonda (Sumbawa) en route, around US$150 per person. Food is included, but admission fee to the Komodo National Park isn't. Check out the boat before agreeing to a tour; some boats are overloaded. It also has a trip that takes in Bajawa, Moni and Kelimutu for US$260 (per group, 4 people maximum).
Perama, T0385 42016. Runs a 2-day trip to Lombok via Rinca costing US$130 for a spot on the deck and US$180 for a cabin. They also offer 4-day tours into the interior of the beautiful island of Flores calling in at Ruteng, Ende, Moni, Kelimutu and finally Maumere for US$360 per car (maximum 4 people). For those who just wish to cruise around Komodo **Perama** offers a 2-night/3-day trip costing US$250 per person.
Princess, Jln Kasimo 3, T0385 41744. Has a boat for charter to Komodo and Rinca. Snorkelling equipment provided.

Komodo *p186*
Diving and snorkelling
The waters around Komodo are finally getting the recognition they deserve as having some of the finest diving spots

in the world. The local diving industry is growing by the year with more and more foreign investors opening up businesses. The waters around the national park are teeming with life and, with improved accessibility over recent years, are seeing increasing numbers of visitors, including liveaboards from as far away as Thailand. The reef is considered to be 99% pristine, with strong currents keeping the water temperature down and preventing the blanching effects of El Niño as seen around the Gili islands. Most companies operate day trips back and forth from Labuanbajo (see Boat, page 190), rather than operating as liveaboards, although this option is available. It takes 1½-2 hrs to reach sites around Komodo. Typically a day trip with 2 dives costs around US$80. Packages are available for 3, 5, and 10 days. Highly recommended are **Reefseekers**, T0385 41433, www.reefseekers.net, whose British owners enthuse about marine life and offer 1½-hr briefings on the journey to the reef on the ecology of the reef relevant to the area being visited. They have built a top notch resort on Pulau Bidadari, which has brought the diving even closer. Also recommended are **Bajo Dive Club**, T0385 41503, www.komododiver.com, and **Dive Komodo**, T0385 41862, www.divekomodo.com.

Note Divers should be warned that currents around the Komodo National Park can be very strong and may not be suitable for inexperienced divers. In Jun 2008, 5 European divers were swept away from their boat in a rip tide. After 9 hrs adrift they managed to get to a remote beach on Rinca where they fought off Komodo dragons and survived on a diet of shellfish for 2 days before being rescued.

There is some great snorkelling off the nearby islands, and around Pantai Merah and Pulau Bidadari in the national park. You need to charter a boat to do this, which can cost between US$50 to US$80. Enquire at one of the agents around town.

⊖ Transport

Labuanbajo *p185*
Air

Komodo Airport is 2 km from town. Airport departure tax is 10000Rp. Flights are met by minivans, and private vehicles. It costs around 15,000Rp to get to the airport from the town. Between **Merpati**, on the way to the airport, T0385 41177; **Indonesia Air Transport**, Jln Kasimo, T0385 41088; and **Trans Nusa**, Jln Soekarno Hatta, T0385 41800, there are daily connections to **Denpasar**. If you want to head to Lombok or Java you must transit in Bali. **Wings Air** (book online through **Lion Air** at www.lionair.co.id) also offers daily connections with Denpasar. **Merpati** is notorious for cancellations. Flights get booked out in advance, so booking early is essential.

Boat

Daily ferries leave at 0800 for **Sape**, **Sumbawa**, 6-8 hrs, US$4-7 depending on class. Buses meet the ferry from Sape and take passengers straight on to Ruteng. Boats travel frequently between Labuanbajo and Lombok, via Komodo on tours. The **PELNI** vessel *Tilongkabila* docks at Labuanbajo twice a month travelling alternately westwards to **Bima**, **Lembar** and **Benoa** (Bali) and northwards to **Sulawesi** with a handy connection to **Makassr**. The PELNI office, T0385 41106, is up a small dirt track past the football pitch. It is in a mechanic's workshop and not signposted.

Bus

There is no bus station; buses cruise the hotels and *losmen* picking up passengers. There are connections with **Ruteng**, 4 hrs, and **Bajawa**, 10 hrs, 1 daily at 0600 – book at any of the tourist information offices in town. It is even possible to make the exhausting journey all the way to **Ende** on a bus that meets the ferry from Sape.

Lansung Indah, T0385 41106, has a small outlet in a mobile phone shop near the port entrance. It sells bus/ferry combination tickets for **Bima**, **Mataram**, **Denpasar**, **Surabaya** and even **Jakarta**.

To Flores from Lombok via Sape, (**Sumbawa**) Many tourists opt to take an overnight bus from Lombok and across Sumbawa on the way to Flores. Typically, buses depart from Mataram (Lombok) around 1500 and travel across Lombok and Sumbawa (with a 2-hr ferry crossing between) arriving in Bima around 0400. Most travellers book a through ticket (Mataram–Sape), and upon arrival in Bima are put on a small bus for the 2-hr ride to Sape. The Mataram–Sape bus ticket will need to be shown to the conductor on this minibus, so don't throw the ticket away. The bus should arrive in time for the 0800 ferry to Labuanbajo (Flores). Some tourists find this heavy going and prefer to stay the night in Sape, or, if the bus breaks or is late, have to stay there. See page 188.

Car hire

Lestari Jaya, (see What to do), and **Manumadi**, Jln Soekarno Hatta, T0385 41457, manumadi@telkom.net, both have vehicles for hire to explore the surrounding countryside.

Ojek

Ojeks for travel around town cost 4000Rp during the day and 7000Rp after sunset.

⊕ Directory

Labuanbajo *p185*

Banks BNI, main road (150 m towards Ruteng from Bajo Beach Hotel), will change cash and TCs from major companies and has an ATM that accepts foreign cards. It is best to also bring some cash in case this breaks down, as the next ATM is a long way from here. **Telephone** Telkom office, south of town, near the PHKA office. Several **Wartel** offices around town.

Sumatra

Although Sumatra does not have Java's historical and archaeological sights, it does offer magnificent natural landscapes. Perhaps
most spectacular of all is the upland crater lake of Danau Toba.
The forests, mountains, rivers and coasts all provide great trekking
and rafting opportunities, some of the finest national parks in the
country and pristine beaches.

There are also over a dozen ethnic groups on the island, who
speak some 20 different dialects, including the peripatetic
Minangkabau of West Sumatra, the Christian Bataks of North
Sumatra, the Ferrant Muslims of Aceh and the tribal peoples of
Nias and Mentawi.

As the world's fourth-largest island (nearly 475,000 sq km),
Sumatra also acts as a 'safety valve' for Java's 'excess' population.
About 60% of Indonesia's transmigrants – four million people –
have been resettled on Sumatra, mostly in the south. Population
densities here are less than one-tenth of those on neighbouring
Java, although some areas – such as Lampung province – are
beginning to suffer the effects of overcrowding.

Sumatra is also crucial to the Indonesian economy. It was in
North Sumatra that Indonesia's first commercial oil well was sunk
in 1871, and over 60% of the country's total petroleum and gas
production comes from the island and the seas that surround it.

Arriving in Sumatra

Where to go

Travelling in Sumatra can be a time-consuming business. Some key destinations – notably
Danau Toba – have no airport. Furthermore, distances can be great and with average road
speeds of around 50 kph, even on the Trans-Sumatran 'highway', it can take a while to get
from A to B. This means that anyone intending to sample Sumatra in anything more than
the most cursory of ways will need to allocate at least 10 days. The classic 'route' is to travel
between Medan and Padang (which both have airports with daily flights), via Berastagi,
Danau Toba and Bukittinggi. This really requires a minimum of 10 days and preferably two
weeks. However, there are opportunities for shorter stays, and people living in the region
regularly come to Sumatra for a week or less for breaks in the cool Batak and Minang

highlands. It is quite feasible to fly into Medan and make for Danau Toba for five days or to Padang and take the bus up to Bukittinggi for a similar length of time. Long-haul visitors, with jet lag to deal with and perhaps a new climate too, would probably find such a short visit exhausting and ultimately less than satisfying.

When to go
Sumatra's climate varies considerably across the island. North of the equator the rainy season extends from October to April, and south of the equator from October to January. Road travel during the dry season is quicker and easier, but overland travel in the wet season is fine on the (largely) all-weather Trans-Sumatran Highway. Most tourists visit between June and October, so travelling out of those months is relatively quiet and hotel rates can often be bargained down.

Getting there
Air Most visitors arrive at Medan, in the north, near the west coast of Sumatra, which offers international connections with Kuala Lumpur (KLIA and Subang), Penang, Hong Kong, Bangkok and Singapore. There are also flights from Singapore to Padang. There are domestic connections with Jakarta from all Sumatran provincial capitals.

Boat The handy Belawan (Medan's port) to Penang international ferry service and the Belawan to Lumut (in Perak, Malaysia) have both been suspended. Check with agents around town for the latest, although it is unlikely these lines will be restored given the number of cheap airlines flying over the Straits. An alternative route into or out of Indonesia is to catch a regular high-speed ferry from Singapore's World Trade Centre or Tanah Merah pier to Batam or Bintan islands in the Riau archipelago (40 minutes). From there it is possible to catch a boat – fast or very slow – to Pekanbaru, up the Siak River on the Sumatran 'mainland', from where it is a five-hour bus ride to Bukitinggi. There are also ferry connections between Melaka and Dumai, although this is not a very popular entry/exit point. The most important domestic entry/exit point is Bakauheni on Sumatra's south tip; hourly ferries link Bakauheni with Merak (West Java). The **PELNI** ship *Kelud* calls in on Belawan on loops to Jakarta's Tanjung Priok via Balai Karimun and Batam respectively.

Getting around
Air This is the most convenient and comfortable way to travel around Sumatra. **Garuda** and **Merpati** service all the main provincial cities. The other main domestic airlines on Sumatra are **Lion Air** and **Kartika**. Smallest of all are **SMAC** and **Susi Air**, which tend to service more out-of-the-way places.

Bus Buses are the main mode of long-distance travel. Steady improvements to the 2500-km Trans-Sumatran 'Highway' (a misnomer – some sections are more like a village road, 1½ lanes wide), which runs down the entire island from Banda Aceh in the north to Bakauheni in the south, are making road travel much faster and more comfortable. It used to take 20 hours to travel from Parapat to Bukittinggi, now it takes 10-14 hours depending on the vehicle. Roads off the Trans-Sumatran Highway are still generally poor, and in the rainy season delays of two days are not unknown while floodwaters subside. Travelling through the Bukit Barisan, or along the west coast, is still quite slow, with average speeds of 40-50 kph, as the road follows every turn of the mountain. There are air-conditioned, VIP or express buses plying all the major routes. The most highly regarded private bus companies are **ALS** and **ANS**.

Tourist buses also now ply the popular routes. In particular, the route from Padang, through Berastagi, Danau Toba and Sibolga, to Bukittinggi. These *bis parawisata* (tourist buses) are often eight-seat minibuses that leave at a set hour (roughly) and tend to arrive more quickly than the *bis biasa* (ordinary bus) alternatives. Tourist services are safer; they often pick up and drop off at hotels in towns; and they may also include stops at designated tourist sights en route (the dreaded *objek wisata*). The main disadvantage (other than cost) is that they reduce contact between locals and tourists.

Train There is a limited rail network in Sumatra. In the north, there is a line running from Medan to Rantau Parapat, and from Medan to Tanjung Balai.

Medan

Medan is big, hot, noisy, congested and dirty, with only a few havens of greenery – for example, Merdeka Square – and no obvious 'sights' to enthrall the visitor. However, while the architecture is not notable by international standards it is significant in the Indonesian context, and Medan does provide a vivid and vivacious introduction to Asia for those who are new to the region. In addition, and perhaps because foreign tourists are less in evidence, the local people are generally warm and welcoming. For those coming from other parts of Indonesia, Medan shows the country in quite a different light, sharing plenty in common with Peninsular Malaysia. This is evident in the crumbling Chinese shophouses, with their low walkways and the smell of incense wafting out into the street. Visitors will also note the presence of a permanent Indian population, not seen anywhere else in the archipelago, driving becaks (rickshaws), cooking fine curries and worshipping at garish southern Indian Hindu temples.

Arriving in Medan → *Phone code: 061. Population: 2,109,030.*

Getting there
Medan is an international gateway and an easy one-hour hop by air from Singapore. There are also air connections with several Malaysian cities and many of western Indonesia's larger cities. The airport is in the centre of town. Medan's port of Belawan is visited by **PELNI** vessels that run fortnightly circuits through the Indonesian archipelago. Medan has two bus terminals. The **Amplas** terminal, 8.5 km south of the city centre, serves all destinations to the south. The **Pinang Baris** terminal, about 9 km to the northwest, serves destinations north of Medan. The train system is running, but services are limited. ▸▸ *See Transport, page 201.*

Getting around
Becak, sudaco, mesin becak (motorized becak), bis damri, metered taxi, unmetered taxi and kijang – if it moves, it can be hired. The fare around town on an oplet (minibus) is 3000Rp. For a ride on a becak expect to pay a minimum of 5000Rp; with a bit of bargaining, taxis are often available for the same price as a becak; on a mesin becak, 5000Rp. Becaks can be chartered for about 25,000Rp per hour.

Medan is a nightmare to get around; many of the main access roads are choked with traffic and the one-way system only seems to add to the frustration. However, becak drivers and taxis have become adept at chicken footing down side lanes and avoiding the main arteries.

Tourist information

The **North Sumatran Tourist Office** (Dinas Pariwisata) ① *Jln Jend A Yani 107, T061 452 8436, Mon-Fri 0800-1600*, has maps and good city and regional guides. **Dinas Pariwisata** ① *Jl Brig Jend Katamso 43, no telephone, daily 0900-1700*, is another tourist office but this one is less helpful and a quick peek into the visitor's book shows that around two tourists a month pop in. There is some material available but little English is spoken and it is often closed. Those who are interested in Medan's architectural heritage should try and get hold of *Tours through historical Medan and its surroundings*, by Dirk A Buiskool (1995). The pamphlet is sold in some hotel gift shops and is also available in the Dutch original.

Tours Tour companies have offices in most of the larger hotels and organize half-day city tours, and day tours to Berastagi and to the orang-utans at Bukit Lawang. Longer overnight tours to Danau Toba and to the Nias Islands are also offered by most tour agents.

Places in Medan → *For listings, see pages 197-202.*

Colonial buildings

The greatest concentration of colonial buildings is to be found along Jalan Balai Kota and its continuation, Jalan Jend A Yani, and around Merdeka Square. Few still perform their original functions as the headquarters of plantation companies, European clubs, and stately hotels. As Dirk A Buiskool explains in his pamphlet *Tours through historical Medan and its surroundings* (1995), from which much of the information below is taken, Medan underwent a building explosion during the first decade of the 20th century. The city's wealth and economic importance demanded many new buildings, and as these had to be constructed quickly there was a tendency towards standardization of design – producing what became known as 'normal architecture'.

Walking south from the northwest corner of the 'Esplanade', now **Merdeka Square** (Independence Square), the first building of note is the **Central Post Office** at Jalan Bukit Barisan 1. It was begun in 1909 and completed in 1911 and is refreshingly unchanged. Inside, the main circular hall beneath the domed roof still contains its original post office counters. On the other side of the road was Medan's most stately hotel, the **Dharma Deli**. Today, a new block so dominates the site that the original hostelry is all but invisible. The Dharma Deli was formerly the Hotel De Boer and began life in 1898 as a modest place with just seven rooms. However, as Medan's economic influence grew, so the Hotel De Boer also expanded and by 1930 it had 120 rooms. Among the innovations introduced at the hotel was the so-called 'mosquito-less room': rooms where the windows were entirely enclosed in wire gauze, allowing people to sleep without mosquito nets. Perhaps the most famous person to have stayed at the hotel was the spy, Mata Hari.

The **Padang** itself is notable for its huge, epiphyte-filled trees that skirt the square and provide relief from the sun. On the west side of the square are two more elegant buildings, side by side: the appropriately stolid Bank of Indonesia and the refined Balai Kota. The **Bank of Indonesia**, formerly the De Javasche Bank, was designed by Ed Cuypers in 1910 in Classical style. The **Balai Kota** was probably erected in 1908 and then modernized in 1923. The clock in the elegant tower was donated by Medan's most influential Chinese businessman – Tjong A Fie (see below). The new Balai Kota, or more fully the Kantor Wali Kotyamadya, is just over the river on Jalan Raden Saleh. The architect of this building has drawn on the original Balai Kota for inspiration, most obviously in the domed tower which imitates the original, barring the blank space where the clock should be.

The Chinese community

The strip of buildings running the length of Jalan Jend A Yani from Merdeka Square south to Jalan Pemuda are very different to the buildings on the Padang; the latter is representative of the colonial government and the economic interests that sustained and supported it. These, however, were largely owned by Medan's Chinese business community – they are small **Sino-Dutch shophouses** where families would at the same time run their businesses and live, sleep and eat. Although many are marred by modern facades, they are nonetheless notable for their use of both Dutch and Chinese architectural flourishes and for their variety. Most notable of all is the run-down and romantically decrepit **Tjong A Fie Mansion** at Jalan Jend A Yani 105. This quasi-colonial/quasi-Chinese house, with its green-and-beige paint scheme and peacock-topped entrance arch, was built by a wealthy Chinese businessman, after which it is named. Like other Chinese who found their fortunes in Southeast Asia, Tjong A Fie arrived in Medan from Guangdong (Canton) in 1875 almost penniless – he reputedly had a few pieces of silver sewn behind his belt. In Medan he gained the trust of the Dutch authorities and the sultan, and became the supplier for many of the area's plantations. Before long he was a millionaire and Medan's 'Major' – the highest ranking member of the Chinese community. He was a great philanthropist, giving generously to good causes – a founder, for example, of the Colonial Institute (now the Tropical Institute) in Amsterdam.

Opposite the mansion is the side street Jalan Jend A Yani I, which has a little reminder of the early days of independence in the spelling of the road name: DJln Djenderal A Yani. Walking north towards Merdeka Square a short distance is the **Tip Top Restaurant**, which began serving food and drinks in 1934 and continues to do so in a style redolent of the colonial period. Just across the railway line at the end of Jalan Jend A Yani V is the **Vihara Kong Ti Niong** – Medan's oldest Chinese pagoda.

Temples, pogodas and mosques

Another road with historical buildings is the garden-like Jalan Jend Sudirman (Polonia quarter), southwest of the town square. At the southwest edge of the city is the **Vihara Gunung Timur** ⓘ *Jln Hang Tuah 16, photography is not allowed in the pagoda, remember to remove your shoes before entering the inner sanctuary*, just west of Jalan Cik Ditiro. This building, erected in the late 1970s, is the largest Chinese pagoda in Medan. Set in a peaceful area, the main entrance to the temple is flanked by guardian lions. Filled with lanterns, incense and demons, the temple is a rewarding retreat from the bustle of the city. The highly decorated roof is probably its most notable feature. Locally known as **Candi Hindu** (Hindu temple), the Shri Mariamman is at Jalan H Zainul Arifin 130. The complex serves Medan's large South Asian community and the brightly painted figures of gods and animals stand out a mile. The temple welcomes visitors. This part of town, reasonably enough, is the Indian quarter and the temple has been recently renovated and expanded. However, there has been a Hindu temple on the site from 1884. The **Immanuel Protestant Church**, built in 1921 in art deco style, can be found back towards the town centre at Jalan Diponegoro 25. Almost facing it on the other side of the road is the **Mesjid Agung**, with a towering new minaret.

The attractive **Mesjid Raya** or **Grand Mosque** ⓘ *admission by donation*, with its fine black domes and turquoise tiles, can be found at the corner of Jalan Sisingamangaraja and Jalan Mesjid Raya. The mosque was built in 1906 in 'Moroccan' style by Sultan Makmun Al-Rasyid, and designed by the Dutch architect Dingemans. The marble came from Italy, the chandelier from Amsterdam, and the stained-glass from China. In the grounds is a small plot containing the tombs of the sultans of the Istana Maimun Palace, and a fairy-tale style minaret. It is a shame that the mosque is on such a busy road – it detracts from its beauty.

To the west of the mosque, set back from the road on Jalan Brig Jen Katamso, is the **Istana Maimun** – also known as the **Istana Sultan Deli** ① *daily 0800-1700, 3000Rp*. This impressive building was designed by Captain Theo van Erp, a Dutch architect working for the Royal Dutch Indies Army. It was constructed in 1888 as one element in a complex

Medan

Where to stay 🛏	Novotel Soechi 10	Cahaya Baru 14
Danau Toba International 1	Sri Deli 12	Corner Cafe Raya 1
Garuda Plaza 7	Zakia 15	De Deli Darbar 3
Ibunda 8		Imperial Cakery 6
Inna Dharma Deli 4	**Restaurants** 🍴	M&R 4
Madani 9	Belmondo 2	Merdeka Walk 9

N

200 metres
200 yards

that included the Grand Mosque. The predominant colour is yellow – the colour of the royal house of Deli. It is eclectic architecturally, embracing Italian, Arab and Oriental styles. Inside are photographs of the various sultans and their wives, and a poor oil painting of the Sultan Deli himself who built the palace. The interior includes a few pieces of Dutch furniture and the sultan's throne. His descendants continue to live in one wing of the palace.

Museums and the zoo

The **Museum Sumatera Utara** ① *Jln HM Joni 51, T061 771 6792, Tue-Sun 0830-1200, 1330-1700, 1000Rp*, some distance south of town off Jalan Sisingamangaraja, is an extensive building with an equally extensive – though of variable quality – collection of artefacts. Not surprisingly, it specializes in those of North Sumatran origin and upstairs has some fine wood and stone carvings from the Nias Islands. Unfortunately it is ill-lit and poorly maintained, with little useful explanatory detail. The **Bukit Barisan Museum** ① *Jln H Zainul Arifin 8, T061 453 6927, Mon-Fri 0800-1500, admission by donation*, also known as the Museum Perjuangan Abri or the Military Museum, displays a decaying selection of Sumatran tribal houses and arts and crafts, as well as military paraphernalia.

Medan listings

For hotel and restaurant price codes and other relevant information, see pages 9-12.

● Where to stay

Medan *p193, map p196*

The rock-bottom budget digs in Medan are no great shakes, but there are some good options in the slightly more expensive categories. There is a cluster of hotels on Jln SM Raja (Jln Sisingmangaraja), which is the best area to have a wander and compare prices.

$$$$-$$$ Novotel Soechi, Jln Cirebon 76, T061 456 1234, www.accorhotels.com/asia. This place is crawling with business people, and is deservedly popular for its excellent

RM Famili **5**
Rosvin **7**
Simpang Tiga **8**
Sun Plaza **10**
Tip Top **16**

service, good facilities and spacious smart rooms (some with pool views). Pool, fitness centre. Free Wi-Fi in rooms. Excellent discounts available. Recommended.

$$$$-$$ Danau Toba International, Jln Imam Bonjol 17, T061 415 7000. Sprawling hotel with long list of facilities, including tennis courts and a large pool set in a garden with plenty of outdoors seating. The rooms are a tad antiquated, but comfortable, and some have garden views. Wi-Fi is available in the lobby.

$$$-$$ Hotel Garuda Plaza, Jln SM Raja 18, T061 736 1111. Large hotel with friendly staff, comfortable rooms (some with free Wi-Fi access), cable TV and complimentary newspapers. There is a pool out the back with a pleasant lounging area.

$$$-$$ Hotel Inna Dharma Deli, Jln Balai Kota 2, T061 415 7744, www.innahotels. com. This historical hotel is looking a little rough around the edges nowadays. The rooms are ultra clean, spacious and have cable TV. Free Wi-Fi is available for guests in the hotel café. Pool.

$$$-$$ Madani Hotel, Jln SM Raja 1, T061 735 8000, www.madanihotelmedan.com. There are plenty of Islamic vibes at this plush 4-star hotel, with corridors filled with Lebanese music and cafés without beer. The staff are friendly and the rooms are spotless and clean with cable TV (most foreign-language channels are in Arabic). There is a 25% discount available, making this place excellent value. Recommended.

$$ Dhaksina Hotel, Jln SM Raja 20, T061 732 0000. Garish hotel with a fair selection of clean a/c rooms, although many have no windows. 10% discount available.

$$ Hotel Sumatra, Jln SM Raja 35, T061 732 1551. Big a/c rooms with clean attached bathroom, TV and some with balcony. Staff are friendly. Discounts available for stays of 5 nights or more.

$$-$ Hotel Sri Deli, Jln SM Raja 30, T061 736 8387. Good selection of rooms, including windowless economy rooms with mandi.

Things get better as prices rise, with cleanish standard a/c rooms filled with light.

$$-$ Ibunda Hotel, Jln SM Raja 31-33, T061 736 8787, www.ibundahotel.com. The pea-green facade of the Ibunda is unmissable, and the colour theme continues in the interior, with its confusing staircases reminiscent of an Escher painting. The rooms here are good value, the more expensive ones are huge, and the standard singles, though a little dark, come with a/c and TV.

$ Hotel Zakia, Jln Sipiso Piso 10-12, T061 732 2413. Staff are half conscious, but rooms here are not too bad for the price, with spartan fan rooms on the 2nd storey with veranda overlooking a small garden.

⑦ Restaurants

Medan *p193, map p196*
Medan's large Chinese community means that the Chinese food here is excellent. There are many small eating houses in the street running off Jln Jend A Yani. The Indian area of town is centred on Jln Cik Ditiro and Jln H Zainal Arifin, close to Sri Mariamman Temple.

$$ Belmondo, Jln Zainul Arifin 122, T061 451 8846. Restaurant with sophisticated pretences popular with expats and locals at weekends. There is a good wine list, fusion food, seafood and a convivial atmosphere. Live jazz on Sat nights from 2000.

$$ De Deli Darbar, Jln Taruma 88, T061 415 6858. Open 1100-2230. There is plenty of choice here, with a menu that features both southern Indian veg and non-veg frontier dishes. Good selection of naan bread and tasty tidbits. Recommended.

$$ M&R, Jln Taruma 37, T061 453 6537. Daily 1100-1500 and 1800-2100. Tidy eatery furnished in traditional eastern Chinese style with caged song birds hanging from the ceiling, patrons come to sample *nyonya* (Straits Chinese fusion of Malay and Chinese flavours thought to have originated in Melaka, Malaysia) cuisine. The menu is heavy on seafood, with good crab dishes.

$$-$ Merdeka Walk, Jln Balai Kota (on the western side of Merdeka Square). Daily 1200-2400. Collection of eateries including **Oh La La** (bakery serving filled croissants, lasagne and cakes), **Killiney Kopitiam** (Singaporean franchise offering *kaya* toast, half cooked eggs and plenty of coffee), as well as some smaller stalls serving Indonesian staples.

$$-$ Sun Plaza, Jln Zainul Arifin 7, T061 450 1500. Daily 1000-2200. Shopping mall with plenty of places to eat in clean, a/c comfort. **Dome** and **De'Excelso** are cafés serving sandwiches, pastas, salads and a wide range of coffees and ice cream. **Ya Kun Kaya Toast** is a Singaporean outfit serving *kaya* toast (*kaya* is a rich jam made from coconut), thick coffee and half-cooked eggs. There is also an excellent food court, and branches of **Bread Talk** and **Papa Ron's Pizza**. A reassuring spot for those that have returned from jungle treks.

$ Cahaya Baru, Jln Teuku Cip Ditiro 12, T061 453 0962. Daily 1000-2200. Cheap vegetarian and non-vegetarian Indian cuisine in a clean setting. The menu features biryanis, tasty veg thalis and all the usual favourites at very sensible prices.

$ Corner Café Raya, Jln Sipiso Piso 1, T061 734 4485. Open 24 hrs. English teachers pop in here for the city's coldest beer and roast chicken and mashed potato with gravy served up in a merry ambience.

$ Imperial Cakery, Jln Zainul Arifin 116. T061 451 6230. Daily 1000-2200. Spotless bakery with good range of cakes, also serves simple pasta dishes and good sandwiches. The smoked salmon with scrambled egg on French brioche gets the day off to a good start.

$ RM Famili, Jln S M Raja, T061 736 8787. Open 24 hrs. On the ground floor of the **Ibunda Hotel**, this clean *rumah makan* has some fine *nasi Padang* dishes, good Malay fare including *Ikan asam pedas* (fish cooked in a spicy tamarind sauce) and simple Indonesian favourites. The *sirsak* (soursop) juice here is a tropical delight.

$ Rosvin, Jln Ahmad Yani 114, T061 7786 0446. Small eatery serving up a good range of spicy Acehnese and Malay dishes, including their signature *nasi lemak* (rice cooked in coconut milk with small side dishes).

$ Simpang Tiga, Jln Ahmad Yani 83, T061 453 6721. Glorious *nasi Padang* (spicy West Sumatran food) in full a/c comfort as well as a play area for kids.

$ Tip Top, Jln Ahmad Yani 92, T061 451 4442. Daily 0800-2200. The venue of choice for the city's older generation of Chinese-Indonesians for a morning coffee and a chat, the **Tip Top** has pleasant outdoor seating, plenty of ice cream, a touch of colonial decadence and distinctly average Indonesian and Chinese dishes.

🍷 Bars and clubs

Medan *p193, map p196*
Most hotels in the upper categories have bars, which stay open until around 0200.
Hotel Danau Toba International (see Where to stay). Has 5 venues for boozing, including **Dangdut International** (with, unsurprisingly, live *dangdut* – Indonesian pop music heavily influenced by Bollywood and Arabic music), **Rock Café** and **Tobasa Club** with its different theme evenings including Ladies' Night on Thu and DJs at the weekend.
Zodiac, at the **Novotel Soechi** (see Where to stay). Live music at weekends, and some good drinks promotions.

🎭 Entertainment

Medan *p193, map p196*
Cinema
There is a cinema on the 3rd floor of the **Grand Palladium** (see Shopping) showing all the latest blockbusters, and some Indonesian films (20,000Rp). For information on what is currently showing, phone T061 451 4321.

❋ Festivals

Medan *p193, map p196*
Idul Fitri (Islamic holy day), is a movable feast. Muslims descend on the Maimun Palace in traditional dress to mark the end of the fasting month of Ramadan – a very colourful occasion.
Mar-May Medan Fair is held each year at the Taman Ria Amusement Park on Jln Gatot Subroto. There are also permanent cultural exhibits at the park.

○ Shopping

Medan *p193, map p196*
Antiques Jln Jend A Yani is the main shopping area, with the largest concentration of 'antique' shops. Beware of fakes: old Batak artefacts are cunningly mass produced and there are few real antiques for sale these days.

Books There is a branch of **Gramedia** at the Sun Plaza (see below) with a small selection of English-language books and magazines such as *Time* and *The Economist*.

Malls Sun Plaza, Jln Zainul Arifin 7, T061 450 1500, daily 1000-2200, has clothes shops, opticians, computer hardware and software and restaurants; **Grand Palladium**, Jln Kapten Mohlan Lubis 8, T061 451 4939, daily 0900-2200, cinema, mobile phones, magazines, (a few English language titles) and a huge supermarket in the basement.

Markets One of the greatest attractions of Medan is its markets, known locally as *pajak*. The huge **Pajak Pusat** (Central Market) – in fact an agglomeration of various markets selling just about everything – is located close to Jalan Dr Sutomo. It is renowned for its pickpockets. Safer is the **Pajak Petisar**, on Jln Rasak Baru, just off Jln Gatot Subroto. It is a fruit and vegetable market in the morning (0600), that later develops into a general

market, selling clothes, food and general merchandise. The **Pasar (Pajak) Ikan Lama** (Old Fish Market) is a good place to buy cheap batik, other types of cloth and assorted garments. It is on Jalan Perniagaan, close to Jln Jend A Yani. Visitors may see live fruit bats strung up for sale.

Supermarkets Kedai 24, Jln SM Raja, located near the hotels, open 24 hrs, has most daily necessities. If you can't find what you need here, then head to the top floor of **Yuki Simpang Raya**, opposite the Mesjid Raya, which has a slightly more comprehensive selection.

Textiles Jln Jend A Yani III, which runs off Jln Jend A Yani, has a number of textile outlets. Browsing through the markets can be rewarding – either the massive **Central Market** or the **Old Fish Market**; the latter is the best place to buy batik (see Markets, above). Formal batik can be found at **Batik Danar Hadi**, Jln Zainul Arifin 117, T061 457 4273, daily 0900-2100.

○ What to do

Medan *p193, map p196*
Tour operators
There are travel and tour companies all over town and most will provide a range of services from booking airline tickets through to providing tours and bus tickets. There is a concentration along Jln Katamso, south of the intersection with Jln Letjen Suprapto.
Amalia Amanda Tour and Travel, Jln Katamso 43, T061 452 1666. Ferry tickets to Penang.
Erni Tour, Jln Katamso 43 J, T061 456 4666. Ticketing and money changer.
Mutiara Tour and Travel, Jln Katamso 43 K, T061 456 6700. Ferry tickets and flights to Malaysia.
Perdana Ekspres, Jln Katamso 35C, T061 456 6222. Penang ferry tickets and PELNI agent.

Tobali Tour, Jln SM Raja 79, T061 732 4472. Tourist buses to Danau Toba.

Trophy Tour, Jln Katamso 33, T061 415 5777, www.trophytour.com. International and domestic ticketing. Very well established.

⊖ Transport

Medan *p193, map p196*

Air

Medan's Polonia International Airport is 3 km south of the town – effectively within the city. A taxi from the city centre to the airport costs 20,000Rp. Or take a bus from Pinang Baris terminal (in the direction of Amplas terminal) and get off at the traffic lights on Jln Juanda, the airport is 500 m on the right (3000Rp). There is a fixed-price taxi booth in the airport, on the right just before the exit. The fare to Jln SM Raja is a steep 35,000Rp.

Domestic To **Banda Aceh** daily with Sriwijaya, Garuda Indonesia and Kartika; **Pekanbaru** daily with Sriwijaya; **Padang** daily with Mandala; **Batam** daily with Lion Air and Sriwijaya; **Padang** daily with Mandala and Lion Air; **Yogyakarta** daily via **Padang** with Mandala; **Jakarta** daily with Garuda, AirAsia, Lion Air and Sriwijjaya.

International Daily to **Singapore** with Singapore Airlines and regular connections on Jetstar Asia (www.jetstar.com). AirAsia has daily flights to **Kuala Lumpur**. Also daily direct flights to **Penang** with AirAsia, Lion Air and Kartika Airlines.

Boat

Medan's port, **Belawan**, is 26 km north of the city. Shuttle buses meet passengers from the ferry. The fare into town is 9000Rp. However, ferry companies provide transport to Belawan from their offices as part of the cost of the ticket to **Penang**. Town buses for Belawan leave from the intersection of Jln Balai Kota and Jln Guru Patimpus, near the TVRI offices. Oplets also travel to Belawan (the destination is displayed). The PELNI vessels *Kelud* and *Sinabung*

call into Belawan on their way to Jakarta's Tanjung Priok. Of most use to travellers is the *Sinabung*, which stops at **Batam** (30-min ferry ride from Singapore), before heading to **Java**. This vessel departs every Tue. Check the latest PELNI schedule at the booking agent **Perdana Ekspres**, Jln Katamso 35C, T061 4566 2222.

Various companies run ferries: Perdana Ekspres, Jln Katamso 35C, T061 456 6222, and their partner **Amalia Amanda**, Jln Katamso 43, T061 452 1666, have express boats to **Penang** sailing Tue, Thu, Sat at 1000. The journey takes 5-6 hrs. The one-way fare is US$36 plus US$3 seaport tax. The return fare is US$60 plus US$3 seaport tax. Transport to **Belawan** is provided free by the company, but the trip from Belawan to **Medan** is charged at 9000Rp. Perdana Ekspres has an office in Penang at Ground Floor PPC Building, Pesara King Edward, T04 262 0802. Ferries leave **Penang** Mon, Wed, Fri at 0900. Fares are the same. Tickets can also be booked at www.langkawi-ferry.com.

Bus

Medan has 2 main bus terminals: Amplas and Pinang Baris. **Amplas terminal** is on Jln Medan Tenggara VII, 8.5 km south of the city centre off Jln Sisingamangaraja, and serves all destinations south of Medan including **Bukittinggi**, **Parapat** and **Danau Toba** (6 hrs, 25,000Rp), **Jakarta**, **Bali**, **Jambi**, **Dumai**, **Pekanbaru**, **Palembang** and **Sibolga**. Get there by yellow oplet running south (Nos 24, 52 or 57), 3000Rp. Major bus companies like **ALS** have their offices on Jln Sisingamangaraja close to the terminal (at the 6.5 km marker). The most comfortable way of getting to **Danau Toba** is to take the tourist minibus service offered by Tobali Tour, Jln SM Raja 79C, T061 732 4472, for 80,000Rp. The bus departs at 0900. Phone ahead to book a seat and ask to be picked up at your hotel.

The **Pinang Baris terminal** is on Jln Pinang Baris (off Jln Gatot Subroto, which becomes Jln Binjei), about 9 km northwest of the city centre, and serves **Banda Aceh** and other destinations north of Medan including **Bukit Lawang** (leaving every 30 mins, 3 hrs, 15,000Rp – don't pay the touts who wait for tourists, pay the driver at the end of your journey); and **Berastagi,** 2 hrs, 7000Rp. Get to the terminal by orange or green microlet running along Jln Gatot Subroto. The best way of getting to Berastagi is to catch microlet No 41 from the front of Yuki Simpang Raya heading to **Padang Bulan**, 3000Rp. Tell the driver you want to get off at Simpang Pos, where the streets are lined with buses heading to Berastagi and **Kebonjahe**, 2 hrs, 7000Rp. **Jakarta**, US$38; **Yogyakarta**, US$40; **Padang** and **Bukittinggi**, 20-22 hrs, US$14 or a/c US$24.

Bus companies It makes sense to book a seat over the phone rather than traipsing all the way to the offices the day before departure. Your hotel should be able to help you. Pelangi, Jln Gajah Mada 56, T061 457011, runs to Pekanbaru, Palembang, Banda Aceh and Jakarta. PMTOH, Jln Gajah Mada 57, T061 415 2546, serves **Banda Aceh**, **Yogya**, **Solo**, **Jakarta**. ANS, Jln SM Raja 30, T061 786 0667, super executive buses to Jakarta, Bukittinggi, Padang and Bandung. ALS, Jln SM Raja Km 6.5, T061 786685, has services to Dumai (for ferries to Batam and for Melaka, Malaysia), Jakarta, Banda Aceh, Yogya and Solo.

Car hire

National Car Rental, Hotel Inna Dharma Deli, see Where to stay. Cars with driver can be rented from the Sri Deli Hotel, see Where to stay.

Taxi

Can be rented by the day; ask at your hotel. Fares within Medan range from 10,000Rp to 25,000Rp (more if buying from the fixed-price booth at the airport). Most taxi companies are located at Jln Sisingamangaraja 60-107.

Train

The station is on Jln Prof M Yamin. The schedule from the train station is a little erratic. There are a couple of daily departures to **Rantau Parapat** (4-5 hrs, 55,000Rp/75,000Rp). Check the latest schedule at the station.

ⓘ Directory

Medan *p193, map p196*
Banks If travelling from Penang to Medan via Belawan Port, it is advisable to change money in Georgetown (Penang) before departure – the exchange rate is much better than in Medan. Duta Bank offers cash advances against Visa and MasterCard. The Hong Kong Bank has a 24-hr ATM. There are also a number of money changers on Jln Katamso. Bank Central Asia, Jln Bukit Barisan 3, will provide cash advances on Visa). Money changers include: King's Money Changer, Jln Pemuda 24; and PT Supra, Jln Jend A Yani 101. **Embassies and consulates** For Indonesian embassies and consulates abroad and for foreign embassies in Indonesia, see http://embassy.goabroad.com. **Immigration** Jln Binjai Km 6.2, T061 451 2112. **Medical services** Bunda Clinic (open 24 hrs), Jln Sisingamangaraja, T061 7032 1666; Herna Hospital, Jln Majapahit 118A, T061 414 7715; Gleneagles Hospital, Jln Listrik 6, T061 456 6268, is reputed to be the best in town. **Police** Jln Durian, T061 452 0453. **Telephone** At the General Post Office, Jln Bukit Barisan 1 (at Central Post Office) for overseas calls. There are other Wartel offices all over town, including on Jln Sisingamangaraja (next to the Hotel Deli Raya and opposite the Mesjid Raya) and on Jln Irian Barat (just north of the intersection with Jln Let Jend MT Haryono). Calls can also be placed from the Tip Top Café on Jln Jend A Yani.

Bukit Lawang

Bukit Lawang, sometimes also named 'Gateway to the Hills', is a small community on the edge of the Gunung Leuser Nature Reserve, an area of beautiful countryside. A few years ago Bukit Lawang was a thriving place with thousands of tourists coming to see the orang-utans. This is no longer true. The downturn in tourism in Indonesia has hit Sumatra hard. Things got worse for the town in November 2003 when a flash flood swept away much of the infrastructure and killed hundreds of residents. However, there is a real sense of resilience and community here, and the people are working hard to get the town firmly back on the tourist trail. Visitors will note the effort made to keep the area clean, with recycling and rubbish bins along all the paths in the village.

Arriving in Bukit Lawant → *Phone code: 061.*

Getting there
Direct buses leave from Medan's Pinang Baris terminal every 30 minutes (three hours, 15,000Rp). From Berastagi catch a bus to Medan and get off at Pinang Baris; from here, catch a regular bus to Bukit Lawang. Taxis can be hired in Medan, the journey will take two hours. **>>** *See Transport, page 206.*

Tourist information
The **Visitor Information Centre** ① *daily 0700-1500*, has free maps and can offer advice on hiking. It also sells a useful booklet on the park and its wildlife and flora (12,000Rp). You can get park permits here, including long-term research permits.

For free maps and a price list of guided tours, contact the guides association, HPI ① *opposite the Visitor Information Centre, T081 3707 30151, daily 0800-1500.*

Orang-Utan Rehabilitation Centre

Just outside the village is the famous centre established in 1973 – now one of Sumatra's most popular tourist destinations. The work of the centre is almost entirely supported by revenue from tourism. The orang-utan (*Pongo pygmaeus*) is on the verge of extinction throughout its limited range across island Southeast Asia, and the centre has been established by the Worldwide Fund for Nature to rehabilitate domesticated orang-utans for life in the wild. The problem is that there is a ready black market for orang-utans as pets and in Medan they sell for US$350. However, when the young, friendly animals grow up into powerful, obstreperous adult apes, they are often abandoned and some end up at Bukit Lawang. Locals come from Medan to frolic in the river, not to see the apes, so while the river may be busy, feeding time is comparatively quiet.

Getting there
The entrance to the reserve is a 30-minute walk from the village, following the Bohorok River upstream, which then has to be crossed by boat; from there it is another 20 minutes or so up a steepish path to the feeding point. Alternatively, buses and minibuses travel down Jalan Gatot Subroto, which becomes Jalan Binjei, leaving from the Central Market (45 minutes, 3000Rp). Leave Bukit Lawang an hour before feeding time to allow for the journey.

Entry to the park

Visitors can see the apes during feeding times (0800-0900 and 1500-1600, you should aim to get there five minutes beforehand). The times do sometimes change, so check at the PHKA office in Bukit Lawang. Guides can be hired from the PHKA office for one-, two- or three-day treks of varying difficulty and visitors have reported seeing gibbons, monkeys and orang-utans. All visitors must obtain a permit from the PHKA office (one day: 20,000Rp, plus 50,000Rp for camera and 150,000Rp for video camera) before entering the park. A passport must be shown before a permit is issued (although this is not strictly enforced). Afternoons are more crowded, especially at weekends; it is best to stay the night and watch a morning, weekday, feed if possible.

Next door to the PHPA office is a **Visitor Information Centre** ① *daily 0700-1500, donation requested*, which shows films in English on Monday and Friday at 2000 (when equipment is working), and also has a study room and a display.

Around Bukit Lawang

There are a number of caves in the vicinity. For the **Bat Cave** ① *5000Rp*, take a torch and non-slip shoes; it is not an easy climb and a guide is recommended (10,000Rp). There is also a **rubber processing plant** close by – ask at the visitors centre for a handout and map.

Tubing

Floating down the Bohorok River on an inner tube has become a popular excursion. Tubes can be hired for 10,000Rp per day in the village for the 12 km (two to three hours) journey to the first bridge. There is public transport from the bridge back to Bukit Lawang. For US$50 you can trek upstream and return in the late afternoon by inner tube. Dry bags are provided for cameras and other valuables. Beware of whirlpools and watch out for low branches; tourists have drowned in the past.

Hiking

Hiking is the best way to experience the forest and see the wildlife. The visitor centre has handouts and maps of hiking trails and guesthouses, and may be able to provide information about guides for jungle treks. Head to the Association of Indonesian Guides, **HPI** ① *near the visitor centre*, T081 3707 30151, *daily 0800-1500*, for a map, price list for treks and other information. Bukit Lawang has more than 130 guides, massively outnumbering the tourists and so there is some pressure to take one. The HPI office recommends getting a guide directly from their office, where they can match a guide to your interests and ensure the correct price. Note that all official guides carry an HPI identity card. Languages include English, German, Spanish, French and Dutch. Prices for all hikes are fixed by the HPI office. A three-hour hike costs US$22, one-day hike US$36 (plus US$14 to tube down the river back to Bukit Lawang after the trek), two days for US$80 (plus US$14 for tubing) and three days for US$100. All prices include guide, transportation, permit, food and tent.

It is possible to hike to **Berastagi** in three days at a cost of US$118. This trek is less popular because so much of the route has been deforested. Instead, those visitors wishing to trek through true jungle should opt for the five- to seven-day hike to **Kutacane**, US$300. Most treks require a minimum of three to four people. Note that these are arduous treks requiring fitness and hiking boots; check the credentials of guides – many lack experience (they should be able to produce a legal licence and permit). During the rainy season (around August-December) there can be very heavy downpours and good waterproofs are essential.

Whitewater rafting

The HPI offer rafting trips on the nearby Wampu River, costing around US$60 per person per day. These are sometimes combined with a trek.

Tangkahan → *For listings, see pages 205-206.*

Tangkahan lies about 40 km north of Bukit Lawang, next to the Gunung Leuser National Park and there is only one resort here, the **Bamboo River Guesthouse** (see Where to stay, page 206). What is special about this place is its proximity to unspoilt lowland rainforest, and the absence of tourists. No trekking is promoted here, so bird and animal life is more active. It is possible to hike (guide strongly recommended), take a canoe trip down the Batang Serangan River, or visit some hot sulphur springs.

Getting there

Tangkahan is a five-hour chartered bus ride from Bukit Lawang, ask at the tourist office for more information. From Medan, catch a bus from the Pinang Baris terminal to Tangkahan (three hours). At the river crossing in Tangkahan, shout for the raft man.

Bukit Lawang listings

For hotel and restaurant price codes and other relevant information, see pages 9-12.

● Where to stay

Bukit Lawang *p203*
The road ends at the bus stop, so reaching guesthouses further upstream means as much as a 25-min slog on foot. About 15 or so *losmen* line the Bohorok River up to the crossing-point for the reserve. Many guesthouses were damaged by the flood in 2003, and some were forced out of business. The slowdown means it is easy to find somewhere to sleep. The views and jungle atmosphere are best upriver, towards the park entrance.

A recent venture being organized through the Visitor Information Centre involves camping on the edge of the national park, a 2-hr walk from the village past the Bat Cave. The campsite is on the edge of a river and is very secluded. A great way to escape the crowds and witness nature first-hand. Enquire at the HPI office. There are currently no tents available to rent.
$$-$ Bukit Lawang Eco Lodge, T081 2607 9983. Set in lovely gardens, which produce some tasty vegetables for evening meals. With plenty of eco-friendly ideals, this hotel is one of the more popular places. The rooms are clean and comfortable, although don't have the views of some of the places further up the river. Recommended.
$$-$ Jungle Inn, T081 3753 24015, a.rahman3775@yahoo.co.id. The most popular guesthouse in Bukit Lawang with an extraordinary selection of rooms. The cheapest, out the back, have a balcony next to a small waterfall and gushing stream. There is one room with a rockface as a wall. The more expensive rooms are large and decadent (for Bukit Lawang) with 4-poster beds, thoughtful decoration and stunning views. The staff here are friendly, and the sunset sees guitars and bongos being taken from their hiding places for a Sumatran sing-along. Recommended.
$ Bukit Lawang Indah Guesthouse, T081 5276 15532. 38 clean and spacious rooms with fan and squat toilet. 24-hr electricity.
$ Garden Inn, T081 3968 43235. Rickety wooden structures with perilous stairs. Rooms have balcony with sublime river views, and bathrooms with squat toilet. Recommended.

$ Jungle Tribe, T081 3751 26275. Offers 1 room, more planned. Spacious, with balcony.
$ The Lizard Guesthouse. Friendly place right on the river with simple rattan-walled rooms. The café downstairs has a TV and selection of DVDs. The owner speaks superb English and is a good source of information.
$ Sam's Guesthouse, T081 3700 93597. The rooms that have been finished are pleasant, some with beautiful views over the river and comfy beds with mosquito nets.

Tangkahan *p205*
$ Bamboo River Guesthouse, on the Buluh River, Tangkahan, 40 km north of Bukit Lawang, no telephone, communication is by walkie-talkie. Owned by an English woman and a local senior guide. Has 10 rooms and an evening meal costs around 25,000Rp.

🍴 Restaurants

Bukit Lawang *p203*
There are plenty of stalls near the bridges offering simple local fare. Most of the hotels have decent menus (all **$**).
$ Green Hill Café. Pool table and simple snacks in a breezy riverine setting.

$ The Jungle Inn. Fine potato and pumpkin curries and juices made with local honey.
$ Jungle Tribe. Macaroni cheese and pizzas somewhat overshadowed by the extensive cocktail list for those wanting a jungle party.
$ Rock Inn Café and Bar. Daily 0900-2400. Built into a rockface, with a motorbike hanging from the wall, this local hang-out offers curries, soups, tacos and spaghetti.
$ Tony's Restaurant. Daily 0700-2300. Small bamboo eatery serving up fair pizzas. The owner is proud of her fettuccine, which she says gets top marks from European visitors.

🚌 Transport

Bukit Lawang *p203*
Bus
There are no direct buses from Bukit Lawang to Berastagi. Instead head back to Pinang Baris and jump on a Berastagi-bound bus (2 hrs, 7000Rp).

ⓘ Directory

Bukit Lawang *p203*
Banks *Losmen* and tour companies change money, but rates are poor so bring sufficient cash. **Telephone** Wartel office in main 'village'. Mobile reception gets poorer the further up the river you go.

Berastagi

Berastagi, is a hill resort town, lying 1400 m above sea level on the Karo Plateau among the traditional lands of the Karo Batak people. Though Berastagi may not be a one-horse town, it gives the impression of being a one-road town. There is also the distinct feel that it has become a way-station, a sort of trucking stop between other more important places.

Arriving in Berastagi → *Phone code: 0628.*

Getting there
Berastagi is 68 km from Medan and 147 km from Parapat. There are regular bus connections with Medan (two hours, 7000Rp). Getting from Parapat on a public bus is a little more complicated as it involves changes. The bus station is at the south end of the main road, Jalan Veteran. ▶▶ *See Transport, page 211.*

Getting around

Visitors can travel easily around town on foot, by bicycle and using oplets. For the surrounding villages and towns cars can be hired and oplets service some routes. Dokars can also be used for short local journeys; in Berastagi these are known as *sados*.

Tourist information

Staff at **Dinas Pariwisata** ⓘ *Jln Gundaling No 1, T0628 91084*, speak good English and are a useful source of local information. Their guided hikes up the nearby volcanoes are some of the cheapest in town. The **Sibayak Guesthouse** ⓘ *Jln Veteran 119*, and the **Wisma Ginsata** ⓘ *Jln Veteran 79*, are also excellent sources of information. The Sibayak keeps a particularly useful comments book.

Places in Berastagi → *For listings, see pages 209-212.*

The town does not have many specific sights of interest, but its position, surrounded by active volcanoes, is memorable. Unfortunately, Berastagi has a rather uncared-for feel, and it is somewhat featureless. Nonetheless, it is a good place to cool off after the heat and bustle of Medan, and go for a mountain hike. It is also a good base from which to explore the surrounding countryside.

For those without the time to visit the Batak villages outside Kabanjahe, there is a Batak village of sorts – **Peceren** ⓘ *2000Rp for admission to village,* just outside town on the road to Medan, 100 m past the **Rose Garden Hotel**. It is rather run down and dirty, with a few Batak houses interspersed with modern houses; however, it is in some respects more authentic than those that have been preserved, showing how living communities are adapting to the changing world. Just 200 m or so up Jalan Gundaling from here is a strange Buddhist temple – the **Vihara Buddha**. How the architect managed to arrive at this fusion of styles is not clear, but 'ungainly' would not be an unkind description. The general goods market behind the bus station is worth a wander.

Around Berastagi

Kabanjahe

ⓘ *12 km south of Berastagi. Easily accessible by bus, regular departures from the bus station on Jln Veteran, 25 mins, 3000Rp.*
Meaning 'Ginger garden', Kabanjahe lies on the main road and scores of buses and oplets make the journey. It is a local market town of some size and little charm, but it is worth visiting on Monday market day. Kabanjahe is also an important communication town. From here it is possible to walk to traditional villages of the Karo Batak people (see below).

Lingga and Barusja

ⓘ *Catch a bus from the bus station on Jln Veteran to Kabanjahe, and from there a microlite or bemo onwards; in Kabanjahe they leave from the intersection of Jln Pala Bangun, Jln Veteran and Jln Bangsi Sembiring. To visit Lingga, an 'entrance fee' of 2000Rp must be paid at the tourist information centre in the main square (visitors with a guide may not have to pay).*
Karo Batak villages are to be found dotted all over the hills around Berastagi. The more traditional villages are not accessible by road and must be reached on foot; to visit these communities it is recommended to hire a guide (ask at your hotel or the tourist centre). It can make sense to charter a bemo for the day – a lot more ground can be covered.

Two villages that can be visited with relative ease from Kabanjahe are Lingga and Barusjahe. Both can be reached by microlite from Kabanjahe. This ease of access has inevitably resulted in rather 'touristy' villages. **Lingga**, is about 4 km northwest of Kabanjahe and is a community of some 30 Batak houses, of which there are about a dozen traditional longhouses. There are overpriced carvings for sale. Photographs of the local people might require payment. **Barusjah** is slightly more difficult to get to and as a result is marginally more 'traditional', but can still be reached by microlite from Kabanjahe. It is rather a dirty village with very few houses in the traditional style, but there are a few over two centuries old (and as a result are decaying badly). The soaring roofs are particularly impressive.

Dokan

ⓘ *Catch a Simas bus at the bus terminal in Kabanjahe and ask to be set down at the Dokan turn (13 km from Kabanjahe), it is then a 3-km walk to the village, a donation is expected. Buses on to Sipisopiso are usually pretty crowded.*

Dokan is a fine Karo Batak village that lies halfway between Kabanjahe and Sipisopiso, where villagers are less inclined to hassle.

Sipisopiso waterfalls

ⓘ *24 km from Kabanjahe, a 1-hr drive southeast of Berastagi. Catch a bemo to Pemangtangsiantar and ask to get off at Simpang Sitanggaling. The falls are a 30-min walk from here or a quick ojek ride away. Entry to the falls is 2000Rp.*

The falls cascade through a narrow gap in the cliffside and then fall 120 m to **Danau Toba**. It is possible to walk along a spur to a small gazebo for a good view of the falls, or to walk to the bottom and back takes about one hour. There is the usual array of souvenir stalls and *warungs*. In spite of the commercialism, the falls are a pretty spectacular sight. There is no accommodation here, but from Sipisopiso towards **Parapat** is **Siantar Hotel**, a nice place to stop for coffee and fried bananas. In its garden and restaurant you have a superb view of the lake, but despite its name you cannot sleep there, it is only a restaurant.

Mount Sibayak

Sibayak lies northwest of Berastagi at 2095 m and can be climbed in a day, but choose a fair weather day and leave early for the best views (and to avoid the rain). Take the trail from behind Gundaling Hill, ask at your hotel for directions before setting out. Guides can be easily found (again, ask at your hotel – they will charge US$7-15 depending on the size of the party), and a map of the route is available from the **Tourist Information Office**. Information is also available from either the **Ginsata** or **Sibayak** guesthouses. Wear good walking shoes and take a sweater as it can be chilly. It takes about two to three hours to reach the summit, along a logging road, or alternatively there is a jungle trek that is quicker if you take a bemo to Semangat Gunung, in the Daulu Valley. Over the summit, the descent is down 2000 steps to reach the hot water and **Sulphur Springs** ⓘ *daily 0800-2300, 5000Rp.* The sulphur is collected by local people and is used as medicine and as a pesticide.

Mount Sinabung

Sinabung, which rises to 2454 m to the west of Berastagi, is another popular climb. There are now three routes up the volcano. One of the routes is well marked but it is best to take a guide as heavy rain and mist can make it very dangerous (see note, below). Seven people disappeared here in 1996/1997, when mist made it impossible for them to find the path. Maps are available from the Sibayak guesthouses.

To climb the mountain without a guide, catch a bus to Danau Lau Kawar (one hour, 6000Rp). The path from the village passes a restaurant; fork left just after the restaurant (do not continue along the main path). This path then passes a house and on the left you will see a small hut; you need to turn left again onto another path that passes the hut. The route then works its way through the forest for one hour and is relatively well marked with arrows and string. As the path leaves the forest it becomes very steep and enters a rock gully (also steep). The route passes an old campsite and then a cliff overhang decorated with graffiti. (This makes a good shelter in bad weather as hot steam issues through vents.) After around three to four hours in total, the path reaches the summit. Paths skirt the crater lip but care is needed.

Take good hiking boots, a jumper, a change of clothes, and a water bottle. Tents can be hired from the Sibayak guesthouses. Leeches can sometimes be a problem.

Note The Tourist Information Service recommends that visitors take a guide with them on mountain hikes as the weather is very unpredictable and the thick jungle on the flanks of the mountains leads into the massive Gunung Leuser National Park where it is very easy to get lost. The Tourist Information Service and Ginsata have a list of recent tourist mishaps on the mountain, including details of an Austrian tourist who got lost on Sibayak in 2007, and was found nine days later unconscious in a garden in a small town on the edge of the park. He claimed he was led further into the jungle by the ghosts of two German tourists, missing since 1997, a claim locals – with their appreciation of anything connected to the supernatural – seem to believe heartily.

Sidikalang

This is a small, unremarkable town, 75 km southwest of Berastagi, which serves an important 'linking' function. From here it is possible to travel north, along the valley of the Alas River to Kutacane and the Gunung Leuser National Park, and from there to Takengon and the Gayo Highlands, and finally to Banda Aceh at the northern tip of Sumatra. Alternatively, it is possible to travel west to the coast and then north along the coast, again to Banda Aceh. The countryside around here is locally known for the quality of its coffee.

Tongging

Tongging is a small town on Danau Toba's northern shore. Like the much more popular Samosir Island, it is possible to swim in the lake and generally relax, although the tourist infrastructure here is not nearly as developed. It is a good base to see the Sipisopiso falls (see above) and also a number of relatively untouristy Batak villages, including **Silalahi**. Tongging can also be used as an alternative route to Samosir – there are boats from Tongging to Samosir via Haranggaol every Monday at 0730.

Berastagi listings

For hotel and restaurant price codes and other relevant information, see pages 9-12.

⬤ Where to stay

Berastagi *p206*
Berastagi is not a particularly attractive town, but it does have a selection of some of the best *losmen* in Sumatra. Not only

are the rooms clean and well maintained, but the owners go out of their way to provide travellers with information on the surrounding area. They arrange trips to traditional ceremonies, inform travellers on the best way to climb the mountains and on hikes, and are generally highly constructive. Breakfast is not usually included in the price.

$$$$-$$$ Sibayak Internasional Hotel,
Jln Merdeka, T0628 91301, www.hotel
sibayak.com. A 4-star hotel perched on
a hillside overlooking the town. Rooms
are clean, with cable TV. There is a pool,
tennis court, disco, putting green and
free Wi-Fi access in the lounge area.
40% discount available.

$ Ginsata Hotel and Guesthouse,
Jln Veteran 27, T0628 91441. The hotel is
on the noisy main road and has clean
rooms with cold-water shower. The
guesthouse (enquire at hotel office) around
the corner is much quieter and has tidy
simple rooms. The owner is an excellent
source of local information. Recommended.

$ Hotel Melati Bangkit Nan Jaya, Jln
Pendidikan 82, T081 2646 5006. Relaxed
place out of town, with pleasant rooms,
some with TV. There is no restaurant, but
they can prepare a simple evening meal
on request. Bargain for a decent price.

$ Sibayak Losmen, Jln Veteran 119, T0628
91095. This *losmen* is reached by walking
through a travel agent's office. One of the
more homely options in town, the staff here
are friendly and offer excellent information
on tours. The rooms with attached bathroom
(cold water, squat toilet) on the 2nd floor
are clean, but some are windowless. The
cheaper rooms on the top floor have shared
bathroom and access to a lovely roof terrace.
Hot-water showers are available for 5000Rp.

$ Sibayak Multinational Guesthouse,
Jln Pendidikan 93, T0628 91031, irnawati_
pelawi@yahoo.co.id. 2 km out of town on
the road leading towards Gunung Sibayak,
this place is set in sprawling gardens with
excellent views and a quiet atmosphere.
More expensive rooms are big with hot-
water showers. The smaller, old-style rooms
are passable, but have no hot water.

$ Wisma Sibayak, Jln Udara 1, T0628
91104, bhirinxz@yahoo.com. What looks
like a Malay doll's house from the outside, is
home to the best budget accommodation
in town, with excellent local information,
spotless rooms with or without attached

bathroom (cold water), lots of communal
space and friendly vibes. Recommended.

$ Wisma Sunrise, Jln Kaliaga 5, T0628
92404. Simple, clean rooms with cold-water
shower. This place has superb views over
the town and down to the plains beyond.
The owner works at the tourist office in
town and can arrange tours to Danau
Toba and Bukittinggi. There are no eating
facilities here.

Restaurants

Berastagi *p206*

There are a good number of restaurants
along Jln Veteran – serving mainly Padang
food. Fruits grown in the area include
avocados and *marquisa* (passion fruit);
the latter is made into a delicious drink.

$ Eropa, Jln Veteran 48G, T0628 91365.
Daily 0700-2100. Simple eatery with a long
list of Chinese dishes and some Western
dishes such as soups, pasta and steaks.
Good for those needing a dose of pork.

$ Losmen Sibayak. Decent Western and
Indonesian fare.

$ Mexico Fried Chicken, Jln Veteran 18,
T0628 93252. Open 0800-2300. Fast-food
fans might want to pop in. The entrance
has a sign with a Hispanic man wearing a
panama hat with MFC emblazoned on it.
Fried chicken set meals, burgers and coffee
form the menu.

$ Raymond Café, Jln Trimurti, T0813 9742
8979. Daily 0700-2300. Friendly and a
good place to meet travellers, chat with
locals and get a taste of the delicious local
vegetables. The avocado salad with a
lemon juice dressing is superb, as are the
juices. Simple Western and Indonesian fare
is good value here. Recommended.

$ Wisma Sibayak. Serves traveller-friendly
Western and Indonesian fare.

Foodstalls

There are many open-air *warungs* serving
good, fresh food, using the temperate fruit
and vegetables grown in the surrounding

countryside. **Jln Veteran** has the best selection. The market near the monument just off Jln Veteran sells fresh produce.

⊙ Shopping

Berastagi *p206*
Antiques and handicrafts Sold in several shops along Jln Veteran. **Mamaken** at Jln Veteran 16, T0628 91256, daily 0800-2100, sell mostly Batak pieces.

⊙ What to do

Berastagi *p206*
Hiking
It is possible to hike through spectacular countryside, all the way to Bukit Lawang from Berastagi in 3 days. However, the government is anxious about visitors disturbing this culturally sensitive area and trekkers should take the time and care to organize trips properly. Ask in town at the Sibayak Guesthouse or at the Tourist Information Service, Jln Gundaling 1, for trekking information. There are numerous guides offering treks to Bukit Lawang; this is a difficult and demanding trek requiring a degree of fitness and good walking boots. Most people trek this route in the other direction, from Bukit Lawang to Berastagi (see page 204). Many of the guides have little experience so check credentials carefully.

Tour operators
The best are those attached to the Sibayak and Ginsata *losmen*. They can arrange canoe or raft trips along the Alas River to the northwest of Berastagi. The journey passes through the Gunung Leuser National Park with traditional villages and tropical rainforest. An all-inclusive 3-day trip, costs US$110. 3-day guided jungle treks are also available for about US$110. Other places worth visiting for tour information include: **CV Berastagi View**, Jln Veteran 4 (inside post office), T0628 92929, brastagiview@yahoo.co.id.

Dinas Parawisata, Tourist Information Service, Jln Gundaling 1, T0628 91084.

⊖ Transport

Berastagi *p206*
Bus
In order to get to **Parapat** (for Danau Toba) by public bus, it is necessary to change twice: once in Kabanjahe and then in Pemangtangsiantar.

From Berastagi, minibuses and oplets travel to **Kabanjaje** continuously (25 mins, 3000Rp). From there, buses leave for **Pemangtangsiantar** (every 30 mins 0800-1500, 3 hrs, 15000Rp). From Pemangtangsiantar, there are buses to Parapat (every 30 mins, 1 hr, 15,000Rp). There are a couple of alternative and less used routes to **Toba** and **Samosir**. One is to catch a bus to **Haranggaol**, on the north side of Danau Toba. For **Bukit Lawang** catch a Pinang Baris bound bus (2 hrs, 8000Rp), and connect with a Bukit Lawang-bound bus (3 hrs, 15,000Rp).

Tongging
Boat
A boat goes from Tongging to **Haranggaol** every Mon at 0730, which links with the 1500 boat from Haranggaol to **Ambarita**.

Bus
From Berastagi there are direct bus connections with **Tongging**, about 1 per hr in the afternoon, from Jln Kapiten Mumah Purba (10,000Rp). Alternatively, take a bus or bemo to **Kabanjahe** (3000Rp) and from there a minibus to **Simpang Situnggaling** (1 hr, 6000Rp). From here there are minibuses to **Tongging** (1 hr, 6000Rp). Leave enough time as buses only run until about 1600 and there is a lot of hanging around.

⊙ Directory

Berastagi *p206*
Banks There are several banks and money changers in town, and they will change

most TCs. **Medical services** Health centre, Jln Veteran 30. **Telephone** Wartel office for international telephone calls, Jln Veteran (by the Bank Negara Indonesia).

Danau Toba

Danau Toba and the surrounding countryside is one of the most beautiful areas in Southeast Asia. The cool climate, pine-clothed mountain slopes, the lake and the sprinkling of church spires give the area an almost alpine flavour. After Medan or Padang, it is a welcome relief from the bustle, heat and humidity of the lowlands. The vast inland lake lies 160 km south of Medan and forms the core of Batakland in both a legendary and a geographical sense. The lake covers a total of 1707 sq km and is the largest inland body of water in Southeast Asia (87 km long and 31 km across at its widest point). Lodged in the centre of the lake is Samosir Island, one of Sumatra's most popular destinations (see page 216).

Danau Toba was formed after a massive volcanic explosion 75,000 years ago, not dissimilar – although far more violent – to the one that vaporized Krakatoa in the late 19th century. The eruption of Toba is thought to have been the most powerful eruption in the last million years. The area is now volcanically dormant, the only indication of latent activity being the hot springs on the hill overlooking Panguraran (see page 219). The fact that Danau Toba's water is so warm for a lake at close to 1000 m leads one to assume that there must be some heat underwater too.

Arriving in Danau Toba

Getting there
There is only one way to get to Danau Toba and that is by road. It is 147 km from Berastagi, 176 km from Medan and 509 km from Bukittinggi. The vast majority of visitors either approach from Medan (although some take the troublesome route from Berastagi) or from the south via Padangsidempuan (the road to Bukittinggi and Padang). Taking the Trans-Sumatran Highway from Medan via Tebingtinggi is a fairly fast and direct route, taking about four hours on a good day. The main bus terminal is on Jalan Sisingamangaraja (Jalan SM Raja) – aka the Trans-Sumatran Highway – around 1 km from the centre of town. Some buses stop at bus agencies and others run from the ferry terminal to/from Samosir.

Getting around
Bemos can be hired for 2500Rp for trips around town. There are also various forms of water transport. Danau Toba's two main destinations are the town of Parapat on the mainland and the island of Samosir (see page 216). Buses drop passengers off in Parapat and from here there are regular passenger ferries to Samosir Island. A car ferry runs from Ajibata, just south of Parapat. ▶ *See Transport, pages 215 and 223.*

Parapat → *For listings, see pages 213-216.*

Parapat is a small resort on the east shores of Danau Toba frequented by the Medan wealthy. It was established by the Dutch in the 1930s, although today most Western visitors merely breeze through en route to Samosir Island (but must pay 1000Rp entrance for the privilege, although this is not strictly enforced). There are stunning views over the lake, but unfortunately there doesn't seem to have been any coherent attempt to plan the development of the town. This means that there are architectural monstrosities side-by-side with elegant villas.

Parapat has the air of a 1950s European beach resort, with its pedaloes, metal railings, light blue paint and low-rise villa accommodation. This would be a great selling point for nostalgists, but unfortunately all the most attractive hotels are being allowed to slide into ruin, unloved and under-invested. Instead money is being poured into new, large and rather insensitive places. Nowadays, most foreign visitors get out of Parapat as soon as possible and head to the more sedate and rural charms of Samosir.

Tourist information

The tourist office, **Pusat Informasi**, is on Jalan P Samosir, under the archway that welcomes visitors to the town. However, there is virtually no information available here and it is hard to know why it exists.

Places in Parapat

There are few sights in Parapat. The best **beaches** are a little way out of town – like those at Ajibata village, about 1 km south of Parapat – but easily walkable. Saturday is market day when Bataks selling local handicrafts and 'antiques' converge on the town and particularly on the market area at **Pekan Tigaraja**, close to the ferry dock for Samosir. A smaller market is also held here on Tuesday and Thursday. The bright, rust-red roofed church above the town sits in well-cared for gardens, with views over the lake. On Sunday, services have as many as eight to 10 hymns.

Haranggaol → *For listings, see pages 213-216.*

This is a small, sleepy, rather run-down town on Danau Toba's northeastern shore. Few tourists visit the town, but there is an excellent **market** on Monday and Thursday – when there are early morning boat connections with Samosir from Ambarita and/or Simanindo – and good walks in the surrounding countryside. If visitors wish to experience the wonder of Toba, without the crowds at Parapat and on Samosir, then this is the place to come.

Arriving in Haranggaol

Haranggaol lies off the main bus route, so it can take a time to reach the town. There are bus connections from Kabanjahe (easily accessible from Berastagi) to Seribudolok, and from there bemos run to Haranggaol. Getting to or from Parapat to Haranggaol is not easy; it involves three bus changes and it usually takes eight hours to cover the 50-odd km. Taking the ferry is easier. ⏵ *See Transport, page 216.*

Danau Toba listings

For hotel and restaurant price codes and other relevant information, see pages 9-12.

🛏 Where to stay

Parapat *p212*

Most tourists merely breeze though Parapat on market day or on their way to or from Samosir. However, there is a fair range of

options for those who miss the last ferry or have an early morning bus to catch.
$$$-$$ Hotel Inna Parapat, Jln Marihat 1, T0625 41012. With a distinct 1970s design, this 3-star hotel has a range of comfortable rooms with TV and bath. The rooms at the back are best, with beautiful views of the lake, and a balcony. There is a good swimming beach and jet skis for hire. Free Wi-Fi access in the lobby. Discounts available (30%).

$$ Toba Hotel, Jln Pulo Samosir 8, T0625 41073. Though the corridors here are virtually pitch black at noon and the furniture is rather ancient, the rooms are right on the shoreline, and there is access to a beach and relaxed outdoors seating. Upstairs rooms are comfortable, with better views.

$$-$ Mars Family Hotel, Jln Kebudayaan 1, T0625 41459. The cheap rooms here are dark, but clean. Paying a little more gets a spotless room, with lake views and TV. Peaceful and well-run hotel. Recommended.

$ Charlie's Guesthouse, Tigaraja, T0625 41277. The owner of this place is a popular Batak pop star, and speaks English with the peculiar cockney accent the locals develop here. Near the harbour for boats to Tuk Tuk, so is ideal for late-night arrivals intending on leaving town the next morning. Homely and chaotic hotel with simple and comfortable rooms, although a little dark.

Haranggaol *p213*
$ Haranggaol, situated in town rather than on the lake shore. The best place to stay. Some rooms have hot water. There's a large eating area, used to catering for tour groups.

$ Segumba Cottages, 3 km out of town. Bali-style cottages situated in a beautiful, quiet position. Some rooms with *mandi*.

🍴 Restaurants

Parapat *p212*
There are 2 concentrations of restaurants: on Jln Haranggaol and along Jln Sisingamangaraja. Haranggaol restaurants are geared more to tourists, while locals and Indonesians tend to eat at those on Jln Sisingamangaraja. The Indonesian (and Chinese) restaurants along Jln Sisingamangaraja are generally better than those on Jln Haranggaol.

$ Hong Kong, Jln Haranggaol 91, T0625 41395. Daily 0800-2100. Clean place serving up good portions of Chinese food and a smattering of Western fare. Recommended.

$ Istana, Jln SM Raja 68, towards the bus terminal. Good *nasi Padang*. Recommended.

$ Paten, Jln SM Raja (opposite the entrance gateway to Parapat). One of the better Chinese restaurants in this strip. Well priced.

$ Restoran Asia, Jln SM Raja 80-82, T0625 41450. Daily 0700-2200. Chinese and Indonesian food, with excellent seafood and sweet-and-sour dishes. Also some fair steaks.

$ Rumah Makan Islam Murni, Jln Haranggaol 84. Daily 0700-2200. Small but tasty selection of Malay cuisine. The *nasi soto* (chicken in rich coconut-based soup with potato patty served with rice) is excellent.

$ Rumah Makan Marina, Jln Haranggaol 48. Daily 0800-2100. Indonesian dishes, clean.

$ Sederhana, Jln Haranggaol 38. One of the best Padang restaurants in town, good *kangkung*, clean and well-run.

🎭 Entertainment

Parapat *p212*
Batak cultural shows are held on public holidays and during the **Danau Toba Festival** in Jun at the Open Air Stage on Jln Kebudayaan. The more expensive hotels (eg Inna Parapat) also sometimes organize cultural shows.

✺ Festivals

Parapat *p212*
Jun/Jul Pesta Danau Toba (Danau Toba Festival) (movable), held over a week. Hardly traditional, but there are various cultural performances and canoe races on the lake.

🛍 Shopping

Parapat *p212*
Jln Sisingamangaraja and Jln Haranggaol are the main shopping areas, and both have the same type of souvenir shops. **Batak Culture Art Shop**, towards the bottom of Jln Haranggaol, is better than most and sells some authentic Batak pieces. There's

a market at **Pekan Tigaraja** near the ferry jetty, on Sat – a good place to buy batik and handicrafts. On other mornings there is a small food market.

⊙ What to do

Parapat *p212*
Cruises
Boats can be hired from near the **Toba Hotel**. Trips around Samosir cost US$137, or a 1-hr ride around the lake can be had for US$44. These prices are highly ambitious and good bargaining should bring the price down significantly.

Rafting
Day-trips down the Asahan River (80 km from Parapat) for US$80 per person (minimum 2 people). Price includes all equipment, food and transportation.

Swimming
There is a decent beach for swimming in front of the **Hotel Inna Parapat**.

Tour operators
Tour companies in Parapat have gained a rather poor reputation. Usually they are just used to book bus tickets and confirm flights, rather than arrange tours.
Dolok Silau, Jln S Raja 56 and at the harbour near **Charlie's Guesthouse**, T0625 41467. ANS bus tickets to destinations in Sumatra and beyond. Also arranges rafting trips down the Asahan River.
Planet Wisata, Jln Haranggaol 97, T0625 41037. Bus and plane tickets. Also books AirAsia flights.
Raja Taxi, Tigaraja, opposite **Charlie's Guesthouse**. Minibuses to Medan.

Watersports
Water-scooters and pedal boats on the waterfront and from the **Hotel Inna Parapat**.

⊖ Transport

Parapat *p212*
Boat
Parapat is the main port for **Samosir Island**, and ferries leave the town from the jetty in the Tigaraja market at the bottom of Jln Haranggaol (0930-1730, 30 mins, 7000Rp). Most ferries dock at Tuk Tuk on Samosir and they will drop off at the various hotel jetties, so state your destination. Some continue north to Ambarita, while others also dock at Tomok just south of the Tuk Tuk Peninsula. Most of the hotels and guesthouses have a ferry timetable posted. For further details, see page 223. Note that arriving after dark makes it difficult to reach Samosir the same day. The only ferry operating after 1930 is the car ferry (see below). For those who arrive in Parapat after the last ferry has departed, and can't bear the thought of spending a night in town, it is possible to charter a boat for around US$40 (bargain hard).
   Car ferry There is a car ferry from Ajibata, just south of town, to **Tomok**, every 3 hrs, 0830-2130, 4000Rp for foot passengers, 150,000Rp for a car.

Bus
There are no direct buses to **Berastagi** – it is necessary first to travel to **Pemangtangsiantar** (1 hr, 15,000Rp), and then change to a **Kebonjahe** bus (3 hrs, 15,000Rp), before finally getting on a bus bound for **Berastagi** (25 mins, 3000Rp).
   For **Medan**, minibuses pick passengers up off the ferry from Tuk Tuk and drive to the Amplas terminal (5 hrs, 60,000Rp). More comfortable minibuses are available from Raja Taxi (see Tour operators) for 80,000Rp.
   Economy buses to Medan depart from the terminal on Jln SM Raja (6 hrs, 25,000Rp), and drop passengers at Medan's Amplas terminal. Other destinations include **Bukittingi** (15 hrs, economy US$12, a/c executive US$19); **Padang** (17 hrs, economy US$15, a/c executive US$22); **Jakarta** (50 hrs, economy US$40, a/c executive

US$60). For masochists there are buses to **Yogyakarta** and **Denpasar**, which are more expensive than flights and take days.

Note It is much more expensive getting tickets from travel agencies and hotels in Parapat and Tuk Tuk, than buying them directly from the bus station. Prices given above reflect prices of tickets bought at the bus station. **Andilo Nancy**, Parapat bus terminal, T0625 41548, sells ANS tickets for a/c buses to **Bukittinggi**. Avoid seats numbered 33, 34 and 35 as these are right at the back of the bus next to the toilet and do not recline.

Haranggaol *p213*
Boat
A ferry connects Haranggaol with **Tuk Tuk** and **Ambarita** on Samosir Island on Mon and Thu at 1300 and 1500, 4 hrs. See page 223 for the time of journeys in the other direction. From Samosir there are many ferries across to **Parapat** for onward buses to Berastagi and Medan (see page 224).

ferries across to **Parapat** for onward buses to Berastagi and Medan (see page 224).

⊙ Directory

Parapat *p212*
Banks Rates are poor in Parapat, but even worse on Samosir. It is best to arrive with sufficient cash for your stay, although that may present risks in itself. There is a series of places that will change money on Jln Haranggaol and in the market area. **Pura Buana International**, Jln Haranggaol 75, money changer.
Medical services Hospital, Jln P Samosir.
Police Jln Sisingamangaraja (close to the inter-section with Jln P Samosir).
Telephone Warpostel, Jln Haranggaol 74 (for fax and telephone), the most conveniently located of the telephone offices; Warpostel at Jln Sisingamangarja 72 (for fax and international telephone).

Samosir Island

With a large number of traditional Batak villages, fine examples of rumah adat (traditional houses), cemeteries, churches, enigmatic stone carvings, good swimming, hiking, cheap lodgings and few cars, Samosir Island has proved a favourite destination for travellers. Surrounded by the lake and mist-cloaked mountains, which rise precipitously from the narrow 'coastal' strip on the eastern shore, it is one of the most naturally beautiful and romantic spots in Southeast Asia.

Accommodation is concentrated on the Tuk Tuk Peninsula, Tomok and Ambarita, although there are basic guesthouses scattered across the island. Rooms with a lake view are double the price of those without. Camping is also easy on Samosir. Food on the island is good and cheap; there are a number of warungs in Tomok, Ambarita and on the Tuk Tuk Peninsula.

Arriving on Samosir Island → *Phone code: 0645.*

Getting there
There are regular passenger ferries to Samosir Island from Danau Toba. It is possible to charter a speedboat for around US$40 (bargain hard). A car ferry runs from Ajibata, just south of Parapat. Passenger ferries drop passengers off at various points on the Tuk Tuk Peninsula, usually close to their chosen guesthouse or hotel. The crossing takes about 35 minutes. ▸▸ *See Transport, pages 215 and 223.*

Getting around
Numerous guesthouses and tour companies have motorbikes for hire, in varying states of repair. Prices vary accordingly but range between US$6-8 per day. A driving licence is

not required. This is a recommended way to see the island, although accidents are all too frequent on the narrow roads. Note that although it is possible to drive across the island, there is no assistance available should you get a puncture – which means a long walk to the nearest motorbike repair outfit. Better still, hire a bicycle and slow the pace or embark on a hike or a walk.

A minibus runs every 20 minutes in the morning between Tomok and Ambarita, and then on to Pangururan; less frequently in the afternoons. The bus does not take the route around the lakeshore on the Tuk Tuk Peninsula – it cuts across the neck of the peninsula.

Places on Samosir Island → *For listings, see pages 220-224.*

The various places of interest on Samosir are listed under the town entries below. However, there are two aspects of the island that are everywhere. First there are the **tombs**. These can be seen throughout the Batak area, but it is on Samosir where people find themselves, so to speak, face to face with them. Some are comparatively modest affairs: the tomb itself is topped with a restrained Batak house made of brick and stucco. Others are grandiose structures, with several storeys, pillars and ostentatious ornamentation. Still others seem to be tongue-in-cheek: the one surmounted with a Christmas tree, decorated with fairy lights just out of Ambarita on the road to Simanindo, is a case in point. All, though, show an imaginative fusion of Batak tradition and Christian symbolism. The need to construct these tombs must have been strong (the tradition is dying) as many took up valuable rice land.

The other aspect of Samosir are the **fish 'tanks'** known as *deke ramba*. These have been laboriously constructed on the lake edge, rocks carefully fashioned and then placed close enough together to allow the water in, while also keeping the fish in. Some appear to be very old, and most are still in use. Many have become ornamental, containing sometimes gargantuan *ikan mas*; others are still used to raise fish for the pot. The main fish raised are *ikan mas* (which are also eaten) and *mujahir*, which are native to Danau Toba. Fingerlings are caught in the lake and then raised in the tanks for about two years before being sold.

Tomok
Situated around 3 km south of the Tuk Tuk Peninsula, this was a traditional Batak village. and is a popular day-trip from Parapat. This means that there are a host of souvenir stalls, drinks shops and *warungs*, but none that you would go out of your way to patronize. Tomok is also the docking point for the car ferry, which means that lorries roar through this rather sad place.

However, the town is not an entirely lost cause, as it contains some fine high-prowed **Batak houses** and **carved stone coffins, elephants** and **chairs**. Walking from the jetty inland, there is a path lined with souvenir stalls that winds up a small hill. Half way up (about 500 m) is the **Museum of King Soribunto Sidabutar** ⓘ *admission by donation (about 2000Rp)*, housed in a traditional Batak house, containing a small number of Batak implements and photographs of the family.

Walking a little further up the hill, on from the mass of stalls and taking the path to the right, there is a carved stone coffin, the **King's Coffin**, protected by what remains of a large but dying *hariam* tree. The sarcophagus contains the body of Raja Sidabutar, the chief of the first tribe to migrate to the area. The coffin is surrounded by stone elephants, figures, tables and chairs. Further up the main path, past the stalls, is another grave site with stone figures arranged in a circle. The **church services** at the town and elsewhere on Samosir are worthwhile for the enthusiasm of the congregations – choose between no fewer than three churches.

Tuk Tuk Peninsula

Tuk Tuk is the name given to the peninsula that juts out rather inelegantly from the main body of Samosir Island, about 4 km north of Tomok. It is really just a haven for tourists, with nothing of cultural interest. There is a continuous ribbon of hotels, guesthouses, restaurants, minimarts, curio shops and tour companies following the road that skirts the perimeter of the peninsula. This might sound pretty dire, but in fact the development is not as overbearing as it might be – the nature of the topography means that you don't get confronted with a vision of tourism hell. And in spite of the rapid development, Tuk Tuk is still a peaceful spot, with good swimming, sometimes great food and good-value accommodation. There are various places on Tuk Tuk that masquerade as **tourist information centres**, when they are actually tour companies and travel agents. Nonetheless, they can be a good source of information.

If you decide to walk, it will take approximately one hour to get to Tomok and 1½ hours to reach Ambarita. Mountain bikes can be hired from many of the guesthouses and hotels for 25,000Rp per day and this is a recommended way to see the island; make sure you check over the bike carefully. Motorbikes can be hired for US$6-8 per day.

Ambarita

The pretty town of Ambarita, on the lakeshore north of Tuk Tuk, has more in the way of sights but nowhere to stay. There are guesthouses and hotels along the road running north towards Simanindo and the track that follows the coast to Tuk Tuk. Most visitors staying in these hotels rent their own wheels from Tuk Tuk. If you choose to walk allow 1½ hours to Tuk Tuk; seven hours to reach Simanindo at the north tip of the island.

Places in Ambarita   There are several **megalithic complexes** in the vicinity of the town. The most important of which is near the jetty at **Siallagan village** ① *2000Rp*. There are lots of 'freelance' guides waiting to pounce on tourists here, some of whom explain the sight quite dramatically. Expect to pay between US$1-3 for a tour. The first group of chairs, arranged under a hariam tree, are 300 years old and were used as the site for village councils, where disputes were settled and punishments decided. The chief would sit in the armchair, while other village elders sat in the surrounding chairs. The person on trial would sit on the small chair closest to the table – having been incarcerated for seven days in the small cage close to the stone chairs. A medicine man would consult his diary to decide on the best day for any sentence to be meted out. A stone figure mysteriously occupies one of the seats. Guides hang around to recount the chairs' gruesome past with a certain amount of relish. The really gruesome part of the traditional legal system is associated with the second group of megaliths. The criminal sentenced to death would be blindfolded, tied hand and foot and carried to the large stone block. He would then be sliced with a small knife and chilli, garlic and onions were reputedly rubbed into the wounds before a mallet – like a meat tenderizer – would be used to prepare the 'meat' for consumption (by pounding the man, already, no doubt, in a certain amount of pain). Having been sufficiently trussed and pummelled, the unfortunate would be carried to the block and his head cut off. The (strength-giving) blood was collected and drunk by the chief, while the meat was distributed to the villagers. The bones, finally, were collected up and thrown into the lake – which was unclean for a week and no activity occurred during this time. The chief's staff is carved with the faces of past chiefly generations. This gruesome tradition came to an end in 1816 when a German missionary (by the name of Nommensen – there's a university in Medan named after him) converted the population to Christianity. Facing the complex is a row of well-preserved **Batak houses**.

Also here is the **tomb of Laga Siallagan**, the first chief of Ambarita. To get there, turn right (coming from Tomok) off the main road in Ambarita, shortly after the post office walk past the football field and police post, and turn left to walk past tombs and ricefields to the complex, about 500 m in all, it is possible to approach from Tuk Tuk via the side road.

Simanindo

Simanindo is at the north tip of Samosir. The house of a former Batak chief, Raja Simalungun, has been restored and turned into an **Ethnological Museum** (**Huta Bolon**) ① *daily 1000-1700, 5000Rp*, containing a musty collection of Batak, Dutch and Chinese artefacts. The brief labels in English reveal little. There are souvenirs for sale in Batak houses.

Close by is a well-preserved fortified **Batak community** ① *shows are staged Mon-Sat 1030-1110, 1145-1239, and Sun 1145-1230, if a minimum of 5 tourists show up, 30,000Rp*, with fine examples of richly carved Batak houses. This is the best maintained of the various 'preserved' communities on Samosir. Visitors sit through a lengthy sequence of 12 dances, performed by a rather lacklustre crew – many of the dances seem more like loosening up exercises prior to a workout. The requisite audience participation number and the final dance gives an opportunity for guests to add a donation to their entrance fee.

Pangururan

Pangururan, the capital of Samosir, is on the west coast, close to the point where the island is attached to the mainland by a small bridge. It is a dusty, ramshackle little town. There is no reason to stay here and most people visit the town on the way to the **hot springs** on Mount Belirang. Pangururan is also probably the best place from which to set out to hike across the island to Tomok (see Hiking, page 223).

From Pangururan, a bus service operates to the interior village of Roonggurni Huta. An occasional service has begun operating in the south part of the island between Tomok and Nainggolan, and then on to Pangururan.

Mount Belirang hot springs

① *2.5 km or 1 hr from Pangururan if you walk, 1000Rp.*

The sulphurous gases and water have killed the vegetation on the hillside, leaving a white residue – the scar can be seen from a long way off on Samosir. Cross the stone bridge and turn right (north). They are about a third of the way up Mount Belirang (also known as Mount Pusuk Buhit). It is too hot to bathe at the point where they emerge from the ground, but lower down there are pools where visitors can soak in the healing sulphurous waters. There are separate bathing pools for men and women and some *warungs* nearby for refreshments. Views of the lake are spoilt by uncontrolled, unattractive development, and even the spring site itself leaves rather a lot to be desired: plastic pipes and moulded concrete make it look, in places, more like a plumber's training site.

Samosir Island listings

🛏 Where to stay

Tuk Tuk Peninsula *p218*

Tuk Tuk is almost overloaded with lodgings, from very simple affairs to large, comfortable hotels. Almost all accommodation is situated along the road (really just a lane) that skirts around the edge of the peninsula. To the north and south there is a relatively steep drop into the lake, so the chalets seem to cling precariously to the hillside. To the east the land slopes more gently into the lake, so there is room for larger gardens and bigger guesthouses and hotels. Be sure to bargain for your accommodation; stays of 3 or more nights often see prices dropping sharply.

$$$-$ Tabo Cottages, T0625 451318, www.tabocottages.com. Those in the know stay here, in beautiful Batak cottages overlooking a large garden and the lake. The mid-priced rooms are clean and have hot water, and some have outdoor bathrooms. Economy rooms are good value, with cold water and lake views. There's also a smashing vegetarian restaurant. Recommended.

$$-$ Samosir Cottages, T0625 41050, www.samosircottages.com. Sprawling and impersonal resort-style place that fills up with Indonesian tourists at weekends. Rooms are clean and the family room can sleep 4 and has cable TV, fridge and kitchen. Internet access available (expensive).

$ Anju Cottage, T0625 451265. Good selection of rooms, ranging from Batak houses to tiled concrete chalets in a breezy setting. There is decent swimming here and a diving board. Prices include breakfast.

$ Bagus Bay, T0625 451287. Well-run and friendly place with a selection of spotless rooms in Batak houses, some with lake views. 4 attractive rooms set in a leafy garden.

Extensive gardens with badminton and volleyball courts and children's play area. Good range of facilities including Internet café, 10,000Rp per hr, book exchange and satellite TV in the restaurant. Recommended.

$ Carolina Cottage, T0625 41520, carolina@indosat.net.id. By far the most popular place in Toba, with convenient access from Parapat, excellent swimming area with pontoon for diving, and well-manicured gardens. Selection of rooms in Batak houses, most with great lake views, the more expensive rooms have hot water and a breezy balcony. Recommended.

$ Christina Guest House, T0625 451027. On the road heading out towards Ambarita, rooms here are comfortable and fronted by an attractive lily pond with expansive views of the lake. The family house is superb value, with space for 5 people. There is a restaurant with cable TV. Internet café.

$ Horas Homestay, T081 3960 13643. Access to these rooms is via **Horas Chillout Café**, and down crumbling and overgrown steps that lead to the shoreline. Basic clean rooms. This place possesses a rural charm not found in most other Tuk Tuk lodgings and will satisfy those in need of some peace and quiet.

$ Liberta Homestay, T0625 451035. Collection of Batak houses, some in a better state of repair than others, set in a lovely garden. This is a popular place, and gets busy at weekends. Locals bring along their guitars for musical evenings, and often like to challenge visitors to games of chess in the laid-back restaurant. Recommended.

$ Sibigo, down a small track next to **Carolina**, T0625 451017. Sleepy and quiet. Rooms are adequate and have beautiful views, but are sorely in need of a good clean.

Ambarita *p218*

The hotels and guesthouses listed here are scattered along the road towards Simanindo (over a distance of about 9 km from town) and the smaller road leading towards Tuk Tuk (over about 2 km). They are quieter than those in Tuk Tuk. They are also quite isolated, so you will need to hire a bicycle or motorcyle if you want to try other restaurants and bars. This part of the island is also rather treeless near the lake shore, but has some good swimming. Guesthouse owners will often pick visitors up from Tomok or Tuk Tuk if they phone ahead. Otherwise, catch a minibus from Tomok heading towards Simanindo (3000Rp) and tell the driver which hotel you wish to alight at. All the hotels mentioned have restaurant attached.

$$ Sapo Toba, T0625 700009. Collection of smart chalets built on a hillside overlooking the lake. All the rooms are identical and have hot water, TV, fridge and bathroom with bath. The reception is at the bottom of the hillside inside the restaurant on the left, just keep following those eternal steps down. Internet 35,000Rp per hr.

$ Barbara Guest House, T0625 41230. Down a small track and neighbouring **Thyesza**, accommodation is a little down at heel, but the friendly staff makes up for peeling paint. Some rooms have a lake view and hot water. Restaurant and good swimming.

$ Mas, T0625 451051. Gorgeous views, a peaceful setting and a good selection of clean tiled rooms in a concrete block fronted by a small fish farm with swirling koi. This is a fine option for those wishing to stay far enough outside of Tuk Tuk to escape the overtly touristy atmosphere, but close enough to have good dining options nearby. Tuk Tuk is a leisurely 30-min stroll away. Rooms downstairs have hot water. Recommended.

$ Thyesza, 4 km to the north of Ambarita, down a small track leading to the shoreline, T0625 41443, www.flowerofsamosir.com. Well-maintained place with 6 tidy tiled rooms in a flower covered concrete block slightly set back from the lake. Also a cheaper Batak house right on the shore. This

part of the coast has excellent swimming and clear water. The restaurant is good. Recommended.

$ Tuk Tuk Timbul, about 1 km south of Ambarita towards Tuk Tuk, T0625 41374. Collection of smart cottages in a great isolated position off the road and down on the lakefront on a small headland. The restaurant serves good food including home-baked bread. There is a large fish pond and good swimming.

● Restaurants

Tomok *p217*

There are several *warung* around the village, eg **Islam**. Nothing outstanding, but passable whether European, Chinese, Minang or standard Indonesian fare.

Tuk Tuk Peninsula *p218*

There is an increasing number of good restaurants on Tuk Tuk; many specialize in vegetarian travellers' food.

$ Bamboo. Daily 0800-2200. Good spot for sunsets, cocktails and a range of simple Western food and Indonesian staples. The best option here is the beach BBQ when the owner grills fresh lake fish and serves them with a variety of lip-smacking sauces.

$ Jenny's. Daily 0800-2200. Popular place with friendly staff in a colourful setting serving sandwiches and good salads. There is often live Batak folk music here in the evenings.

$ Juwitas, T0625 451217. Daily 0800-2200. Small wooden café with chatty owner serving decent vegetarian grub, curries and lake fish.

$ Popy's Fish Farm, T0625 451291. Daily 0800-2200. Fresh fish cooked in every conceivable way in a breezy setting. The menu also features some Chinese dishes and curries.

$ Rumba's Pizzeria, there are 2 branches. One is on the southeastern side of the peninsula, T0625 451310, daily 0800-2300, reasonable create-your-own pizza with a variety of toppings. The other is on the western side of the peninsula, T0625 451045, daily 1200-2100, considerably cheaper, with sunset views and good pizzas.

Guesthouse restaurants
Some of the best dining is in Tuk Tuk's guesthouses, which generally serve food daily 0700-2200.

$ Bagus Bay. Pizza, tasty veg curry and a breakfast menu featuring rare treats such as baked beans with cheese on toast.

$ Liberta Homestay. Mellow setting for a beer, healthy grub with lots of vegetarian offerings in a convivial setting.

$ Sibigo. Excellent fresh lake fish grilled and served with limes and local sauces. This place also serves chips with all manner of sauces including *sate* and *sambal*.

$ Tabo Cottages. This is a haven for vegetarians with hearty soups accompanied by fresh bread, good salads and aloe vera power drinks. Carnivores are not forgotten, with a few fish and chicken dishes on the menu. There is a good breakfast menu here, with a superb-value buffet breakfast. At weekends the kitchen struggles to cope with demand and it can take some time for meals to materialize. Recommended.

Ambarita *p218*
There are a couple of coffee shops and *warungs* in town, but nothing that stands out. The best place to eat is at a nice little *warung* next to the police post (turn off the main road and walk past the football field).

$ Joe's Vegetarian Restaurant, Pindu Raya (a hamlet between Tuk Tuk and Ambarita). Known for its home-made cakes and coffee.

$ No Name Pizzeria, 7 km or so north of town on the road to Simanindo just in front of the **King's Hotel**. Curiously, there is currently no pizza on offer despite the name, but the menu features simple Western food and some standard Indonesian dishes. This place doubles up as a *tuak* (toddy) shop at night and can be a fun place to meet locals.

Guesthouse restaurants
Of the guesthouses on the strip between Ambarita and Simanindo, **Barbara's** and **Thyesza** (both **$**) are the most traveller savvy, and **Thyesza** cooks up authentic Batak dishes (including dog meat on request), simple Western fare and serves excellent fresh fruit juices including refreshing *marquisa* juice.

🎵 Bars and clubs

Tuk Tuk Peninsula *p218*
Locals head to *tuak* (toddy) shops of an evening for a drink and chat. These can look fairly inconspicuous from the outside. Ask at your hotel which one is most accessible. Expect to pay 1500 to 2000Rp for a glass.
Brando's Blues Bar, T0625 451084. Open 1800-0200. Reggae, blues and a smattering of house music at this place, which has a small dance floor, some outdoors seating, a pool table and cheap, strong spirits to get the legs swaying to a different tune.

🎭 Entertainment

Tuk Tuk Peninsula *p218*
Traditional dance Batak folk song and dance performances every Wed and Sat, 2015 at **Bagus Bay** (see Where to stay). A very popular and a fun way to spend an evening.

🛍 Shopping

Tuk Tuk Peninsula *p218*
Books Gokhon Bookshop, offers a postal service; **Bagus Bay Bookshop**, for second-hand novels; **Penny's Bookshop**, has an excellent book-lending section, maps and some DVDs to rent – for 8000Rp you can watch a DVD in the shop. There are a number of other places around the peninsula that sell second-hand books.
Crafts There are scores of craft and curio shops selling woodcarvings, medicine books, leather goods, Batak calendars, carved chess

sets and wind chimes. The chess sets are a good buy here but they vary enormously in quality and price, it's worth shopping around.

⚙ What to do

Samosir Island *p216*
Hiking
Hiking across Samosir's central highlands is one of the most rewarding ways to see the island. The distance from east to west is only about 20 km as the crow flies, but the route is a steep and circuitous climb of 750 m, making the real walking distance about 45 km. It is just possible to walk the route in a day if hiking from west to east (eg from Panguraran to Tomok), but it is best to stay overnight at the interior village of Roonggurni Huta to recuperate from the climb. A number of homestays here charge about US$2-3 for a bed.

The hike from Roonggurni Huta to Tomok or vice versa is about 29 km: 10 hrs if walking uphill, 6 hrs down. There are also trails to Ambarita and (longer still) to Tuk Tuk, although these are less well marked. From Roonggurni Huta to Panguraran it is a less steep 17 km, about 3 hrs walking. There is also a bus service for the terminally exhausted between Panguraran and Roonggurni Huta. It is probably best to climb from west to east as this misses out the steep climb up to Roonggurni Huta from Tomok. Catch a bus to Panguraran and set off from there. A map marking the hiking trails and giving more details about the routes is available from **Penny's Bookshop** in Tuk Tuk.

Tours
There are no regular tours around the island, due to lack of tourists, but they can be arranged at one of the tour companies. Most of the hotels will provide a map, and suggest a coherent day-trip itinerary taking in Tomok, Siallangan, Sangkal (weaving village), Simanindo, and over to the hot springs on near Pangguran. Many of the

guys working in the hotels will offer to guide tourists for US$5-10.

Tuk Tuk Peninsula *p218*
Cooking classes
Juwita's (see Restaurants). Visitors can choose from a list of Batak and Indonesian dishes and learn to cook them with the vivacious owner in a 3-hr class, US$20 (negotiable).

Massage
Traditional massage available at guesthouses around the peninsula, about 50,000Rp per session. Ask at **Tabo Cottages** or **Bagus Bay**.

Tour operators
There are plenty of operators around the peninsular, browse for a good price. The companies listed here will book bus tickets (very expensive – cheaper from the **Audilo Nancy** office at the bus terminal) and help arrange a tour of the island:

Anju Cottage, T0625 451265.
Bagus Bay Information, T0625 451287.

⊖ Transport

Samosir Island *p216*
Boat
Most visitors get to Samosir by ferry from **Parapat**. The ferry leaves about every hour and takes 30 mins (7000Rp). Most ferries dock at Tuk Tuk on Samosir and they will drop off at the various hotel jetties, so state your destination. Some continue north to **Ambarita**, while others also dock at **Tomok** just south of the Tuk Tuk Peninsula. Most of the hotels and guesthouses have a ferry timetable posted. Check the schedule.

The 1st ferry from Parapat leaves at 0930, from Samosir at 0730. The last departs Parapat at 1730, Samosir at 1630.

The **car ferry service** from Ajibata, just south of Parapat to Tomok, runs every 3 hrs from 0830-1730 with a final sailing at 2130,

4000Rp for foot passengers, 150,000Rp for a car.

A ferry also links Tuk Tuk and Ambarita with **Haranggaol** on Danau Toba's north shore, but this only runs on Mon – market day in Haranggaol. The ferry leaves Ambarita at 0700 and takes 2-3 hrs, largely because it stops to pick up market-goers all along the eastern shore. See Haranggaol Transport, page 216. For onwards buses from Parapat, see page 215.

Tomok *p217*
Bus
In theory, a bus runs every 20 mins to **Pangururan** and all stops along the route.

Car ferry
There is a car ferry to **Ajibata**, just south of Parapat every 3 hrs 0830-1730, last departure at 2100, 4000Rp for foot passengers, 150,000Rp for a car.

Tuk Tuk Peninsula *p218*
Boat
Ferry connections with **Parapat** about every hour, 7000Rp.

Bus
Walk to the main road to catch one of the buses running between **Tomok** and **Pangururan**, every 20 mins, 12,000Rp.

Ambarita *p218*
Bus
Connections every 20 mins with **Tomok**, 3000Rp, and all stops to **Pangururan**.

❶ Directory

Samosir Island *p216*
Banks Rates of exchange on Samosir are poor, worse than in Parapat, although the larger hotels and some travel agents will change TCs and cash. There is also a money changer in Ambarita. **Telephone** International calls can be placed from many of the hotels and tour and travel agencies.

Tomok *p217*
Telephone Wartel office, on the northern edge of town on the main road.

Tuk Tuk Peninsula *p218*
Banks PT Andilo Nancy travel agent changes money at a better rate than other places. **Medical services** Clinic (Puskesmas), on the southern side of the peninsula. **Telephone** Many guesthouses, hotels and tour companies offer IDD phone facilities and fax.

Ambarita *p218*
Medical services Clinic (Puskemas), in town.

Bukittinggi and around

Visitors to West Sumatra spend most of their time based in and around the highland settlement of Bukittinggi, its cultural heart. This is entirely understandable as it is one of the most attractive towns in Sumatra and has many places of interest in the immediate vicinity. The accommodation is good, the climate invigorating and the food excellent. The highly mobile Minang people who view this area as their ancestral home are fascinating, and the surrounding countryside is some of the most beautiful in Sumatra. There are peaceful highland lakes, like Maninjau and Singkarak, rivers for rafting and mountain treks.

In July 2008, Bukittinggi was thrust into the international limelight as Indonesian police foiled a plot by Jemaah Islamiyah to blow up the Bedual Café. The suspects, who were arrested in Palembang, claimed that the bombs had at one stage even been put inside the café. However, they realized that with the downturn of tourism in Sumatra, any attack would in fact take more Muslim lives than tourist lives, and subsequently pulled out.

Arriving in Bukittinggi → *Phone code: 0752.*

Getting there
The nearest airport is on the fringes of Padang, a two-hour bus journey away. Most people get to this popular destination by bus; the journey overland from Medan via Danau Toba is pretty gruelling, just over 500 km or 15 hours' drive in total (if the bus doesn't break down, an all too frequent occurrence), however, owing to its popularity, the range of buses and destinations is impressive for a town that is relatively small. ►► *See Transport, page 234.*

Getting around
Bukittinggi itself is small and cool enough to negotiate on foot. One of the great attractions is the surrounding countryside, but trying to get around on public transport can be a bit of a drag so many visitors choose to charter a bemo, hire a motorbike or bicycle, or take a tour. Bemos cost about 2000Rp per trip. Motorbikes and mountain bikes can be hired from many guesthouses and tour companies; motorbike hire costs about 65,000Rp per day and mountain bikes 25,000Rp.

Visitors arriving at Aur Kuning may be encouraged to take a taxi to town; regular (red) opelet ply the route for a fraction of the price (2000Rp), or a bemo can be chartered for the trip to Jalan A Yani for 15,000Rp.

Places in Bukittinggi → *For listings, see pages 230-235.*

The geographic and functional centre of Bukittinggi is marked by a strange-looking **clock tower** at the south end of Jalan Jend A Yani, the town's main thoroughfare. The Jam Gadang, or 'Great Clock' as it is known, was built by the Dutch in 1827. It is a veritable Sumatran 'Big Ben' and has a Minangkabau-style roof perched uneasily on the top. The **central market** is close to the clock tower. Although there is a market every day of the week, market day is on Wednesday and Saturday (0800-1700) when hordes of Minangkabau men and women descend on Bukittinggi. The market – in fact there are two, the Upper Market (*Pasar Atas*) and Lower Market (*Pasar Bawah*) – covers an enormous area and sells virtually everything. Good for souvenirs, handicrafts, jewellery, fruit, spices and weird foods.

The north end of Jalan Jend A Yani runs between two hills that have recently been linked by a footbridge. On top of the hill to the west is **Fort de Kock**, built by the Dutch in 1825 as a defensive site during the Padri Wars. Very little of the fort remains apart from a few rusting cannon and a moat. The centre of the decaying fortifications is dominated by a water tower. However, the views of the town and the surrounding countryside are worth the trip (although trees are beginning to obscure the view). To the east, and linked by a footbridge, on the other side of Jalan Jend A Yani, is Bukittinggi's high point, **Taman Bundokandung** ('Kind-Hearted Mother Park'). The park contains both a museum and a zoo. The **Bukittinggi Zoo** ⓘ *daily 0730-1700, fort and zoo: 5000Rp (8000Rp on public holidays)*, is hardly a lesson in how to keep animals in captivity, but it does have a reasonable collection of Sumatran wildlife, including orang-utans and gibbons. Within the zoo is a **museum** ⓘ *daily 0730-1700, 1000Rp*, established in 1935 and the oldest in Sumatra. The collection is housed in a traditional *rumah adat*, or Minangkabau clan house, embellished with fine woodcarvings and fronted by two rice barns. The museum specializes in local ethnographic exhibits, including fine jewellery and textiles, and is not very informative. There are also some macabre stuffed and deformed buffalo calves here.

To the southwest of the town is the spectacular **Sianok Canyon**, 4 km long and over 100 m deep. A road at the end of Jalan Teuku Umar leads down through the canyon, past the back entrances to the Japanese tunnel system. A path leaves the road at a sharp bend (there is a snack bar here) and continues to a bridge at the foot of the chasm and steep steps on the opposite side of the canyon. Follow a road through a village and across paddy fields for about two hours until you eventually arrive at **Kota Gadang**. Many small silversmiths sell their wares throughout the village. This is a good place to buy smaller silver items; recommended is **Silversmith Aino** ① *at the coffee shop, Jln Hadisash 115*. There is a large tourist gift centre, **Amai Satia**, in Kota Gadang (walk to the mosque and turn right at the T-junction). From Kota Gadang, either retrace your steps, or head for the crossroads in Kota Gadang where you can catch a blue oplet to Aur Kuning (4000Rp).

Also at the southern edge of town and overlooking the canyon is **Panorama Park** ① *3000Rp (4000Rp on public holidays)*, a popular weekend meeting place for courting couples. Within the park is the entrance to a **maze of tunnels** ① *entrance included in price of entrance ticket to park*, excavated by the Japanese during the Occupation, with ammunition stores, kitchens and dining rooms. Guides gleefully show the chute where dead Indonesian workers were propelled out into the canyon to rot. Opposite the park, on Jalan Panorama (formerly Jalan Imam Bonjol), is the **Army Museum** (**Museum Perjuangan**) ① *daily 0800-1700, 2000Rp (although it looks distinctly under-staffed nowadays)*, which contains military memorabilia from the early 19th century through to the modern period. There are some interesting photographs of the disinterring of the army officers assassinated by the PKI during the attempted coup of 1965.

Around Bukittinggi

One of the attractions of Bukittinggi is the array of sights in the surrounding area. The Minang Highlands around Bukittinggi constitute the core – or *darek* – of the Minang homeland. Below are the main excursions, although there are also additional hikes, waterfalls, traditional villages, lakes and centres of craft production.

Many of the sights and places of interest listed here are under separate headings following the Bukittinggi entry. These are: **Danau Maninjau**, **Payakumbuh** and the **Harau Valley**, **Batusangkar** and **Danau Singkarak**, and **Padang Panjang**. Seeing these sights, particularly if time is short, is easiest on a tour. Getting around the Minang area on public transport is time consuming (renting a motorbike for the day makes for greater mobility).

A guide should, in theory, be able to offer some insights into the rich Minang culture. It is worth asking around and getting some first-hand assessments from travellers who have just returned from tours and who may be able to recommend a guide. If possible, find a guide and arrange a tour directly; the tour companies usually use the same guides and because they take a commission the rate rises. The guides working out of the **Orchid Hotel**, the **Canyon Café** have been recommended. See What to do, page 233.

From Bukittinggi to Maninjau

This trip is spectacular. After leaving the main Padang– Bukittinggi route at Kota Baru, the road twists through the terraced countryside to the town of **Matur**. Locals are said to call this stretch of road the Mercedes Bends, and the story is charming even if it might not be true. During the Dutch period there were two sugar cane processing plants at Matur and the Dutch manager of one owned the only car in the area: a Mercedes. When he drove to Bukittinggi local people would line the road to watch the strange machine wind its way to Kota Baru, earning this stretch of road the name the Mercedes Bends. On reaching the crater lip – an awesome spectacle – the road descends through 44 hairpin bends, each of which has been numbered (and sponsored by a cigarette company) by some bureaucratic mind, before arriving at the lake edge village of Maninjau.

A rewarding and spectacular hike from Bukittinggi, easily possible in a day for even the modestly energetic, is to walk to the crater edge at **Puncak Lawang** (Lawang Top) and then down the steep crater sides to the lake-side village of **Bayur**, before catching a bus back to Bukittinggi. To do this, take a bus from Bukittinggi's Aur Kuning bus terminal to Lawang – sometimes called Pasar Lawang (Lawang Market) to distinguish it from Puncak Lawang (8000Rp). From Lawang walk the 4 km to Puncak Lawang at the lip of the crater and 1400 m up – a spectacular view – before taking the path down (a walk of around another two to three hours). The path can be narrow at times, and slippery when wet. Alternatively, catch a bus straight to Maninjau village on the lake shore, navigating the 44 hairpin bends on the way down (one to two hours, 10,000Rp). The last bus leaves Maninjau village for Bukittinggi between 1600 and 1700, later on market days (Monday to Friday). Check there is no mist before departing.

Danau Singkarak
ⓘ *Take a bus heading south towards Solok.*
The Minang area's other lake is Danau Singkarak. It is not as beautiful as Maninjau, but it is possible to come here on a circular journey via Batusangkar.

Batang Palupuh
ⓘ *Catch a bus to Batang Palupuh on the Trans-Sumatran Highway, or take an oplet and then walk to the reserve (30mins).*
This reserve, situated 12 km north of town, is for the monstrous **rafflesia** flower. Ask staff at your guesthouse when the flower will next be in bloom; a guide from the village will point it out for a small fee.

Pandai Sikat and other craft villages
ⓘ *Take a red oplet towards Padang Panjang from the Aur Kuning terminal, get off at Kota Baru and either walk the last 3 km or take an omprengan (a non-licensed bemo) from the intersection.*
One of a number of villages specializing in traditional craft production. Pandai Sikat is situated 13 km south of town at the foot of Mount Singgalang, 3 km off the main road to Padang Panjang, and is a cloth and woodcarving centre. The carvings tend to use natural motifs (trees, animals, flowers, etc), as does the famous *songket* cloth that is produced here. About 1000 women weave richly patterned cloth. Note that the warp may be rayon, imported from Japan, and only the weft, cotton or silk.

Other craft villages include **Desa Sunga**, 17 km south of town, which specializes in brasswork; and **Sungaipua**, on the slopes of Mount Merapi, which specializes in metalwork (knives, swords).

Mount Merapi
ⓘ *Catch a bus to Kota Baru from the Aur Kuning terminal (1st departure 0500), and then hike.*
This active volcano, southeast of town, stands at a height of 2891 m and last erupted in 1979. The difficult climb to the summit takes between four and six hours. Enquire at the Police Station in Kota Baru for more information. Register here before ascending and ask for directions; the route is indistinct in places. The best way to see the volcano is to hire a

guide and climb up at night (US$25), arriving at the summit for sunrise and thus avoiding the heat of the day and the mist that envelopes the mountain by 1100. Wear warm clothes as it is cold on the summit. The ground around the crater is loose and hikers should keep away from the lip. Many hotels and cafés can arrange tours and a good place to enquire is at the **Orchid Hotel** or **Canyon Café**. On Saturday nights hoards of locals climb the volcano, following them is possible but not advisable as many do not know the way.

Mount Singgalang

ⓘ *Take an oplet to Kota Baru from the Aur Kuning terminal. From where you are dropped, turn right at the mosque and walk down to Kota Baru. In the centre of the village is a right-hand turn with the RTCI 4 km sign (referring to the radio installation situated 2 km above Pantai Sikat). Follow this track for 2 km to Pandai Sikat. The mountain path starts to the right of the RTCI installation behind a refreshment hut (often closed). For speed, it is possible to hire a motorbike to the RTCI site. Buses back to Bukittinggi run late, but it is advisable not to descend in darkness.*
Singgalang, which lies to the southwest of Bukittinggi, stands at a height of 2878 m and offers a less arduous climb than Mount Merapi. The trail starts at the village of Pandai Sikat, and the climb takes about four or five hours. It's a disappointing dirty footpath. Near the summit, the ground is scree, so good footwear is recommended. Start early, as mist often descends over the mountain later in the day. Tours are available from the **Canyon Café** and **Orchid Guesthouse** for US$25.

Payakumbuh

ⓘ *Regular oplets from Bukittinggi, 1 hr, these run through Piladang.*
This key centre of Minang culture lies about 10 km east of Bukittinggi (see page 224). En route is the colourful local Friday market at **Piladang**, while on the other side of Payakumbuh is the **Harau Canyon** (see below).

Harau Canyon

ⓘ *Take one of the many buses from Bukittinggi to Payakumbuh. From there catch a white oplet – or a 'sago' as they are called locally – running towards Sarialamat to the turn-off for the Harau Valley (see the main entry for more details on the walk from there).*
The canyon lies around 44 km from Bukittinggi, off the road leading through Payakumbuh towards Pekanbaru.

Pariangan and other Minang villages

ⓘ *There are no direct buses from Bukittinggi, catch an oplet from Bukittinggi to Batusangkar, and then one heading towards Kota Baru – which passes through Parianagan. From Bukittinggi it is necessary to first catch an oplet to Batusangkar, and then a Solok-bound bus.*
Pariangan is a peaceful Minang village on the slopes of Mount Merapi. Balimbiang is about 10 km south of Batusangkar, and 1 km off the main road.

Danau Maninjau → *For listings, see pages 230-235.*

Danau Maninjau is one of the most beautiful and impressive natural sights in Sumatra, rivalling Danau Toba. It is a huge, flooded volcanic crater with steep 600-m-high walls. To the west and south the crater walls are largely forested, dropping straight into the lake and leaving scarcely any scope for cultivation and settlement. This part of the crater supports a fair amount of wildlife. To the east and north there is some flat land and this is where

Maninjau's small settlements are to be found. Once a popular stop on a jaunt around Sumatra, Maninjau has suffered chronically in the downturn in tourism. Many hotels and restaurants have been forced out of business. If it's tourist-free isolation that you crave, it can be found here in abundance.

Arriving in Danau Maninjau
Regular buses service the route from Bukittinggi, taking 1½ hours. Bicycles and motorcycles can be hired from most guesthouses and provide an ideal means of getting around the lake and reaching surrounding villages. Bicycles cost about US$2-3 per day and motorcycles US$5-6 per day.

Places in Danau Maninjau
The lake offers reasonable swimming (although close to the shore it can be murky), fishing and waterskiing. In 1996, discharges of sulphur from hot underwater springs killed many of the fish that are raised here in cages along the shore. The springs explain why the water is surprisingly warm for a lake over 500 m above sea level.

Maninjau village lies on the east shore of the lake at the point where the road from Bukittinggi reaches the lake. It is a small but booming market and administrative centre. Most of the places to stay are in (and beyond) the northern extent of the village. Around 3 km north of Maninjau village is the small and charming hamlet of **Bayur**. This is quite simply a gem of a community. Most of the houses and other buildings are made of wood or are white stuccoed brick, and date from the Dutch period. On the northern edge of the village are several more guesthouses, some of the most peaceful in the area. Wandering around Bayur it is easy to imagine what villages were like before individualism and licence destroyed the bonds of community. Continuing further around the lake the road passes through Muko Muko and then onto Lubuk Basung, where the buses terminate. Most buses from Bukittinggi terminate in Lubuk Busung, a few kilometres past Bayur. Tourists who wish to stay in Bayur should inform the driver, and ask to alight at the desired guesthouse.

There are hiking trails through the surrounding countryside. Because the village is some 500 m above sea level, it is cool even during the day and can be chilly at night.

Around Danau Maninjau
From Maninjau village, a worthwhile walk or bicycle ride is around the north edge of the lake to the village of **Muko Muko**, 16 km in all (buses also ply the route). Just before Muko Muko there are the **Alamada Hot Springs** (rather small and insignificant), an excellent fish restaurant and a hydropower station. The total distance around the lake is about 50 km: 20 km on a good road; 30 km on a dirt track. Bicycles can be hired from many of the guesthouses and coffee shops (US$2-3 per day).

It is also possible to hike up to, or down from, **Lawang Top** (**Puncak Lawang**), on the crater lip. The trail to the crater edge begins in the middle of Bayur, 3 km north of Maninjau village.

Bukittinggi and around listings

*For hotel and restaurant price codes and other
relevant information, see pages 9-12.*

🛏 Where to stay

Bukittinggi *p224*

Most of the travellers' hotels and
guesthouses are concentrated along the
north end of Jln Jend A Yani. Quieter,
smaller and often cleaner homestays
are located on the hills either side of Jln
Jend A Yani. The downturn in tourism has
meant that a lot of hotels have not been
well maintained, and so tourists tend to
congregate in the same few places.

Board and lodging in return for English
conversation lessons is offered in the town
of Batu Sangkar, 1 hr from Bukittinggi.
Teaching duties are for 3 hrs a day. Contact
Mr Edy at **Family International English
School (FIES)**, T0752 71099 or T081 2672
1599. The length of stay is negotiable.

$$$ The Hills, Jln Laras Datuk Bandaro,
T0752 35000, www.thehillsbukittinggi.com.
This large hotel has a definite North African
feel, with its arched entrance, Moroccan
fountains and huge atrium. Rooms are a bit
of a shock, with bright mint green colour
scheme and fairly old furniture. All come
with bath, hot water and TV. The de luxe
rooms have views of the hills. Pool and spa
service. No discounts, but a longer stay gets
a room upgrade.

$$$-$$ Hotel Lima's, Jln Kesehatan 35,
T0752 22641. This place is popular with
Indonesian tour groups and has a range
of rooms in concrete blocks on a hillside.
Superior rooms are carpeted and have hot
water, bath, TV and a range of complimentary
goodies. The cheaper rooms are fronted by a
small garden, and have TV and hot water.

$$$-$$ Royal Denai Hotel, Jln Dr A Rivai
26, T0752 32920, www.royaldenaihotel.
com. Sprawling 3-star hotel crowned with
a Minangkabau roof. Rooms are clean. The
cheapest are a bit tatty. Discounts available.

$$ Hotel Benteng, Jln Benteng 1, T0752
21115, www.bentenghotel.com. Perched
on a hilltop next to the fort, the rooms
have superb views and sizeable hot-water
bathrooms. Discounts.

$$-$ The Gallery, Jln H Agus Salim 25,
T0752 23515. The de luxe rooms are
nothing special, and have soft beds and
average views. The economy rooms have a
lovely sun terrace with marvellous views.

$$-$ Hotel Asia, Jln Kesehatan 38,
T0752 625277. The large reception area is
combined with a comfortable Chinese-
inspired lobby, and makes for a nice
spot for a morning tea. De luxe rooms
are spacious and have balcony with
exceptional views over the town and to
the mountains beyond. Cheaper rooms
have shared bathroom but still have good
views, some with access to a roof terrace.
Recommended.

$ Hotel Dahlia, Jln A Yani 106, T0752
627296, osrina@yahoo.com. Well run, with
hot-water rooms, but low on atmosphere.
The pricier rooms have access to a roof
terrace with good views; the cheaper rooms
downstairs are dark. Breakfast is included.

$ Hotel Kartini, Jln Teuku Umar 6, T0752
22885. Homely hotel offering spotless
rooms with TV and hot water. The more
expensive rooms downstairs are next to the
lobby and can be quite noisy. The rooms
upstairs are quiet and very comfortable. Ask
for the room at the front with a balcony.
Recommended.

$ Hotel Singgalang, Jln A Yani 130, T0752
628709. Rooms are clean but have no
natural light. All have TV, the slightly more
expensive ones have hot-water showers.

$ Merdeka Homestay, Jln Dr A Rivai 20,
T0752 23937. Large rooms with attached
bathroom (cold water) in a villa near a
busy intersection. Can be a little noisy.

$ Minang International Hotel, Jln
Panorama 20A, T0752 21120. Soeharto
stayed here in 1978, and it seems that

little has changed since then. With green and purple carpets, kitsch furniture and peeling wallpaper, this place appeals to a niche audience.

$ Orchid Hotel, Jln Teuku Umar 11, T0752 32634. Currently the most popular cheap place in town, and deservedly so. Rooms are clean, the staff are courteous and helpful. Ask for a room on the side away from the mosque, if you don't want to be disturbed by the call to prayer.

Danau Maninjau *p228*

There are 2 concentrations of guesthouses, in Maninjau village and Bayur, both on the eastern shore. Most places stand empty, and haven't been touched up for years. This is especially noticeable in the cheaper places.

$$-$ Pasir Panjang Permai, T0752 61111. Selection of a/c and non-a/c rooms in 2 concrete blocks. This hotel is geared towards Indonesian tour groups, and gets busy at weekends. More expensive rooms have TV, bath and good views from the balcony. Furniture is a little tatty. Discounts available.

$ Maransay Beach, halfway between Maninjau village and Bayur, T0752 61264. Large wooden hotel built out over the water, with a good restaurant and collection of simple rooms. The ones at the front have a decent amount of natural light. Some rooms have an outside bathroom. There is a small beach beside the hotel. Friendly staff.

$ Tan Dirih, T0752 61461. Tidy, spotless rooms with TV and comfy beds. The large veranda has fine views, and there is free use of tubes here for a day of floating in the lake. You can eat here, but meals need to be ordered well in advance. Recommended.

Bayur

There are fewer places to stay in Bayur than in Maninjau village, although north of the village is a group of 3 peaceful guesthouses down a series of tracks that run from the road, through ricefields, to the lake, where there is a small beach. These guesthouses

are the most peaceful; they are also some distance (3 km) from the main concentration of restaurants and coffee shops. Bemos into and out of Maninjau village stop at 1900, but the walk is beautiful and not far. Try not to arrive here at night, as negotiating the paths through the rice fields in the dark isn't much fun.

$ Arlen Nova's Paradise, T081 5352 04714, www.nova-maninjau.id.or.id. Collection of 5 clean bungalows with attached bathroom set in pleasant garden with lake views.

$ Batu C, next to Lily's. If there is ever an overspill from Lily's, this place might get busy. Simple wooden chalets on the lake.

$ Lily's, T081 3749 01435. The most popular guesthouse around the lake, although still very quiet. Rooms are very simple with shared bathroom. The front ones have excellent views. Staff are friendly and cook up some of the best *nasi goreng* with *tempe* in Sumatra. There is a stony swimming area and a small library of books.

❷ Restaurants

Bukittinggi *p224*

Bukittinggi is renowned for the quality of its food. The climate means that temperate as well as tropical vegetables are available. The number of tourist-oriented cafés has decreased over the last few years, but there are more than enough to cater for the small number of visitors. There are also excellent local restaurants serving Minang/Padang and Chinese dishes, and plenty of foodstalls selling *sate*, *gulai* soup and other specialities.

$ Bedual Café, Jln A Yani 95, T0752 31533. Daily 0800-2300. Chilled music and walls covered in eclectic art, this eatery has plenty of Indonesian and Western food including a roast chicken dinner for 2, a dream for those arriving from the hinterlands. Internet is available for 5000Rp per hr. Recommended.

$ Canyon Café, Jln Teuku Umar 8, T0752 21652. Daily 0700-2300. Popular travellers' hang-out with a friendly atmosphere and

staff offering good local information. The menu is packed with cheap Western food.
$ Family, Jln Benteng 1. Daily 0700-2100. Superb views and good Indonesian food, the house special is *ikan baker* (grilled fish).
$ La Mor Resto, Jln Dr A Rivai 18, T0752 33800. Daily 0700-2100. This popular student hang-out has a long menu of Indonesian dishes such as *nasi goreng* and *soto ayam* and good cold juices.
$ Mona Lisa, Jln A Yani 58, T0752 22644. Daily 0900-2130. Over the years, this place has decreased in size but still serves up fair portions of Chinese food. The best thing here is the create-your-own tropical fruit salad.
$ Selamat, Jln A Yani 19, T0752 22959. Daily 0600-2100. One of the town's better *nasi Padang* places.
$ Simpang Raya, Jln Minangkabau 77, T0752 21910. Daily 0500-2100. With branches all over town, this chain churns out *nasi Padang* to hungry crowds all day. In the evening it is better to arrive earlier: the later it gets the more the selection diminishes.

Foodstalls
The best ones are all in and around the market area; *sate*, fruit, Padang dishes, etc.

Danau Maninjau *p228*
There are several good coffee shops geared to Western tastes in Maninjau village, as well as the usual *warungs* and stalls, concentrated in the market area. Many of the guesthouses offer simple meals. **Maransy** and **Lily's ($)** have the most comprehensive menus and are worth trying. There are lots of roadside stalls serving *otak-otak* (minced fish with spices grilled in a banana leaf – delicious).
$ Bagoes, T0752 61418. Daily 0800-2200. Simple menu of Western and Asian food. Run by John who offers good local information. Internet available, 10,000Rp per hr.
$ Monica Café, T0752 61879. Daily 0800-2200. Quiet eatery with occasional movie screenings. Pancakes, juices and comfy chairs. Internet available, 20,000Rp per hr.

$ Nabila. Daily 0800-2000. Fresh grilled lake fish and simple Indonesian standards.
$ Sambalado, T0752 61020. Daily 0700-2000. Big plates of *nasi Padang*.
$ Waterfront Zalino, T0752 61740. Daily 0800-2200. This clean place is a bit of an anomaly for the area, with well-tended lawns, a spotless interior and a lovely pavilion over the water. There is also a kids' pool, and lots of good local information available. The food is simple Western and Indonesian.

⊙ Entertainment

Bukittinggi *p224*
Minangkabau dances
Dancing, including *Pencak silat*, a traditional form of self-defence, can be seen performed at **Medan Nan Balindung**, Jln Khatib Suleiman 1, Fri-Wed 2030, 40,000Rp.

Minangkabau traditional arts
Music, song, dance and *silat* at **Saayun Salankah**, Jln Lenggogeni 1A, Fri-Sat 2030, 40,000Rp.

⊙ Shopping

Bukittinggi *p224*
Bukittinggi has a good selection of shops selling handicrafts, curios and antiques, and has a particular reputation for its silver and gold jewellery. The shops are concentrated on Jln Minangkabau (close to the Central Market) and along Jln Jend A Yani and Jln Teuku Umar. The most enjoyable way to shop is in the **Central Market** on Wed or Sat (see page 225). At other times it mainly sells products for local consumption – lots of clothes, fruit and vegetables, plastic trinkets, metal goods, fish, dried and otherwise, and so on.

Antiques and curios There is comparatively little for sale that originates from the area around Bukittinggi; most articles are from Nias and Mentawi, from the

Batak areas around Danau Toba, and from further afield, like Kalimantan and Java. The art from Nias and Mentawi is easy to fake and it is likely that much on sale is neither old nor genuine – despite the appearance of authenticity that dust may give. Shops include: **Aladdin**, Jln Jend A Yani 14; **Ganesha**, Jln Teuku Umar 2; **Makmar**, Jln Jend A Yani 10 and **Tanjung Raya Art Shop**, Jln Jend A Yani 85.

Handicrafts There are the handicraft villages like Pandai Sikat, as well as a number of shops in town. Many of the antique shops are really jumped-up handicraft outlets. A place with better goods than most is **Sulaman Silungkang** on Jln Panorama.

Jewellery If interested in buying jewellery, it is worth visiting the Kota Gadang silversmithing village (see page 226), which specializes in producing silver filigree.

⊙ What to do

Bukittinggi *p224*
Buffalo fights
Buffalo fights in the villages around Kota Baru, 10 km to the south of Bukittinggi, have been banned in West Sumatra due to gambling. Ask at your guesthouse.

Rafting
There used to be regular rafting trips down the Batang Anai River and the Sri Antokan rapids, which both flow from Danau Maninjau through the Ngarai Sianok Gorge to Palupuh, and along the Ombilin River that flows out of Danau Singkarak. However, due to a lack of numbers these have been suspended. Enquire at the **Orchid Hotel**.

Rock climbing
In the late 1990s, Bukittinggi began to gain a reputation for the quality of its rock climbing and its rock climbers. Again, the downturn in tourism, and the fact that the local organizer of trips moved to the USA has meant that they are no longer offered. For independent climbers, it might be possible to get a guide from the **Canyon Café** or **Orchid Hotel**. Climbers will need their own equipment, and bear in mind the danger of attempting such climbs without local knowledge.

Baso is a limestone tower around 10 km due east of Bukittinggi, with a number of challenging routes (Australian grading) including Power Pancake (graded 5.12c), Bee Attack (5.11b), Priest (5.10b), Koorong Bana (5.12d) and Bastard (5.12c). The Harau Canyon (see page 228) offers around 24 routes including the technically demanding Liang Limbek (5.13a).

Swimming
The Hills' romantic Romanesque heated pool is open to non-residents, Mon-Fri 25,000Rp, Sat-Sun 30,000Rp, 2000Rp for children. If you have lunch at the hotel they will allow you to swim for free.

Tour operators
Tour companies are concentrated along Jln Jend A Yani. They can reconfirm flights and provide bus tickets, also organize local tours and tours further afield.
Maju Indosari Travel Bureau, Jln Muka Jam Gadang 17, T0752 21671.
Raun Sumatra, Jln A Yani 99, T0752 21133. Professional outfit.
Tigo Balai, Jln A Yani 100, T0752 627235.

Tours
Local tours There are a range of tours organized to Danau Maninjau, Batusangkar, Danau Singkarak and other sights around Bukittinggi. Tours tend to take 1 of 3 routes: the Minangkabau tour, featuring many different places that are representative of the Minangkabau culture, past and present (including Batusangkar, Pagaruyung and Danau Singkarak). Secondly, the Maninjau line (including Kota Gadang and Danau Maninjau), and finally,

the Harau Valley line (including Mount Merapi and the Harau Valley). Most tour/travel agents organize these day-long tours for US$7-15; they are also arranged by many hotels and guesthouses.

Tours further afield Many of the tour operators also organize tours further afield, for example, 10-day trips to the Mentawai Islands. Bukittinggi is an excellent place to arrange a tour to the islands off the West Sumatra coast, but bear in mind that it can take up to 3 days to get to Siberut Island, Mentawai. Again, ask fellow travellers for feedback regarding guides. Expect to pay around US$300 for an 8- to 10-day all-inclusive trip to the islands.

Danau Maninjau *p228*
Tour operators
Kesuma Mekar Jaya, T0752 61300. Offers tours around the region, but they are more expensive than those on offer in Bukittinggi. Door-to-door minibuses can be organized from here, every 2 hrs to Padang, 60,000Rp. Money-changing service and flight ticketing.

⊖ Transport

Bukittinggi *p224*
Air
Given the cheap price of flying in Indonesia, many people fly out of Padang Minangkabau International Airport to Medan or Jakarta rather than facing the Trans-Sumatran Highway. Flights can be booked at all travel agencies in town, and **Raun Sumatra** and **Tigo Balai** (see Tour operators) have shuttle buses to the airport from Bukittinggi for 35,000Rp.

Bus
Local The station is at Aur Kuning, 3 km southeast of town. Buses to local destinations including **Batusangkar** (8000Rp), **Maninjau** (10,000Rp), **Payakumbuh** (8000Rp) and **Padang** (15,000Rp). There are also buses to destinations further afield.

Long distance For **Parapat**, choose the bus company carefully as many people have been overcharged; ensure that you have a ticket with seat numbers. Note that the bus may not connect with the last ferry to **Samosir** (1830), which means a late-night arrival at Parapat and a limited choice of hotels. Also, ensure that your bus is travelling to Parapat, rather than **Pematangsiantar**, as there have been some problems with the roads around Toba. Tickets are also available from travel agents and guesthouses. The Orchid Hotel (see Where to stay) is a reliable place and has tickets for a/c express bus to Parapat for US$19 (including transfer to bus station).

ANS, T0752 22626, and ALS, T0752 21214, offices at bus terminal, have a/c buses to **Parapat**, 15 hrs, US$22; **Medan**, 20 hrs, US$22; **Jakarta**, 30 hrs, US$38; **Pekanbaru**, 6 hrs, US$6.50; and **Bandung**, 36 hrs; US$41.

Taxi
Taxis can be hired, even as far as Medan. Ask at one of the tour offices (see above).

Danau Maninjau *p228*
Air
To reach Padang Minangkabau International Airport, there is a door-to-door minibus service offered by **Raun Sumatra** and **Tigo Balai** (see Tour operators) in Bukittinggi for 35,000Rp. DAMRI buses meet each arriving plane and shuttle passengers to **Padang** or **Bukittinggi** for 15,000Rp.

Domestic To **Batam**, daily with Mandala; **Jakarta**, daily with Lion Air, Mandala, Sriwijaya and Garuda; **Medan**, daily with Mandala. Tickets can be booked at travel agencies in Bukittinggi and Padang.
International Singapore, Tue, Thu, Sat, Tiger Airways. **Kuala Lumpur**, daily with AirAsia.

Bus

Regular buses from Bukittinggi to **Maninjau** village, negotiating 44 bends down from the crater lip to the lake, 1½ hrs, 10,000Rp. Buses also continue on through Bayur to **Muko Muko** on the northwest side of the lake. Those wishing to get back to Bukittinggi need to wait at the road near the entrance to their hotel and flag down a bus from Lubuk Basung to Bukittinggi via Maninjau village. The last bus to Bukittinggi leaves around 1700. From Padang catch a bus to Bukittinggi and ask to be let off at Kuto Tuo, the turn-off for Maninjau, and wait there to catch a bus down to the lake. There is a daily bus to **Pekanbaru**, 7 hrs, 60,000Rp.

Oplets

Some oplets from Bukittinggi continue anti-clockwise around the lake through Bayur and Muko Muko to Lubuk Basung (3000Rp), the end of the road, so to speak.

⏱ Directory

Bukittinggi *p224*
Banks Banks close at 1100 on Sat. Many tour and travel companies change money. Bank Negara Indonesia, Jln Jend A Yani, changes TCs. PT Enzet Corindo Perkasa, Jln Minangkabau 51 (money changer). **Medical services** Dokter Achmad Mochtar Hospital, Jln Rivai (opposite the Denai Hotel). **Telephone** Wartel office, Jln Jend A Yani, for international calls and faxes.

Danau Maninjau *p228*
Medical services Clinic at the southern end of Maninjau village. **Telephone** Jln SMP (facing oplet stop in town), international calls can be made from the office.

Contents

Footnotes

Index

Titles available in the Footprint *Focus* range

Latin America	UK RRP	US RRP
Bahia & Salvador	£7.99	$11.95
Brazilian Amazon	£7.99	$11.95
Brazilian Pantanal	£6.99	$9.95
Buenos Aires & Pampas	£7.99	$11.95
Cartagena & Caribbean Coast	£7.99	$11.95
Costa Rica	£8.99	$12.95
Cuzco, La Paz & Lake Titicaca	£8.99	$12.95
El Salvador	£5.99	$8.95
Guadalajara & Pacific Coast	£6.99	$9.95
Guatemala	£8.99	$12.95
Guyana, Guyane & Suriname	£5.99	$8.95
Havana	£6.99	$9.95
Honduras	£7.99	$11.95
Nicaragua	£7.99	$11.95
Northeast Argentina & Uruguay	£8.99	$12.95
Paraguay	£5.99	$8.95
Quito & Galápagos Islands	£7.99	$11.95
Recife & Northeast Brazil	£7.99	$11.95
Rio de Janeiro	£8.99	$12.95
São Paulo	£5.99	$8.95
Uruguay	£6.99	$9.95
Venezuela	£8.99	$12.95
Yucatán Peninsula	£6.99	$9.95

Asia	UK RRP	US RRP
Angkor Wat	£5.99	$8.95
Bali & Lombok	£8.99	$12.95
Chennai & Tamil Nadu	£8.99	$12.95
Chiang Mai & Northern Thailand	£7.99	$11.95
Goa	£6.99	$9.95
Gulf of Thailand	£8.99	$12.95
Hanoi & Northern Vietnam	£8.99	$12.95
Ho Chi Minh City & Mekong Delta	£7.99	$11.95
Java	£7.99	$11.95
Kerala	£7.99	$11.95
Kolkata & West Bengal	£5.99	$8.95
Mumbai & Gujarat	£8.99	$12.95

Africa & Middle East	UK RRP	US RRP
Beirut	£6.99	$9.95
Cairo & Nile Delta	£8.99	$12.95
Damascus	£5.99	$8.95
Durban & KwaZulu Natal	£8.99	$12.95
Fès & Northern Morocco	£8.99	$12.95
Jerusalem	£8.99	$12.95
Johannesburg & Kruger National Park	£7.99	$11.95
Kenya's Beaches	£8.99	$12.95
Kilimanjaro & Northern Tanzania	£8.99	$12.95
Luxor to Aswan	£8.99	$12.95
Nairobi & Rift Valley	£7.99	$11.95
Red Sea & Sinai	£7.99	$11.95
Zanzibar & Pemba	£7.99	$11.95

Europe	UK RRP	US RRP
Bilbao & Basque Region	£6.99	$9.95
Brittany West Coast	£7.99	$11.95
Cádiz & Costa de la Luz	£6.99	$9.95
Granada & Sierra Nevada	£6.99	$9.95
Languedoc: Carcassonne to Montpellier	£7.99	$11.95
Málaga	£5.99	$8.95
Marseille & Western Provence	£7.99	$11.95
Orkney & Shetland Islands	£5.99	$8.95
Santander & Picos de Europa	£7.99	$11.95
Sardinia: Alghero & the North	£7.99	$11.95
Sardinia: Cagliari & the South	£7.99	$11.95
Seville	£5.99	$8.95
Sicily: Palermo & the Northwest	£7.99	$11.95
Sicily: Catania & the Southeast	£7.99	$11.95
Siena & Southern Tuscany	£7.99	$11.95
Sorrento, Capri & Amalfi Coast	£6.99	$9.95
Skye & Outer Hebrides	£6.99	$9.95
Verona & Lake Garda	£7.99	$11.95

North America	UK RRP	US RRP
Vancouver & Rockies	£8.99	$12.95

Australasia	UK RRP	US RRP
Brisbane & Queensland	£8.99	$12.95
Perth	£7.99	$11.95

For the latest books, e-books and a wealth of travel information, visit us at:
www.footprinttravelguides.com.

Join us on facebook for the latest travel news, product releases, offers and amazing competitions:
www.facebook.com/footprintbooks.